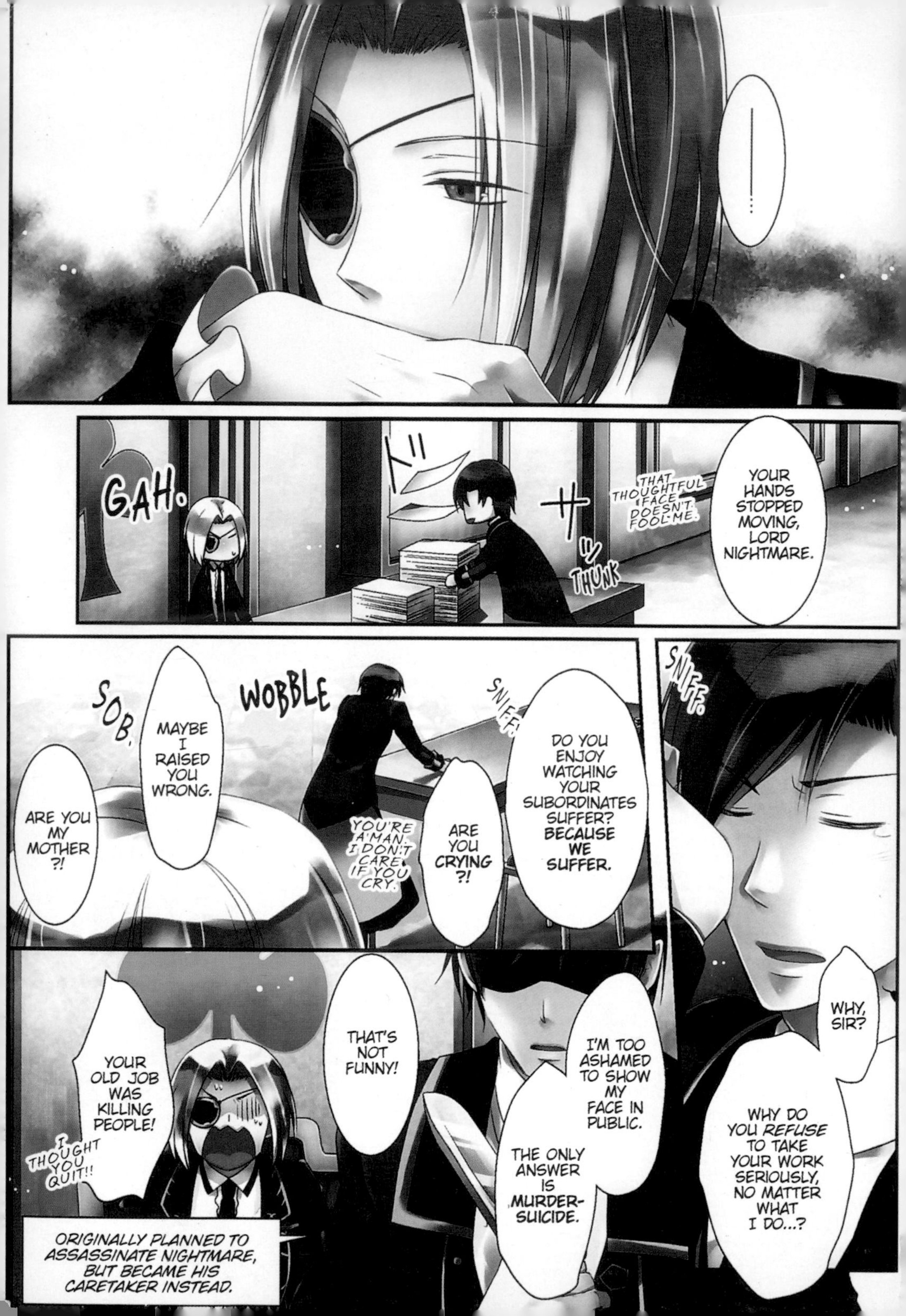
—......
YOUR HANDS STOPPED MOVING, LORD NIGHTMARE.
THAT THOUGHTFUL FACE DOESN'T FOOL ME.
THUNK
GAH.
SNIFF.
WHY, SIR?
WHY DO YOU *REFUSE* TO TAKE YOUR WORK SERIOUSLY, NO MATTER WHAT I DO...?
DO YOU ENJOY WATCHING YOUR SUBORDINATES SUFFER? **BECAUSE WE SUFFER.**
SNIFF.
ARE YOU **CRYING** ?!
YOU'RE A MAN. I DON'T CARE IF YOU CRY.
WOBBLE
MAYBE I RAISED YOU WRONG.
SOB.
ARE YOU MY MOTHER ?!
I'M TOO ASHAMED TO SHOW MY FACE IN PUBLIC.
THE ONLY ANSWER IS **MURDER-SUICIDE.**
THAT'S NOT FUNNY!
YOUR OLD JOB WAS KILLING PEOPLE!
I THOUGHT YOU QUIT!!
ORIGINALLY PLANNED TO ASSASSINATE NIGHTMARE, BUT BECAME HIS CARETAKER INSTEAD.

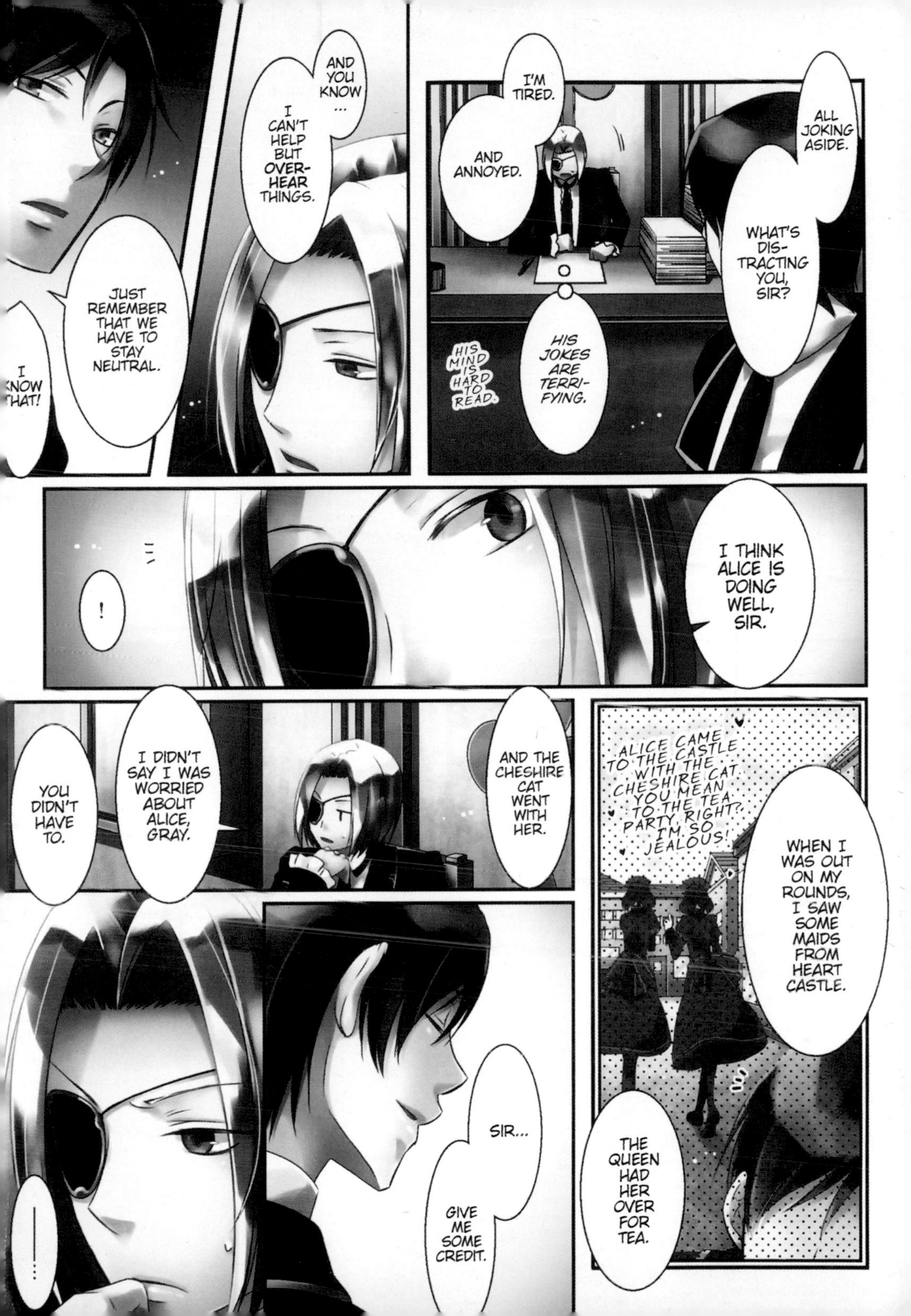
ALL JOKING ASIDE.
WHAT'S DIS-TRACTING YOU, SIR?
I'M TIRED.
AND ANNOYED.
HIS JOKES ARE TERRI-FYING.
HIS MIND IS HARD TO READ.
AND YOU KNOW...
I CAN'T HELP BUT OVER-HEAR THINGS.
JUST REMEMBER THAT WE HAVE TO STAY NEUTRAL.
I KNOW THAT!
I THINK ALICE IS DOING WELL, SIR.
!
WHEN I WAS OUT ON MY ROUNDS, I SAW SOME MAIDS FROM HEART CASTLE.
ALICE CAME TO THE CASTLE WITH THE CHESHIRE CAT. YOU MEAN TO THE TEA PARTY, RIGHT? I'M SO JEALOUS!
THE QUEEN HAD HER OVER FOR TEA.
AND THE CHESHIRE CAT WENT WITH HER.
I DIDN'T SAY I WAS WORRIED ABOUT ALICE, GRAY.
YOU DIDN'T HAVE TO.
SIR...
GIVE ME SOME CREDIT.
......

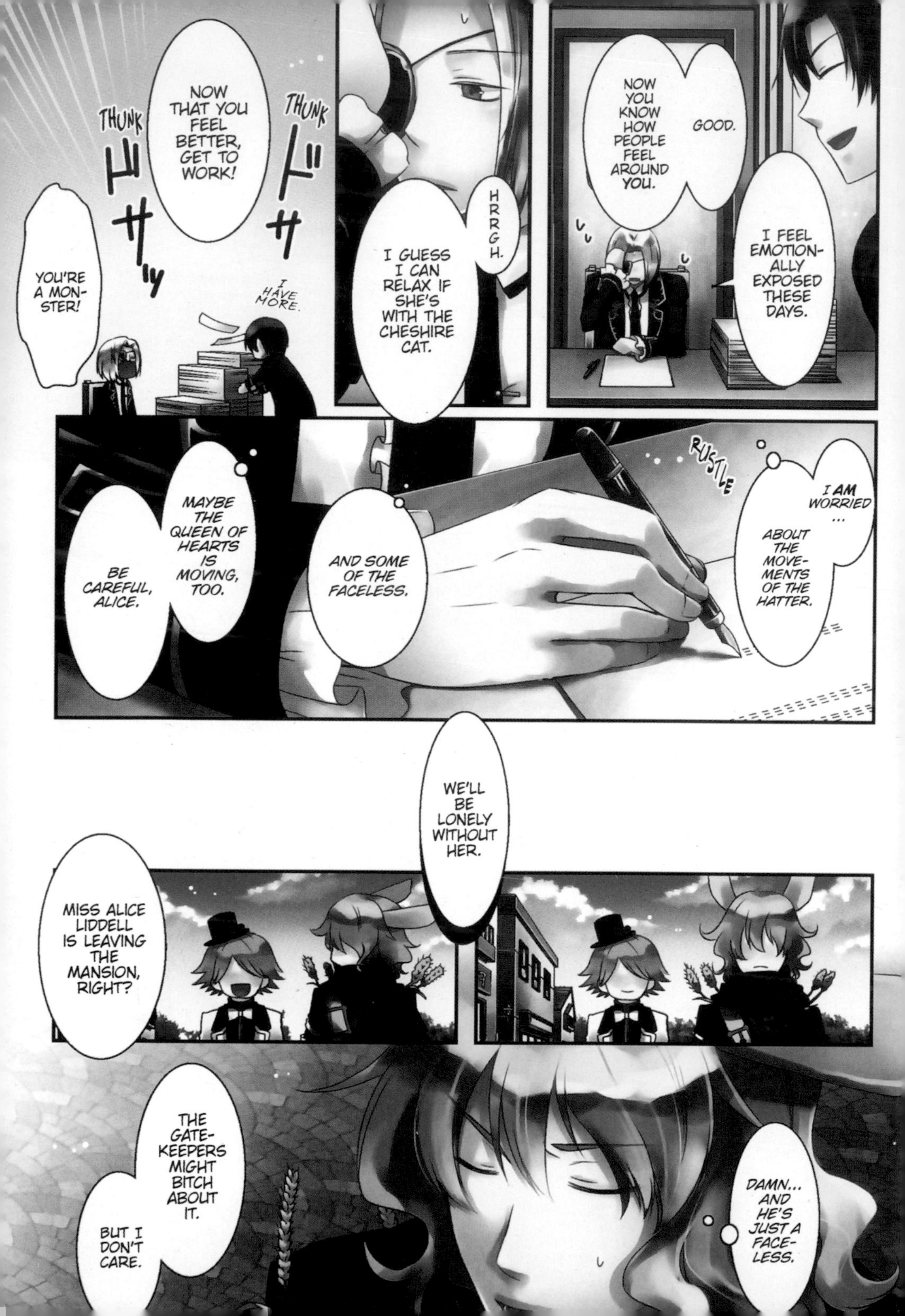
GOOD.
NOW YOU KNOW HOW PEOPLE FEEL AROUND YOU.
I FEEL EMOTION-ALLY EXPOSED THESE DAYS.
HRRGH.
I GUESS I CAN RELAX IF SHE'S WITH THE CHESHIRE CAT.
THUNK
THUNK
NOW THAT YOU FEEL BETTER, GET TO WORK!
I HAVE MORE.
YOU'RE A MON-STER!
RUSTLE
I AM WORRIED...
ABOUT THE MOVE-MENTS OF THE HATTER.
AND SOME OF THE FACELESS.
MAYBE THE QUEEN OF HEARTS IS MOVING, TOO.
BE CAREFUL, ALICE.
WE'LL BE LONELY WITHOUT HER.
MISS ALICE LIDDELL IS LEAVING THE MANSION, RIGHT?
DAMN... AND HE'S JUST A FACE-LESS.
THE GATE-KEEPERS MIGHT BITCH ABOUT IT.
BUT I DON'T CARE.

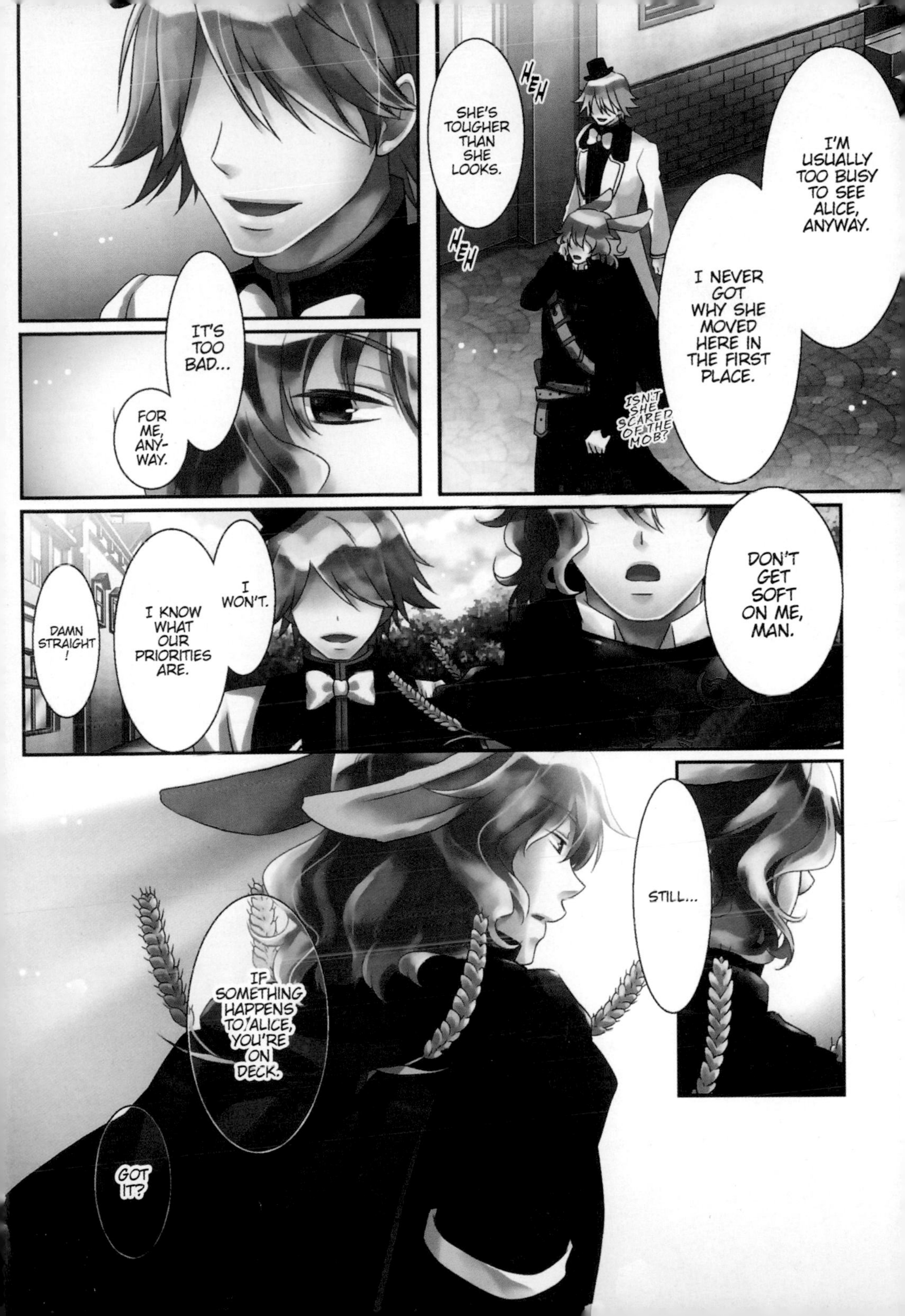
I'M USUALLY TOO BUSY TO SEE ALICE, ANYWAY.
I NEVER GOT WHY SHE MOVED HERE IN THE FIRST PLACE.
ISN'T SHE SCARED OF THE MOB?
HEH
HEH
SHE'S TOUGHER THAN SHE LOOKS.
IT'S TOO BAD...
FOR ME, ANYWAY.
DON'T GET SOFT ON ME, MAN.
I WON'T.
I KNOW WHAT OUR PRIORITIES ARE.
DAMN STRAIGHT!
STILL...
IF SOMETHING HAPPENS TO ALICE, YOU'RE ON DECK.
GOT IT?

Alice in the Country of Clover
~Cheshire Cat Waltz~ **6**

Mamenosuke Fujimaru
藤丸 豆ノ介

Alice IN THE COUNTRY OF Clover
CHESHIRE CAT WALTZ
VOLUME 6

story by **QuinRose**
art by **Mamenosuke Fujimaru**

STAFF CREDITS

translation	**Angela Liu**
adaptation	**Lianne Sentar**
lettering	**Roland Amago**
layout	**Bambi Eloriaga-Amago**
cover design	**Nicky Lim**
proofreader	**Shanti Whitesides**
editor	**Adam Arnold**
publisher	**Jason DeAngelis**
	Seven Seas Entertainment

ALICE IN THE COUNTRY OF CLOVER: CHESHIRE CAT WALTZ VOL. 6
Copyright © Mamenosuke Fujimaru / QuinRose 2011
First published in Japan in 2011 by ICHIJINSHA Inc., Tokyo.
English translation rights arranged with ICHIJINSHA Inc., Tokyo, Japan.

ISBN: 978-1-937867-66-9

Printed in Canada

First Printing: September 2013

10 9 8 7 6 5 4 3 2 1

FOLLOW US ONLINE: www.gomanga.com

READING DIRECTIONS

This book reads from *right to left*, Japanese style.
If this is your first time reading manga, you start
reading from the top right panel on each page and
take it from there. If you get lost, just follow the
numbered diagram here. It may seem backwards
at first, but you'll get the hang of it! Have fun!!

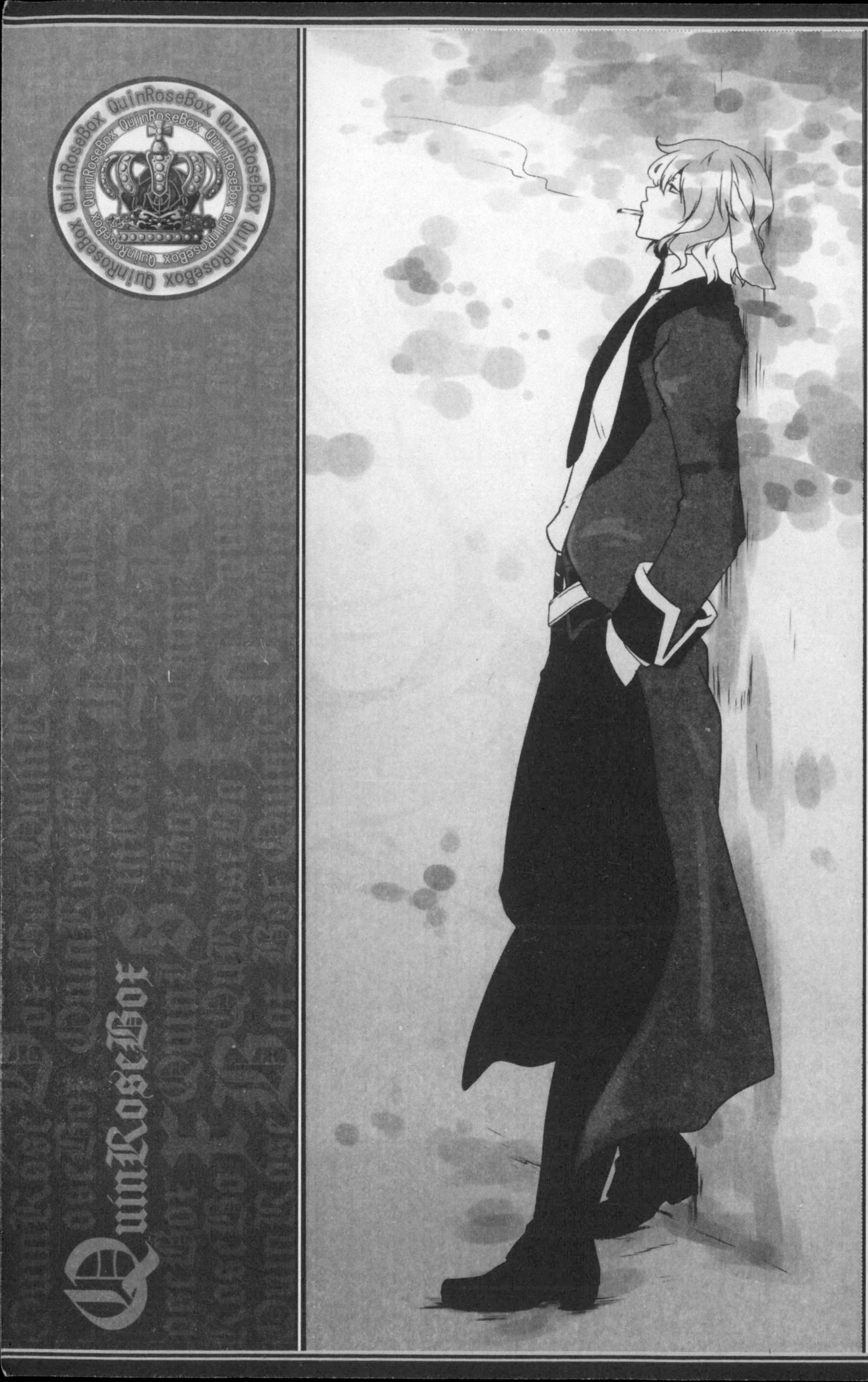

Alice in the Country of Clover

クローバーの国の

アリス

~ Wonderful Wonder World ~

- STORY -

In *Alice in the Country of Clover*, the game starts with Alice having not fallen in love,
but still deciding to stay in Wonderland.

She's acquainted with all the characters from the previous game, *Alice in the Country of Hearts*.

Since love would now start from a place of friendship rather than passion with a new stranger, she can experience a different type of romance from that in the previous game. Her dynamic with the characters is different through this friendship—characters can't always be forceful with her, and in many ways it's more comfortable to grow intimate. The relationships *between* the Ones With Duties have also become more of a factor.

In this game, the story focuses on the mafia. Alice attends the suited meetings (forcefully) and gets involved in various gunfights (forcefully), among other things.

Land fluctuations, sea creatures in the forest, and whispering doors—it's a game more fantastic and more eerie than the first.

Will our everywoman Alice be able to have a romantic relationship in a world devoid of common sense?

Alice in the Country of Clover
Character Information

Elliot March
VA: Tsuguo Mogami

Blood's right-hand man has a criminal past... and a temperamental present. But he's not as bad as he used to be, so that's something. Joining Blood has been good(?) for him.

Blood Dupre
VA: Katsuyuki Konishi

The head of the mafia Hatter Family, Blood is a cunning yet moody puppet-master. Alice now has the pleasure of having him for a landlord.

Alice Liddell
VA: Rie Kugimiya

A normal girl with a bit of a chip on her shoulder. Deciding to stay in the Wonderland she was carried to, she's adapted to her strange new lifestyle.

Vivaldi
VA: Yuuko Kaida

The beautiful Queen of Hearts has an unrivaled temper—which is really saying something in Wonderland. Although a picture-perfect Mad Queen, she cares for Alice as if Alice were her little sister...or a very interesting plaything.

Tweedle Dum
VA: Jun Fukuyama

The second "Bloody Twin" is equally cute and equally scary. In *Clover*, Dum can also turn into an adult.

Tweedle Dee
VA: Jun Fukuyama

One of the "Bloody Twin" gatekeepers of the Hatter territory, Dee can be cute when he's not being terrifying. In *Clover*, he sometimes turns into an adult.

Boris Airay
VA: Noriaki Sugiyama

This riddle-loving cat has a signature smirk—and in *Clover*, a new toy. One of his favorite pastimes is giving the Sleepy Mouse a hard time.

Ace
VA: Daisuke Hirakawa

The unlucky knight of Hearts was a former subordinate of Vivaldi and is perpetually lost. Even though he's depressed to be separated from his friend and boss Julius, he stays positive and tries to overcome it with a smile. He seems like a classic nice guy... or is he?

Peter White
VA: Kouki Miyata

The Prime Minister of Heart Castle—who has rabbit ears growing out of his head—invited (kidnapped) Alice to Wonderland. He loves Alice and hates everything else. His cruel, irrational actions are disturbing, but he acts like a completely different person (rabbit?) when in the throes of his love for Alice.

Gray Ringmarc
VA: Kazuya Nakai

Nightmare's subordinate in *Clover*. He used to have strong social ambition and considered assassinating Nightmare... but since Nightmare was such a useless boss, Gray couldn't help but feel sorry for him and ended up a dedicated assistant. He's a sound thinker with a strong work ethic. He's also highly skilled with his blades, rivaling even Ace.

Nightmare Gottschalk
VA: Tomokazu Sugita

A sickly nightmare who hates the hospital and needles. He has the power to read people's thoughts and enter dreams. Even though he likes to shut himself away in dreams, Gray drags him out to sulk from time to time. He technically holds a high position and has many subordinates, but since he can't even take care of his own health, he leaves most things to Gray.

Pierce Villiers
VA: Souichirou Hoshi

New to *Clover*, Pierce is an insomniac mouse who drinks too much coffee. He loves Nightmare (who can help him sleep) and hates Boris (who terrifies him). He dislikes Blood and Vivaldi for discarding coffee in favor of tea. He likes Elliot and Peter well enough, since rabbits aren't natural predators of mice.

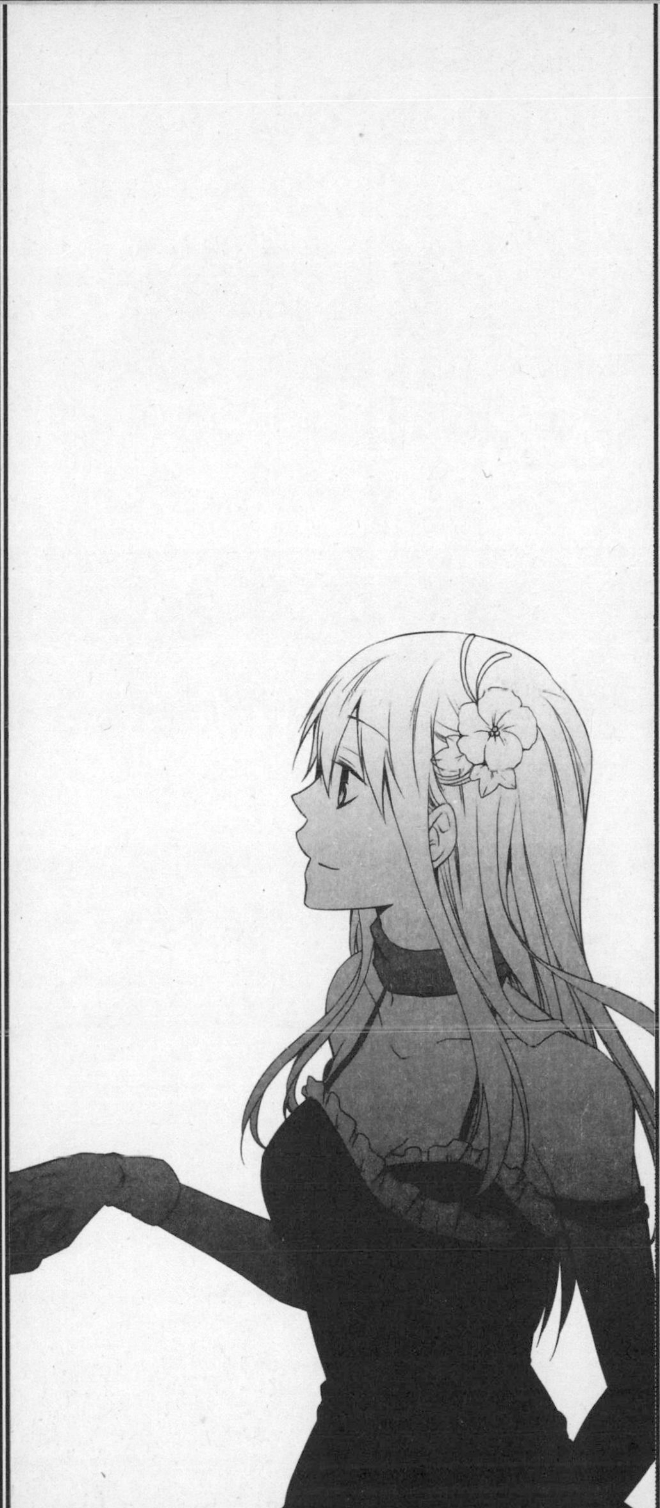

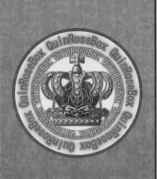

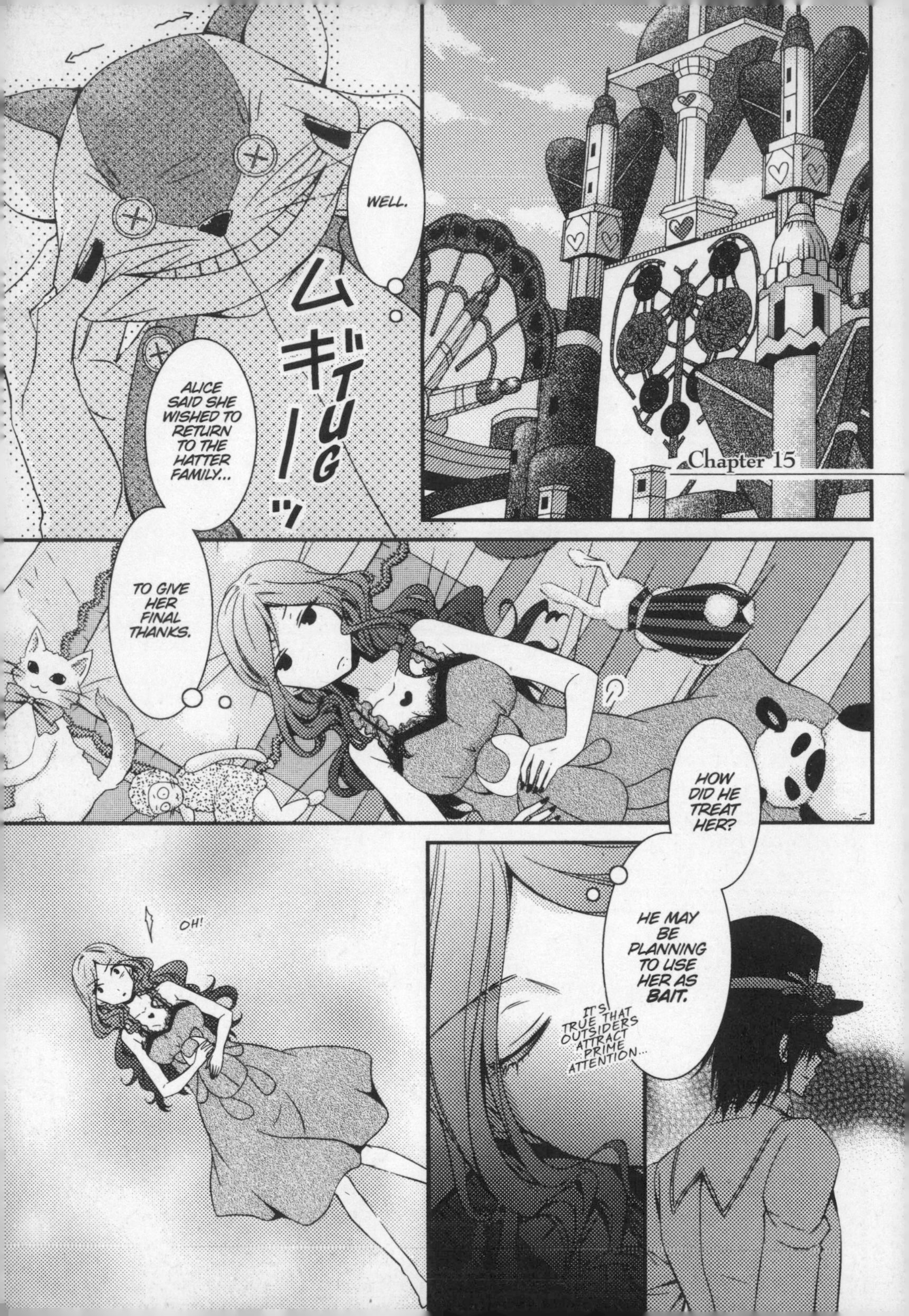
Chapter 15
WELL.
ムギューッ
TUG
ALICE SAID SHE WISHED TO RETURN TO THE HATTER FAMILY...
TO GIVE HER FINAL THANKS.
HOW DID HE TREAT HER?
HE MAY BE PLANNING TO USE HER AS BAIT.
IT'S TRUE THAT OUTSIDERS ATTRACT PRIME ATTENTION...
OH!

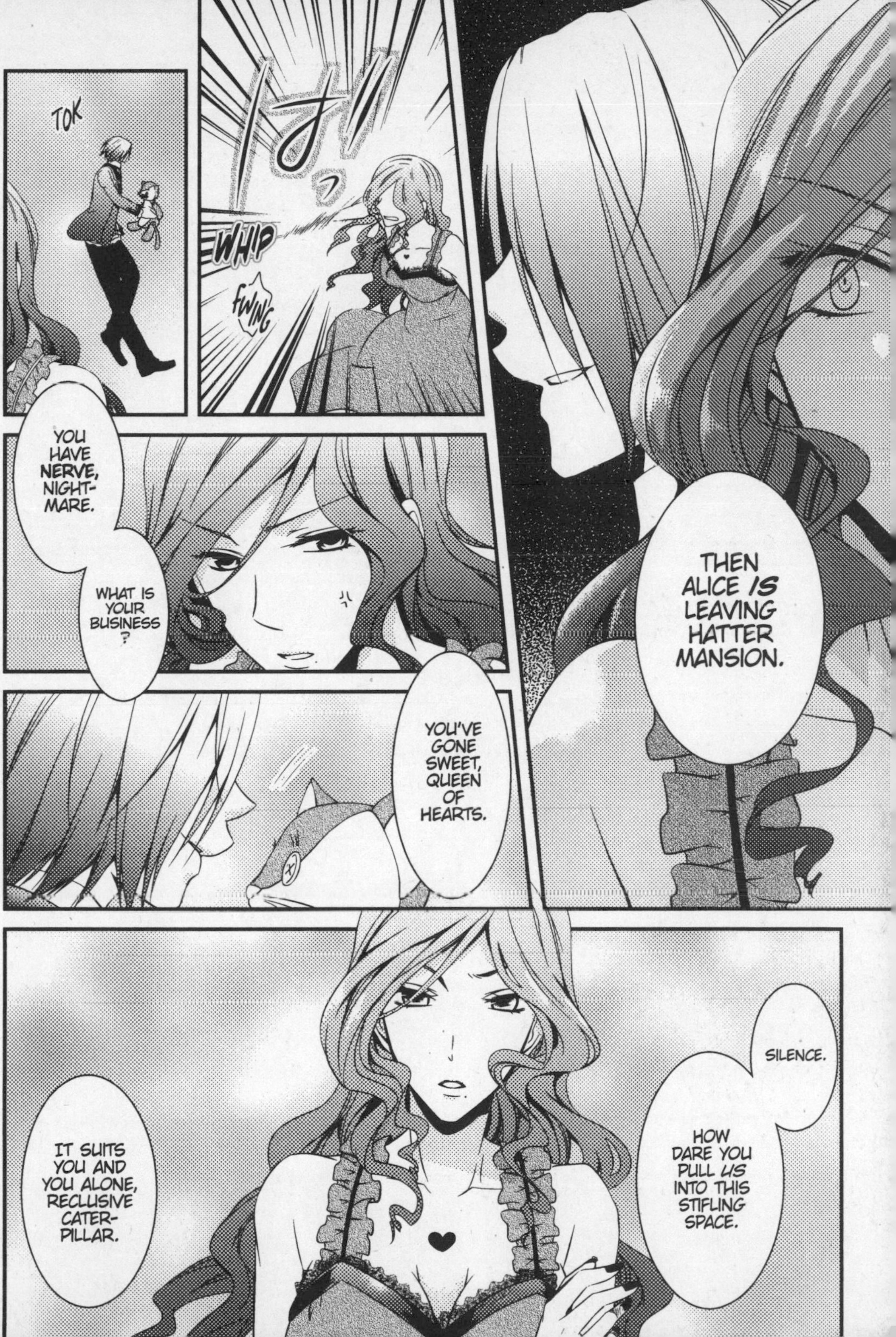
THEN ALICE *IS* LEAVING HATTER MANSION.
WHIP
FWING
TOK
YOU HAVE NERVE, NIGHT-MARE.
WHAT IS YOUR BUSINESS?
YOU'VE GONE SWEET, QUEEN OF HEARTS.
SILENCE.
HOW DARE YOU PULL *US* INTO THIS STIFLING SPACE.
IT SUITS YOU AND YOU ALONE, RECLUSIVE CATER-PILLAR.

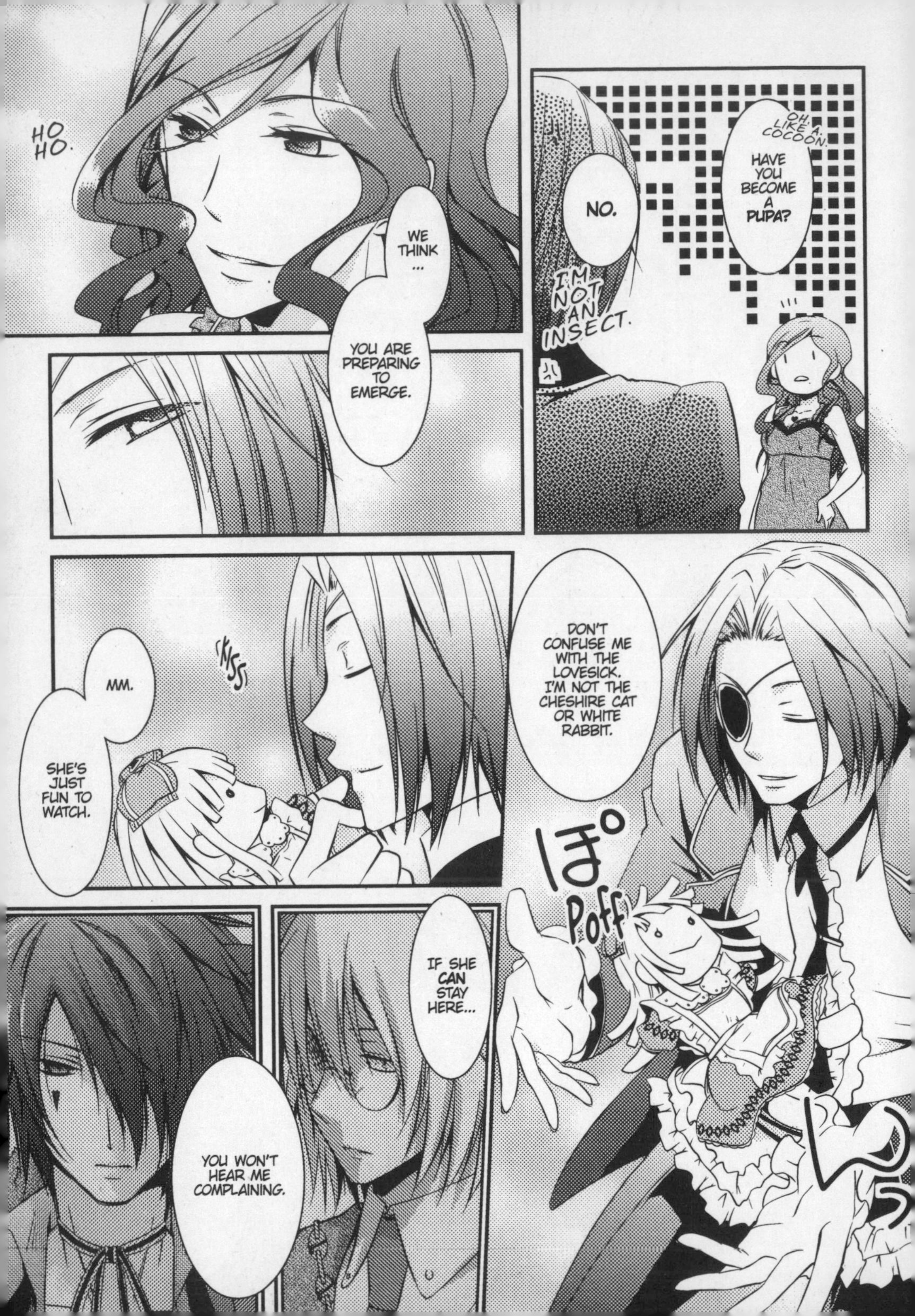
OH, LIKE A COCOON.
HAVE YOU BECOME A PUPA?
NO.
I'M NOT AN INSECT.
HO HO.
WE THINK ...
YOU ARE PREPARING TO EMERGE.
DON'T CONFUSE ME WITH THE LOVESICK. I'M NOT THE CHESHIRE CAT OR WHITE RABBIT.
ぽ
Poff
KISS
MM.
SHE'S JUST FUN TO WATCH.
IF SHE CAN STAY HERE...
YOU WON'T HEAR ME COMPLAINING.

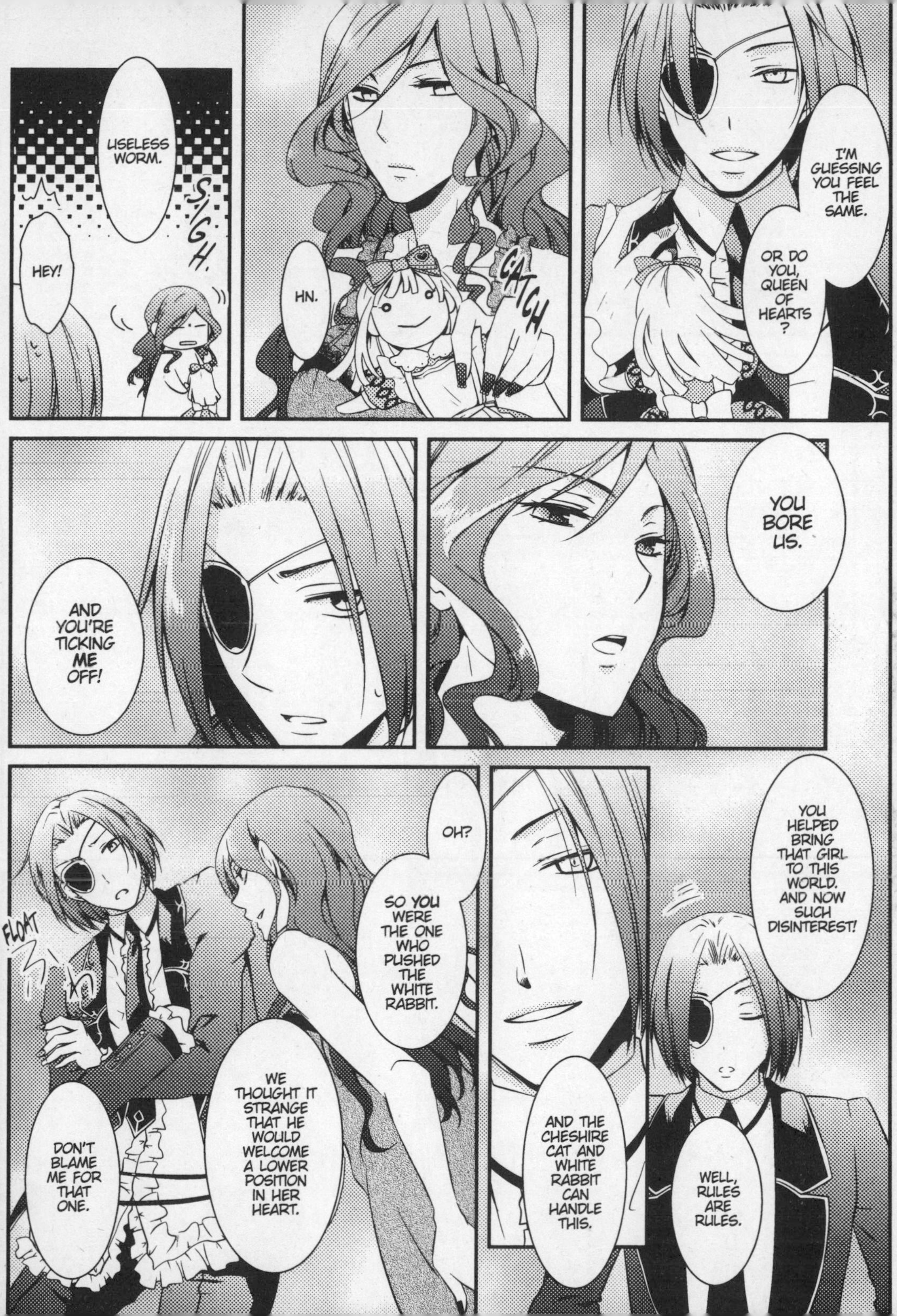
I'M GUESSING YOU FEEL THE SAME.
OR DO YOU, QUEEN OF HEARTS?
CATCH
HN.
USELESS WORM.
SIGH.
HEY!
YOU BORE US.
AND YOU'RE TICKING ME OFF!
YOU HELPED BRING THAT GIRL TO THIS WORLD. AND NOW SUCH DISINTEREST!
WELL, RULES ARE RULES.
AND THE CHESHIRE CAT AND WHITE RABBIT CAN HANDLE THIS.
OH?
SO YOU WERE THE ONE WHO PUSHED THE WHITE RABBIT.
WE THOUGHT IT STRANGE THAT HE WOULD WELCOME A LOWER POSITION IN HER HEART.
DON'T BLAME ME FOR THAT ONE.
FLOAT

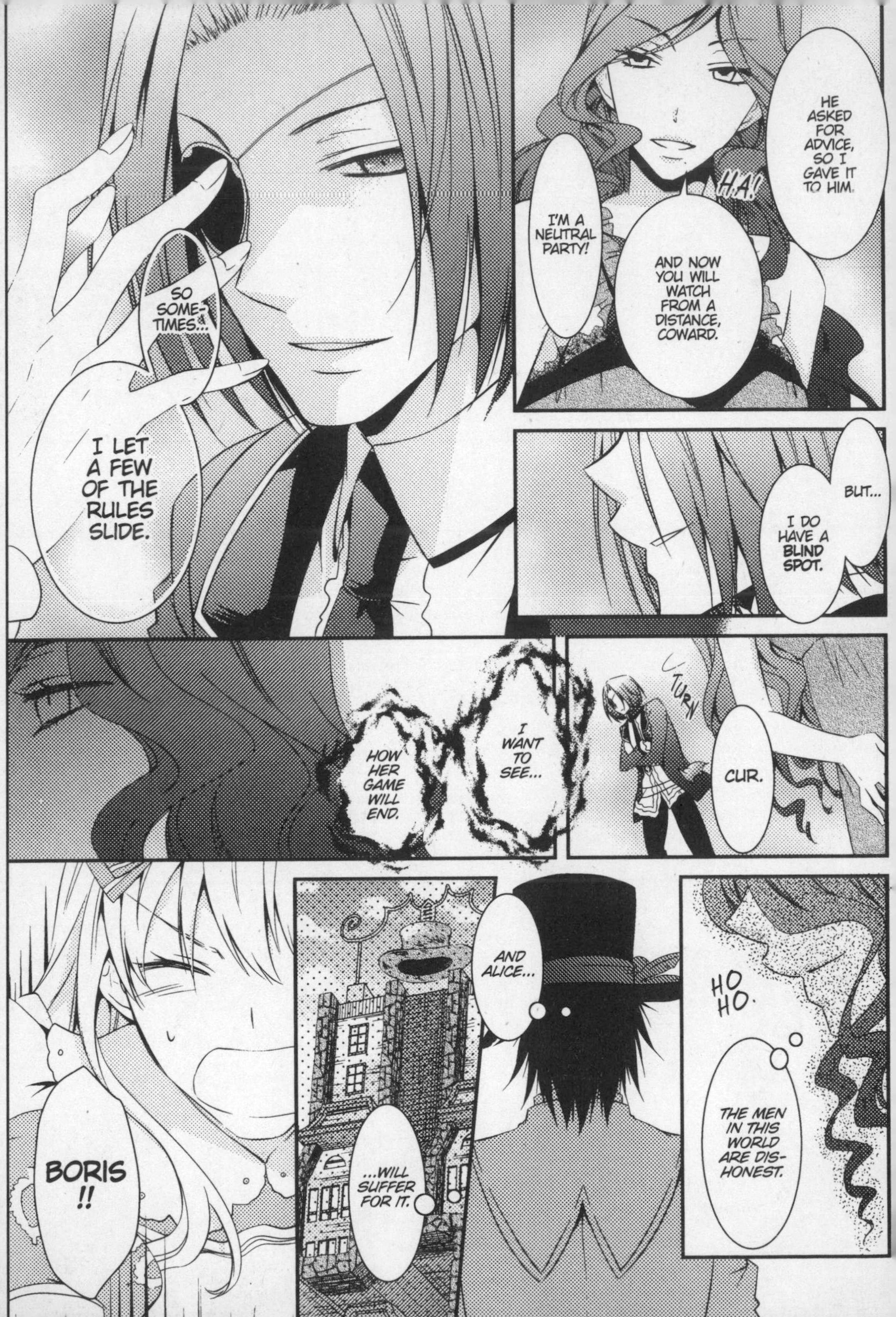
HE ASKED FOR ADVICE, SO I GAVE IT TO HIM.
HA!
I'M A NEUTRAL PARTY!
AND NOW YOU WILL WATCH FROM A DISTANCE, COWARD.
BUT...
I DO HAVE A BLIND SPOT.
SO SOMETIMES...
I LET A FEW OF THE RULES SLIDE.
TURN
CUR.
I WANT TO SEE...
HOW HER GAME WILL END.
HO HO.
THE MEN IN THIS WORLD ARE DISHONEST.
AND ALICE...
...WILL SUFFER FOR IT.
BORIS!!

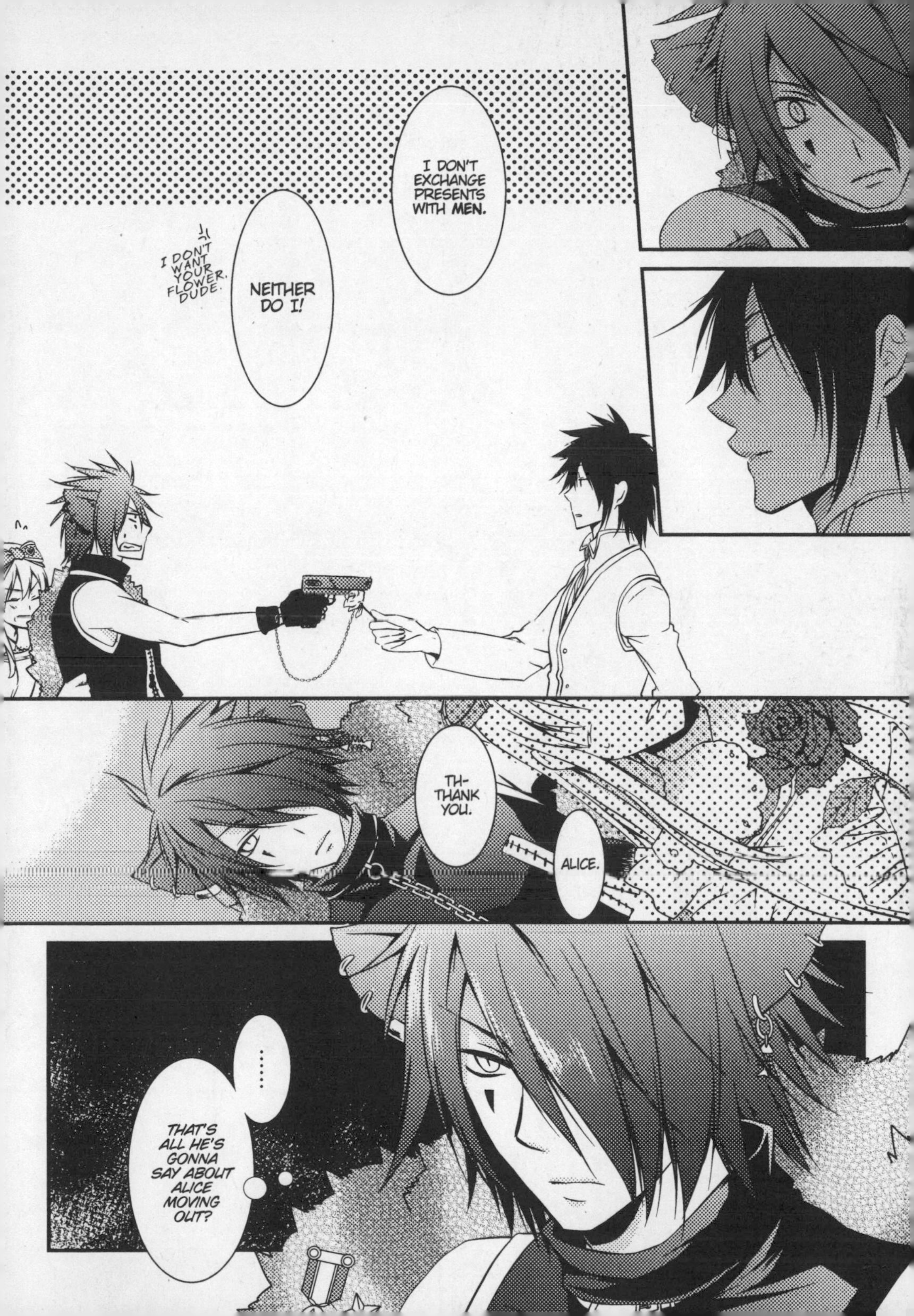
I DON'T EXCHANGE PRESENTS WITH MEN.
NEITHER DO I!
I DON'T WANT YOUR FLOWER, DUDE.
TH- THANK YOU.
ALICE.
......
THAT'S ALL HE'S GONNA SAY ABOUT ALICE MOVING OUT?

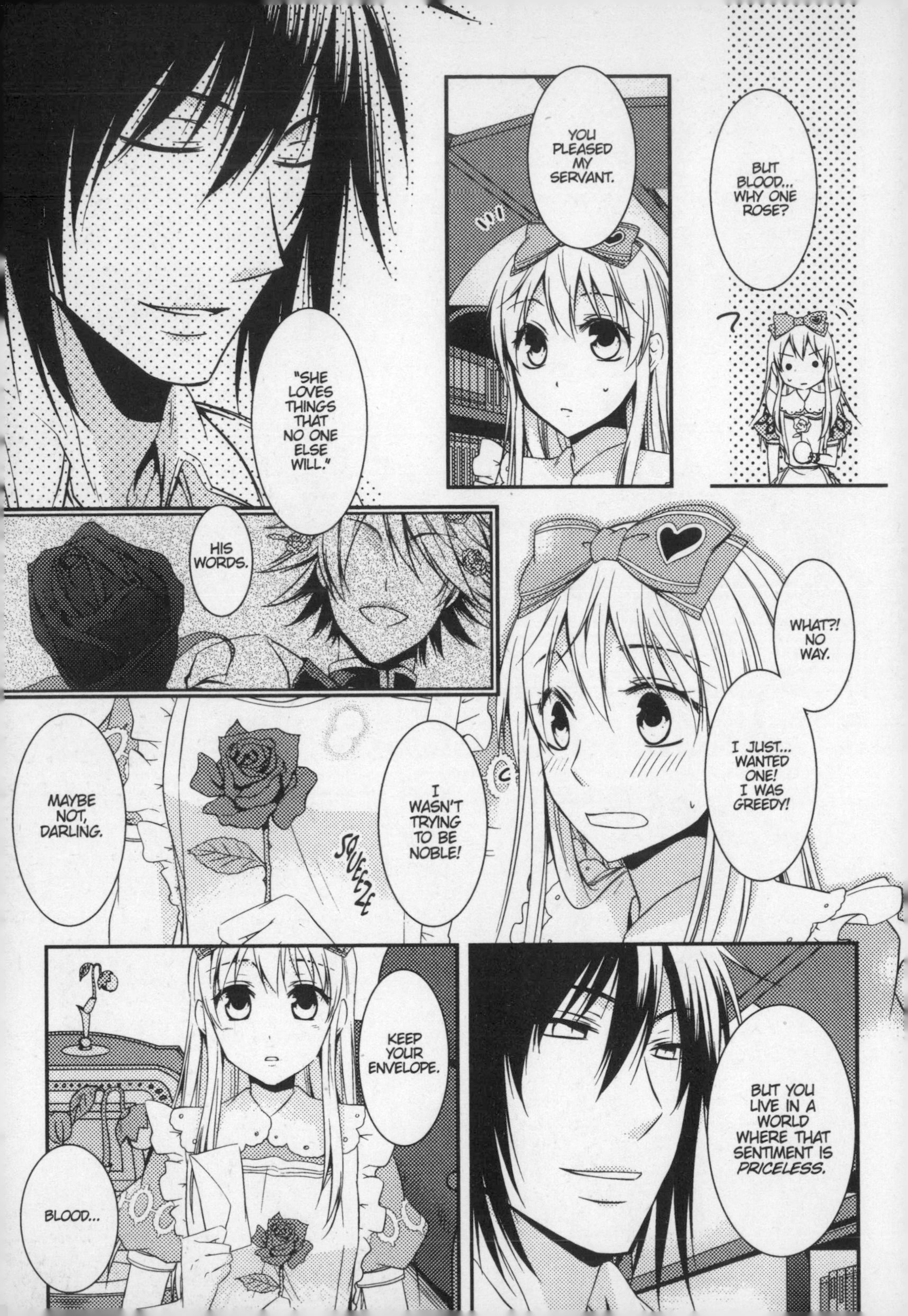
BUT BLOOD... WHY ONE ROSE?
?
YOU PLEASED MY SERVANT.
"SHE LOVES THINGS THAT NO ONE ELSE WILL."
HIS WORDS.
WHAT?! NO WAY.
I JUST... WANTED ONE! I WAS GREEDY!
I WASN'T TRYING TO BE NOBLE!
SQUEEZE
MAYBE NOT, DARLING.
BUT YOU LIVE IN A WORLD WHERE THAT SENTIMENT IS *PRICELESS.*
KEEP YOUR ENVELOPE.
BLOOD...

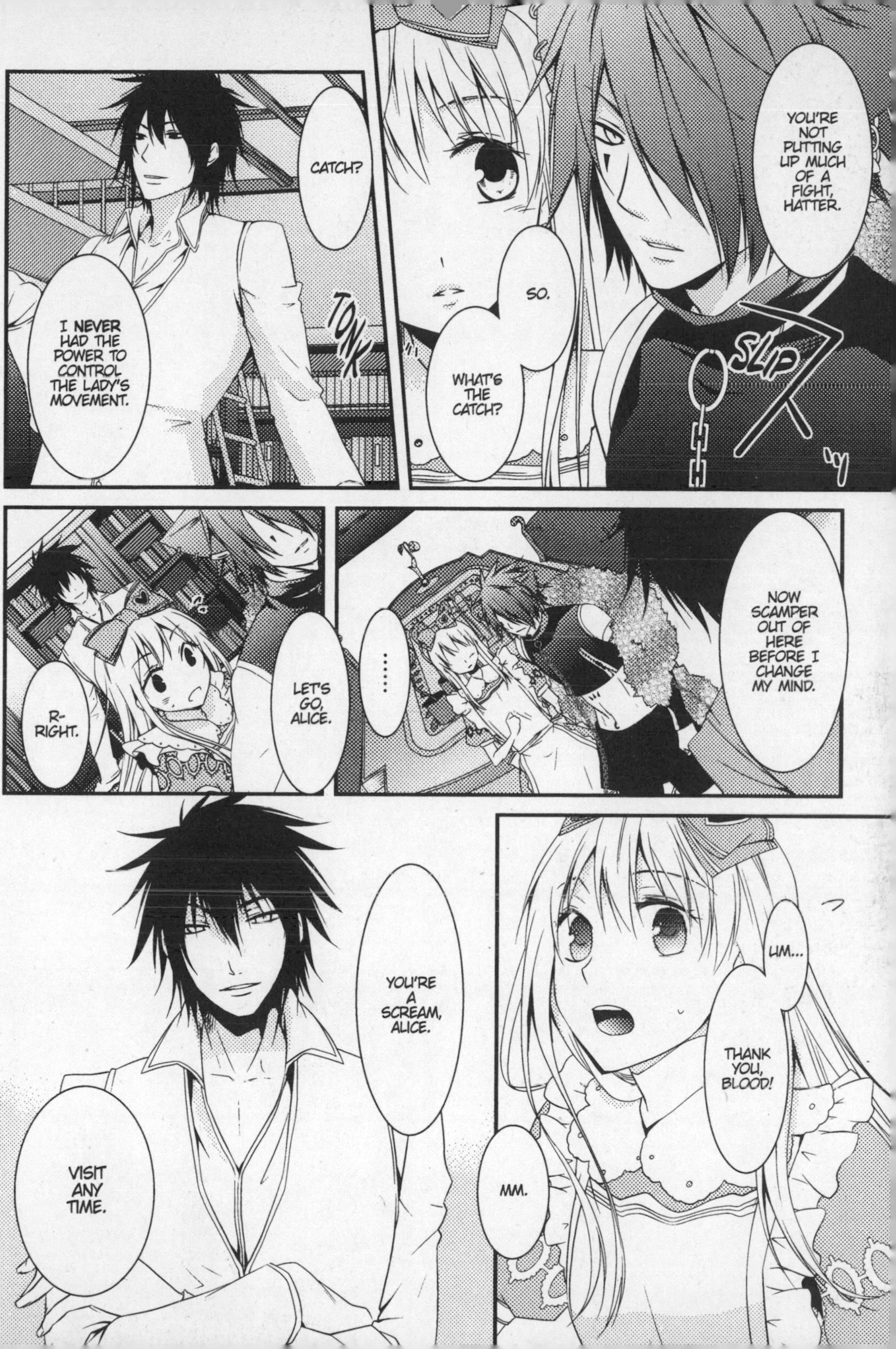
YOU'RE NOT PUTTING UP MUCH OF A FIGHT, HATTER.
SO.
WHAT'S THE CATCH?
SLIP
CATCH?
TONK
I NEVER HAD THE POWER TO CONTROL THE LADY'S MOVEMENT.
NOW SCAMPER OUT OF HERE BEFORE I CHANGE MY MIND.
......
LET'S GO, ALICE.
R-RIGHT.
UM...
THANK YOU, BLOOD!
MM.
YOU'RE A SCREAM, ALICE.
VISIT ANY TIME.

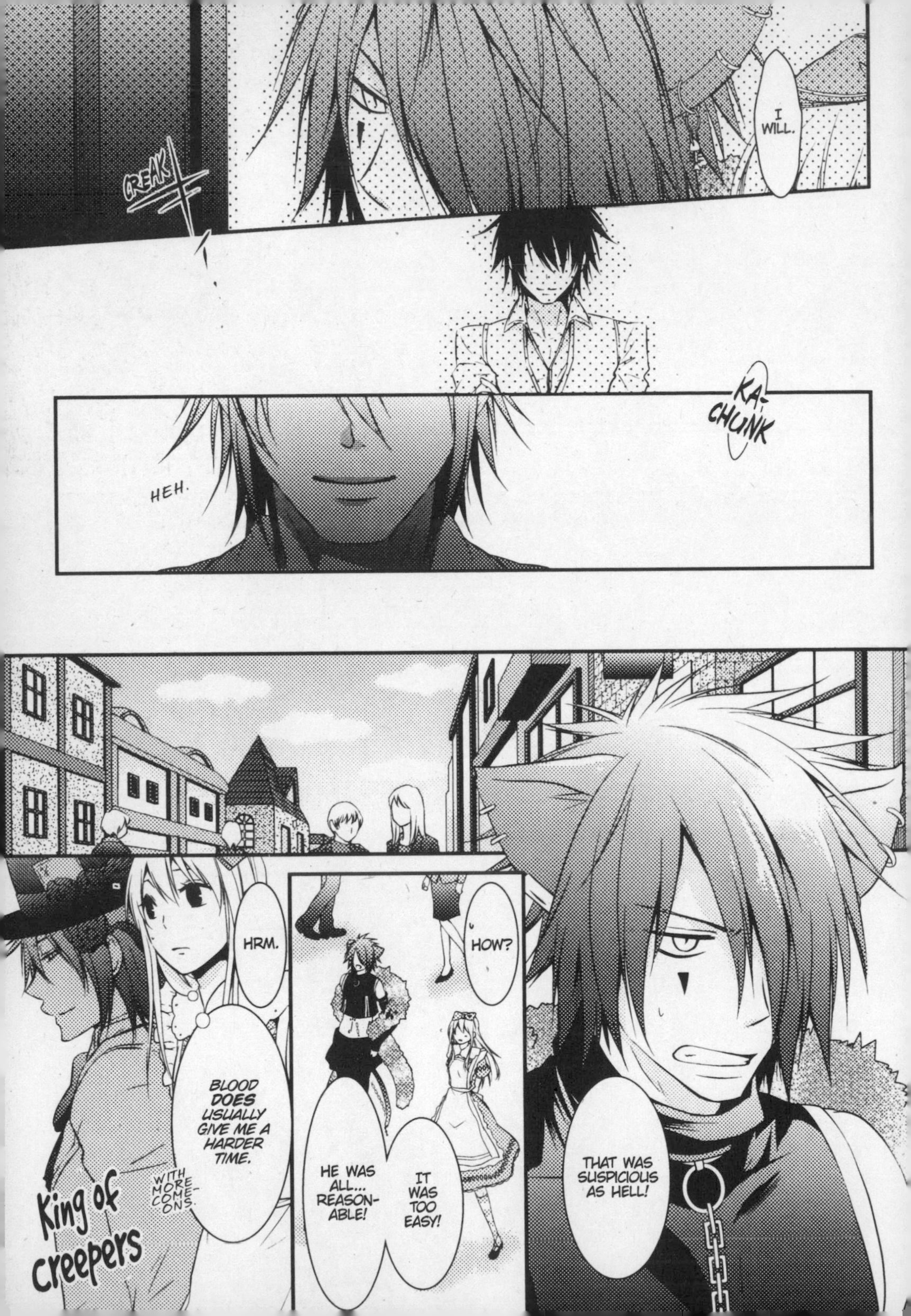
I WILL.
CREAK
KA-CHUNK
HEH.
THAT WAS SUSPICIOUS AS HELL!
HOW?
IT WAS TOO EASY!
HE WAS ALL... REASONABLE!
HRM.
BLOOD DOES USUALLY GIVE ME A HARDER TIME.
WITH MORE COME-ONS.
King of creepers

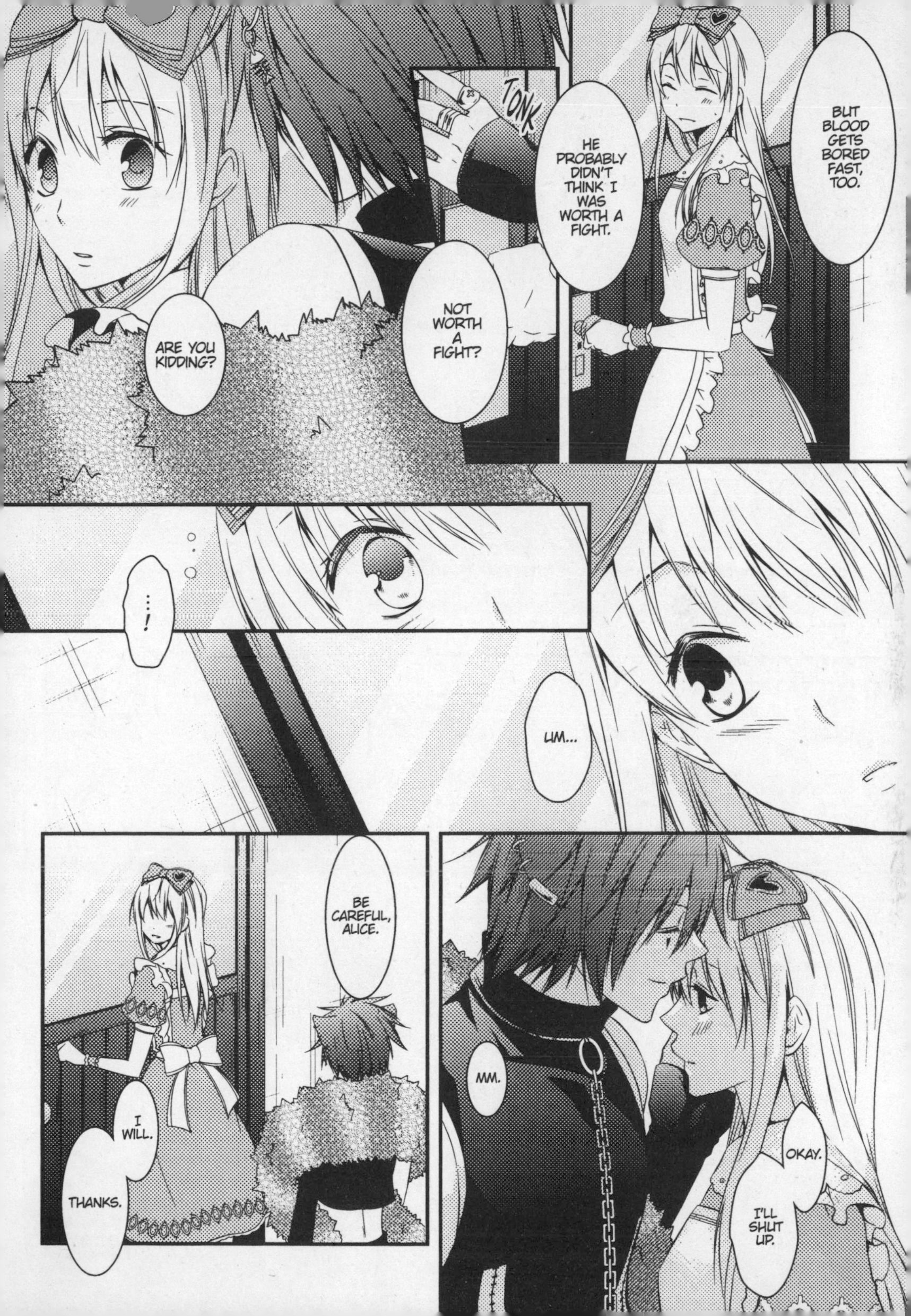
BUT BLOOD GETS BORED FAST, TOO.
HE PROBABLY DIDN'T THINK I WAS WORTH A FIGHT.
TONK
NOT WORTH A FIGHT?
ARE YOU KIDDING?
...!
UM...
MM.
OKAY.
I'LL SHUT UP.
BE CAREFUL, ALICE.
I WILL.
THANKS.

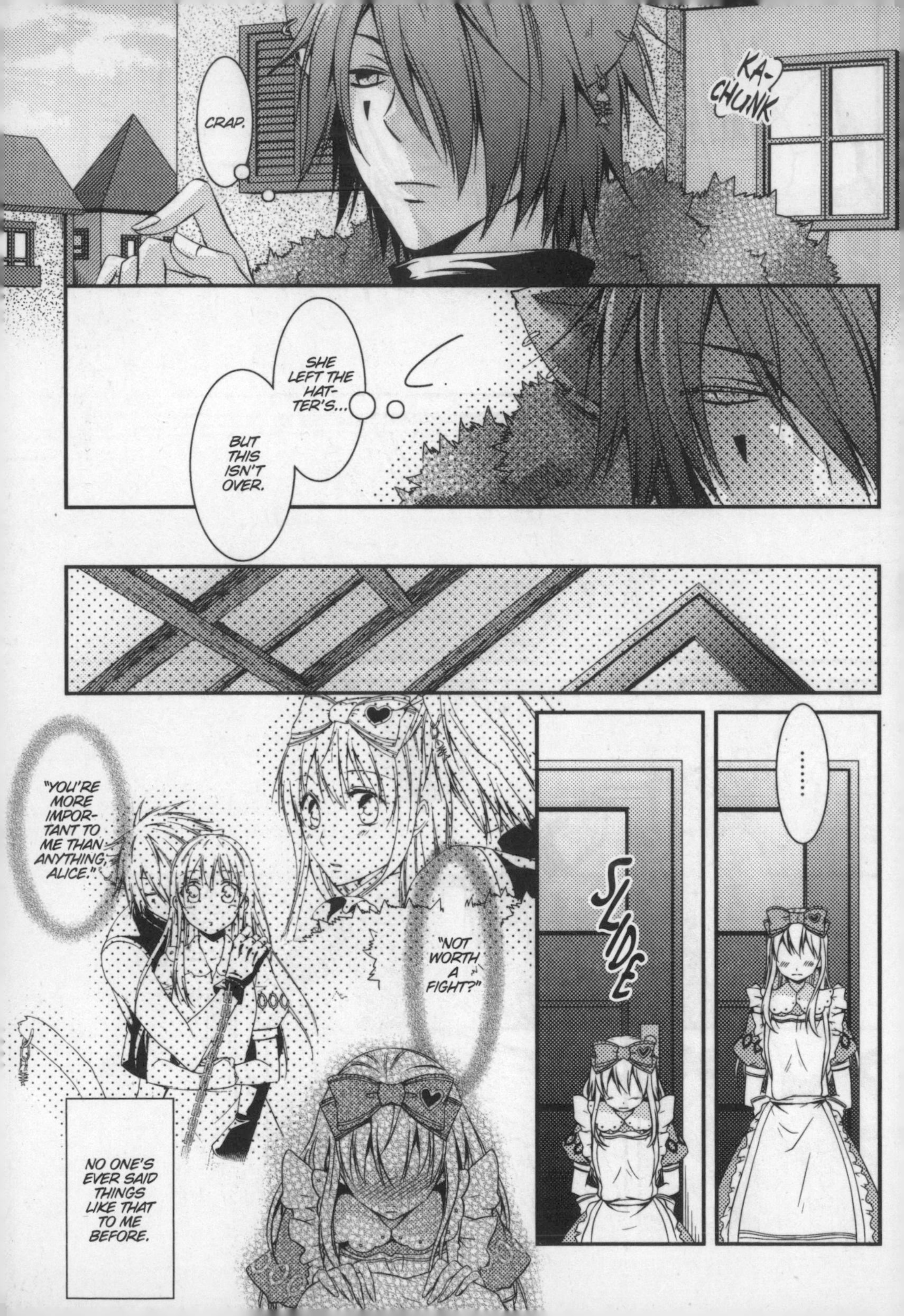
KA-CHUNK
CRAP.
SHE LEFT THE HATTER'S...
BUT THIS ISN'T OVER.
......
SLIDE
"YOU'RE MORE IMPORTANT TO ME THAN ANYTHING, ALICE."
"NOT WORTH A FIGHT?"
NO ONE'S EVER SAID THINGS LIKE THAT TO ME BEFORE.

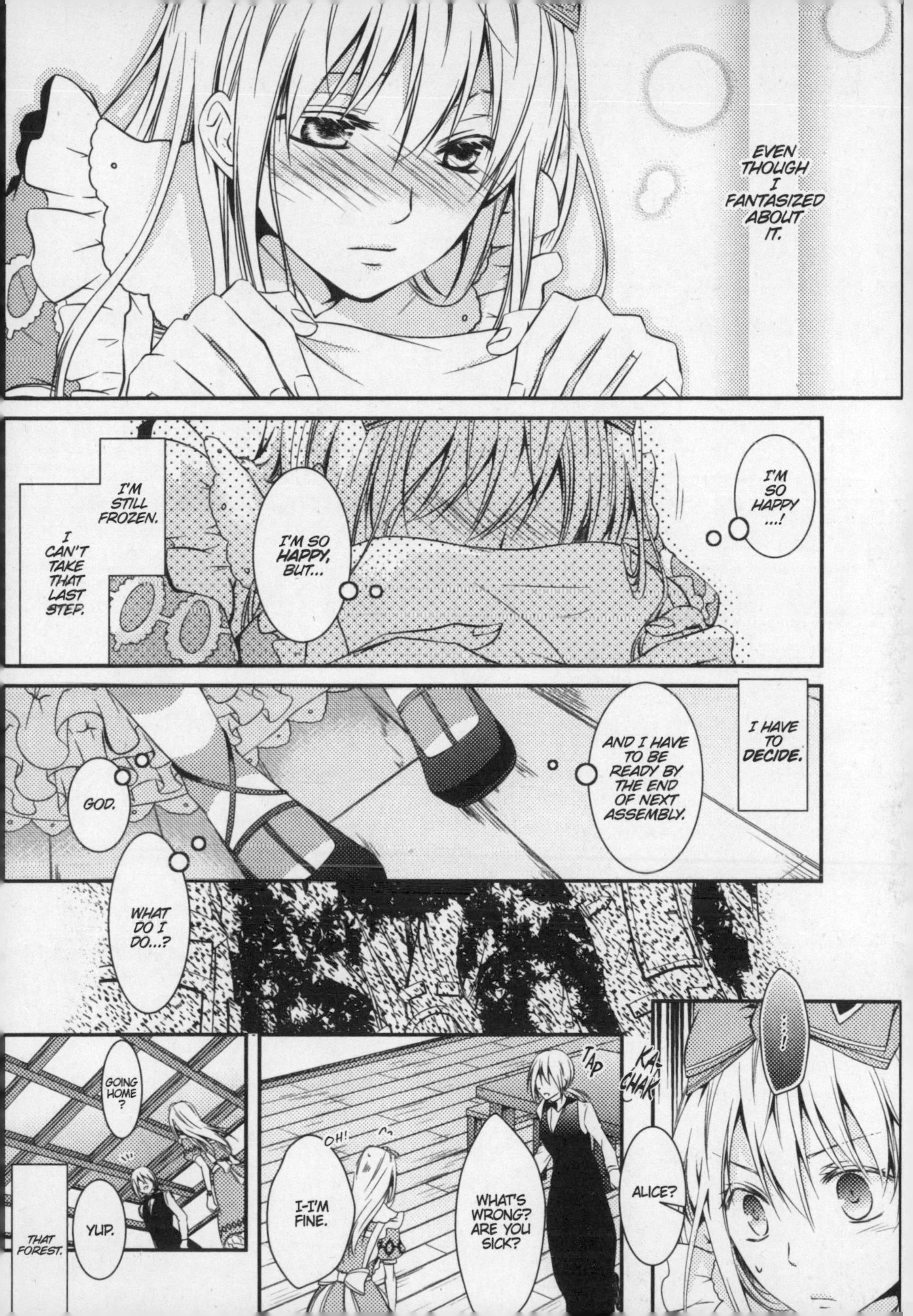
EVEN THOUGH I FANTASIZED ABOUT IT.
I'M SO HAPPY ...!
I'M SO HAPPY, BUT...
I'M STILL FROZEN.
I CAN'T TAKE THAT LAST STEP.
I HAVE TO DECIDE.
AND I HAVE TO BE READY BY THE END OF NEXT ASSEMBLY.
GOD.
WHAT DO I DO...?
...!
KA-CHAK
ALICE?
TAP
WHAT'S WRONG? ARE YOU SICK?
OH!
I-I'M FINE.
GOING HOME?
YUP.
THAT FOREST.

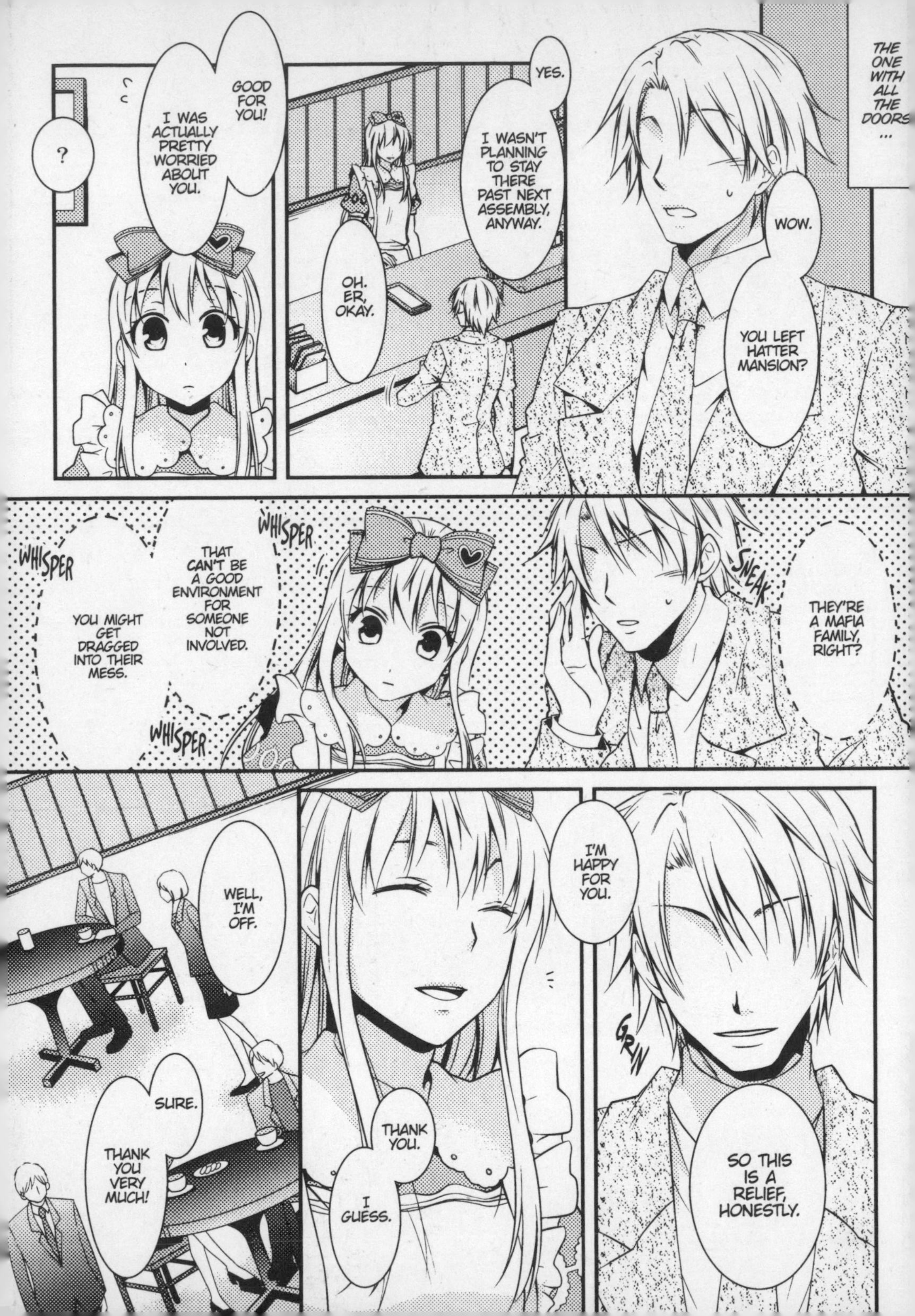
THE ONE WITH ALL THE DOORS...
WOW.
YOU LEFT HATTER MANSION?
YES.
I WASN'T PLANNING TO STAY THERE PAST NEXT ASSEMBLY, ANYWAY.
OH. ER, OKAY.
GOOD FOR YOU!
I WAS ACTUALLY PRETTY WORRIED ABOUT YOU.
?
SNEAK
THEY'RE A MAFIA FAMILY, RIGHT?
WHISPER
THAT CAN'T BE A GOOD ENVIRONMENT FOR SOMEONE NOT INVOLVED.
YOU MIGHT GET DRAGGED INTO THEIR MESS.
WHISPER
WHISPER
I'M HAPPY FOR YOU.
GRIN
SO THIS IS A RELIEF, HONESTLY.
THANK YOU.
I GUESS.
WELL, I'M OFF.
SURE.
THANK YOU VERY MUCH!

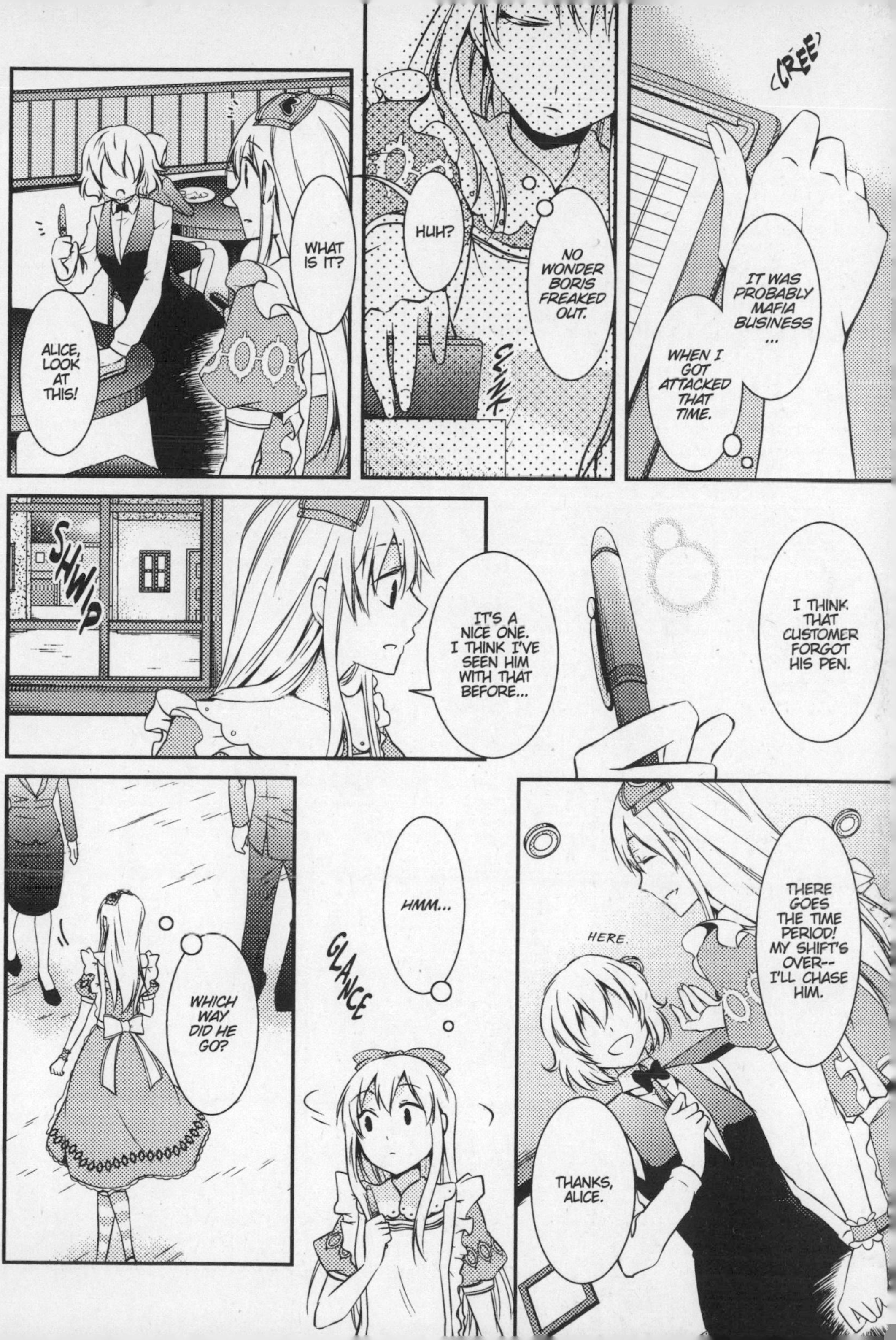
(CREE)
IT WAS PROBABLY MAFIA BUSINESS ...
WHEN I GOT ATTACKED THAT TIME.
NO WONDER BORIS FREAKED OUT.
HUH?
CLINK
WHAT IS IT?
ALICE, LOOK AT THIS!
I THINK THAT CUSTOMER FORGOT HIS PEN.
IT'S A NICE ONE. I THINK I'VE SEEN HIM WITH THAT BEFORE...
SHWIP
THERE GOES THE TIME PERIOD! MY SHIFT'S OVER-- I'LL CHASE HIM.
HERE.
THANKS, ALICE.
HMM...
GLANCE
WHICH WAY DID HE GO?

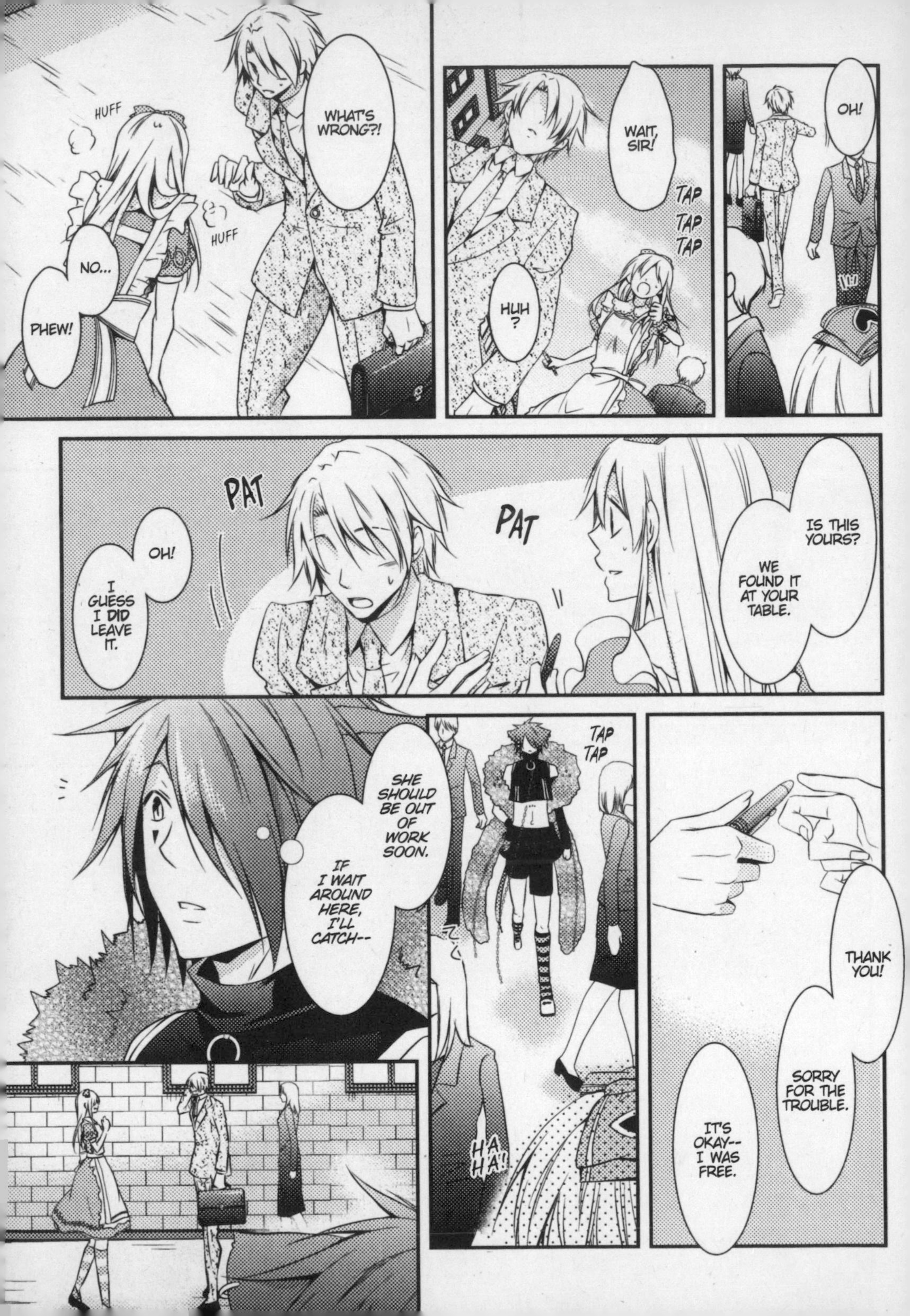
OH!
WAIT, SIR!
TAP TAP TAP
HUH?
WHAT'S WRONG?!
HUFF
HUFF
NO...
PHEW!
IS THIS YOURS?
WE FOUND IT AT YOUR TABLE.
PAT
PAT
OH!
I GUESS I DID LEAVE IT.
THANK YOU!
SORRY FOR THE TROUBLE.
IT'S OKAY-- I WAS FREE.
TAP TAP
HA HA!
SHE SHOULD BE OUT OF WORK SOON.
IF I WAIT AROUND HERE, I'LL CATCH--

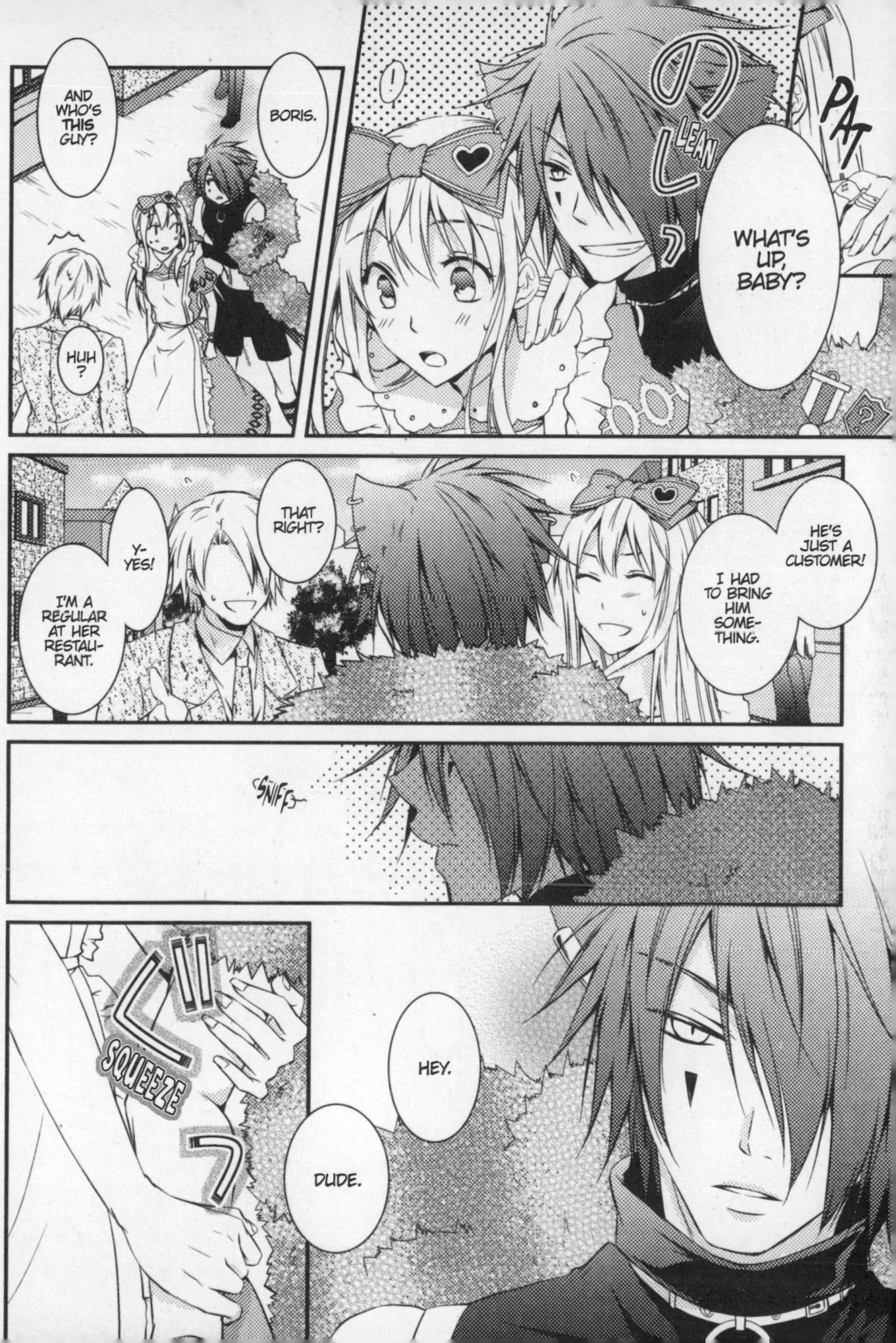
PAT
WHAT'S UP, BABY?
LEAN
!
AND WHO'S THIS GUY?
BORIS.
HUH?
HE'S JUST A CUSTOMER!
I HAD TO BRING HIM SOME-THING.
THAT RIGHT?
Y-YES!
I'M A REGULAR AT HER RESTAU-RANT.
SNIFF
HEY.
DUDE.
SQUEEZE

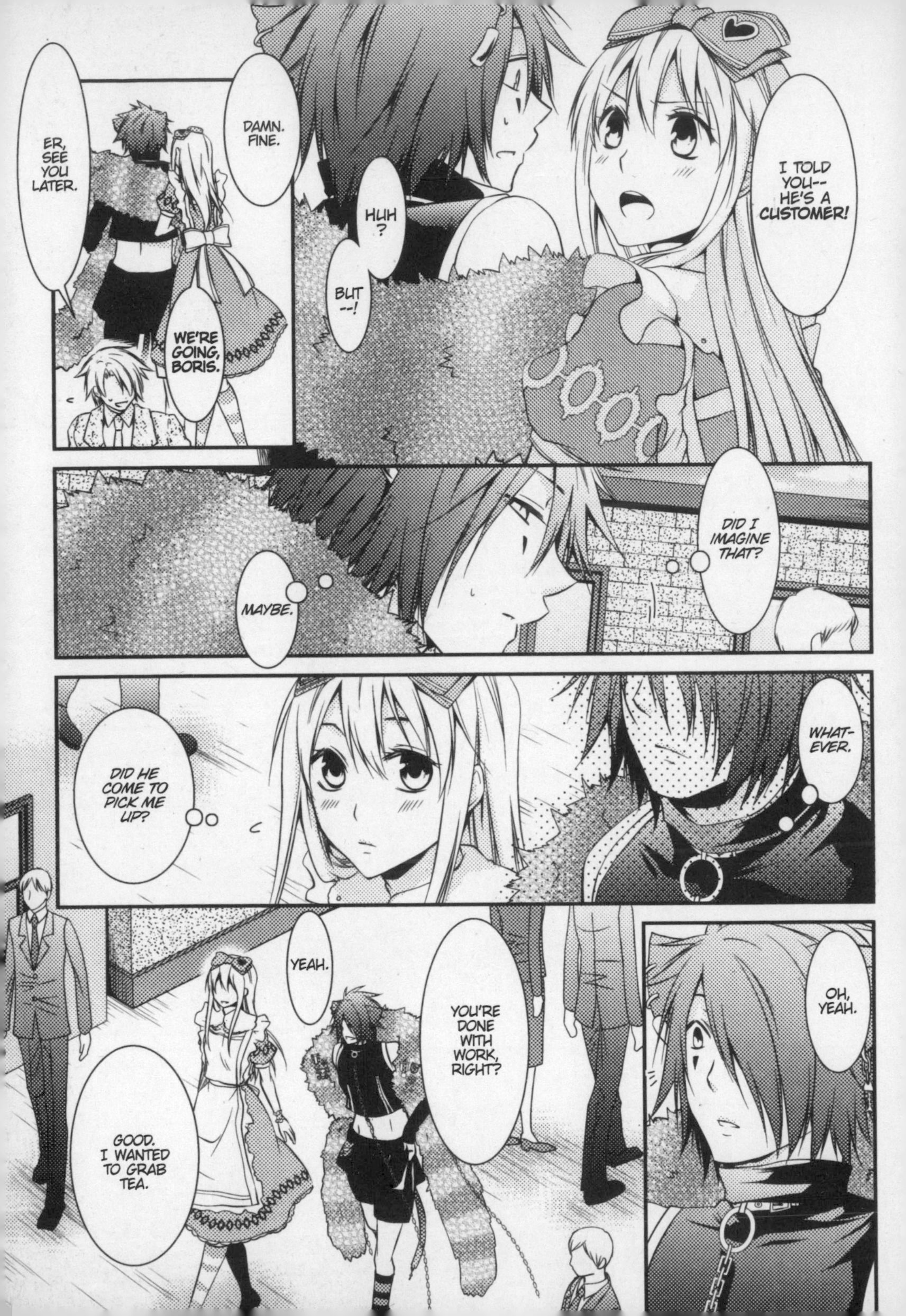
I TOLD YOU-- HE'S A CUSTOMER!
HUH?
BUT--!
DAMN. FINE.
WE'RE GOING, BORIS.
ER, SEE YOU LATER.
DID I IMAGINE THAT?
MAYBE.
WHAT-EVER.
DID HE COME TO PICK ME UP?
OH, YEAH.
YOU'RE DONE WITH WORK, RIGHT?
YEAH.
GOOD. I WANTED TO GRAB TEA.

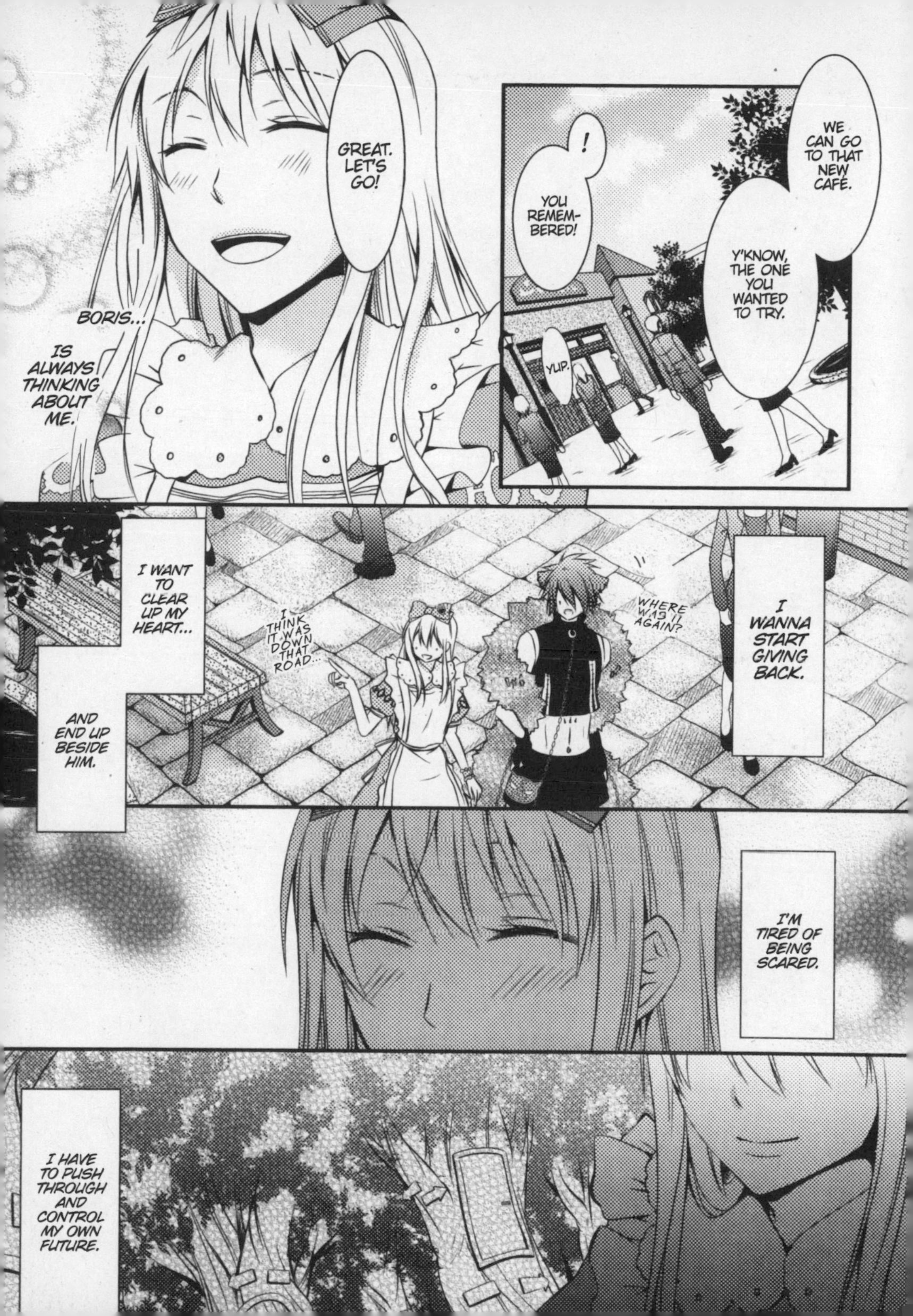
WE CAN GO TO THAT NEW CAFÉ.
Y'KNOW, THE ONE YOU WANTED TO TRY.
!
YOU REMEMBERED!
YUP.
GREAT. LET'S GO!
BORIS...
IS ALWAYS THINKING ABOUT ME.
I WANNA START GIVING BACK.
WHERE WAS IT AGAIN?
I THINK IT WAS DOWN THAT ROAD...
I WANT TO CLEAR UP MY HEART...
AND END UP BESIDE HIM.
I'M TIRED OF BEING SCARED.
I HAVE TO PUSH THROUGH AND CONTROL MY OWN FUTURE.

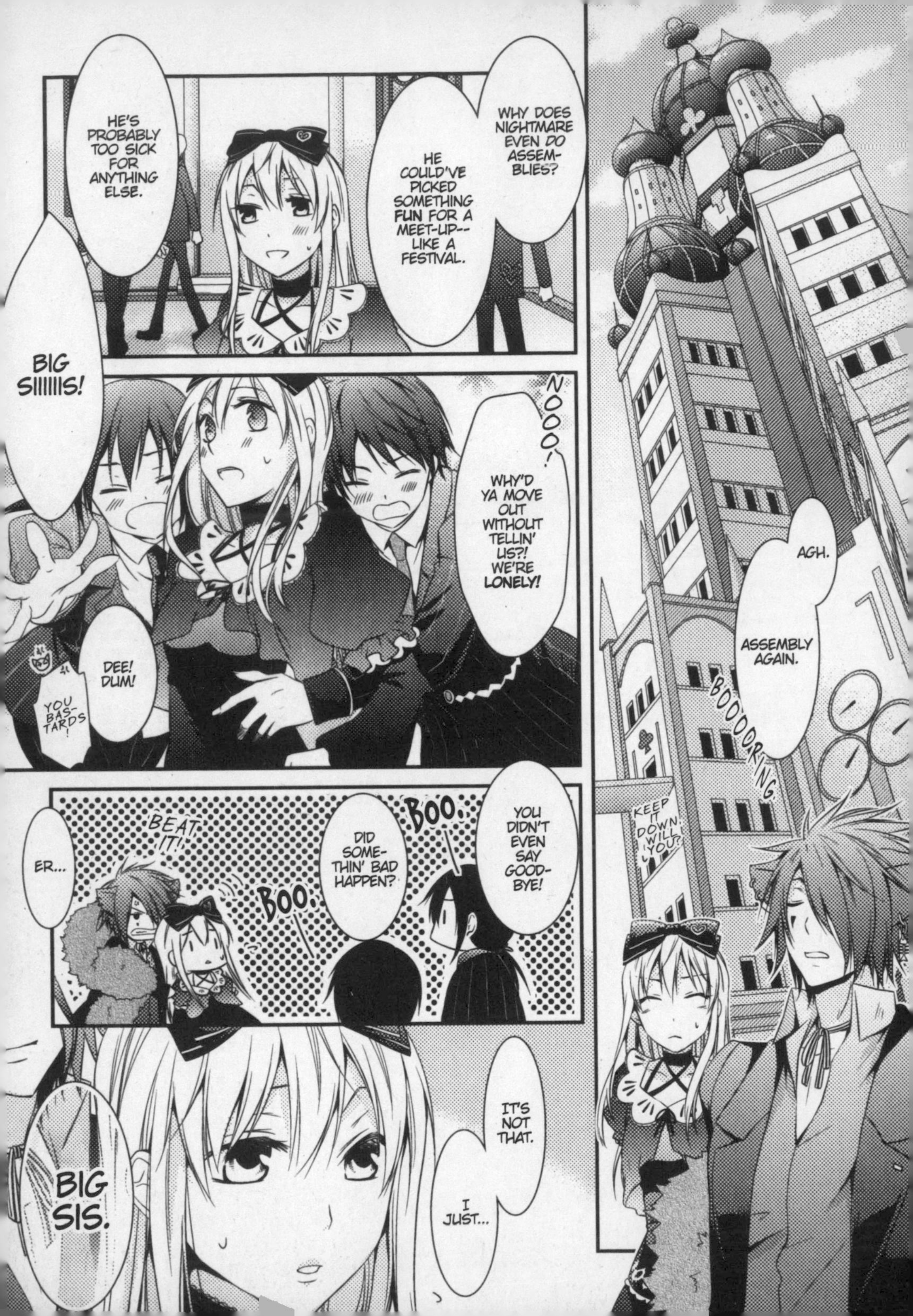
AGH.
ASSEMBLY AGAIN.
BOOOORING.
KEEP IT DOWN, WILL YOU?
WHY DOES NIGHTMARE EVEN DO ASSEMBLIES?
HE COULD'VE PICKED SOMETHING FUN FOR A MEET-UP--LIKE A FESTIVAL.
HE'S PROBABLY TOO SICK FOR ANYTHING ELSE.
NOOOO!
WHY'D YA MOVE OUT WITHOUT TELLIN' US?! WE'RE LONELY!
BIG SIIIIIS!
DEE! DUM!
YOU BASTARDS!
YOU DIDN'T EVEN SAY GOOD-BYE!
BOO.
DID SOMETHIN' BAD HAPPEN?
BOO.
BEAT IT!
ER...
IT'S NOT THAT.
I JUST...
BIG SIS.

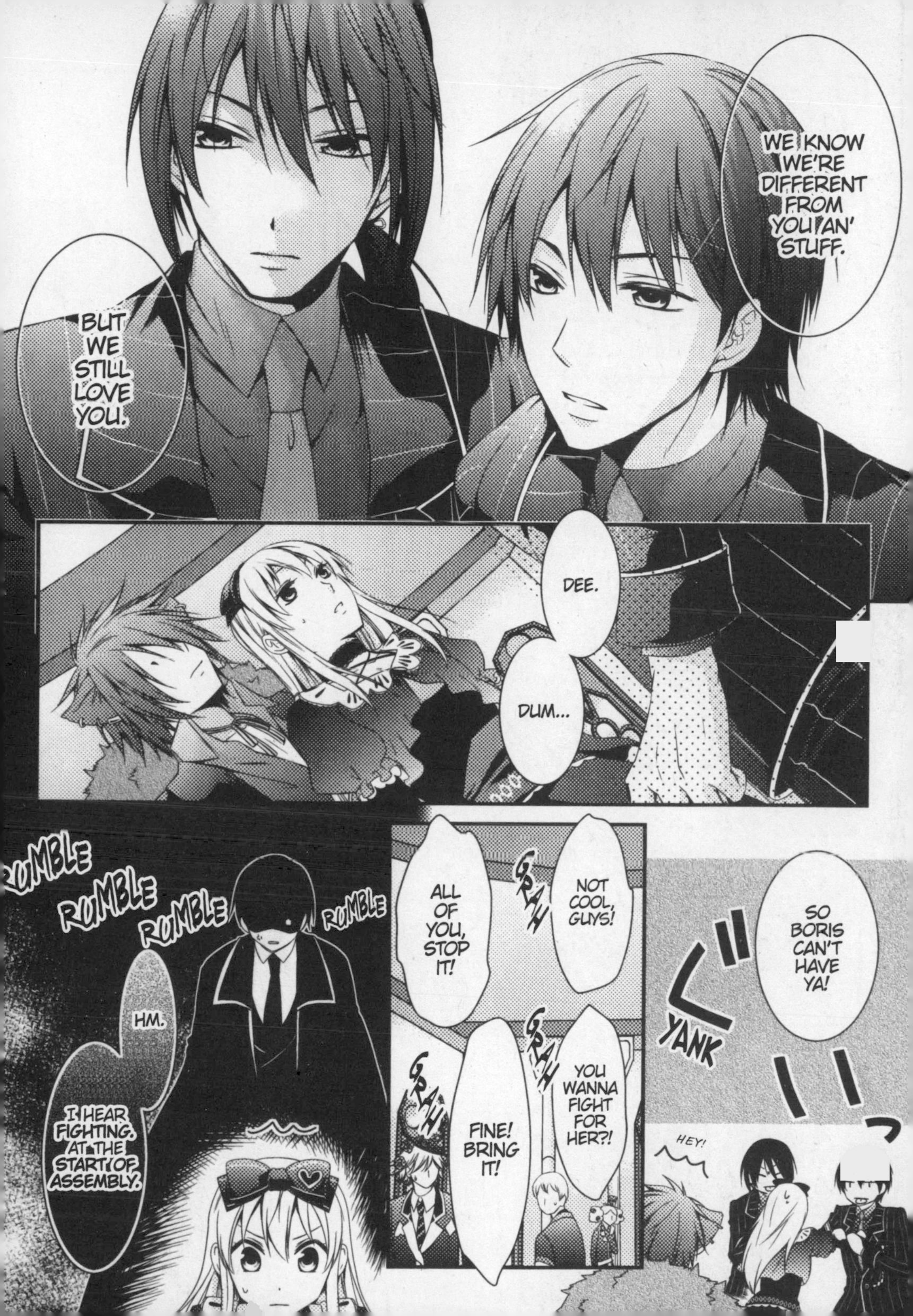
WE KNOW WE'RE DIFFERENT FROM YOU AN' STUFF.
BUT WE STILL LOVE YOU.
DEE.
DUM...
SO BORIS CAN'T HAVE YA!
YANK
HEY!
NOT COOL, GUYS!
GRAH
ALL OF YOU, STOP IT!
GRAH
YOU WANNA FIGHT FOR HER?!
GRAH
FINE! BRING IT!
RUMBLE
RUMBLE
RUMBLE
RUMBLE
HM.
I HEAR FIGHTING. AT THE START OF ASSEMBLY.

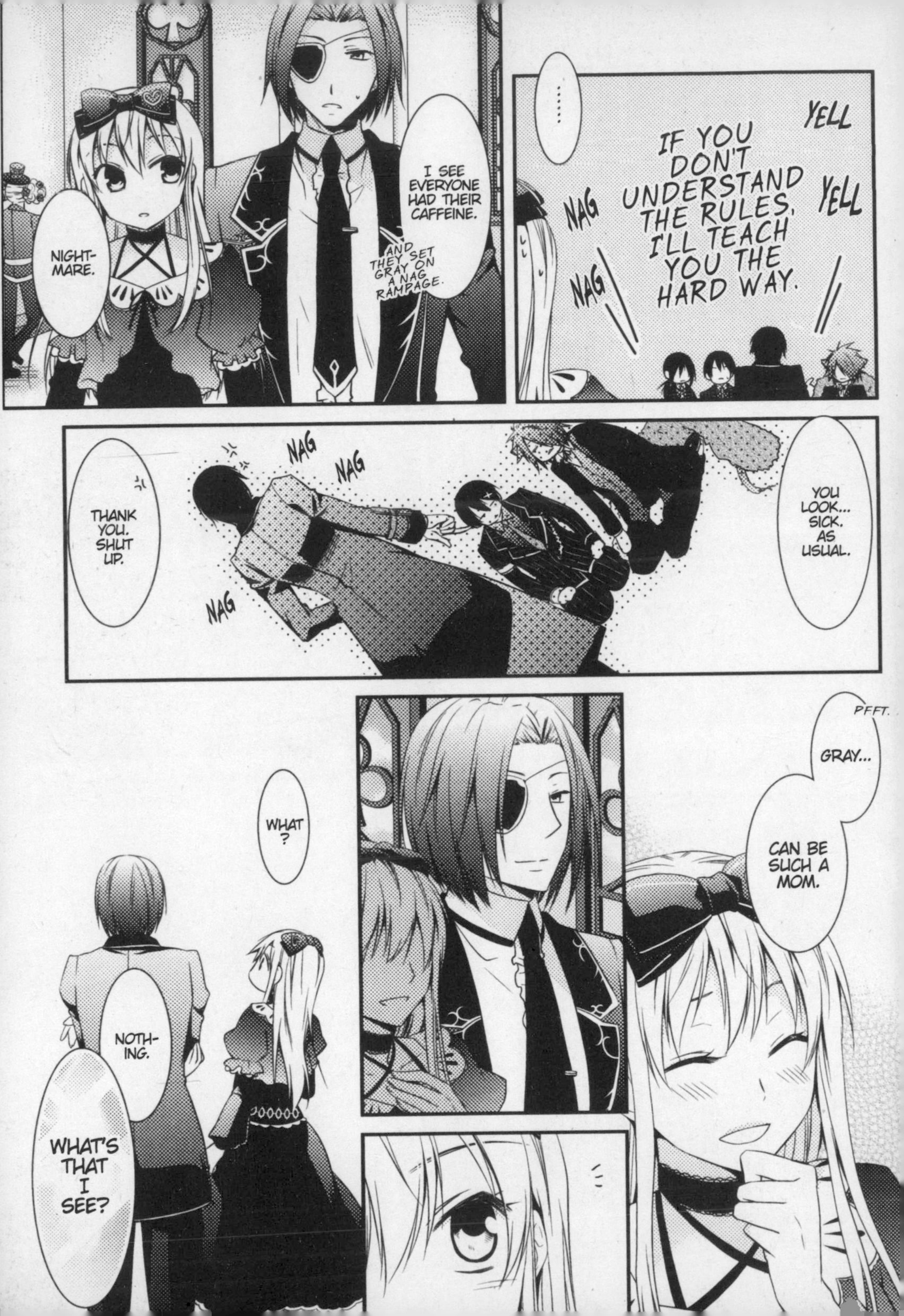
......
IF YOU DON'T UNDERSTAND THE RULES, I'LL TEACH YOU THE HARD WAY.
YELL
YELL
NAG
NAG
I SEE EVERYONE HAD THEIR CAFFEINE.
AND THEY SET GRAY ON A NAG RAMPAGE.
NIGHT-MARE.
YOU LOOK... SICK. AS USUAL.
NAG
NAG
NAG
THANK YOU. SHUT UP.
PFFT.
GRAY...
CAN BE SUCH A MOM.
WHAT ?
NOTH-ING.
WHAT'S THAT I SEE?

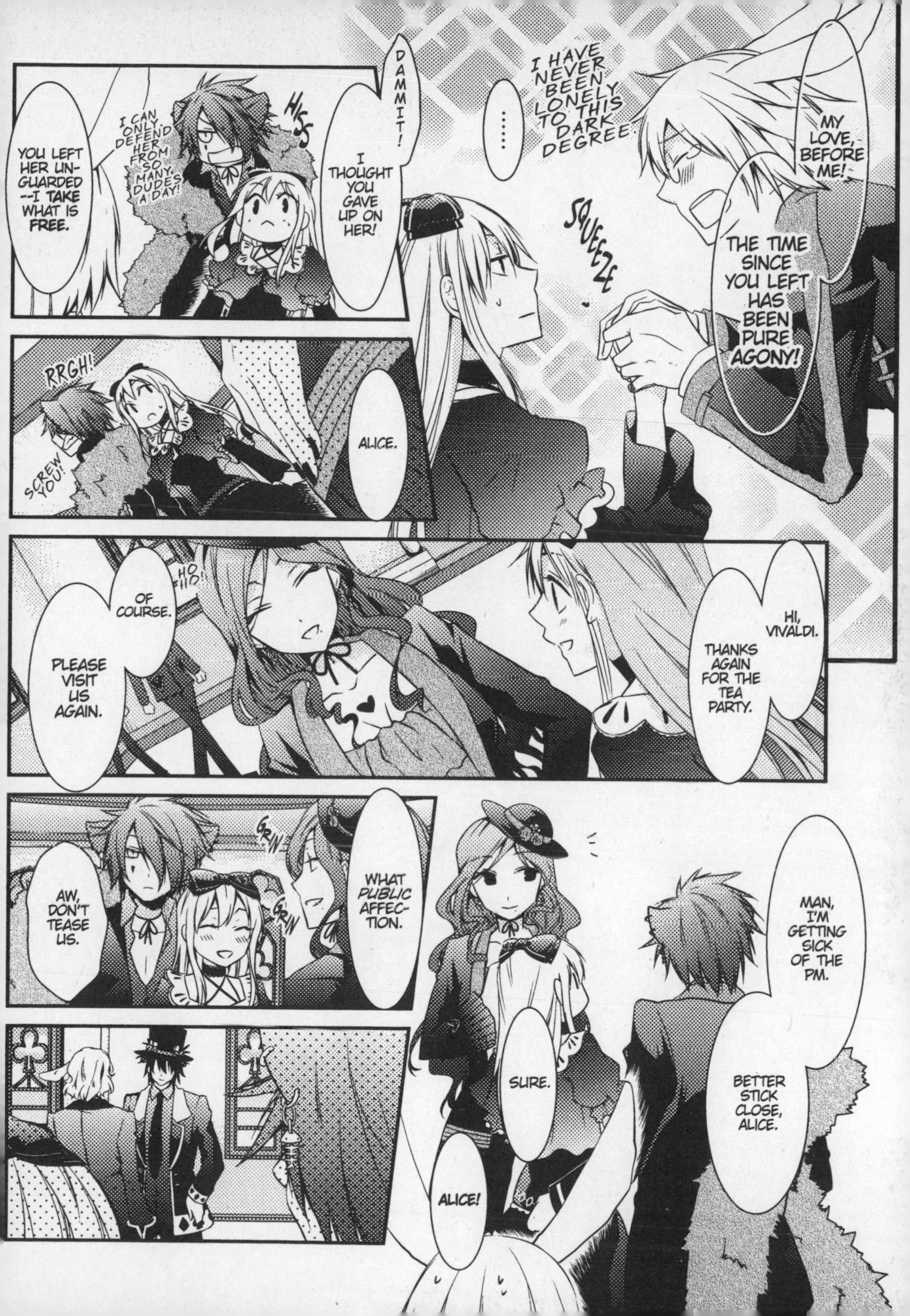
MY LOVE, BEFORE ME!
THE TIME SINCE YOU LEFT HAS BEEN PURE AGONY!
SQUEEZE
I HAVE NEVER BEEN LONELY TO THIS DARK DEGREE.
......
DAMMIT!
I THOUGHT YOU GAVE UP ON HER!
HISS
I CAN ONLY DEFEND HER FROM SO MANY DUDES A DAY!
YOU LEFT HER UN-GUARDED --I TAKE WHAT IS FREE.
ALICE.
RRGH!
SCREW YOU!
HI, VIVALDI.
THANKS AGAIN FOR THE TEA PARTY.
HO HO!
OF COURSE.
PLEASE VISIT US AGAIN.
MAN, I'M GETTING SICK OF THE PM.
BETTER STICK CLOSE, ALICE.
SURE.
ALICE!
WHAT PUBLIC AFFECTION.
GRIN
GRIN
AW, DON'T TEASE US.

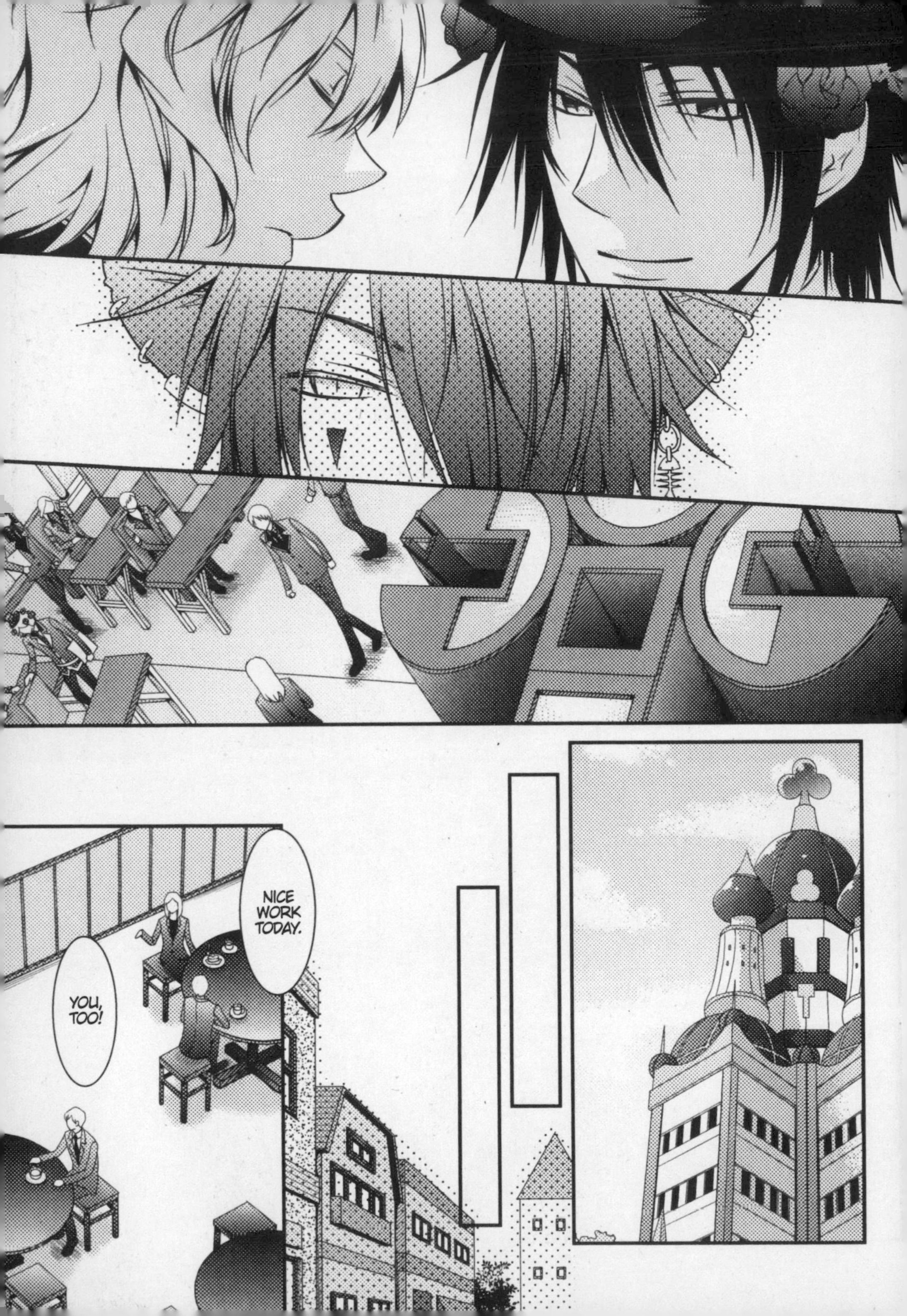
NICE WORK TODAY.
YOU, TOO!

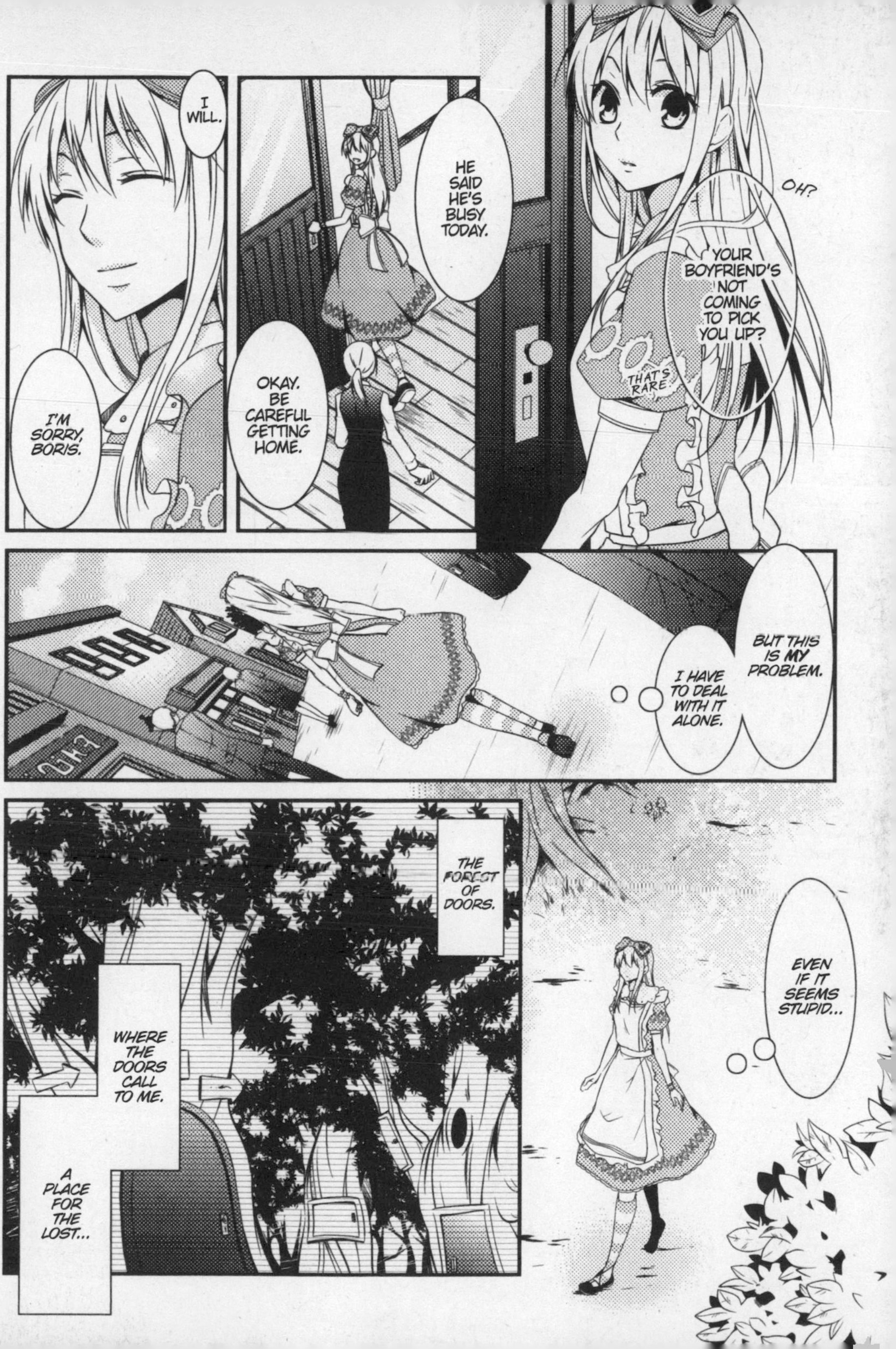
OH?
YOUR BOYFRIEND'S NOT COMING TO PICK YOU UP?
THAT'S RARE.
HE SAID HE'S BUSY TODAY.
OKAY. BE CAREFUL GETTING HOME.
I WILL.
I'M SORRY, BORIS.
BUT THIS IS MY PROBLEM.
I HAVE TO DEAL WITH IT ALONE.
EVEN IF IT SEEMS STUPID...
THE FOREST OF DOORS.
WHERE THE DOORS CALL TO ME.
A PLACE FOR THE LOST...

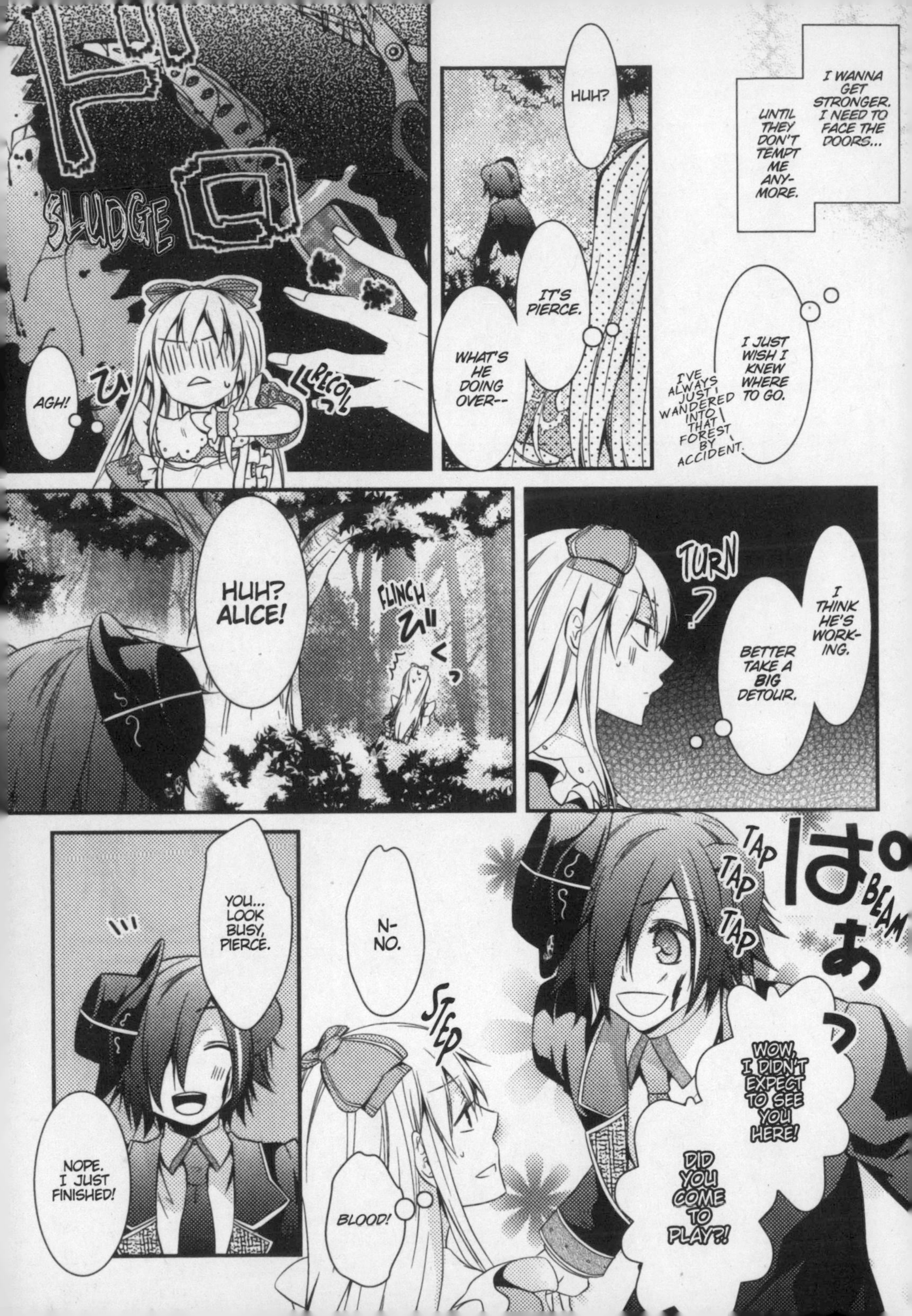
I WANNA GET STRONGER. I NEED TO FACE THE DOORS...
UNTIL THEY DON'T TEMPT ME ANYMORE.
I JUST WISH I KNEW WHERE TO GO.
I'VE ALWAYS JUST WANDERED INTO THAT FOREST BY ACCIDENT.
HUH?
IT'S PIERCE.
WHAT'S HE DOING OVER--
SLUDGE
AGH!
RECOIL
TURN
I THINK HE'S WORKING.
BETTER TAKE A BIG DETOUR.
HUH? ALICE!
FLINCH
TAP
TAP
TAP
BEAM
WOW, I DIDN'T EXPECT TO SEE YOU HERE!
DID YOU COME TO PLAY?!
YOU... LOOK BUSY, PIERCE.
N-NO.
STEP
NOPE. I JUST FINISHED!
BLOOD!

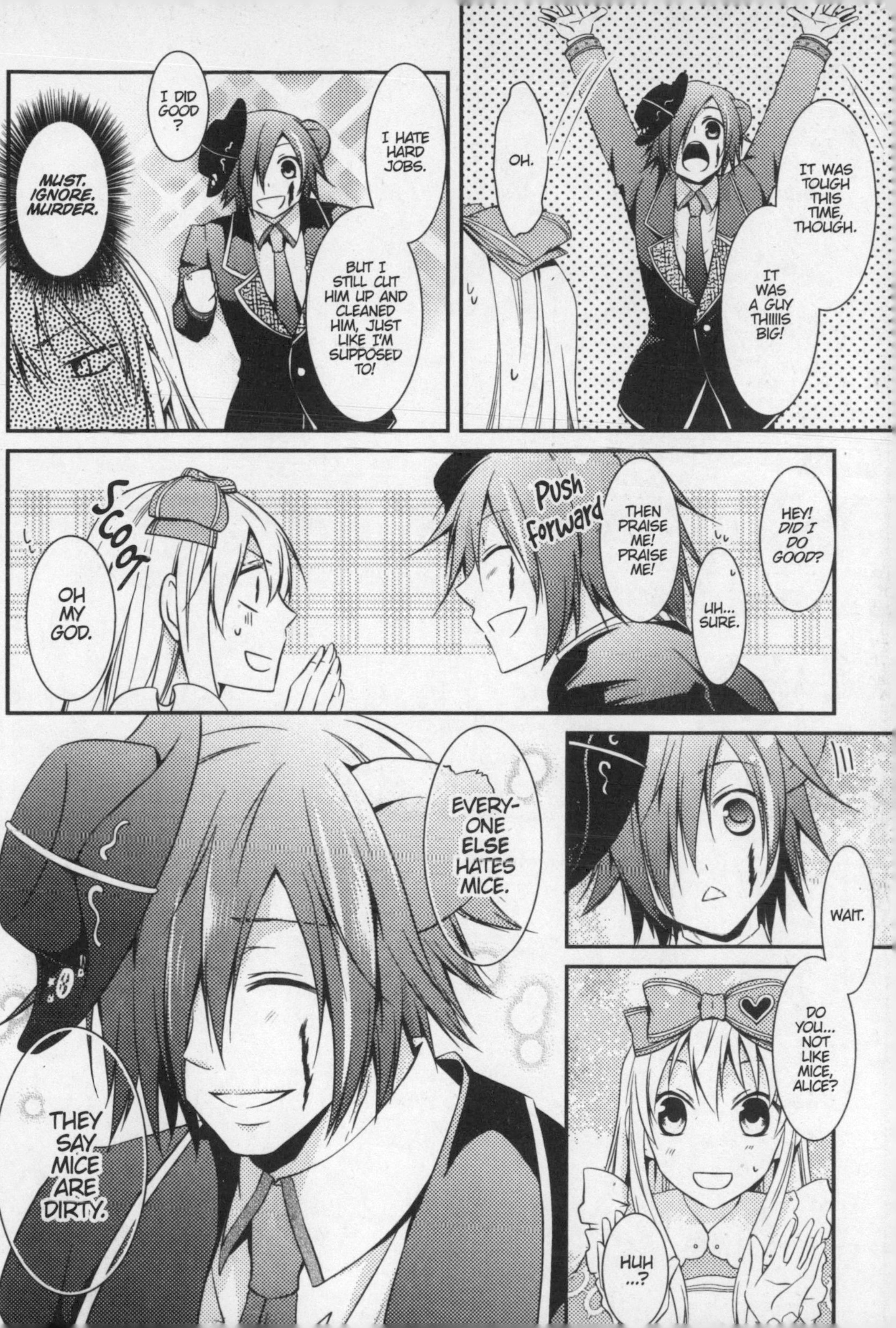
IT WAS TOUGH THIS TIME, THOUGH.
IT WAS A GUY THIIIIS BIG!
OH.
I HATE HARD JOBS.
I DID GOOD?
BUT I STILL CUT HIM UP AND CLEANED HIM, JUST LIKE I'M SUPPOSED TO!
MUST. IGNORE. MURDER.
HEY! DID I DO GOOD?
UH... SURE.
THEN PRAISE ME! PRAISE ME!
Push forward
SCOOT
OH MY GOD.
WAIT.
DO YOU... NOT LIKE MICE, ALICE?
HUH ...?
EVERY-ONE ELSE HATES MICE.
THEY SAY MICE ARE DIRTY.

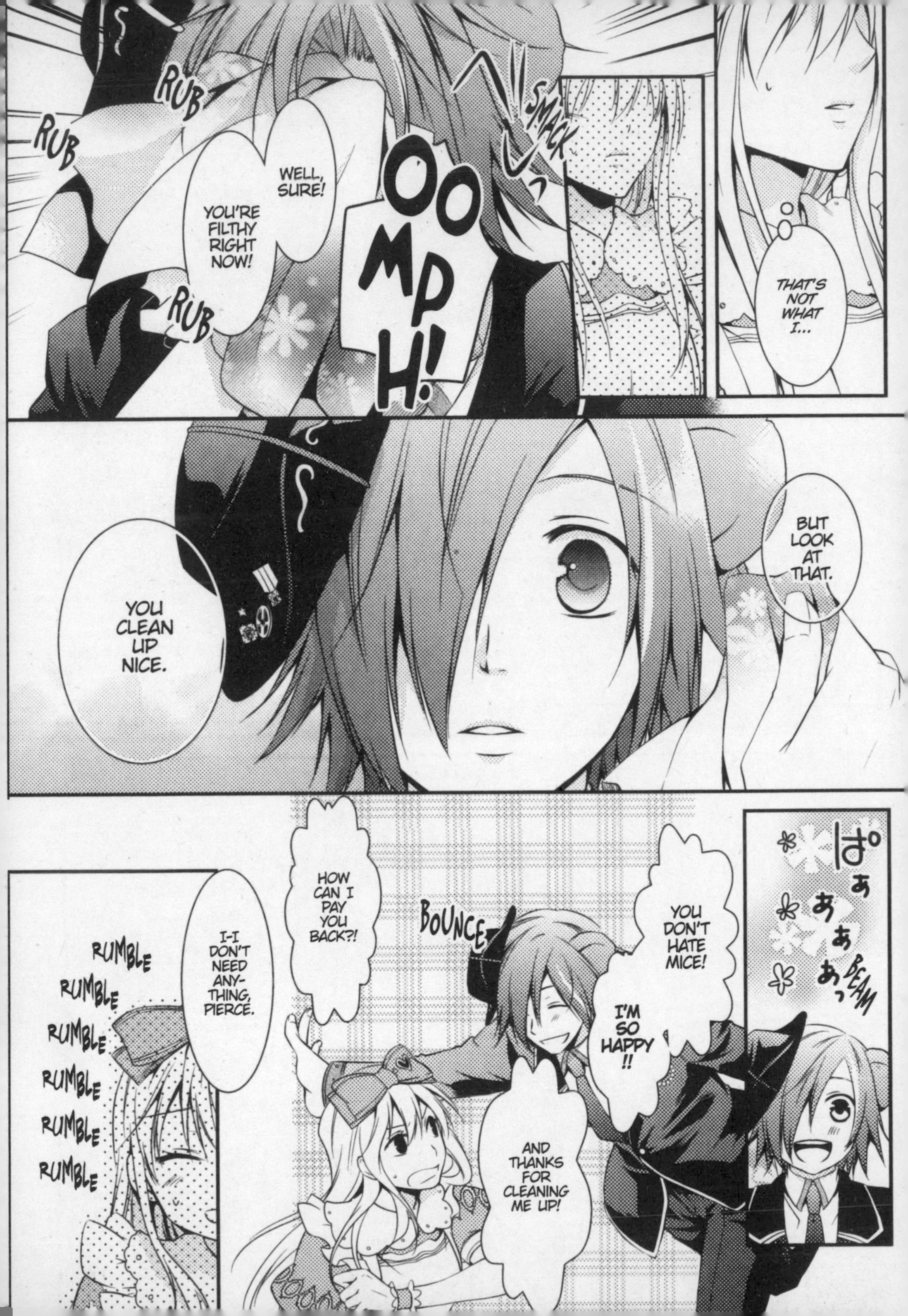
THAT'S NOT WHAT I...
SMACK
OOMPH!
WELL, SURE!
YOU'RE FILTHY RIGHT NOW!
RUB
RUB
RUB
BUT LOOK AT THAT.
YOU CLEAN UP NICE.
ぱぁあぁあっ
BEAM
YOU DON'T HATE MICE!
I'M SO HAPPY!!
BOUNCE
HOW CAN I PAY YOU BACK?!
AND THANKS FOR CLEANING ME UP!
I-I DON'T NEED ANYTHING, PIERCE.
RUMBLE
RUMBLE
RUMBLE
RUMBLE
RUMBLE
RUMBLE

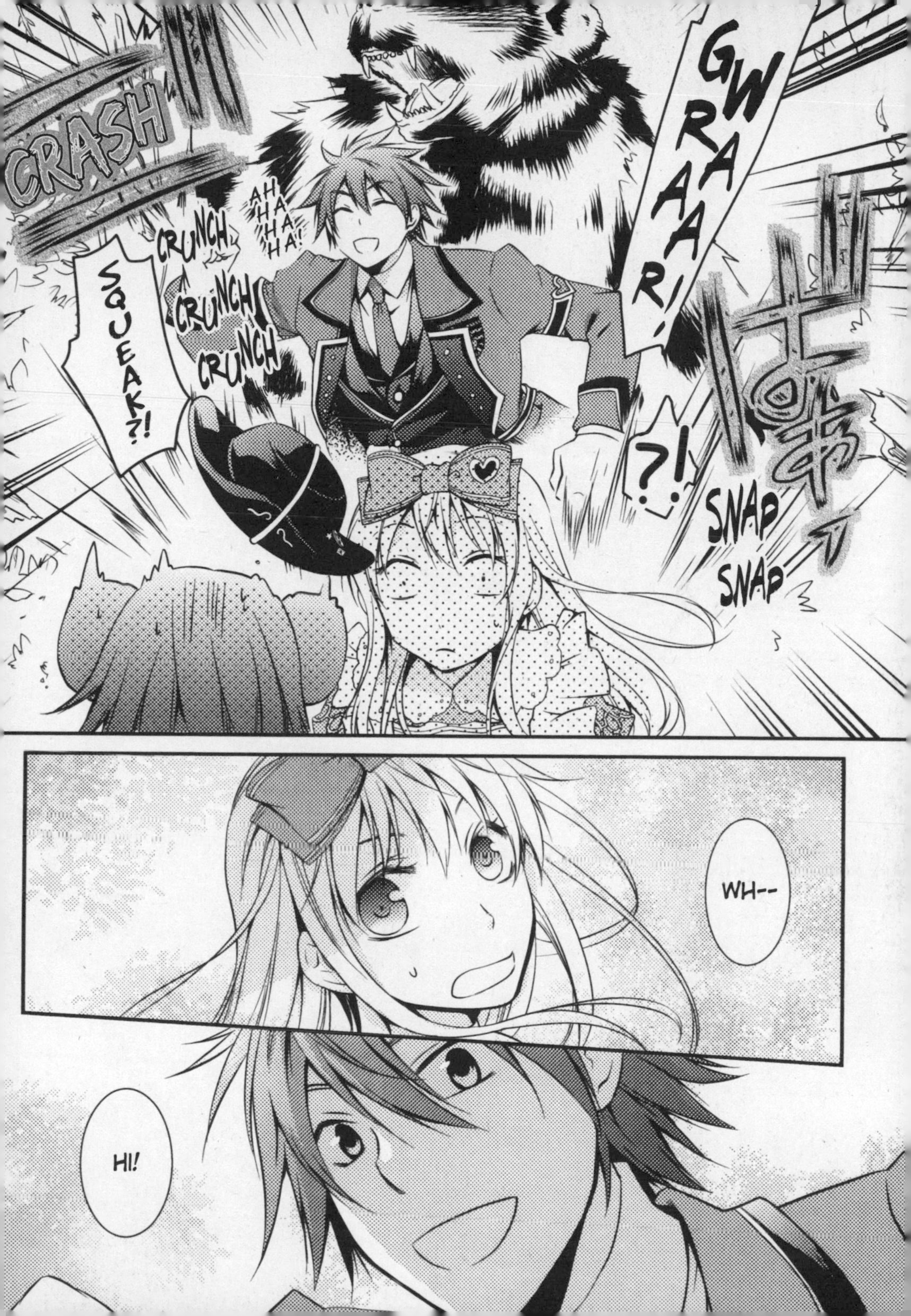
GWRAAAR!
?!
SNAP
SNAP
AHAHAHAHA!
CRASH
CRUNCH
CRUNCH
CRUNCH
SQUEAK?!
WH--
HI!

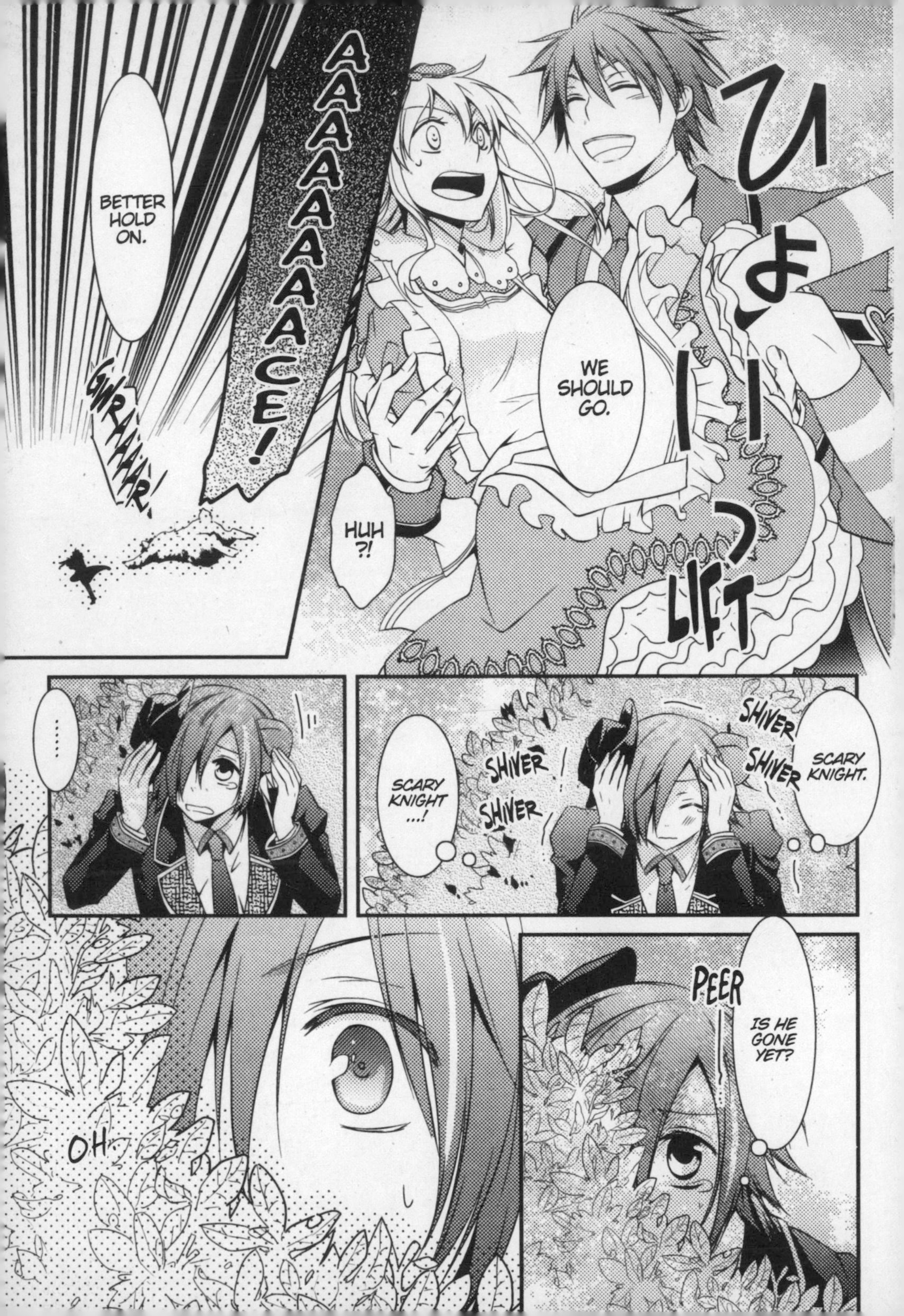

ひょーいっ
LIFT
WE SHOULD GO.
HUH?!
AAAAAAAAAAAACE!
BETTER HOLD ON.
GWRAAAAR!
SHIVER SHIVER
SCARY KNIGHT.
SHIVER SHIVER
SCARY KNIGHT...!
......
PEER
IS HE GONE YET?
OH.

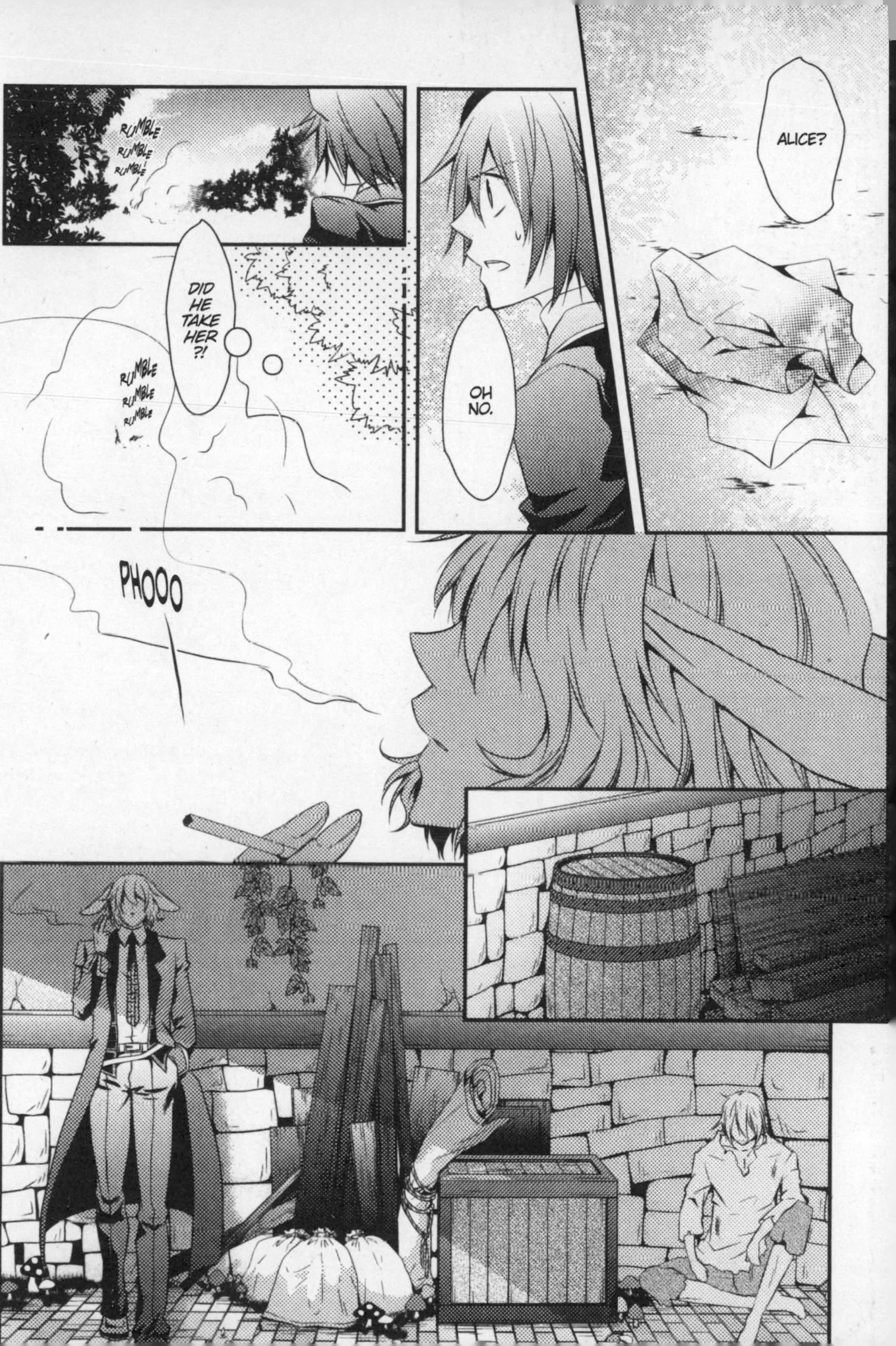
ALICE?
OH NO.
RUMBLE RUMBLE RUMBLE
DID HE TAKE HER?!
RUMBLE RUMBLE RUMBLE
PHOOO

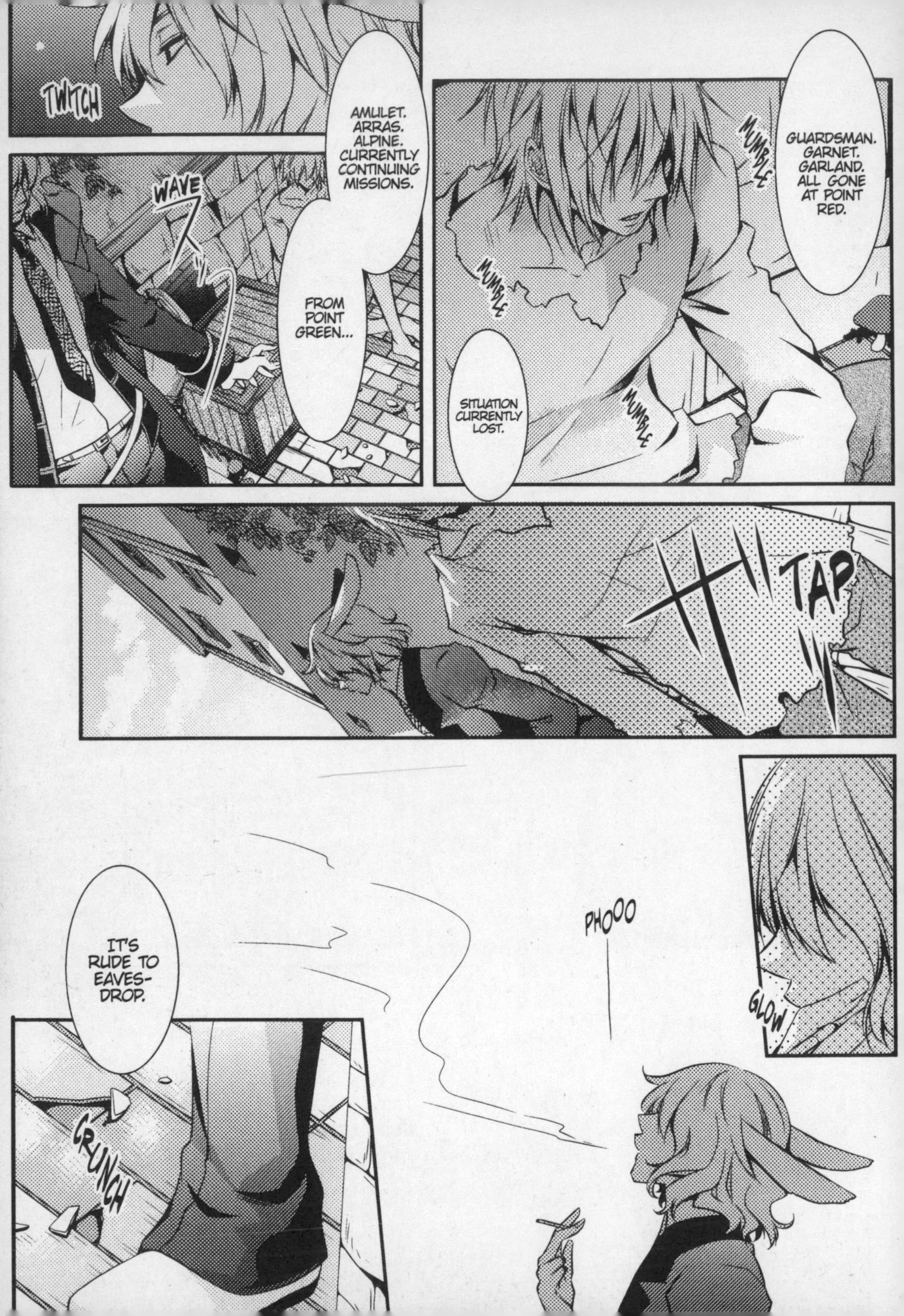
MUMBLE
GUARDSMAN. GARNET. GARLAND. ALL GONE AT POINT RED.
MUMBLE
SITUATION CURRENTLY LOST.
MUMBLE
TWITCH
AMULET. ARRAS. ALPINE. CURRENTLY CONTINUING MISSIONS.
WAVE
FROM POINT GREEN...
TAP
GLOW
PHOOO
IT'S RUDE TO EAVES-DROP.
CRUNCH

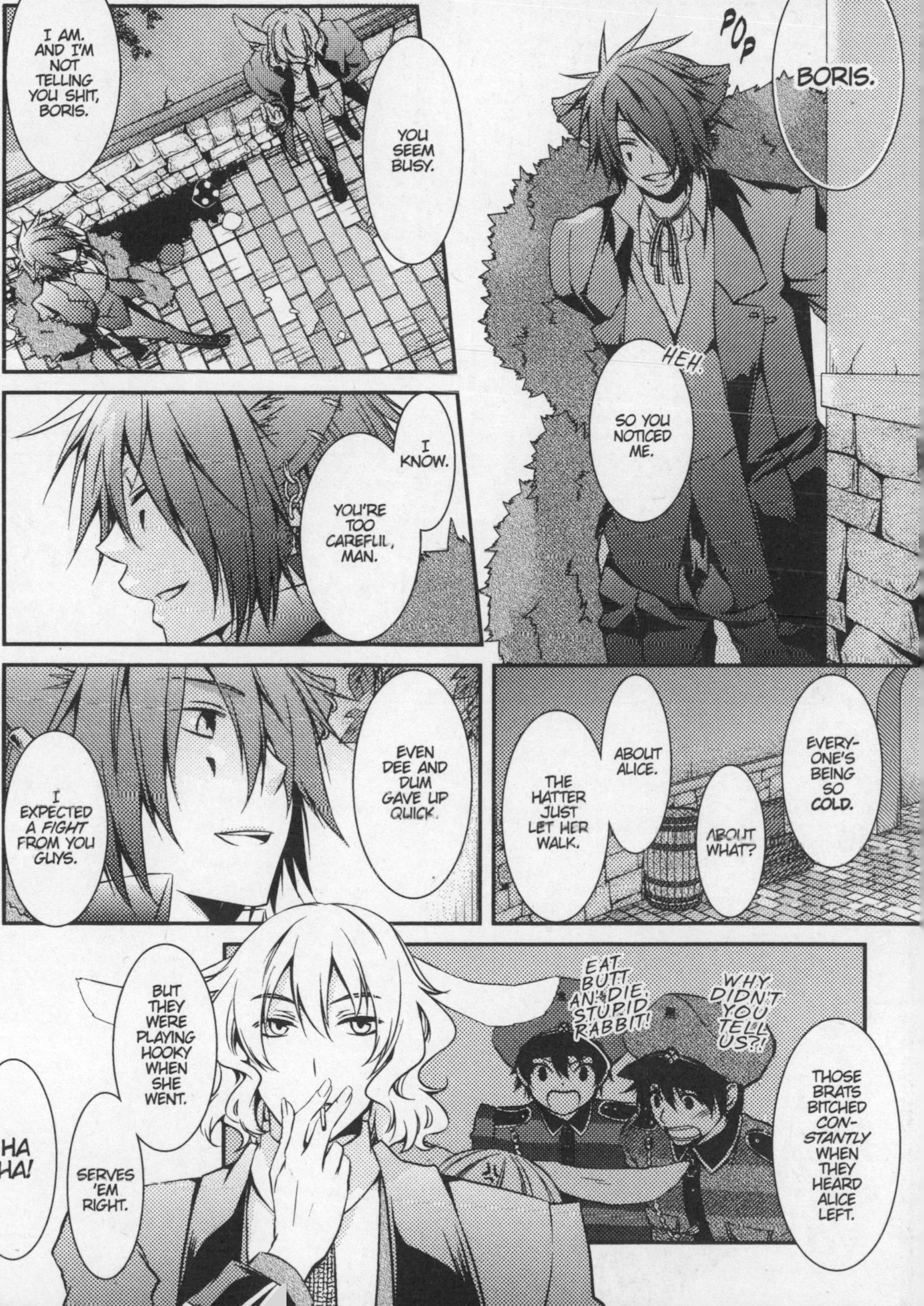
POP
BORIS.
HEH.
SO YOU NOTICED ME.
YOU SEEM BUSY.
I AM. AND I'M NOT TELLING YOU SHIT, BORIS.
I KNOW.
YOU'RE TOO CAREFUL, MAN.
EVERY-ONE'S BEING SO COLD.
ABOUT WHAT?
ABOUT ALICE.
THE HATTER JUST LET HER WALK.
EVEN DEE AND DUM GAVE UP QUICK.
I EXPECTED A *FIGHT* FROM YOU GUYS.
THOSE BRATS BITCHED *CON-STANTLY* WHEN THEY HEARD ALICE LEFT.
WHY DIDN'T YOU TELL US?!
EAT BUTT AN' DIE, STUPID RABBIT!
BUT THEY WERE PLAYING HOOKY WHEN SHE WENT.
SERVES 'EM RIGHT.
HA HA!

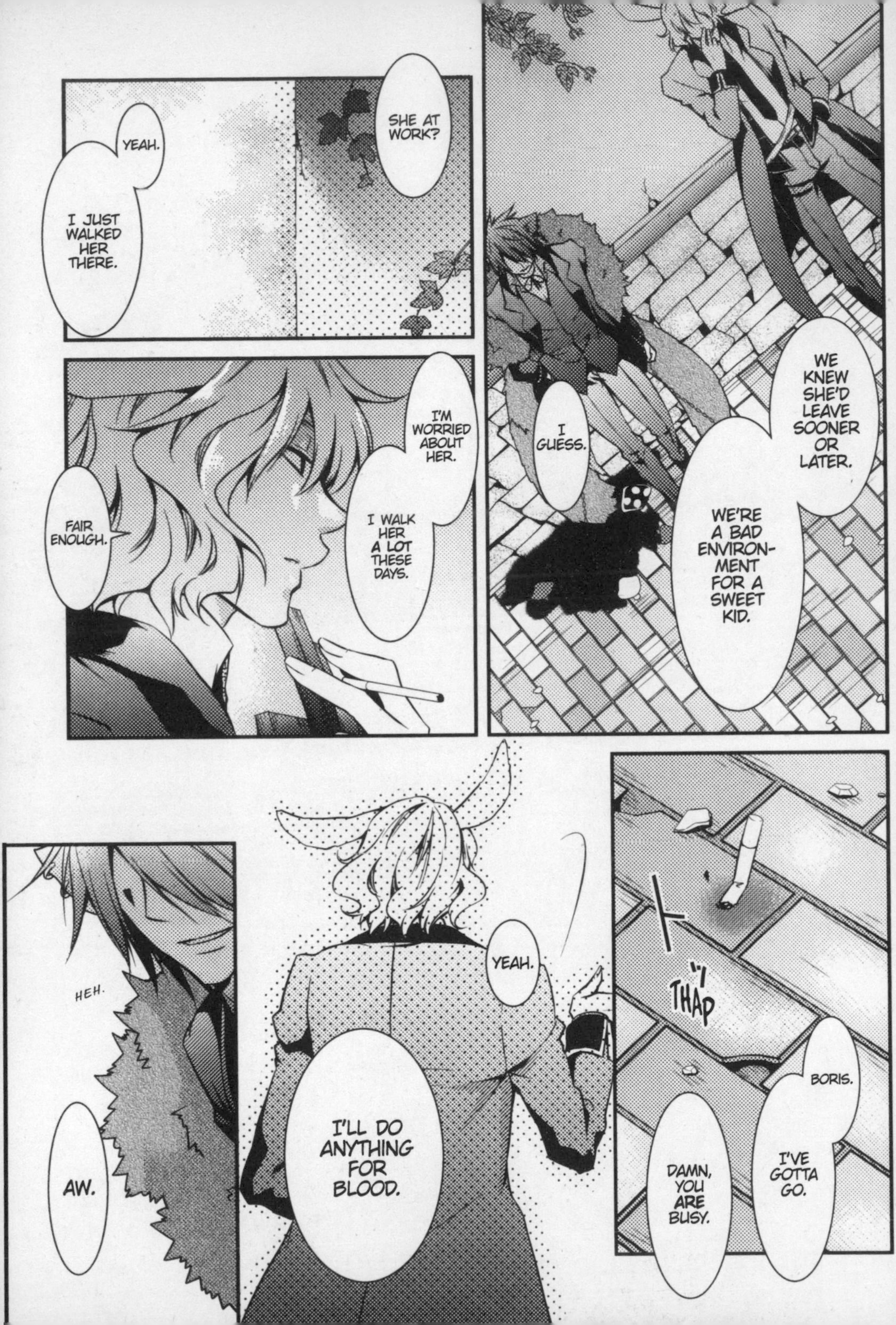
WE KNEW SHE'D LEAVE SOONER OR LATER.
I GUESS.
WE'RE A BAD ENVIRONMENT FOR A SWEET KID.
SHE AT WORK?
YEAH.
I JUST WALKED HER THERE.
I'M WORRIED ABOUT HER.
I WALK HER A LOT THESE DAYS.
FAIR ENOUGH.
THAP
BORIS.
I'VE GOTTA GO.
DAMN, YOU ARE BUSY.
YEAH.
I'LL DO ANYTHING FOR BLOOD.
HEH.
AW.

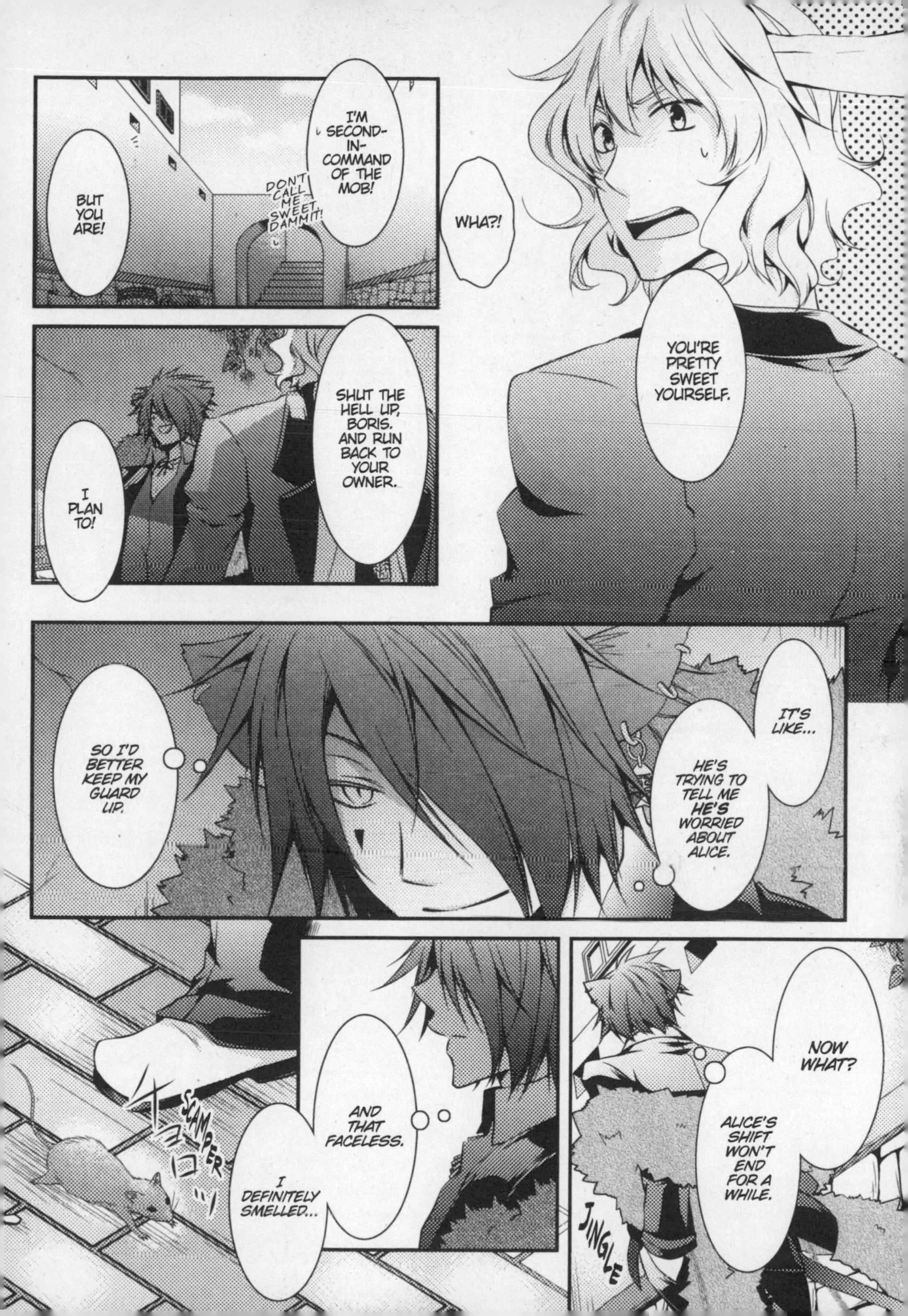
WHA?!
YOU'RE PRETTY SWEET YOURSELF.
I'M SECOND-IN-COMMAND OF THE MOB!
DON'T CALL ME SWEET DAMMIT!
BUT YOU ARE!
SHUT THE HELL UP, BORIS. AND RUN BACK TO YOUR OWNER.
I PLAN TO!
IT'S LIKE...
HE'S TRYING TO TELL ME HE'S WORRIED ABOUT ALICE.
SO I'D BETTER KEEP MY GUARD UP.
NOW WHAT?
ALICE'S SHIFT WON'T END FOR A WHILE.
JINGLE
AND THAT FACELESS.
I DEFINITELY SMELLED...
SCAMPER

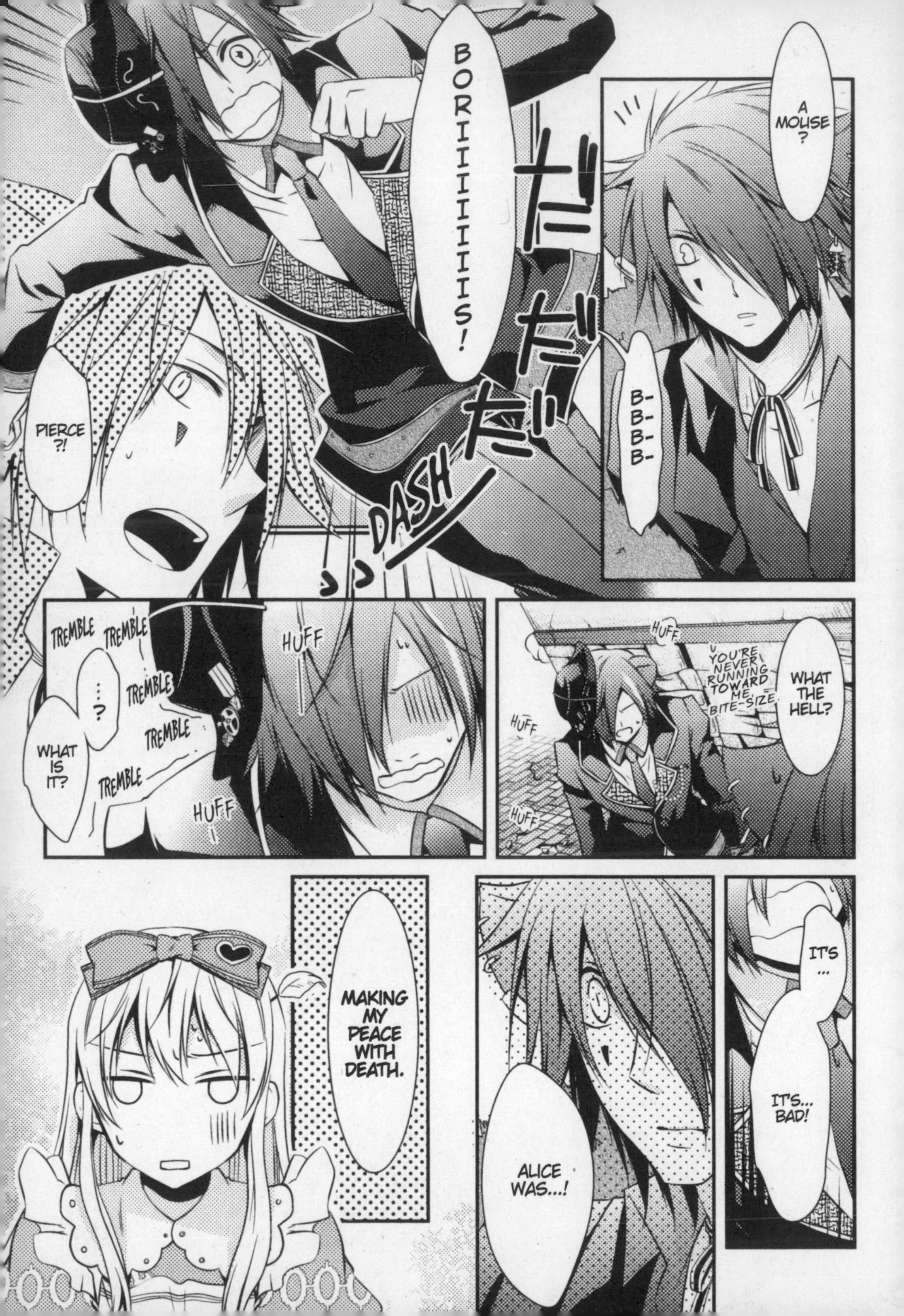
A MOUSE?
B-B-B-B-
BORIIIIIIIIS!
DASH
PIERCE?!
WHAT THE HELL?
YOU'RE NEVER RUNNING TOWARD ME, BITE-SIZE.
HUFF
HUFF
HUFF
HUFF
TREMBLE
TREMBLE
...?
TREMBLE
TREMBLE
TREMBLE
WHAT IS IT?
HUFF
IT'S...
IT'S... BAD!
ALICE WAS...!
MAKING MY PEACE WITH DEATH.

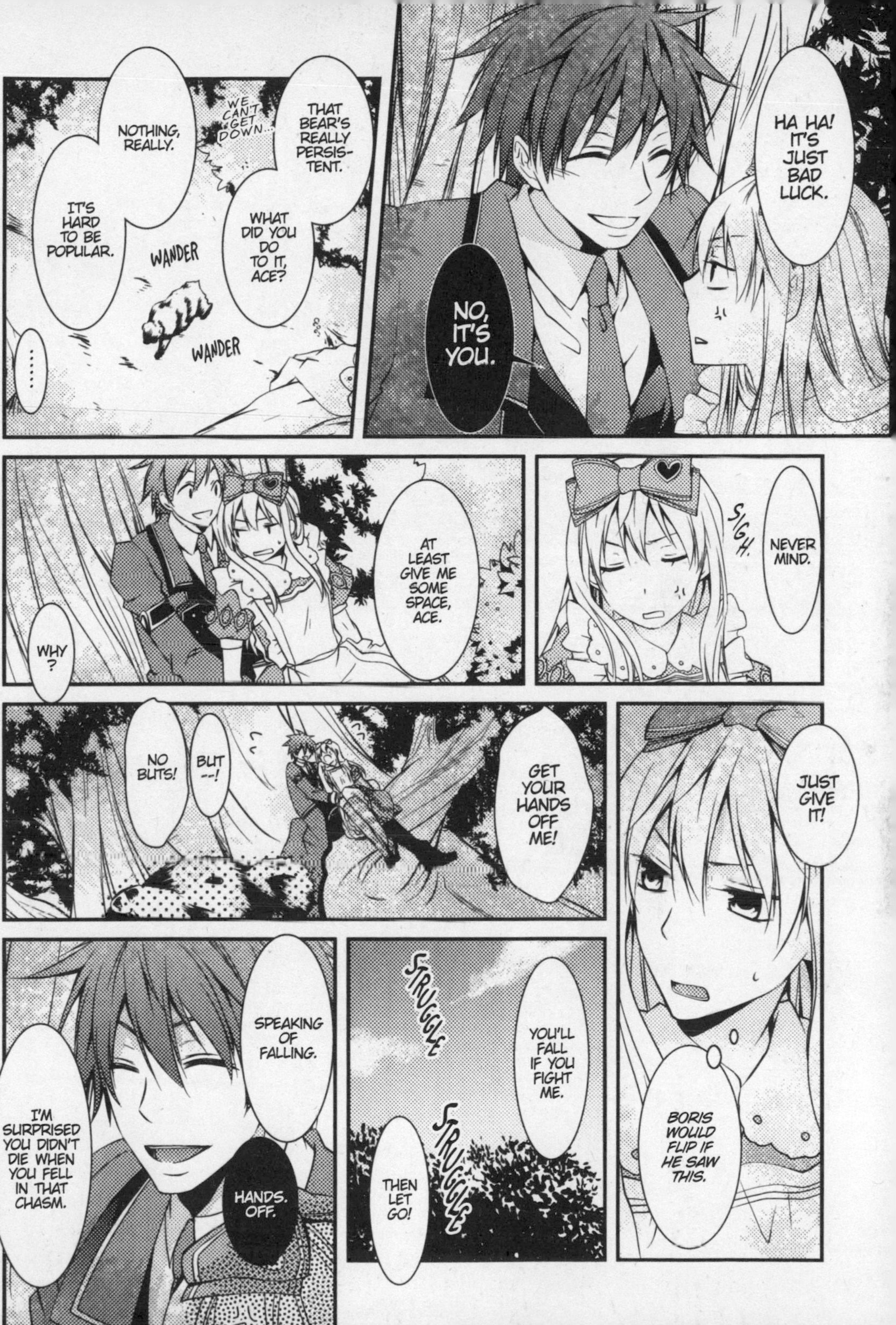
HA HA! IT'S JUST BAD LUCK.
NO, IT'S YOU.
THAT BEAR'S REALLY PERSIS-TENT.
WE CAN'T GET DOWN...
WHAT DID YOU DO TO IT, ACE?
NOTHING, REALLY.
IT'S HARD TO BE POPULAR.
WANDER
WANDER
......
SIGH
NEVER MIND.
AT LEAST GIVE ME SOME SPACE, ACE.
WHY?
JUST GIVE IT!
BORIS WOULD FLIP IF HE SAW THIS.
GET YOUR HANDS OFF ME!
BUT--!
NO BUTS!
STRUGGLE
YOU'LL FALL IF YOU FIGHT ME.
STRUGGLE
THEN LET GO!
SPEAKING OF FALLING.
I'M SURPRISED YOU DIDN'T DIE WHEN YOU FELL IN THAT CHASM.
HANDS. OFF.

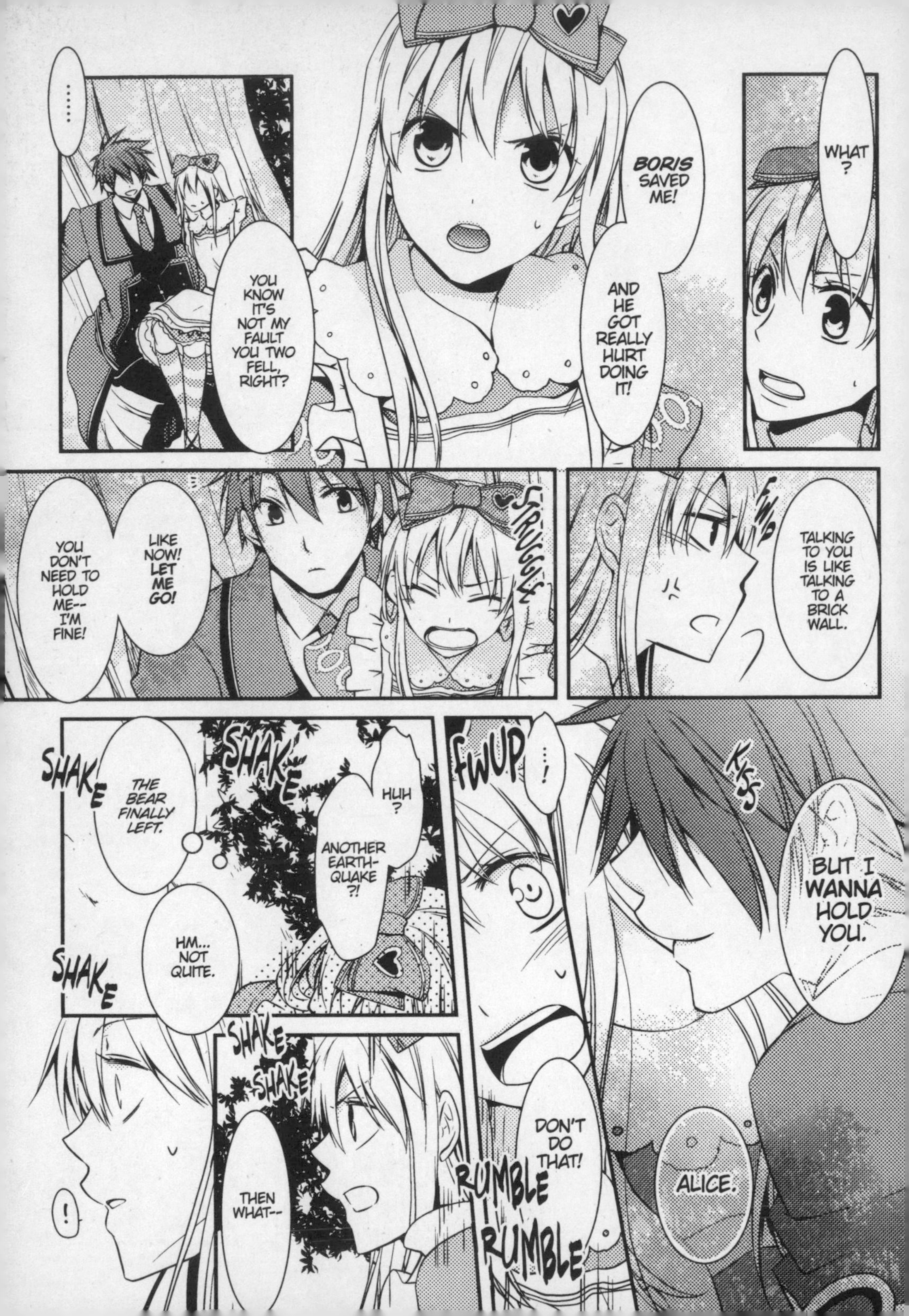
WHAT?
BORIS SAVED ME!
AND HE GOT REALLY HURT DOING IT!
YOU KNOW IT'S NOT MY FAULT YOU TWO FELL, RIGHT?
……
FWIP
TALKING TO YOU IS LIKE TALKING TO A BRICK WALL.
STRUGGLE
LIKE NOW! LET ME GO!
YOU DON'T NEED TO HOLD ME-- I'M FINE!
KISS
BUT I WANNA HOLD YOU.
…!
FWUP
ALICE.
DON'T DO THAT!
RUMBLE
RUMBLE
SHAKE
HUH?
ANOTHER EARTHQUAKE?!
SHAKE
THE BEAR FINALLY LEFT.
HM... NOT QUITE.
SHAKE
SHAKE
SHAKE
THEN WHAT--
!

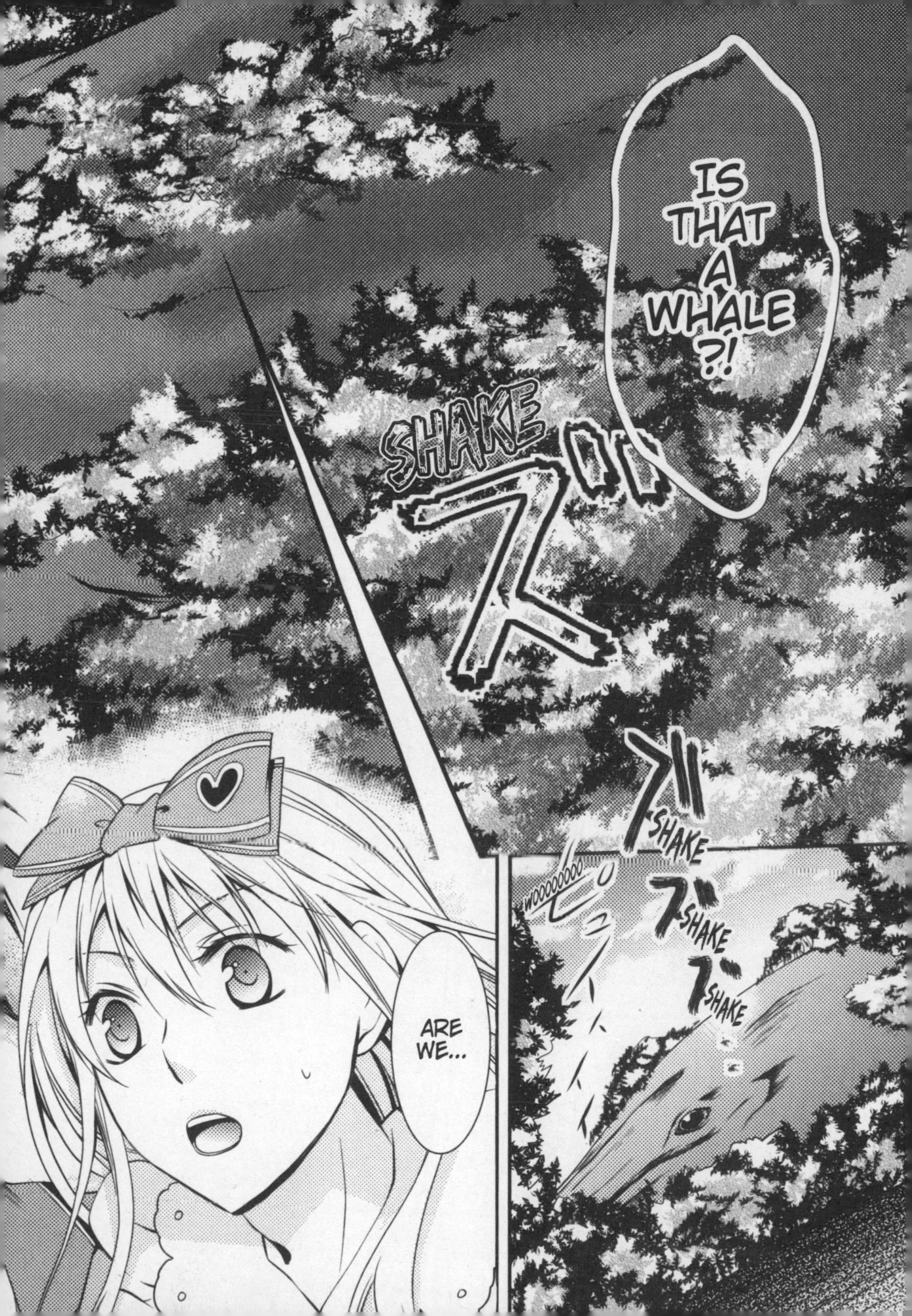
IS THAT A WHALE ?!
SHAKE
SHAKE
SHAKE
SHAKE
WOOOOOOOO
ARE WE...

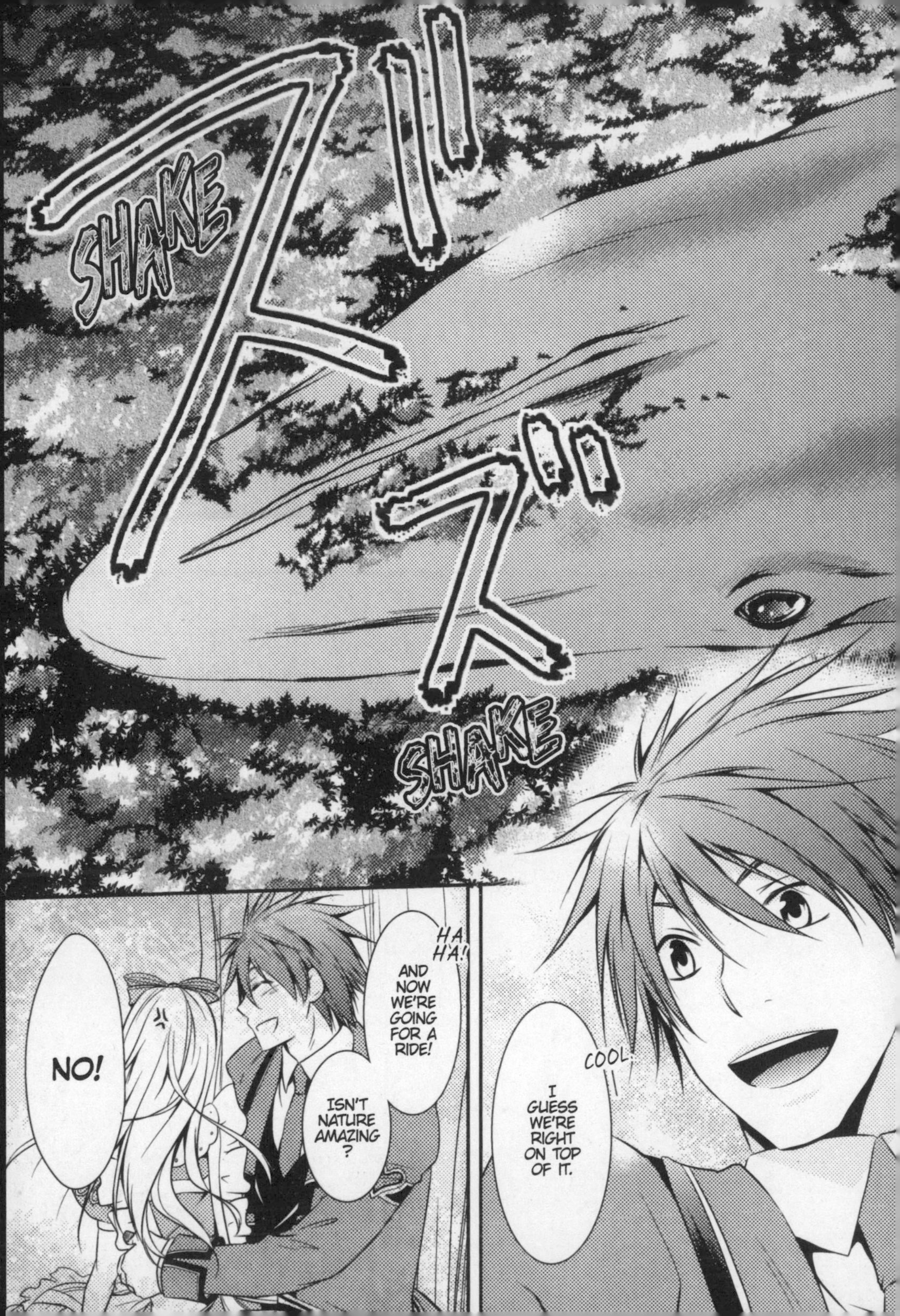
SHAKE
SHAKE
COOL!
I GUESS WE'RE RIGHT ON TOP OF IT.
HA HA!
AND NOW WE'RE GOING FOR A RIDE!
ISN'T NATURE AMAZING?
NO!

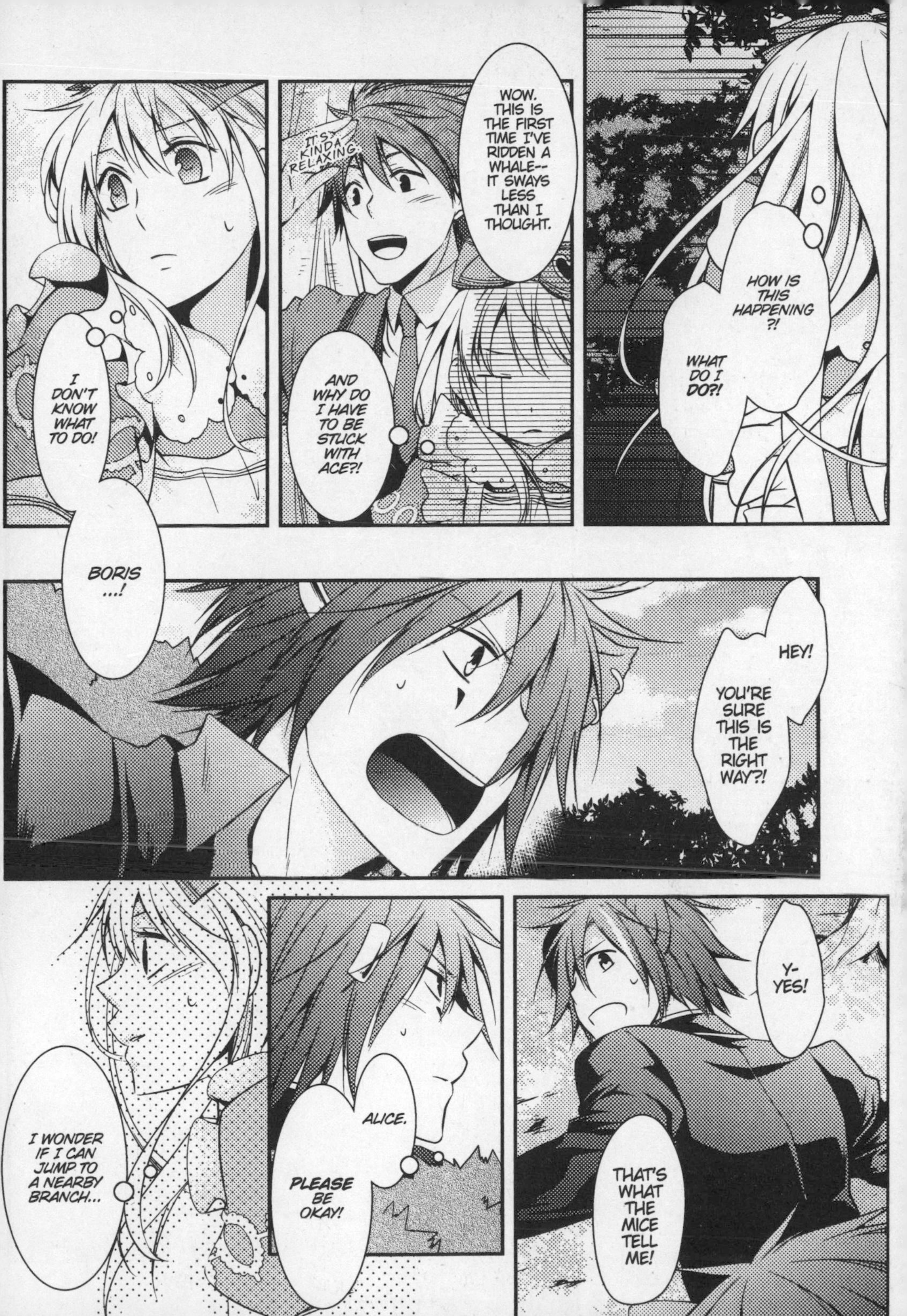
HOW IS THIS HAPPENING?!
WHAT DO I DO?!
WOW. THIS IS THE FIRST TIME I'VE RIDDEN A WHALE-- IT SWAYS LESS THAN I THOUGHT.
IT'S KINDA RELAXING.
AND WHY DO I HAVE TO BE STUCK WITH ACE?!
I DON'T KNOW WHAT TO DO!
BORIS...!
HEY!
YOU'RE SURE THIS IS THE RIGHT WAY?!
Y-YES!
THAT'S WHAT THE MICE TELL ME!
ALICE.
PLEASE BE OKAY!
I WONDER IF I CAN JUMP TO A NEARBY BRANCH...

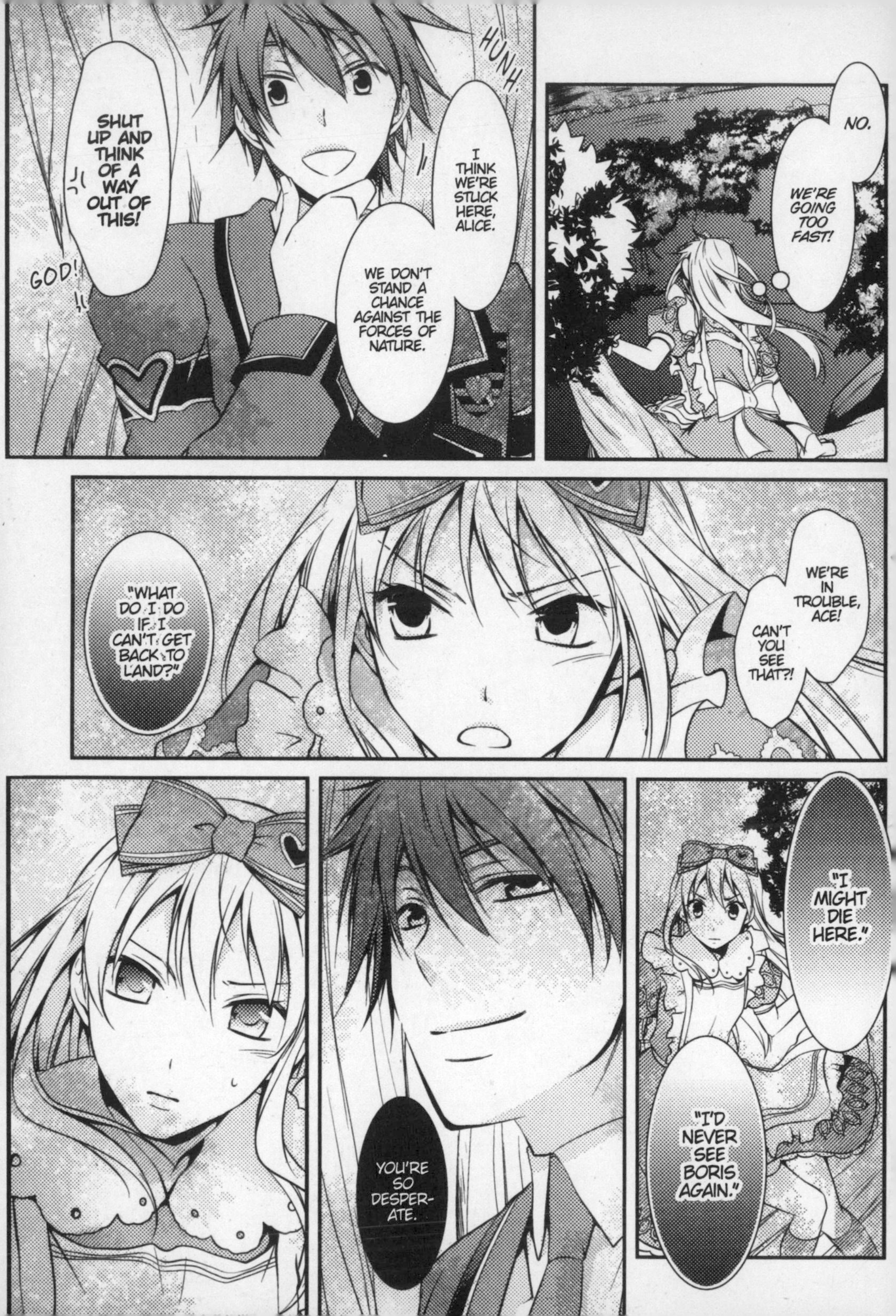
NO.
WE'RE GOING TOO FAST!
HUNH.
I THINK WE'RE STUCK HERE, ALICE.
WE DON'T STAND A CHANCE AGAINST THE FORCES OF NATURE.
SHUT UP AND THINK OF A WAY OUT OF THIS!
GOD!
WE'RE IN TROUBLE, ACE!
CAN'T YOU SEE THAT?!
"WHAT DO I DO IF I CAN'T GET BACK TO LAND?"
"I MIGHT DIE HERE."
"I'D NEVER SEE BORIS AGAIN."
YOU'RE SO DESPERATE.

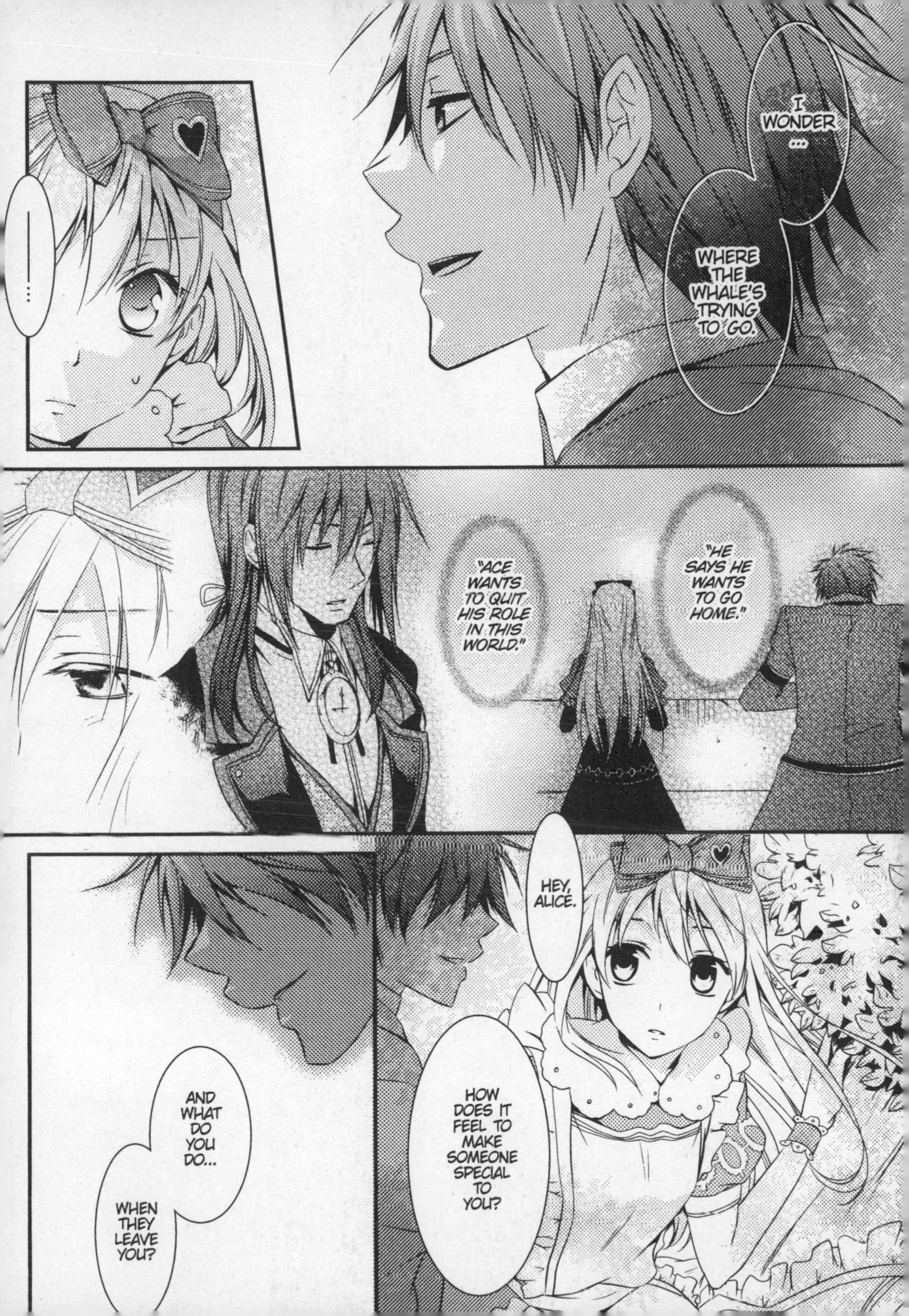
I WONDER...
WHERE THE WHALE'S TRYING TO GO.
—......
"HE SAYS HE WANTS TO GO HOME."
"ACE WANTS TO QUIT HIS ROLE IN THIS WORLD."
HEY, ALICE.
HOW DOES IT FEEL TO MAKE SOMEONE SPECIAL TO YOU?
AND WHAT DO YOU DO...
WHEN THEY LEAVE YOU?

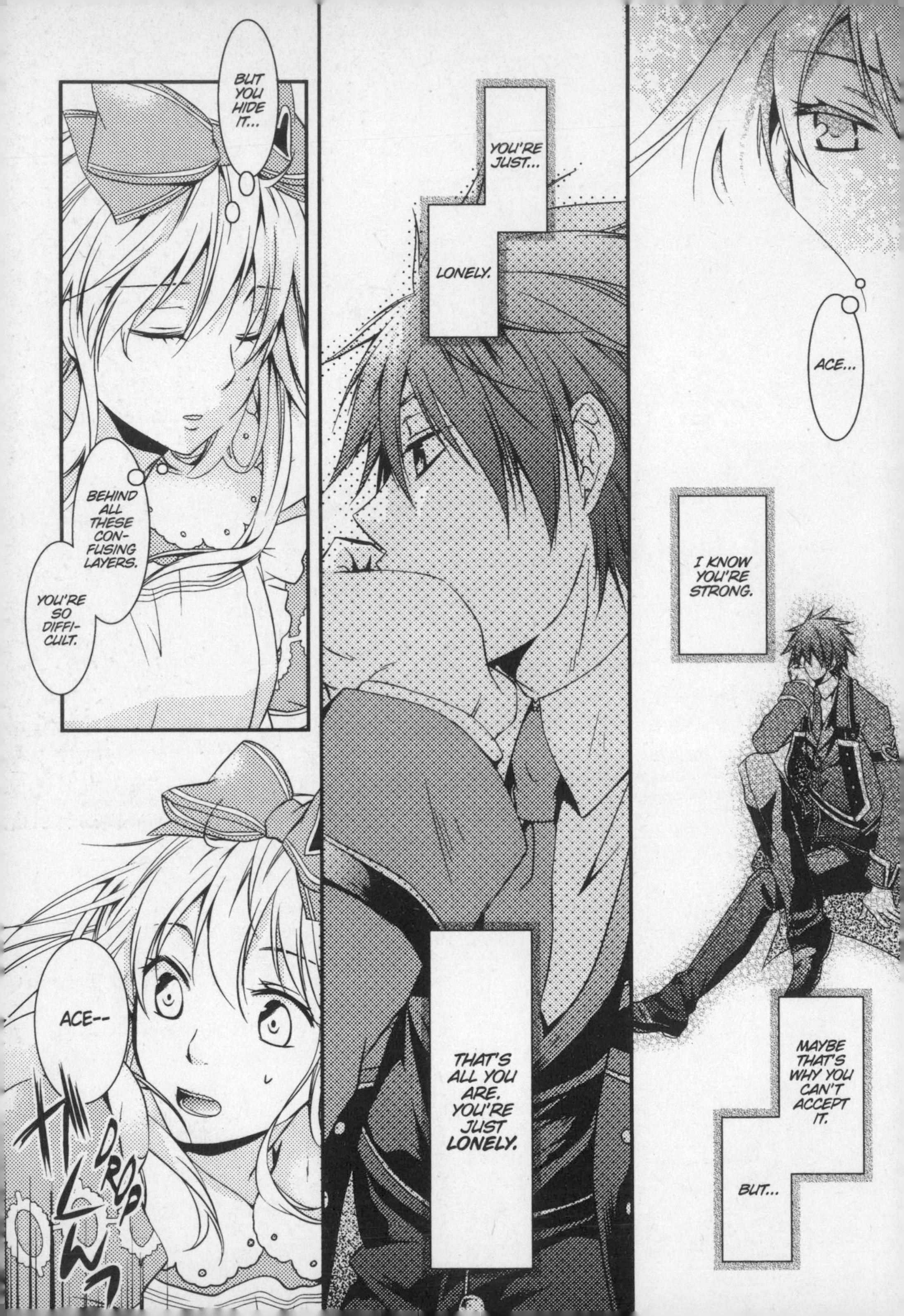
ACE...
I KNOW YOU'RE STRONG.
MAYBE THAT'S WHY YOU CAN'T ACCEPT IT.
BUT...
YOU'RE JUST...
LONELY.
THAT'S ALL YOU ARE. YOU'RE JUST LONELY.
BUT YOU HIDE IT...
BEHIND ALL THESE CONFUSING LAYERS.
YOU'RE SO DIFFICULT.
ACE--
DROP

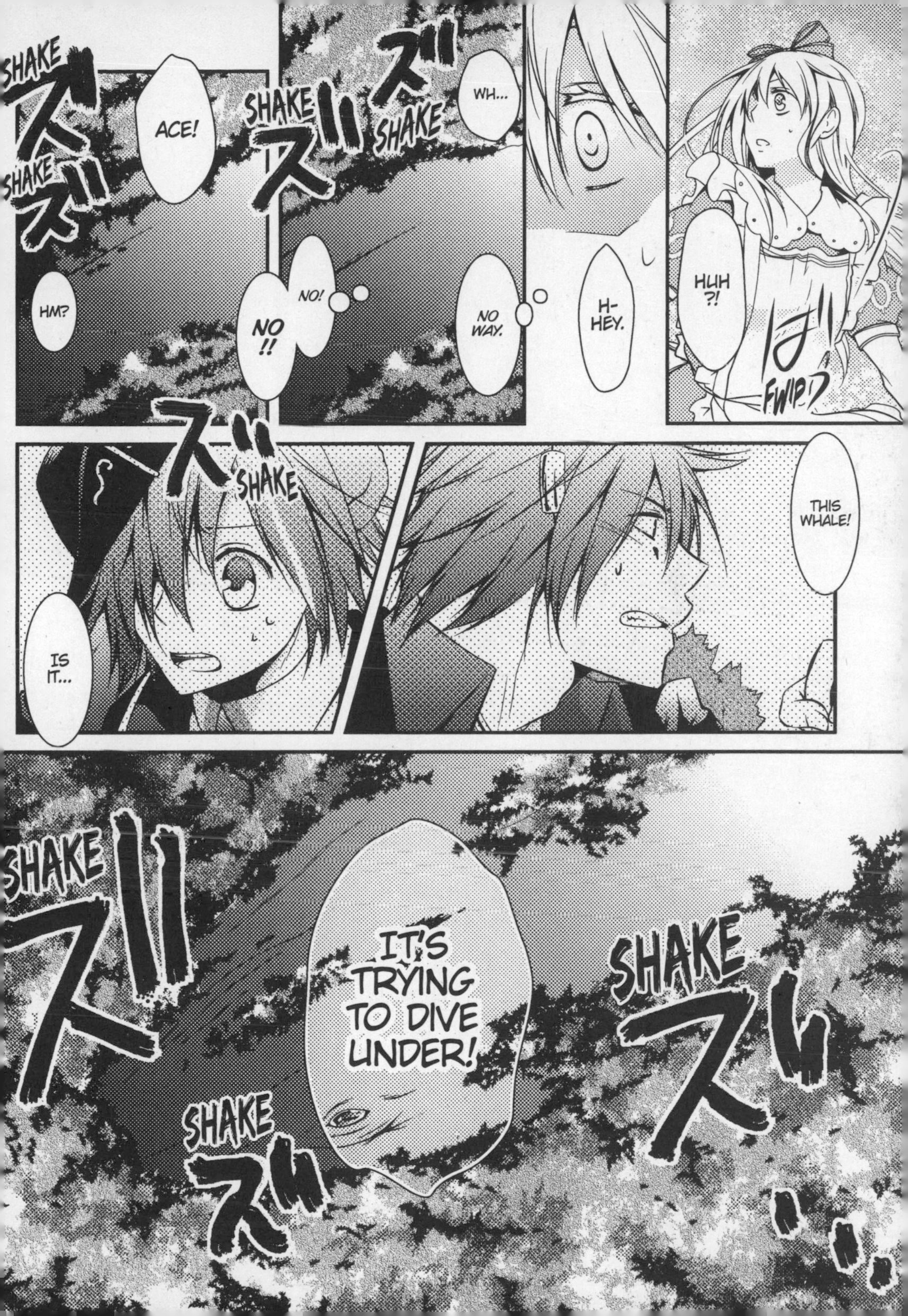
HUH ?!
FWIP
H-HEY.
WH...
SHAKE
SHAKE
NO WAY.
NO!
NO !!
SHAKE
SHAKE
ACE!
HM?
THIS WHALE!
SHAKE
IS IT...
SHAKE
IT'S TRYING TO DIVE UNDER!
SHAKE
SHAKE

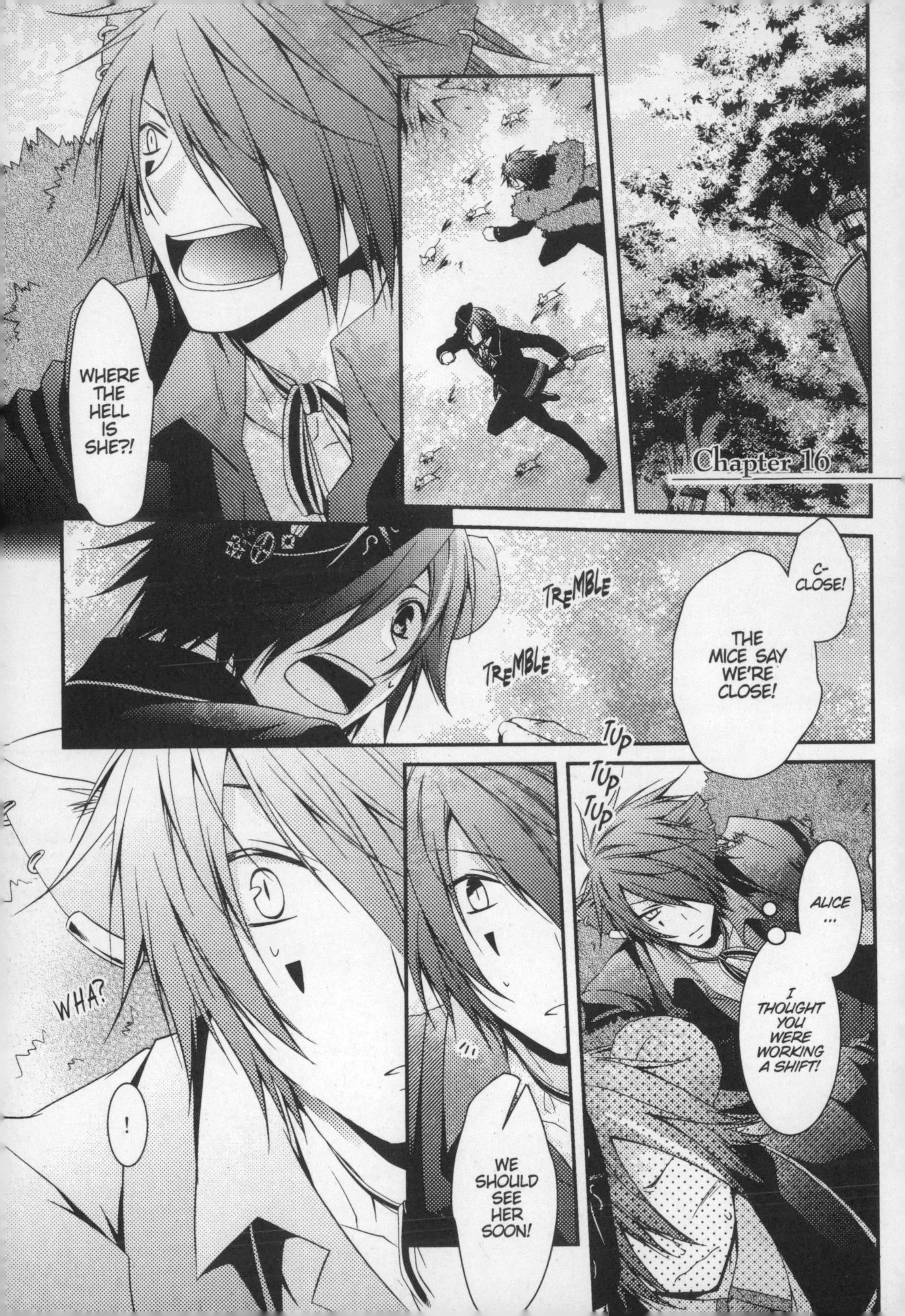
Chapter 16
WHERE THE HELL IS SHE?!
C-CLOSE!
THE MICE SAY WE'RE CLOSE!
TREMBLE
TREMBLE
TUP TUP TUP
ALICE ...
I THOUGHT YOU WERE WORKING A SHIFT!
WE SHOULD SEE HER SOON!
WHA?
!

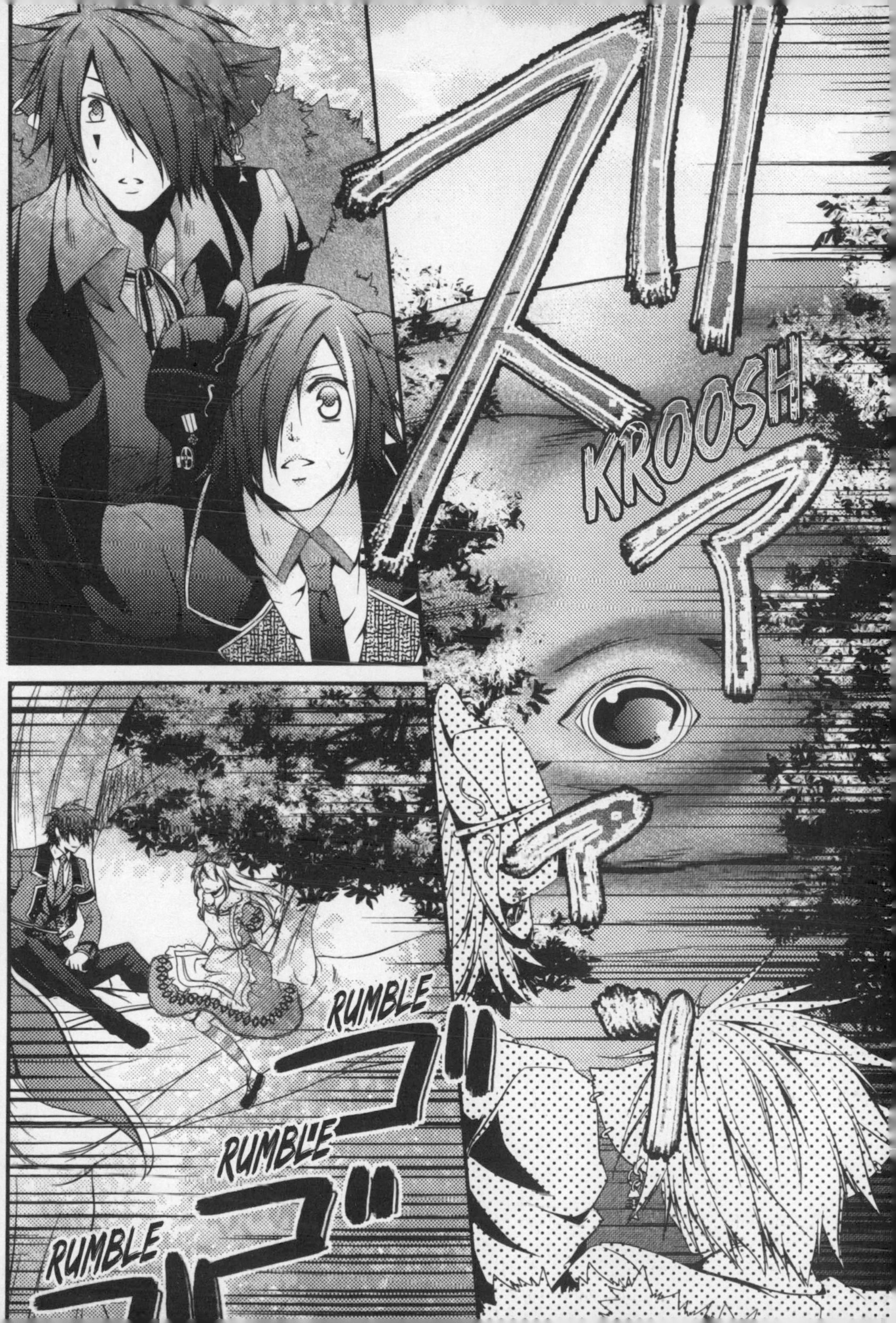
KROOSH
RUMBLE
RUMBLE
RUMBLE

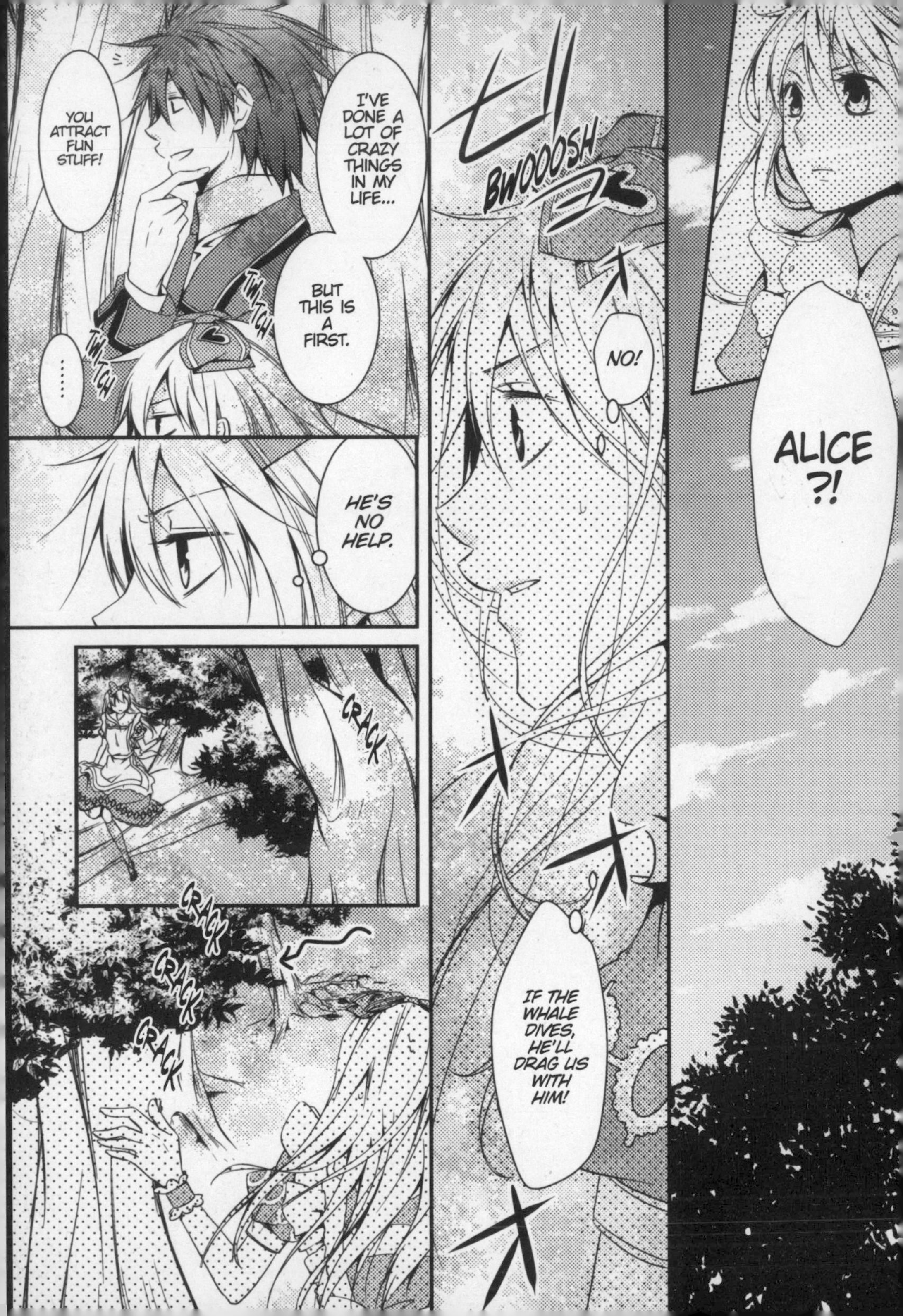
ALICE ?!
BWOOOSH
NO!
IF THE WHALE DIVES, HE'LL DRAG US WITH HIM!
I'VE DONE A LOT OF CRAZY THINGS IN MY LIFE...
YOU ATTRACT FUN STUFF!
BUT THIS IS A FIRST.
TWITCH
TWITCH
......
HE'S NO HELP.
CRACK
CRACK
CRACK
CRACK

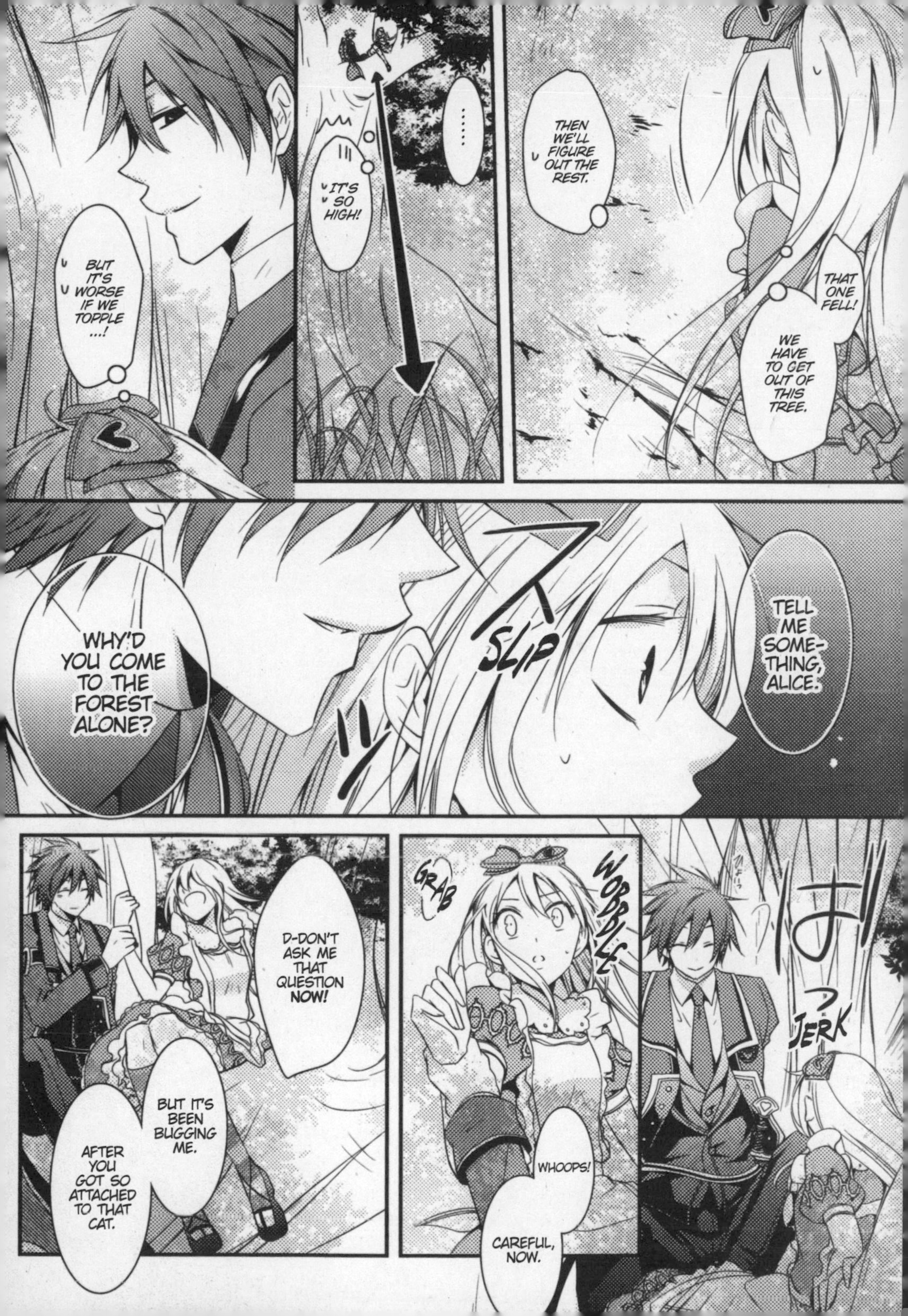
THAT ONE FELL!
WE HAVE TO GET OUT OF THIS TREE.
THEN WE'LL FIGURE OUT THE REST.
......
IT'S SO HIGH!
BUT IT'S WORSE IF WE TOPPLE ...!
TELL ME SOMETHING, ALICE.
SLIP
WHY'D YOU COME TO THE FOREST ALONE?
JERK
WOBBLE
GRAB
WHOOPS!
CAREFUL, NOW.
D-DON'T ASK ME THAT QUESTION NOW!
BUT IT'S BEEN BUGGING ME.
AFTER YOU GOT SO ATTACHED TO THAT CAT.

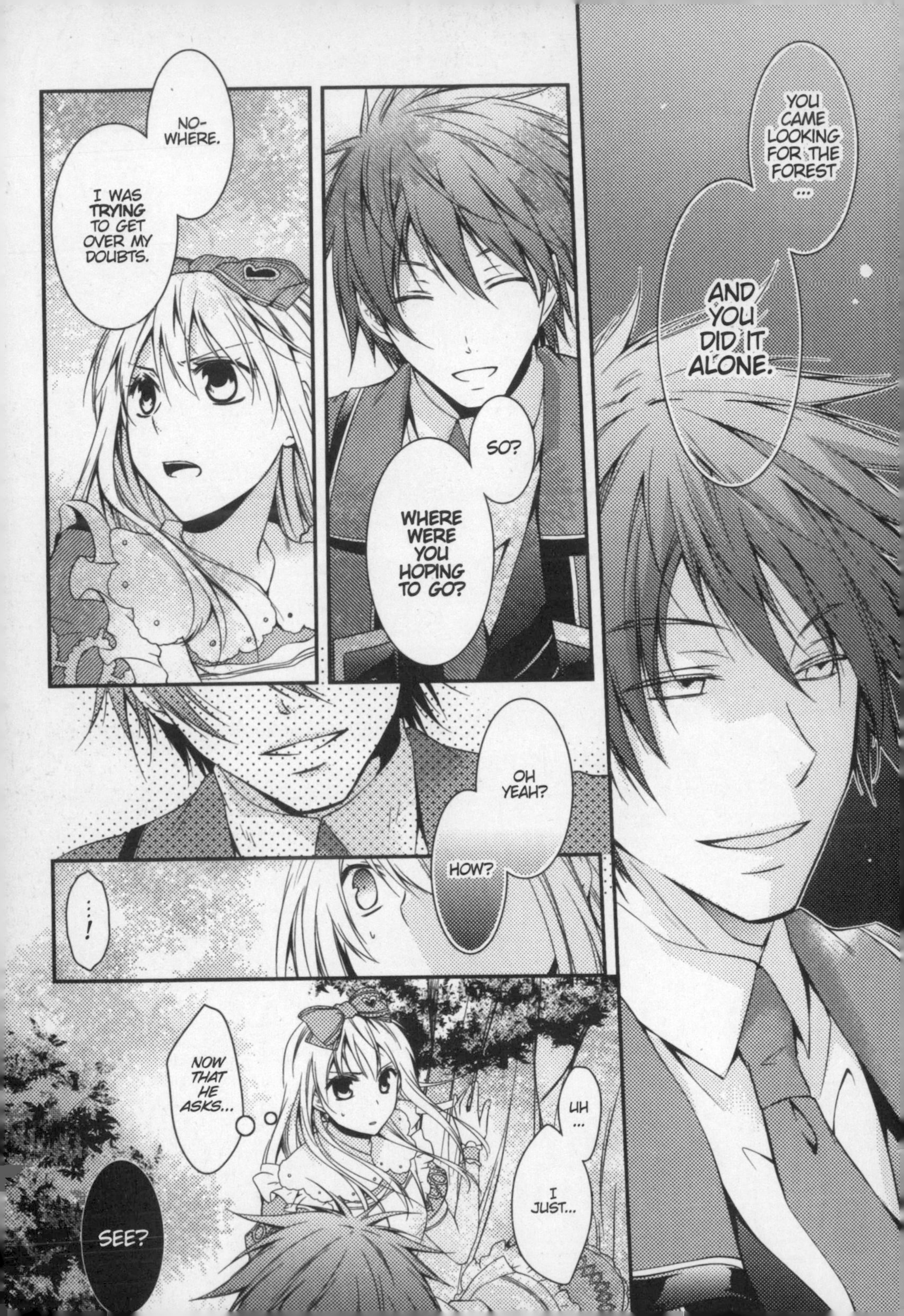
YOU CAME LOOKING FOR THE FOREST...
AND YOU DID IT ALONE.
SO?
WHERE WERE YOU HOPING TO GO?
NO-WHERE.
I WAS TRYING TO GET OVER MY DOUBTS.
OH YEAH?
HOW?
...!
NOW THAT HE ASKS...
UH ...
I JUST...
SEE?

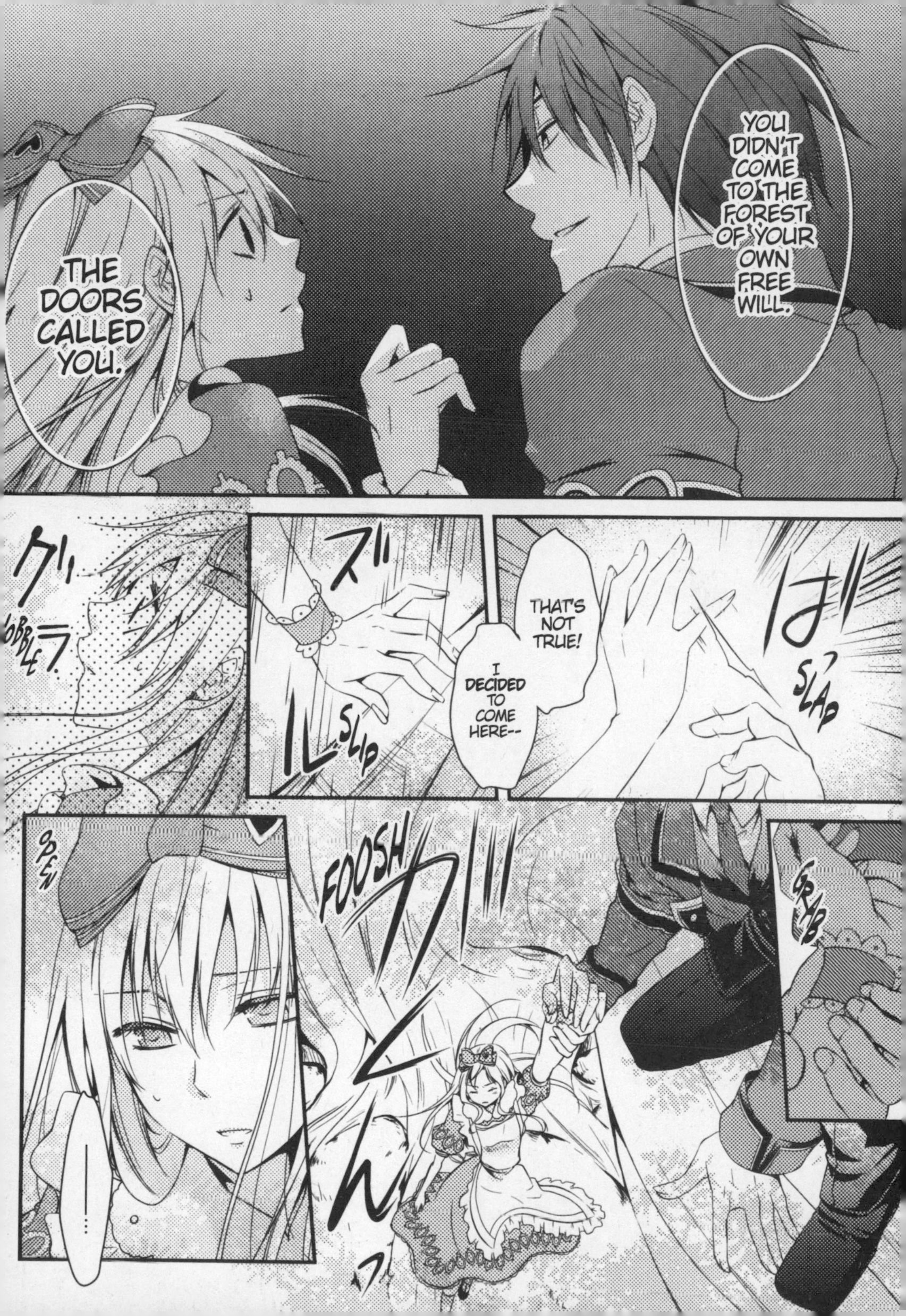
YOU DIDN'T COME TO THE FOREST OF YOUR OWN FREE WILL.
THE DOORS CALLED YOU.
SLAP
THAT'S NOT TRUE!
I DECIDED TO COME HERE--
SLIP
WOBBLE
GRAB
FOOSH
OPEN
......

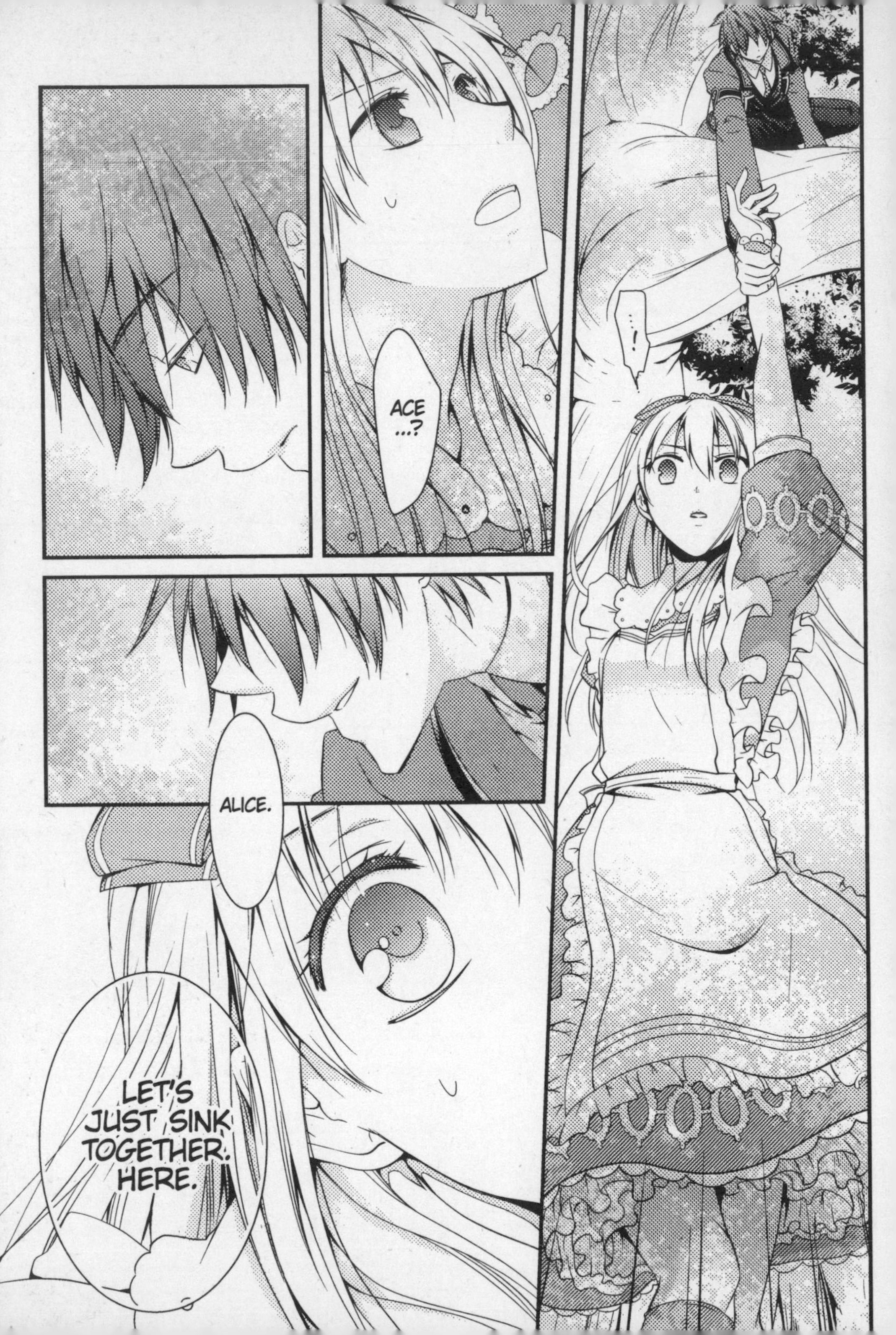
...!
ACE ...?
ALICE.
LET'S JUST SINK TOGETHER. HERE.

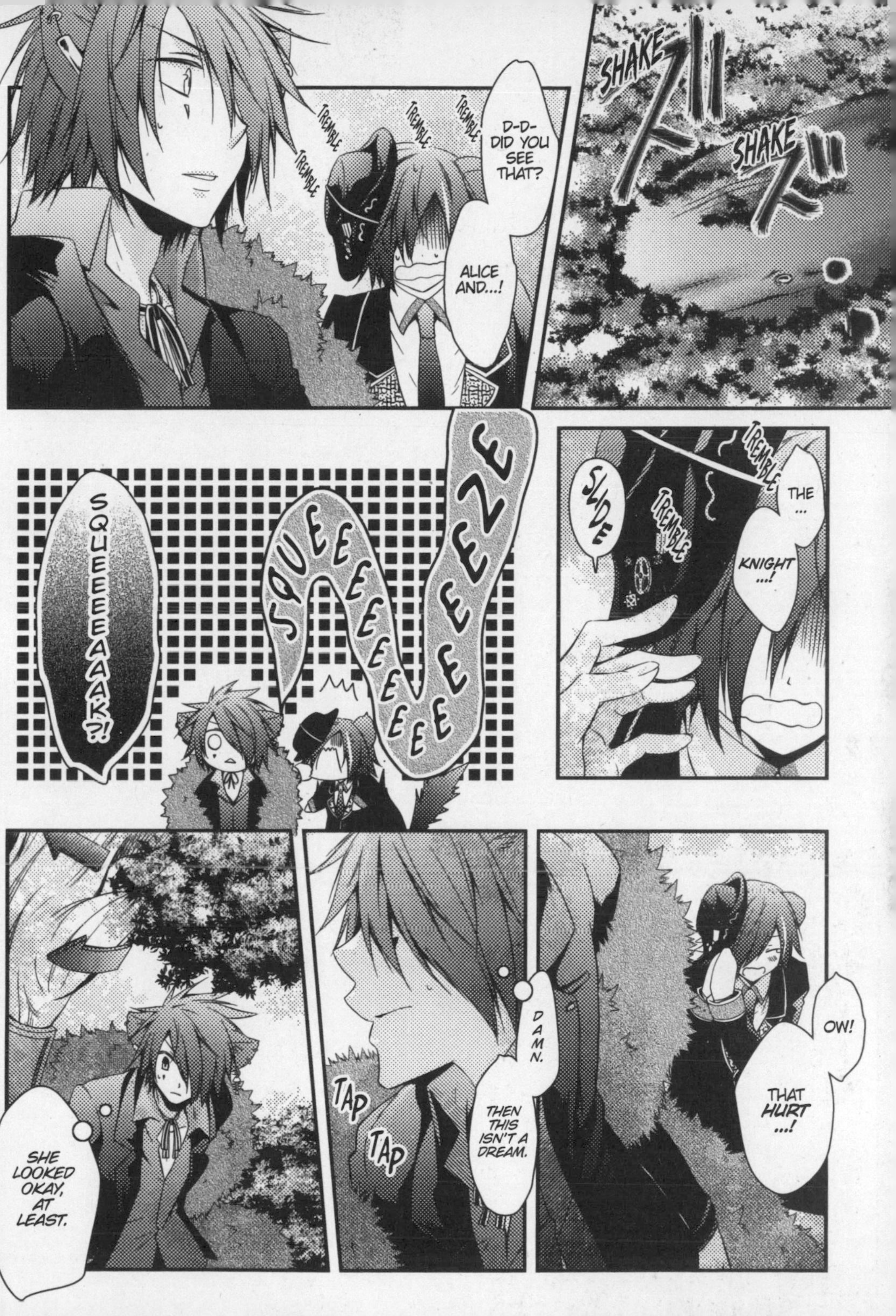
SHAKE
SHAKE
TREMBLE
TREMBLE
TREMBLE
TREMBLE
D-D-DID YOU SEE THAT?
ALICE AND...!
TREMBLE
SLIDE
TREMBLE
THE ...
KNIGHT ...!
SQUEEEEEEEEEEEEZE
SQUEEEEEAAAAK?!
OW!
THAT HURT ...!
DAMN.
THEN THIS ISN'T A DREAM.
TAP
TAP
SHE LOOKED OKAY, AT LEAST.

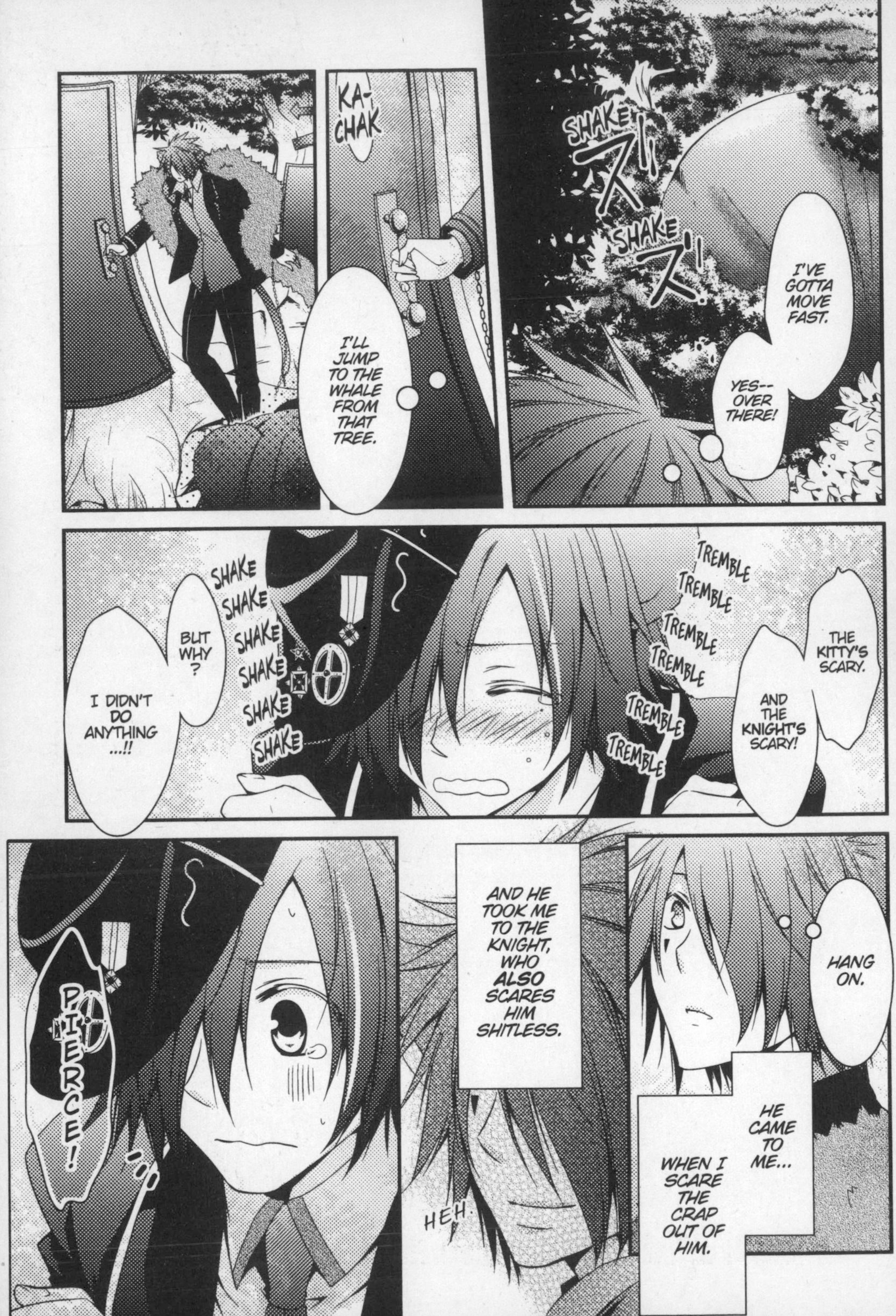
SHAKE
SHAKE
I'VE GOTTA MOVE FAST.
YES-- OVER THERE!
KA-CHAK
I'LL JUMP TO THE WHALE FROM THAT TREE.
THE KITTY'S SCARY.
AND THE KNIGHT'S SCARY!
TREMBLE
TREMBLE
TREMBLE
TREMBLE
TREMBLE
TREMBLE
SHAKE
SHAKE
SHAKE
SHAKE
SHAKE
SHAKE
BUT WHY?
I DIDN'T DO ANYTHING ...!!
HANG ON.
HE CAME TO ME...
WHEN I SCARE THE CRAP OUT OF HIM.
AND HE TOOK ME TO THE KNIGHT, WHO ALSO SCARES HIM SHITLESS.
HEH.
PIERCE!

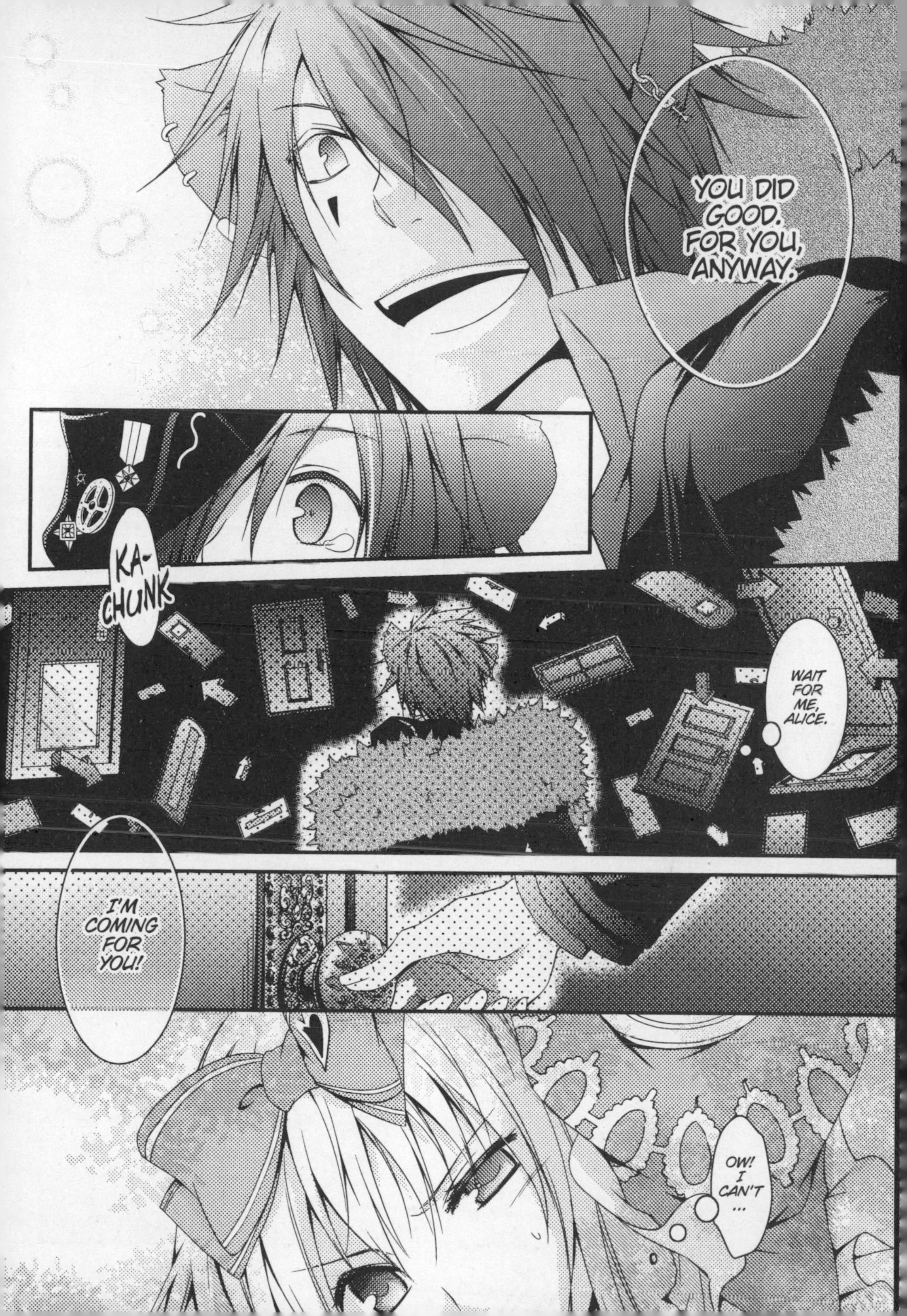
YOU DID GOOD. FOR YOU, ANYWAY.
KA-CHUNK
WAIT FOR ME, ALICE.
I'M COMING FOR YOU!
OW! I CAN'T ...

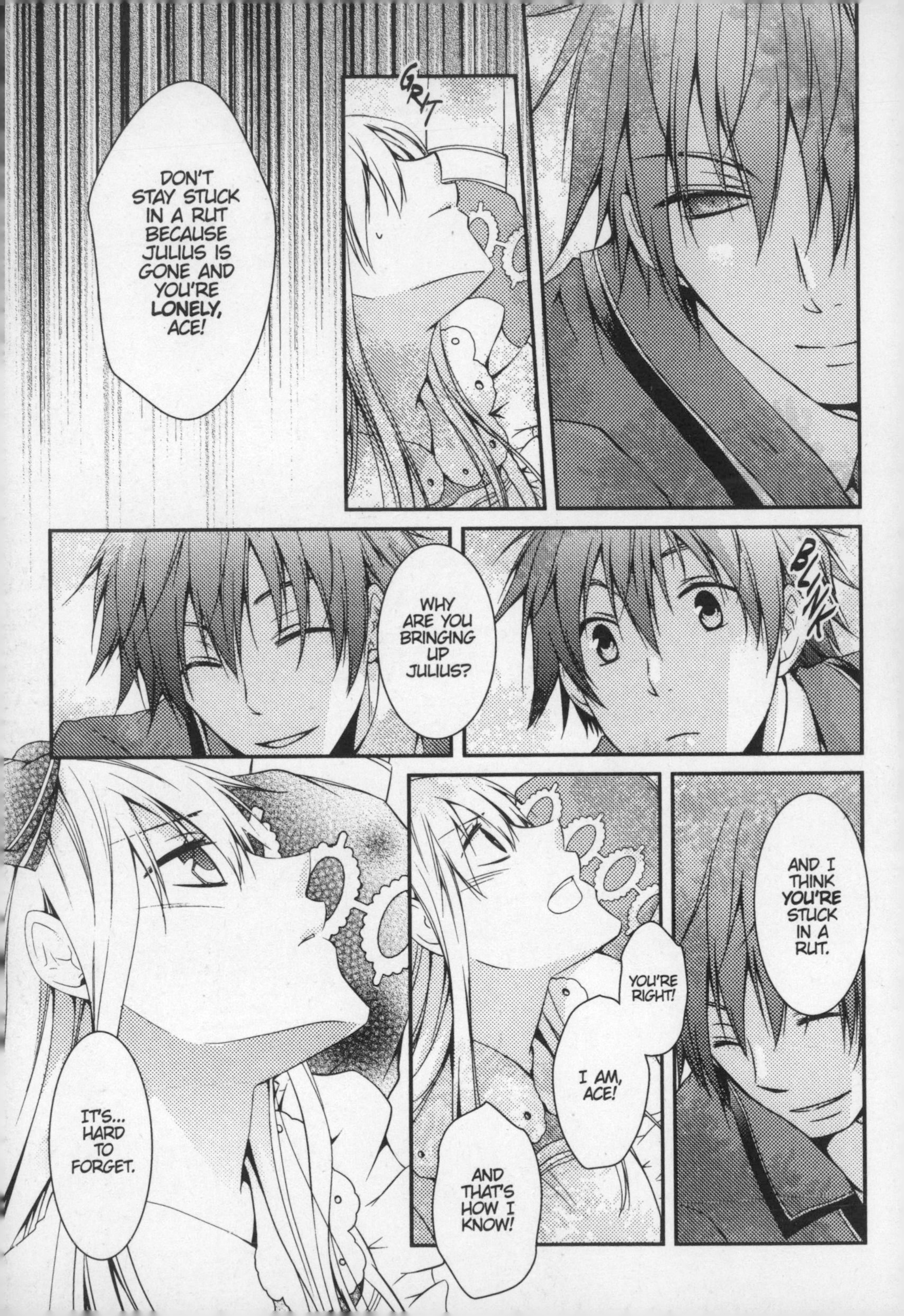
GRIT
DON'T STAY STUCK IN A RUT BECAUSE JULIUS IS GONE AND YOU'RE LONELY, ACE!
BLINK
WHY ARE YOU BRINGING UP JULIUS?
AND I THINK YOU'RE STUCK IN A RUT.
YOU'RE RIGHT!
I AM, ACE!
AND THAT'S HOW I KNOW!
IT'S... HARD TO FORGET.

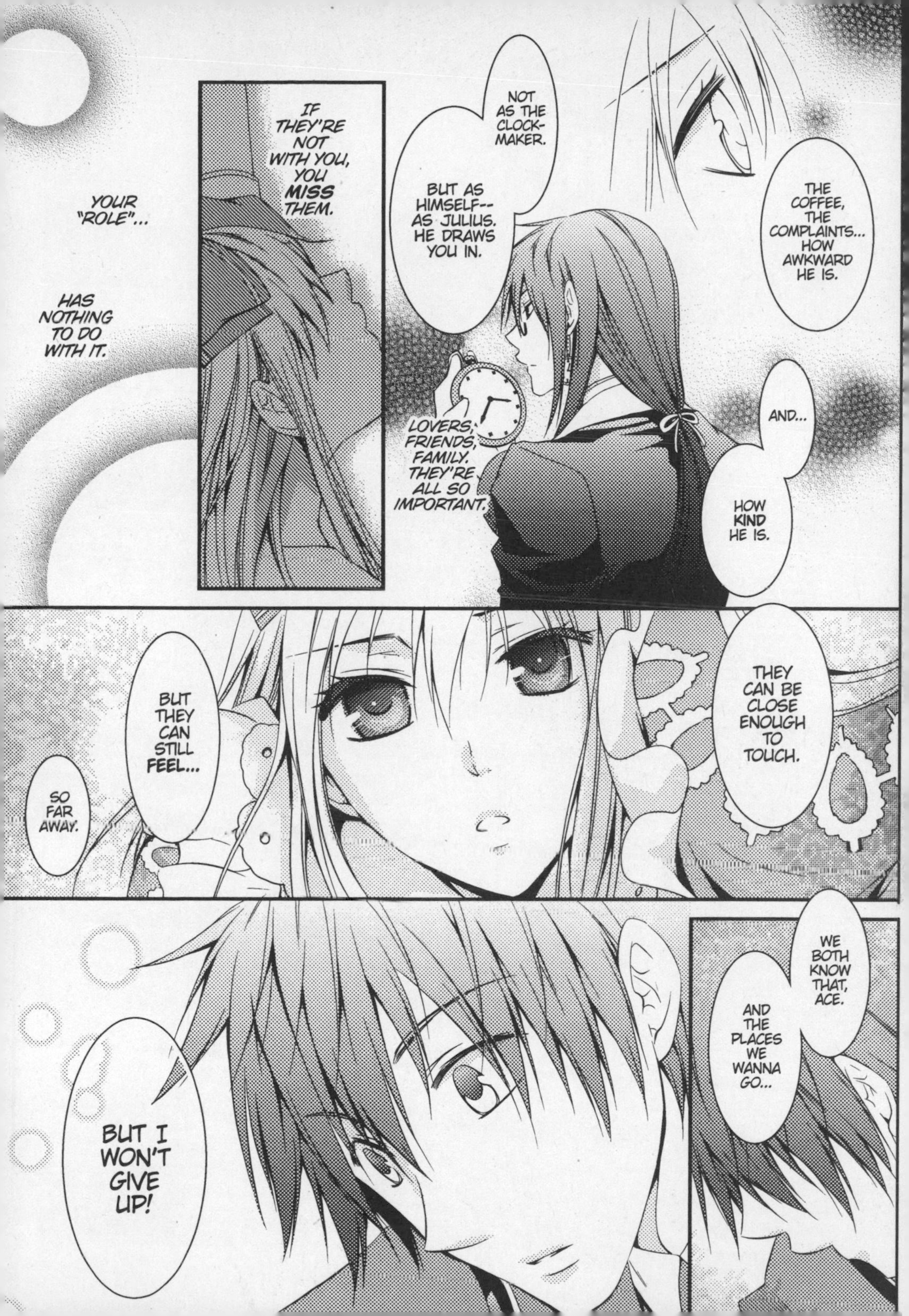
THE COFFEE, THE COMPLAINTS... HOW AWKWARD HE IS.
NOT AS THE CLOCK-MAKER.
BUT AS HIMSELF--AS JULIUS. HE DRAWS YOU IN.
AND...
HOW **KIND** HE IS.
LOVERS, FRIENDS, FAMILY. THEY'RE ALL SO IMPORTANT.
IF THEY'RE NOT WITH YOU, YOU **MISS** THEM.
YOUR "ROLE"...
HAS NOTHING TO DO WITH IT.
THEY CAN BE CLOSE ENOUGH TO TOUCH.
BUT THEY CAN STILL **FEEL...**
SO FAR AWAY.
WE BOTH KNOW THAT, ACE.
AND THE PLACES WE WANNA GO...
BUT I WON'T GIVE UP!

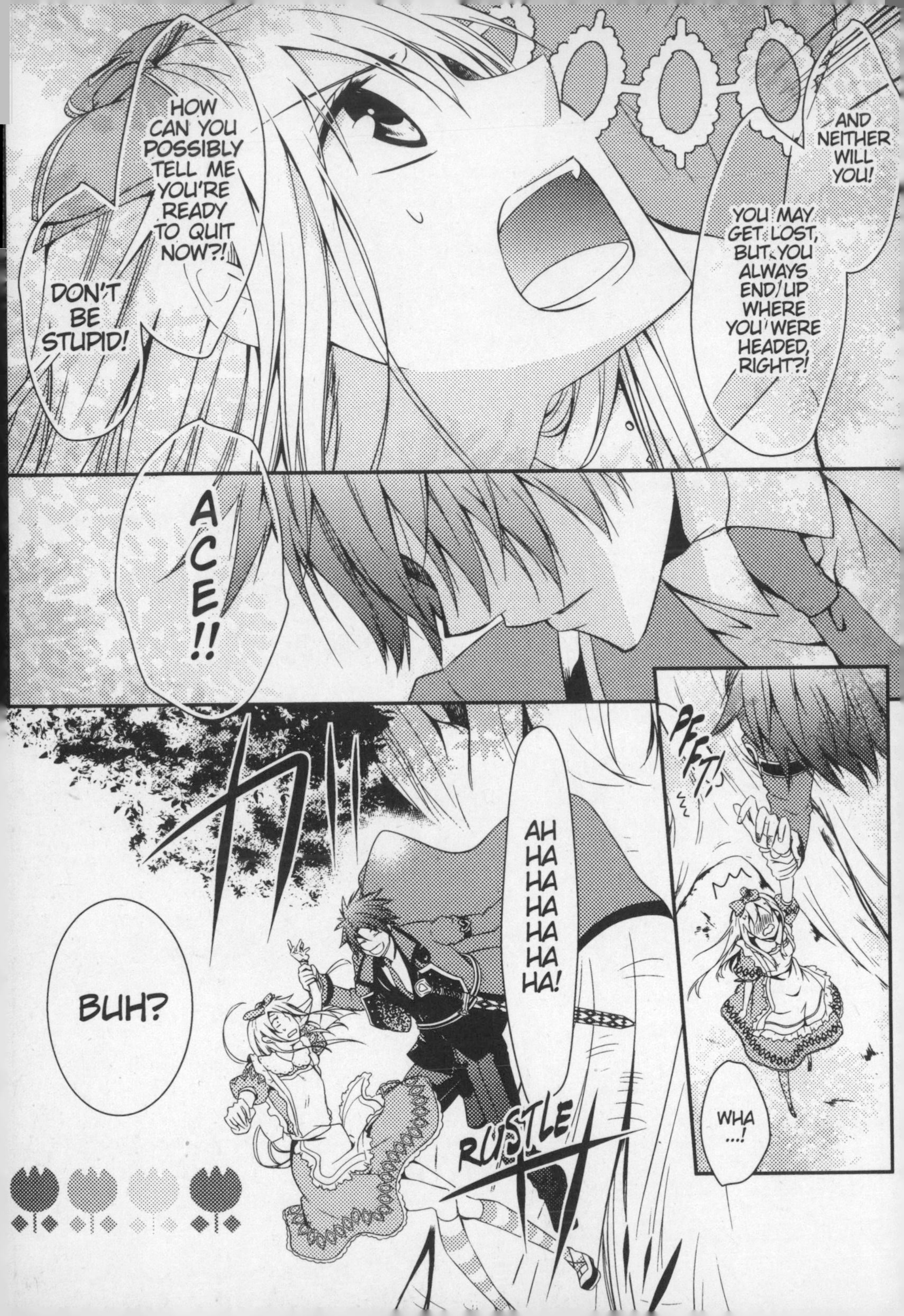
AND NEITHER WILL YOU!
YOU MAY GET LOST, BUT YOU ALWAYS END UP WHERE YOU WERE HEADED, RIGHT?!
HOW CAN YOU POSSIBLY TELL ME YOU'RE READY TO QUIT NOW?!
DON'T BE STUPID!
ACE!!
PFFT!
WHA...!
AH HA HA HA HA HA HA HA!
BUH?
RUSTLE

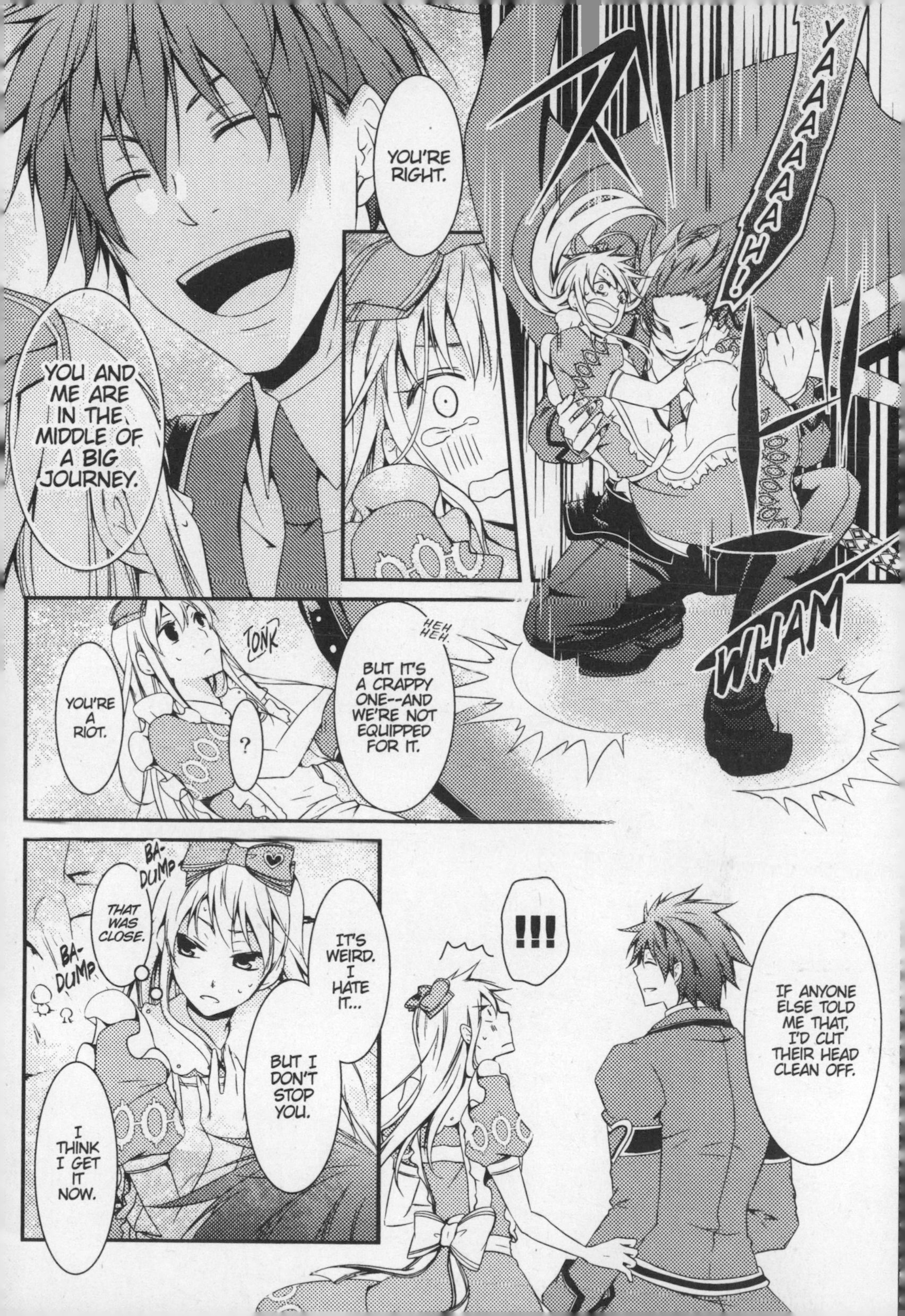
YAAAAAAAH!
WHAM
YOU'RE RIGHT.
YOU AND ME ARE IN THE MIDDLE OF A BIG JOURNEY.
HEH HEH.
BUT IT'S A CRAPPY ONE--AND WE'RE NOT EQUIPPED FOR IT.
?
TONK
YOU'RE A RIOT.
IF ANYONE ELSE TOLD ME THAT, I'D CUT THEIR HEAD CLEAN OFF.
!!!
BA-DUMP
THAT WAS CLOSE.
IT'S WEIRD. I HATE IT...
BUT I DON'T STOP YOU.
BA-DUMP
I THINK I GET IT NOW.

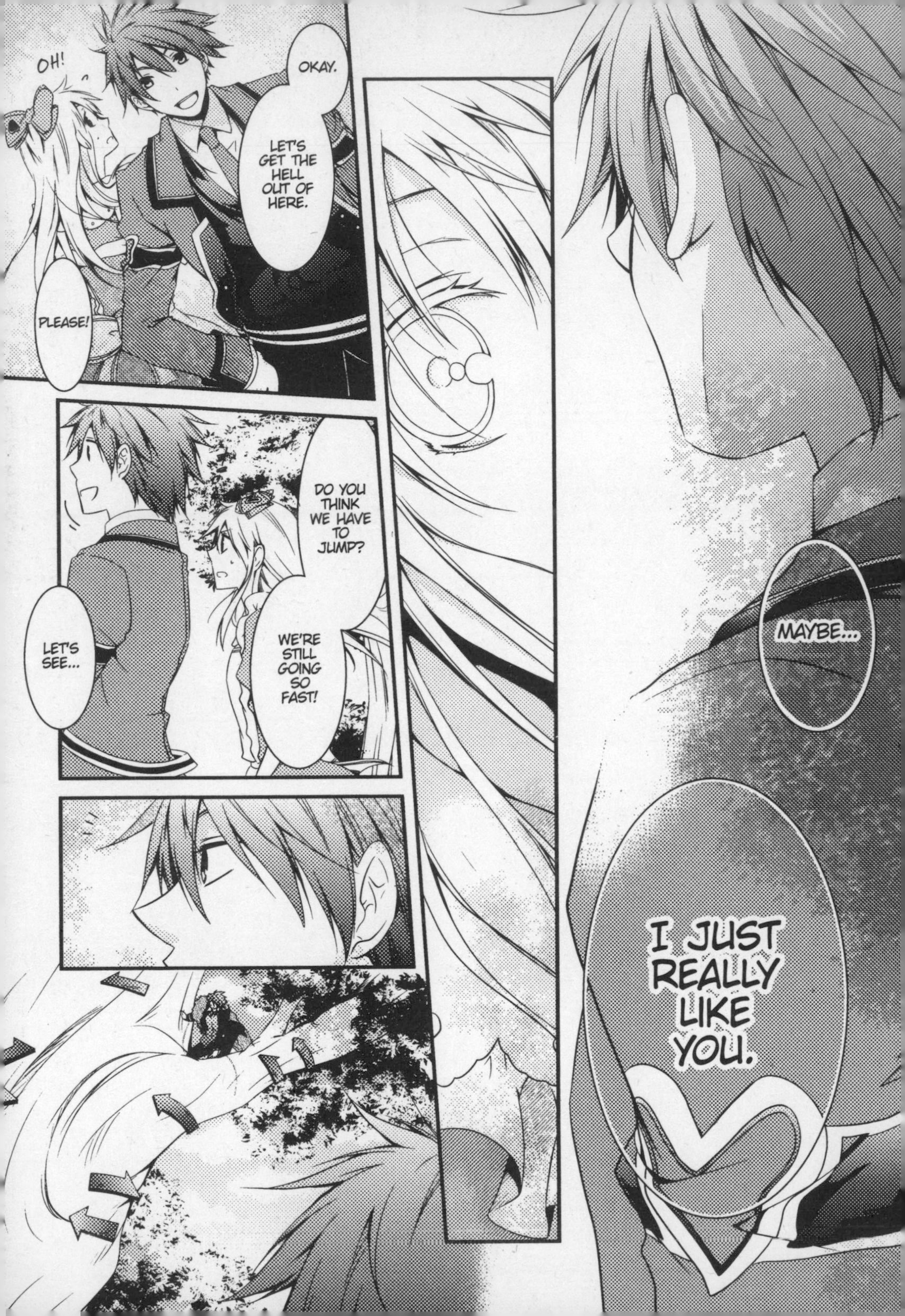
MAYBE...
I JUST REALLY LIKE YOU.
OKAY.
LET'S GET THE HELL OUT OF HERE.
OH!
PLEASE!
DO YOU THINK WE HAVE TO JUMP?
WE'RE STILL GOING SO FAST!
LET'S SEE...

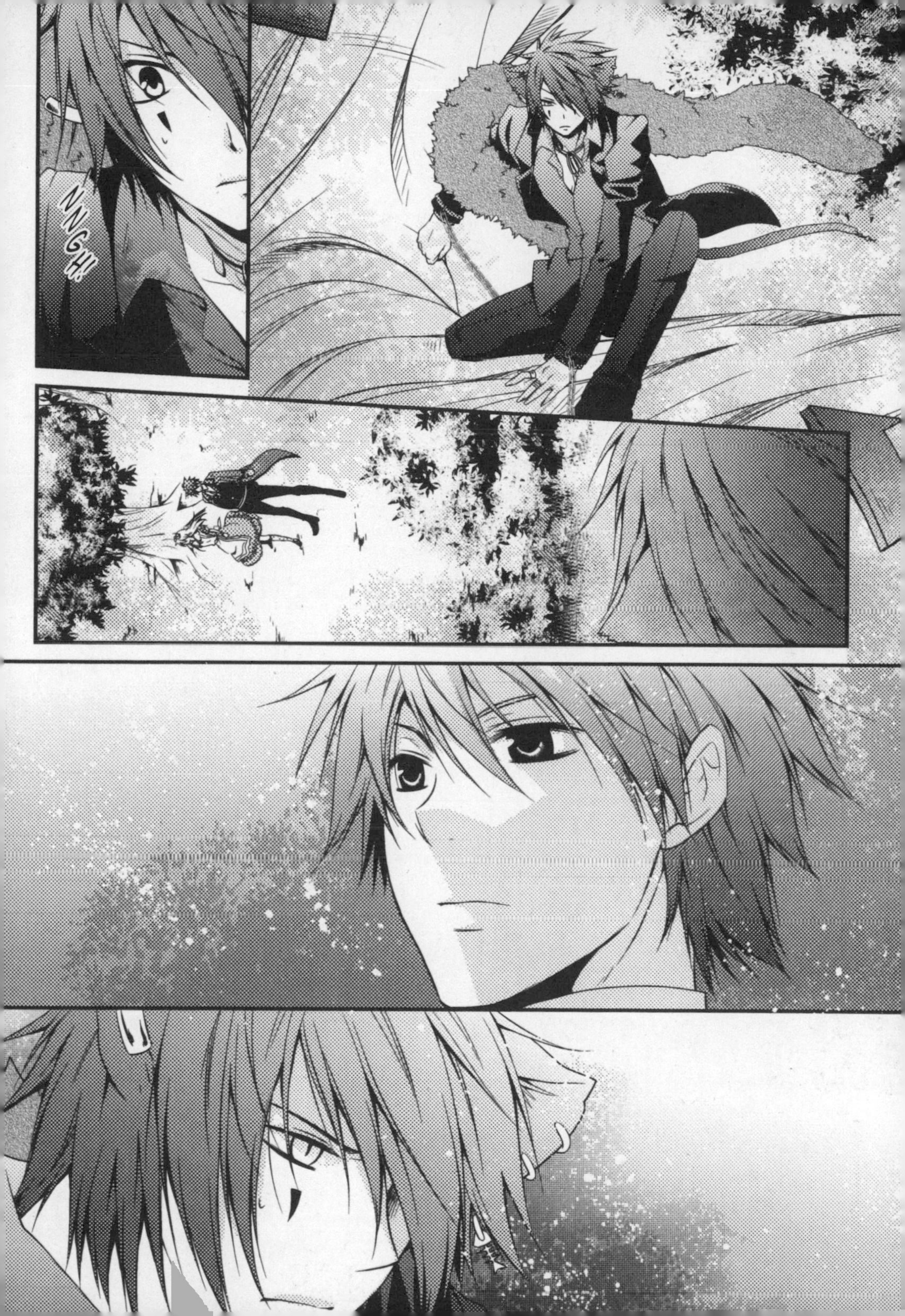
NNGH!

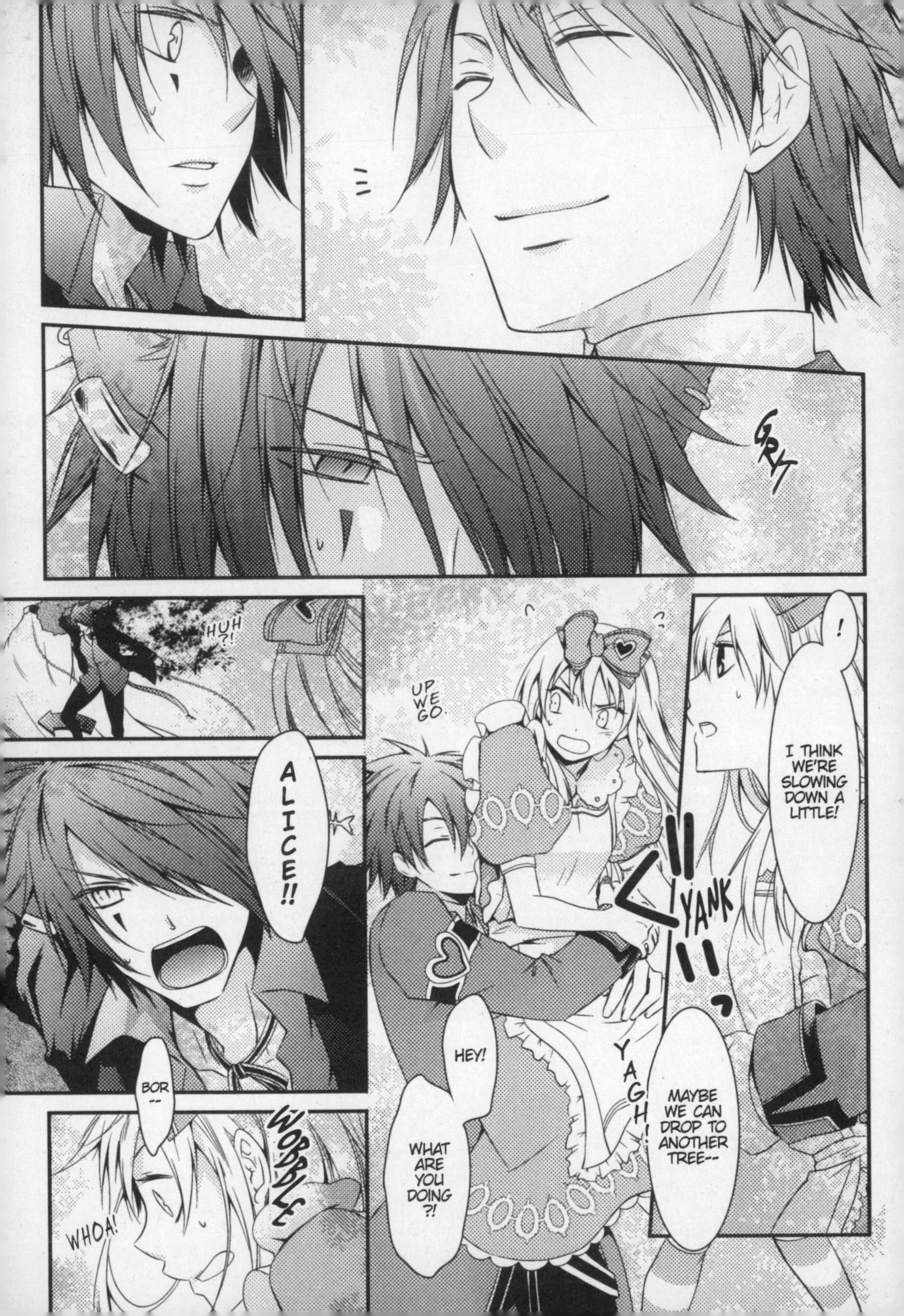
GRK
!
I THINK WE'RE SLOWING DOWN A LITTLE!
MAYBE WE CAN DROP TO ANOTHER TREE--
UP WE GO.
YANK
YAGH!
HEY!
WHAT ARE YOU DOING?!
HUH?!
ALICE!!
BOR--
WOBBLE
WHOA!

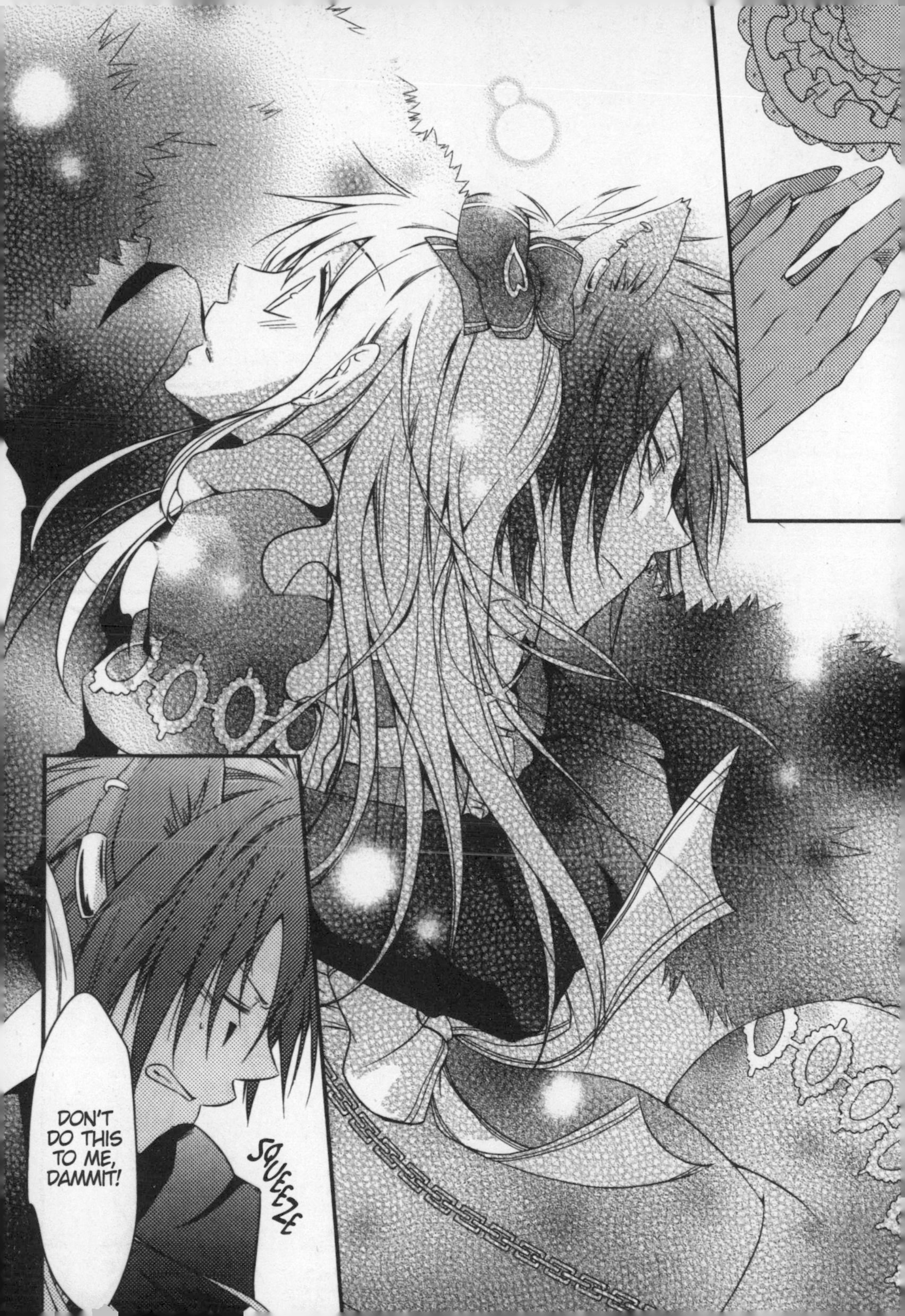
DON'T DO THIS TO ME, DAMMIT!
SQUEEZE

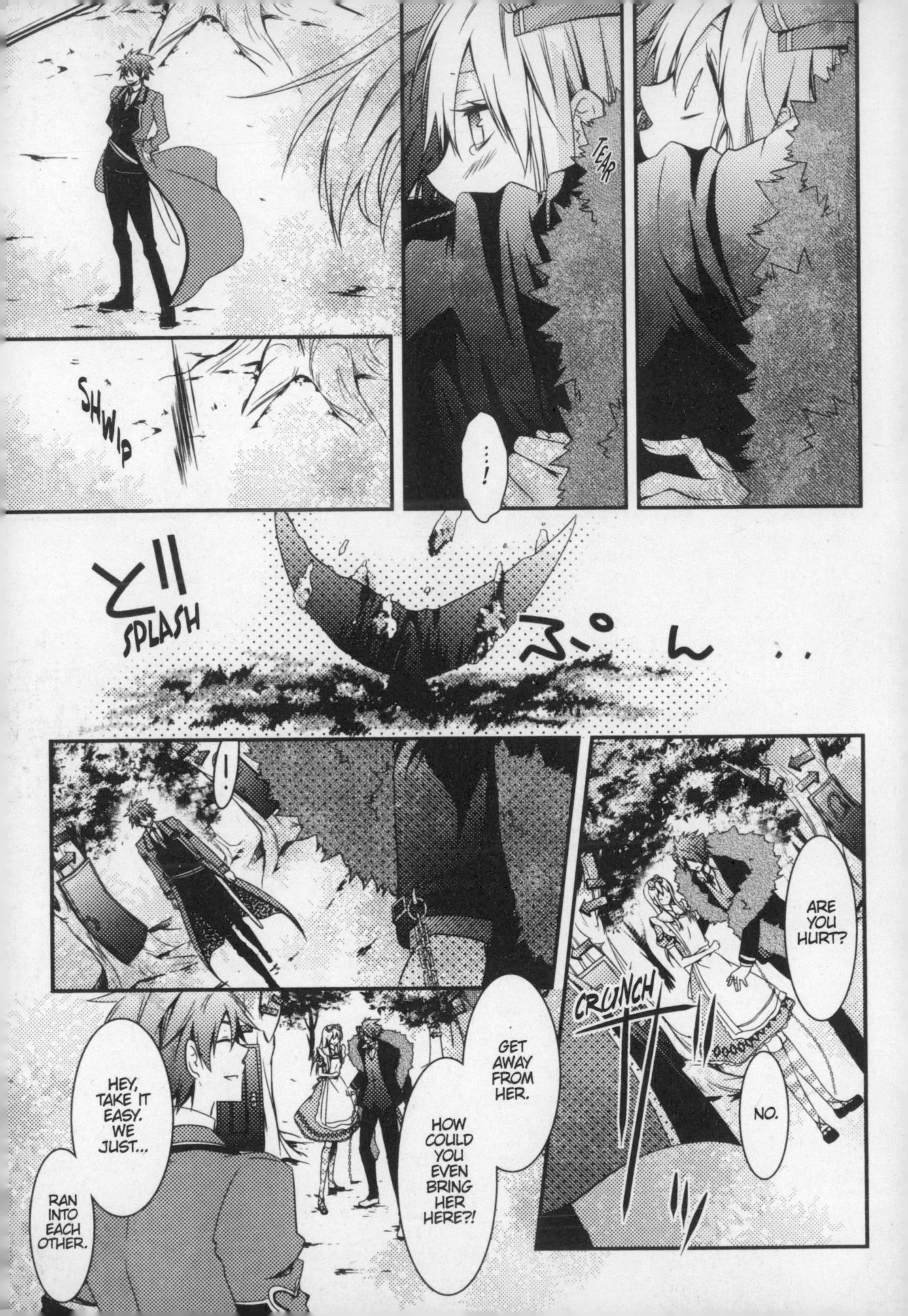
TEAR
...!
SHWIP
SPLASH
ぷん
ARE YOU HURT?
CRUNCH
NO.
!
GET AWAY FROM HER.
HOW COULD YOU EVEN BRING HER HERE?!
HEY, TAKE IT EASY. WE JUST...
RAN INTO EACH OTHER.

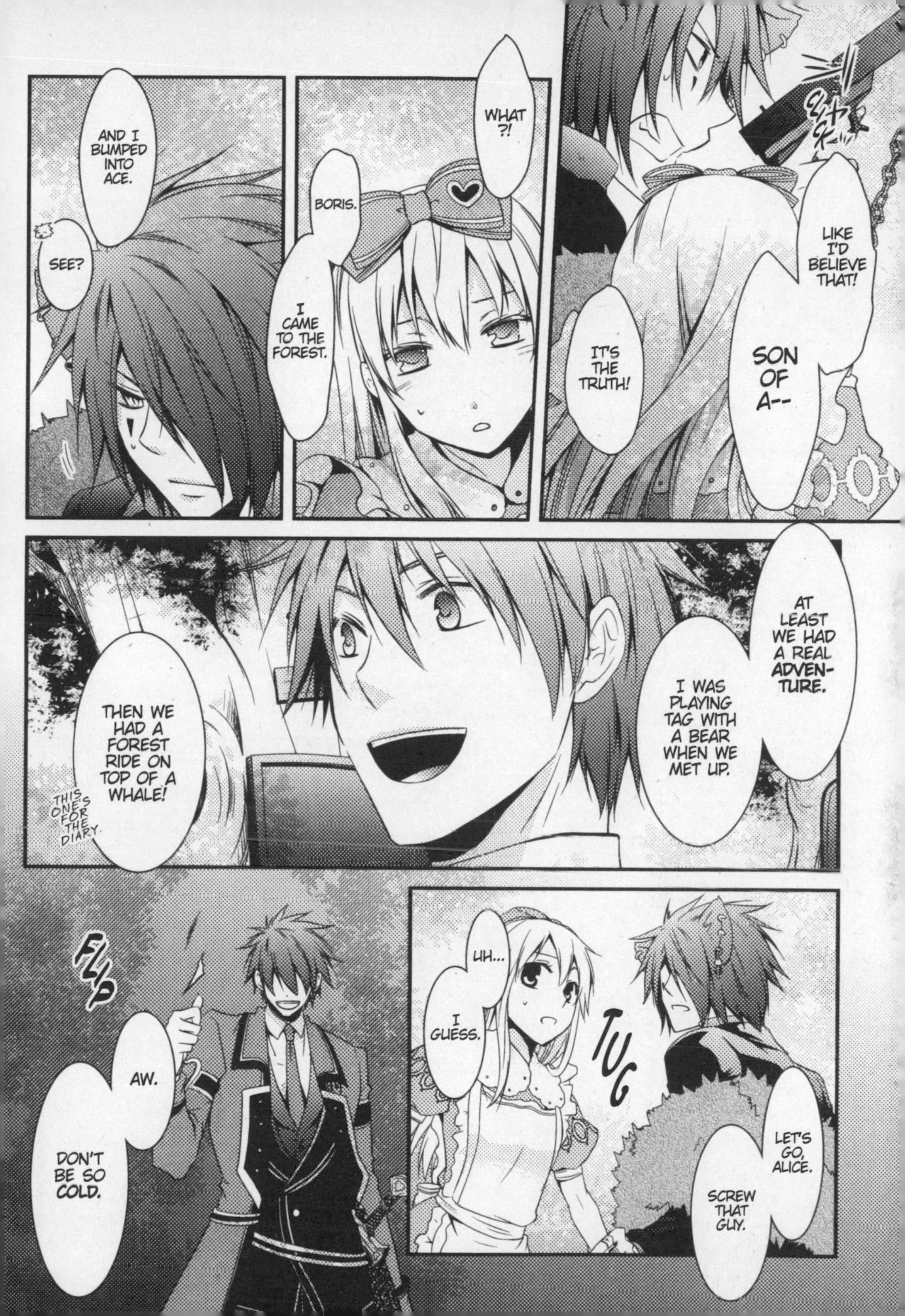
CLICK
LIKE I'D BELIEVE THAT!
SON OF A--
IT'S THE TRUTH!
WHAT ?!
BORIS.
I CAME TO THE FOREST.
AND I BUMPED INTO ACE.
SEE?
AT LEAST WE HAD A REAL ADVENTURE.
I WAS PLAYING TAG WITH A BEAR WHEN WE MET UP.
THEN WE HAD A FOREST RIDE ON TOP OF A WHALE!
THIS ONE'S FOR THE DIARY.
UH...
I GUESS.
TUG
LET'S GO, ALICE.
SCREW THAT GUY.
FLIP
AW.
DON'T BE SO COLD.

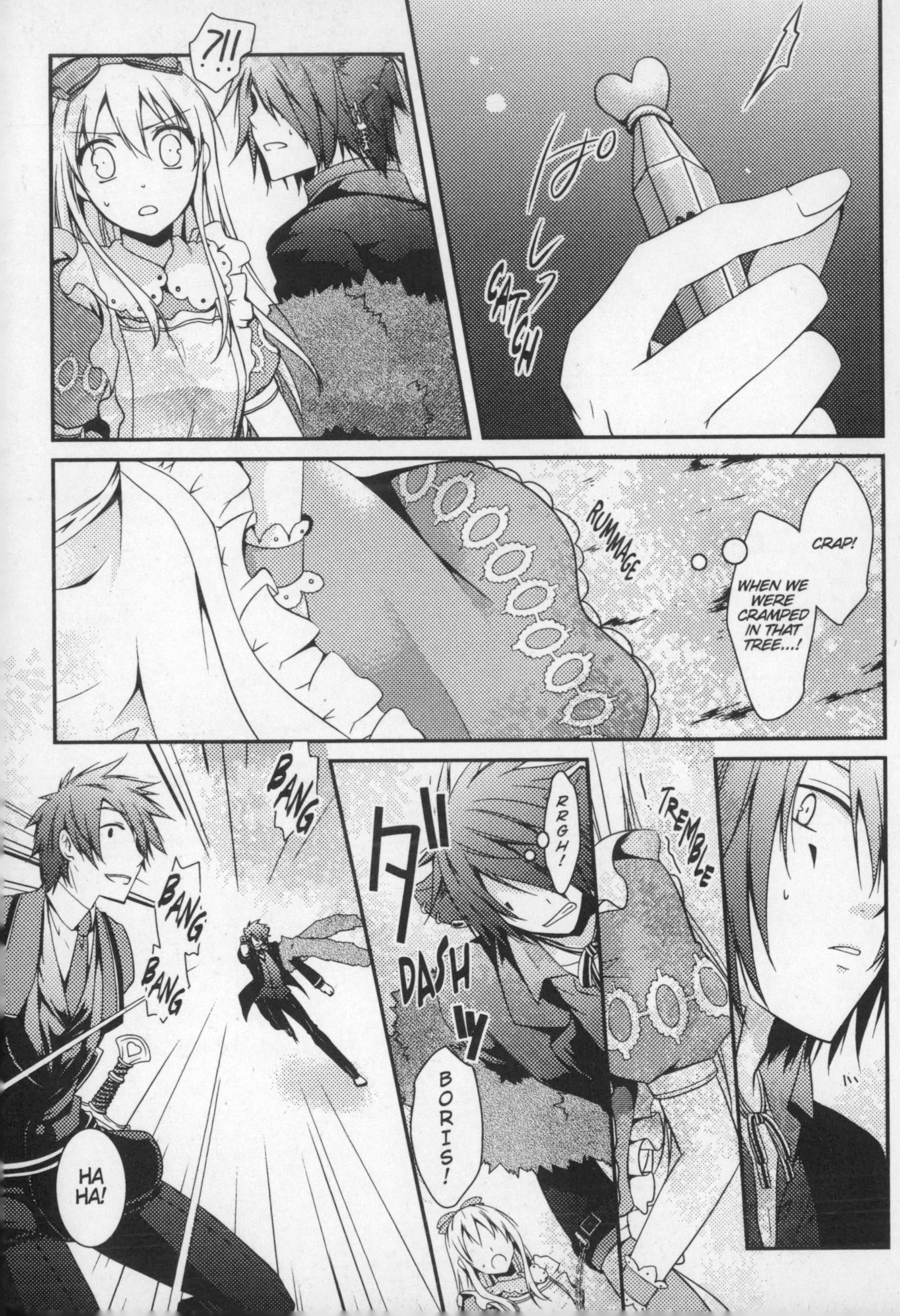
CATCH
?!!
RUMMAGE
CRAP!
WHEN WE WERE CRAMPED IN THAT TREE...!
TREMBLE
RRGH!
DASH
BORIS!
BANG
BANG
BANG
HA HA!

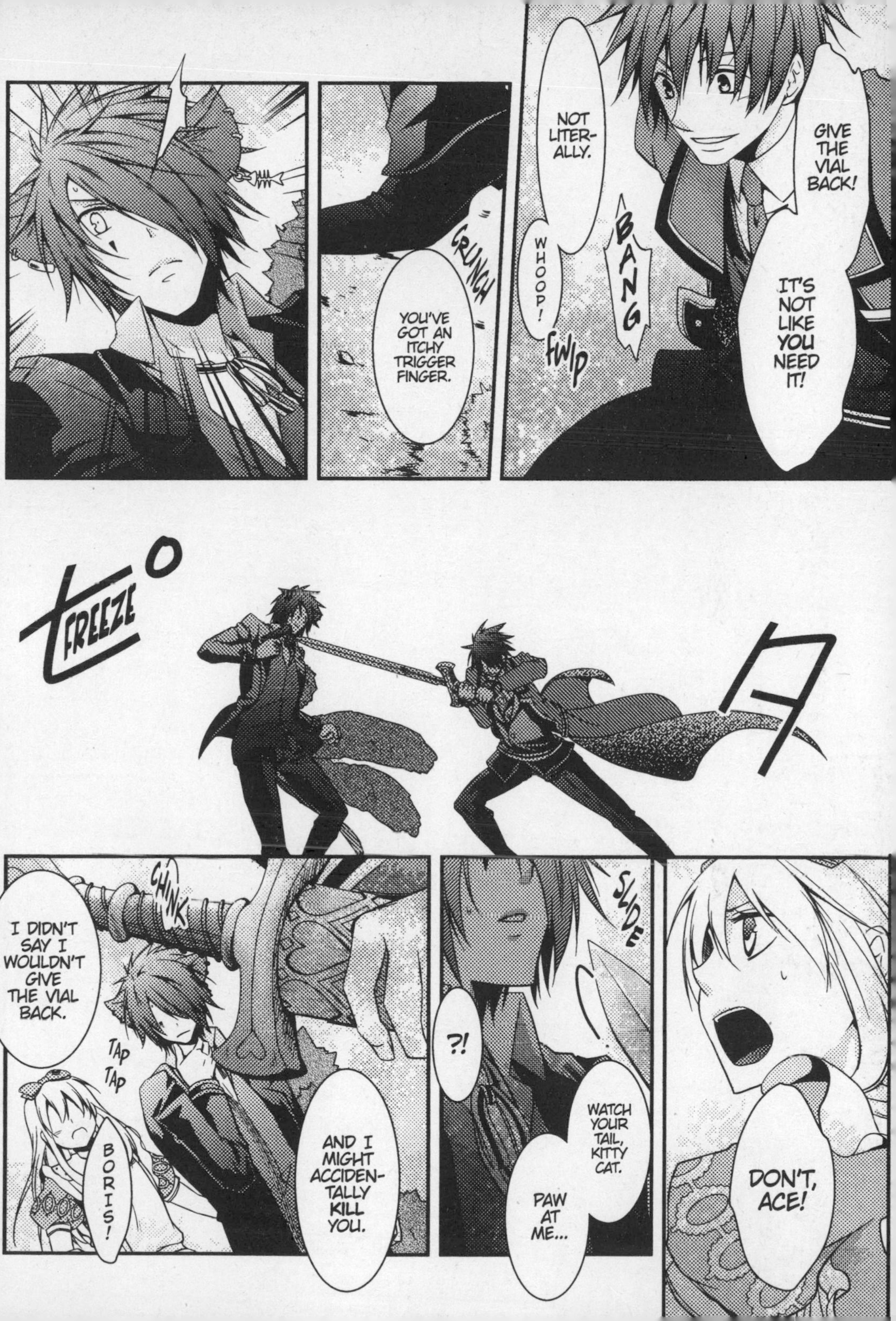
GIVE THE VIAL BACK!
IT'S NOT LIKE YOU NEED IT!
NOT LITER-ALLY.
BANG
WHOOP!
FWIP
CRUNCH
YOU'VE GOT AN ITCHY TRIGGER FINGER.
FREEZE
DON'T, ACE!
SLIDE
?!
WATCH YOUR TAIL, KITTY CAT.
PAW AT ME...
CHINK
I DIDN'T SAY I WOULDN'T GIVE THE VIAL BACK.
AND I MIGHT ACCIDEN-TALLY KILL YOU.
TAP TAP
BORIS!

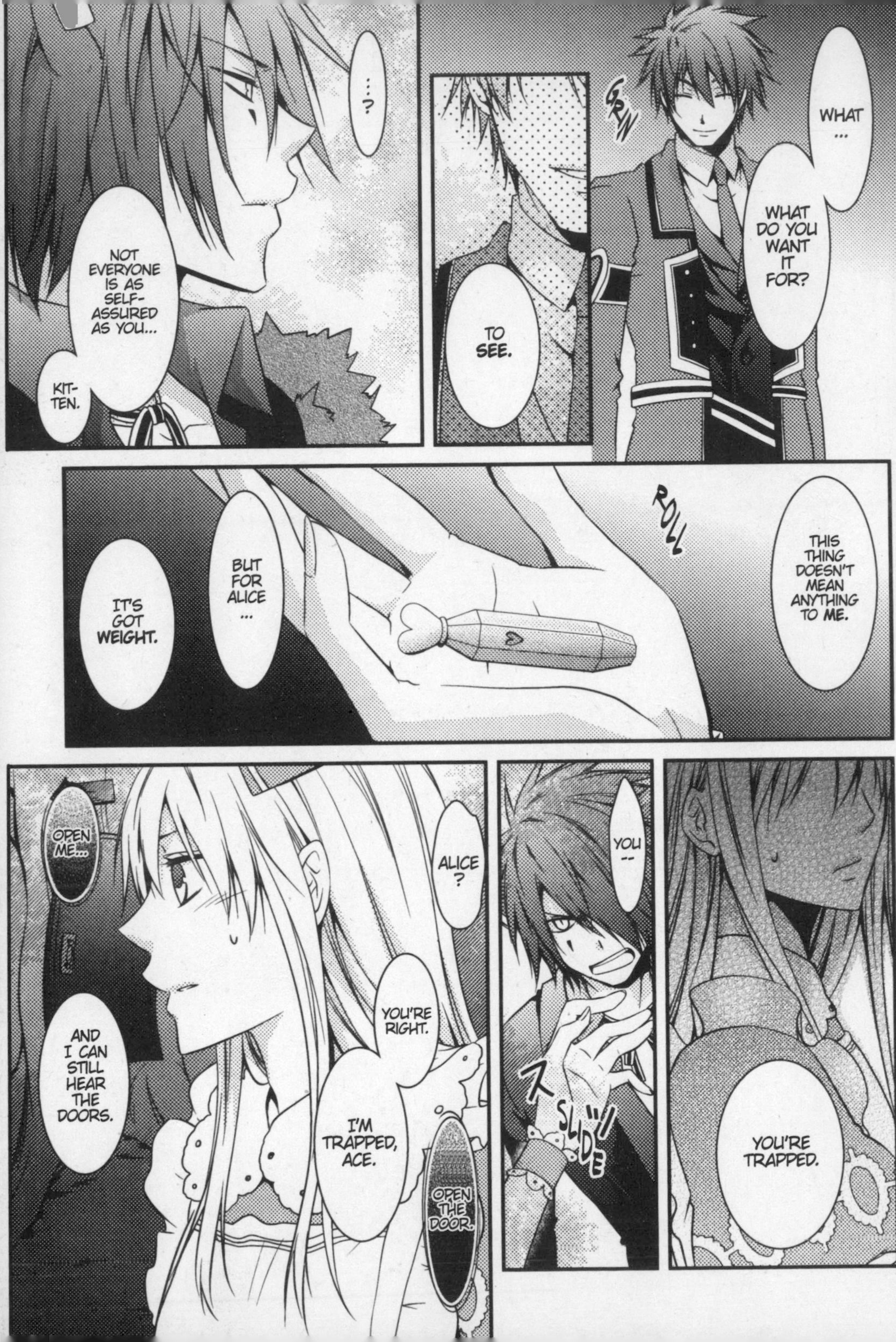
WHAT ...
WHAT DO YOU WANT IT FOR?
GRIN
TO SEE.
...?
NOT EVERYONE IS AS SELF-ASSURED AS YOU...
KIT-TEN.
ROLL
THIS THING DOESN'T MEAN ANYTHING TO ME.
BUT FOR ALICE ...
IT'S GOT WEIGHT.
YOU'RE TRAPPED.
YOU --
SLIDE
ALICE ?
OPEN ME...
YOU'RE RIGHT.
I'M TRAPPED, ACE.
AND I CAN STILL HEAR THE DOORS.
OPEN THE DOOR.

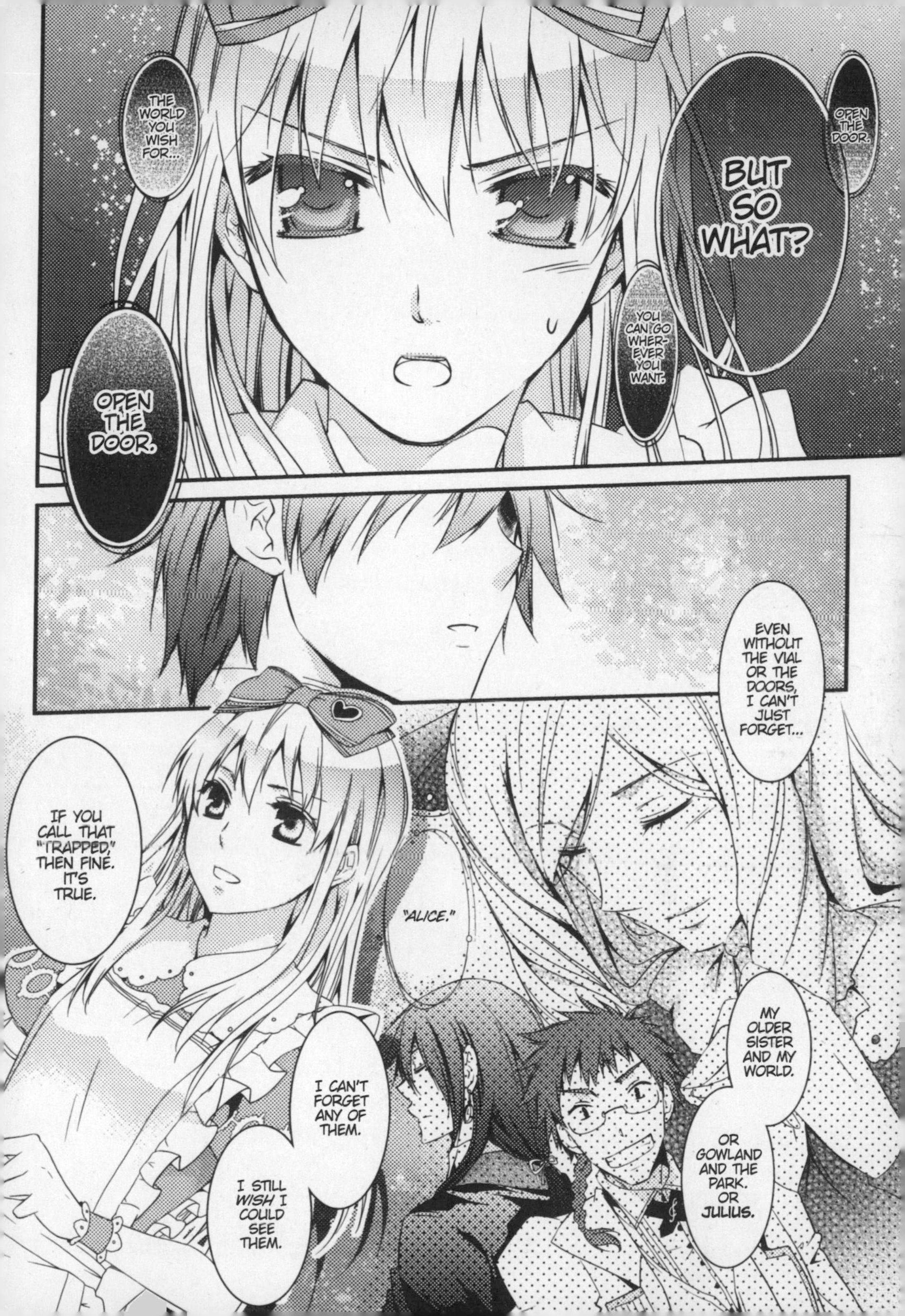

OPEN THE DOOR.
THE WORLD YOU WISH FOR...
YOU CAN GO WHEREVER YOU WANT.
OPEN THE DOOR.
BUT SO WHAT?
EVEN WITHOUT THE VIAL OR THE DOORS, I CAN'T JUST FORGET...
IF YOU CALL THAT "TRAPPED," THEN FINE. IT'S TRUE.
MY OLDER SISTER AND MY WORLD.
OR GOWLAND AND THE PARK. OR JULIUS.
"ALICE."
I CAN'T FORGET ANY OF THEM.
I STILL *WISH* I COULD SEE THEM.

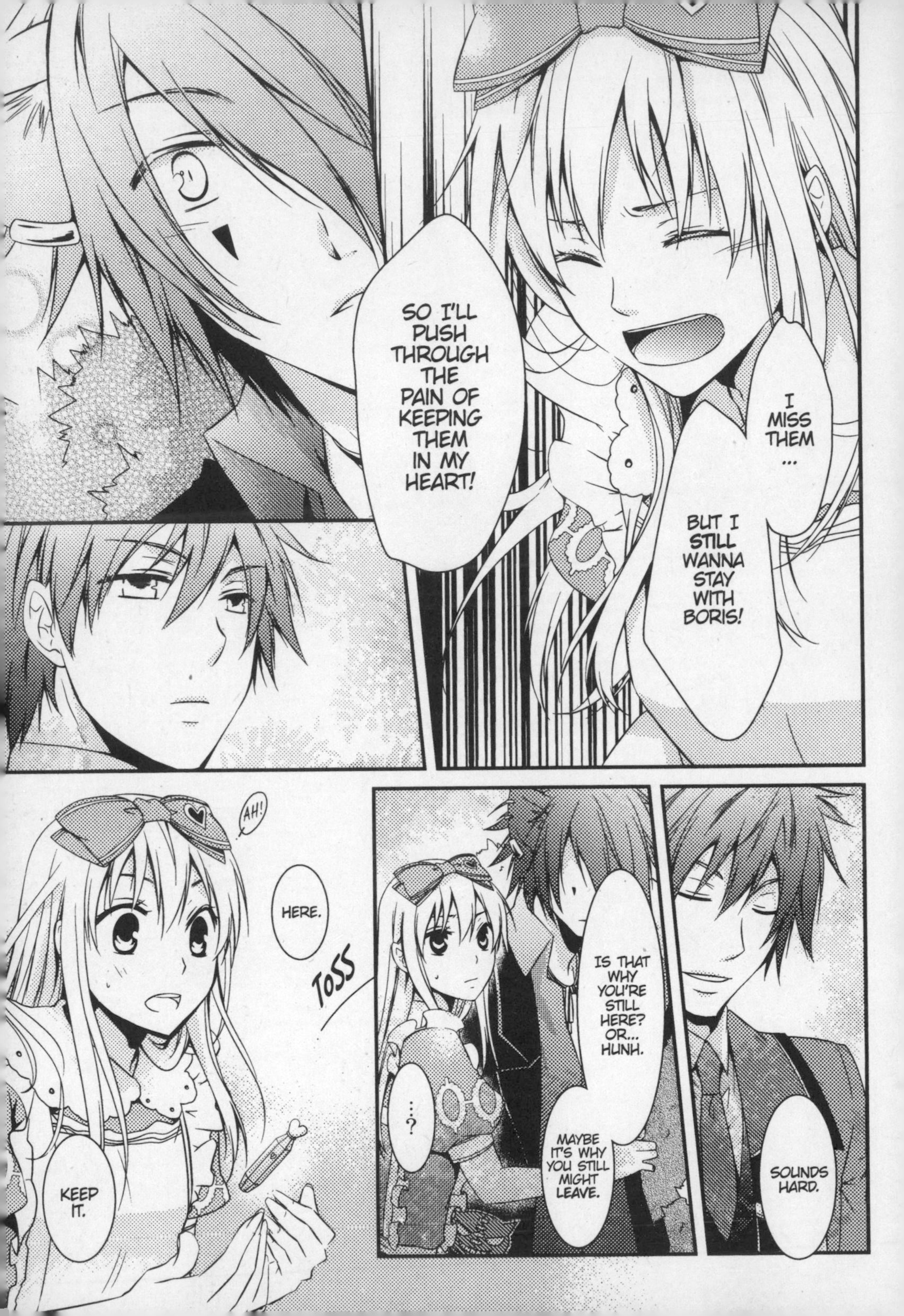
I MISS THEM...
BUT I STILL WANNA STAY WITH BORIS!
SO I'LL PUSH THROUGH THE PAIN OF KEEPING THEM IN MY HEART!
SOUNDS HARD.
IS THAT WHY YOU'RE STILL HERE? OR... HUNH.
MAYBE IT'S WHY YOU STILL MIGHT LEAVE.
...?
AH!
HERE.
TOSS
KEEP IT.

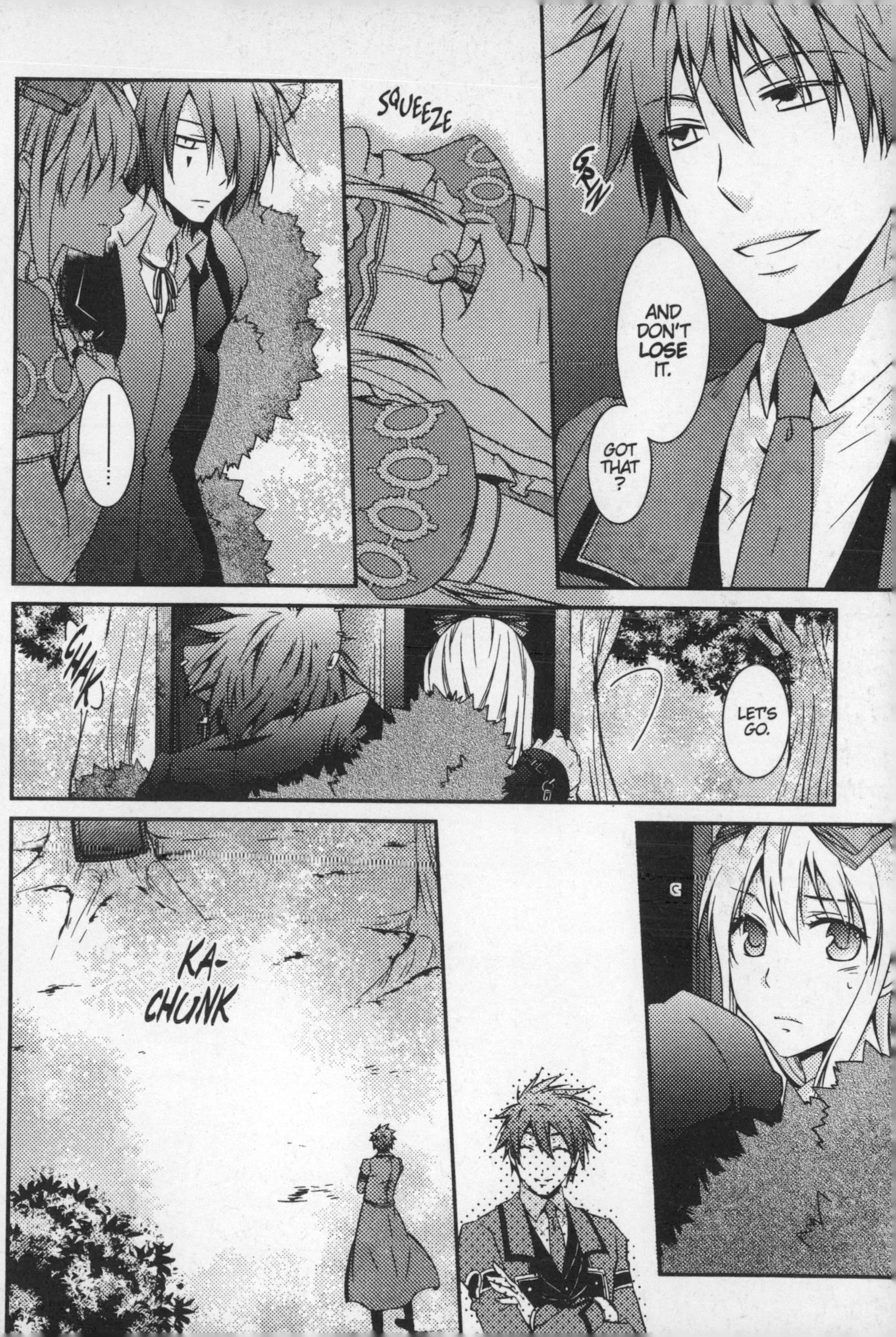
GRIN
AND DON'T LOSE IT.
GOT THAT?
SQUEEZE
—…
LET'S GO.
CHAK
KA-CHUNK

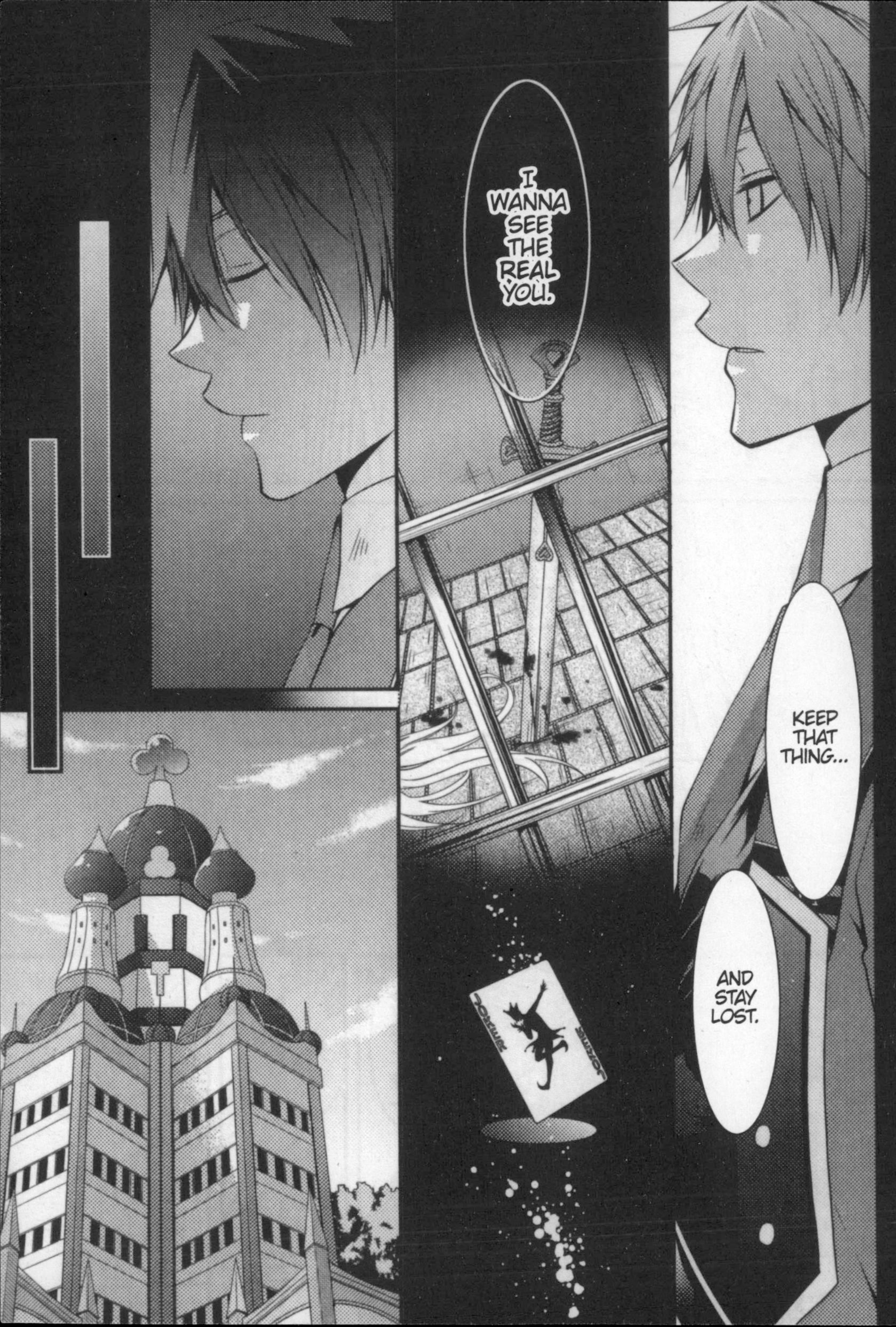
KEEP THAT THING...
AND STAY LOST.
I WANNA SEE THE REAL YOU.

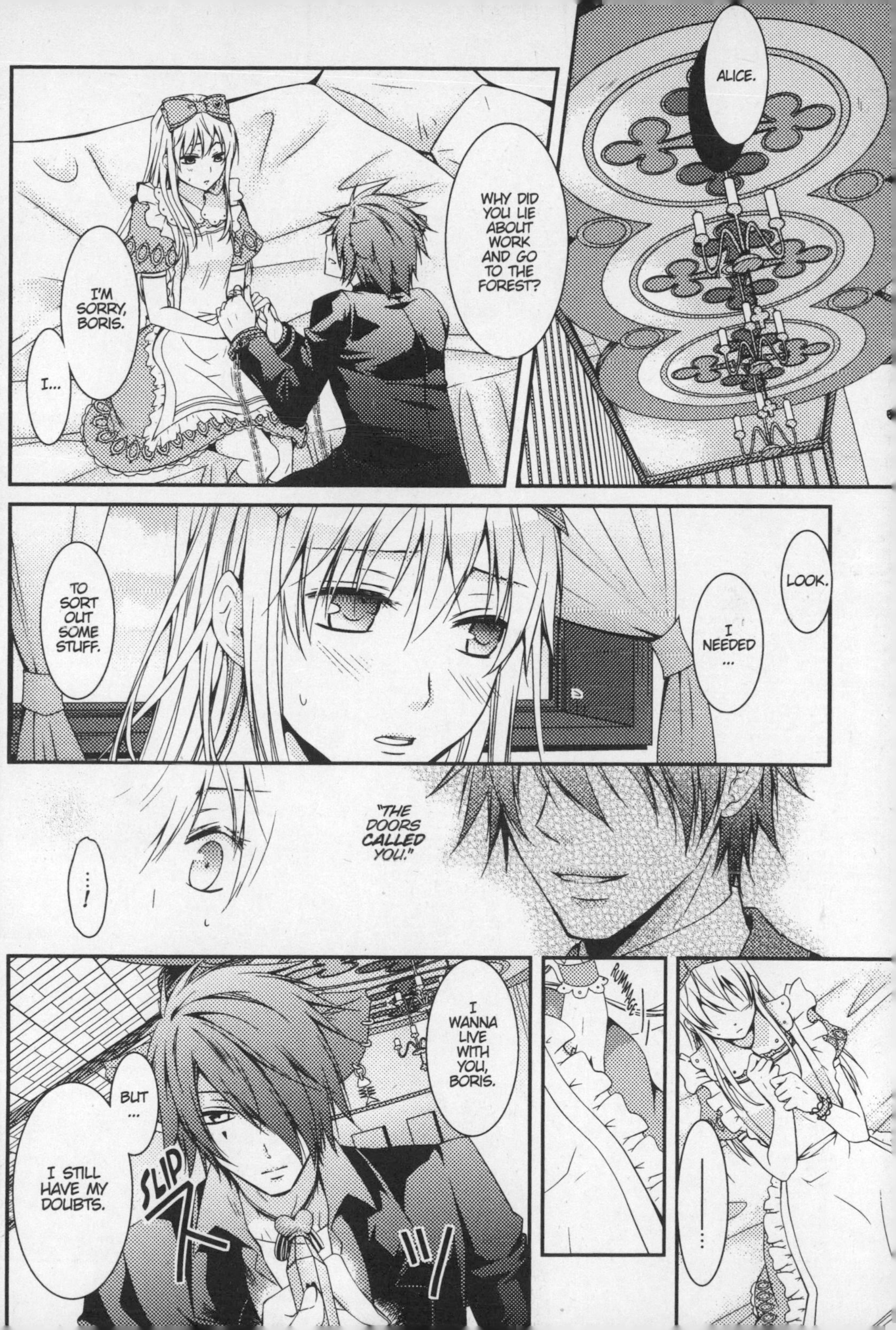
ALICE.
WHY DID YOU LIE ABOUT WORK AND GO TO THE FOREST?
I'M SORRY, BORIS.
I...
LOOK.
I NEEDED ...
TO SORT OUT SOME STUFF.
"THE DOORS CALLED YOU."
...!
......
RUMMAGE
I WANNA LIVE WITH YOU, BORIS.
BUT ...
I STILL HAVE MY DOUBTS.
SLIP

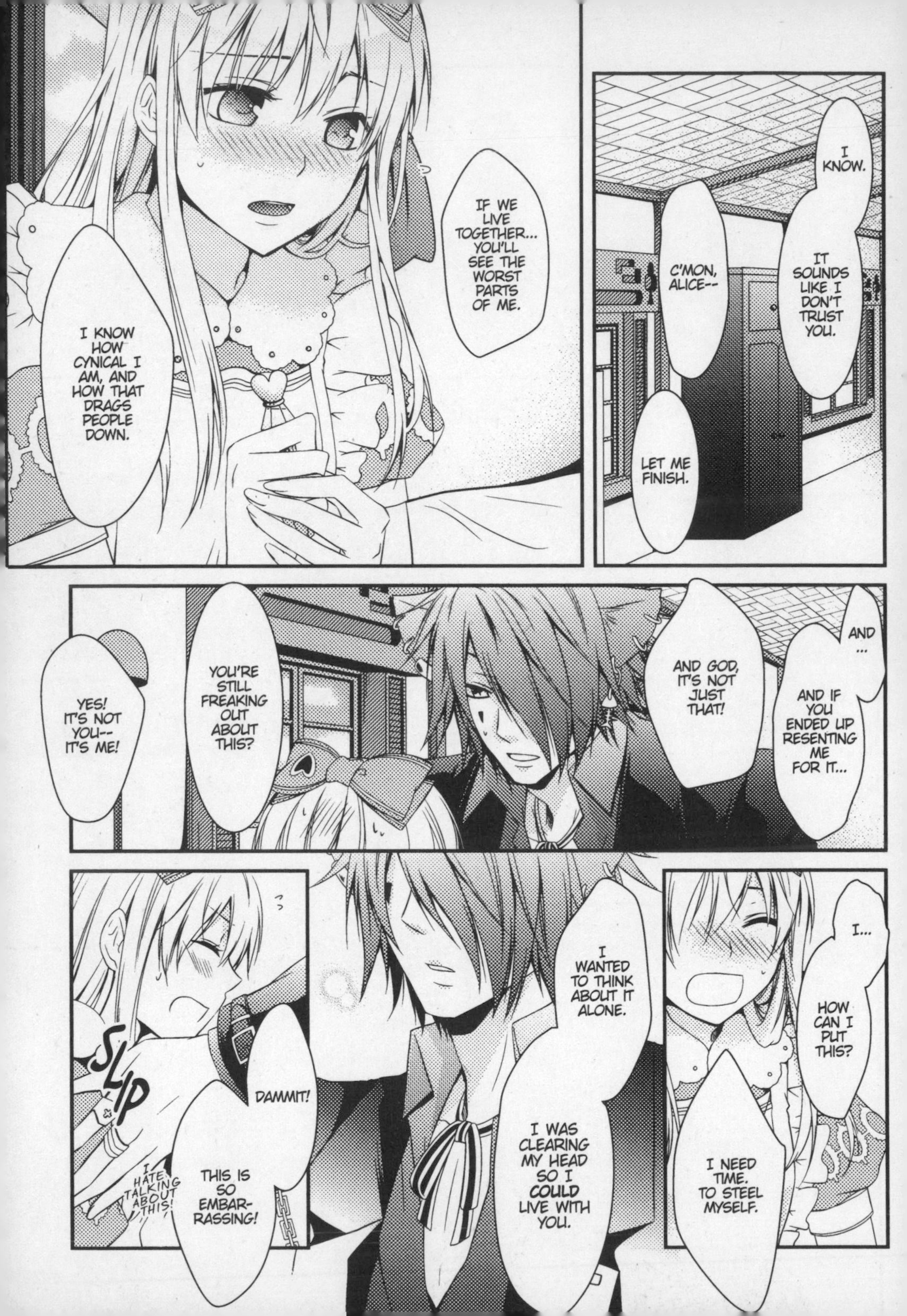

I KNOW.
IT SOUNDS LIKE I DON'T TRUST YOU.
C'MON, ALICE--
LET ME FINISH.
IF WE LIVE TOGETHER... YOU'LL SEE THE WORST PARTS OF ME.
I KNOW HOW CYNICAL I AM, AND HOW THAT DRAGS PEOPLE DOWN.
AND ...
AND IF YOU ENDED UP RESENTING ME FOR IT...
AND GOD, IT'S NOT JUST THAT!
YOU'RE STILL FREAKING OUT ABOUT THIS?
YES! IT'S NOT YOU-- IT'S ME!
I...
HOW CAN I PUT THIS?
I NEED TIME. TO STEEL MYSELF.
I WANTED TO THINK ABOUT IT ALONE.
I WAS CLEARING MY HEAD SO I COULD LIVE WITH YOU.
DAMMIT!
SLIP
THIS IS SO EMBARRASSING!
I HATE TALKING ABOUT THIS!

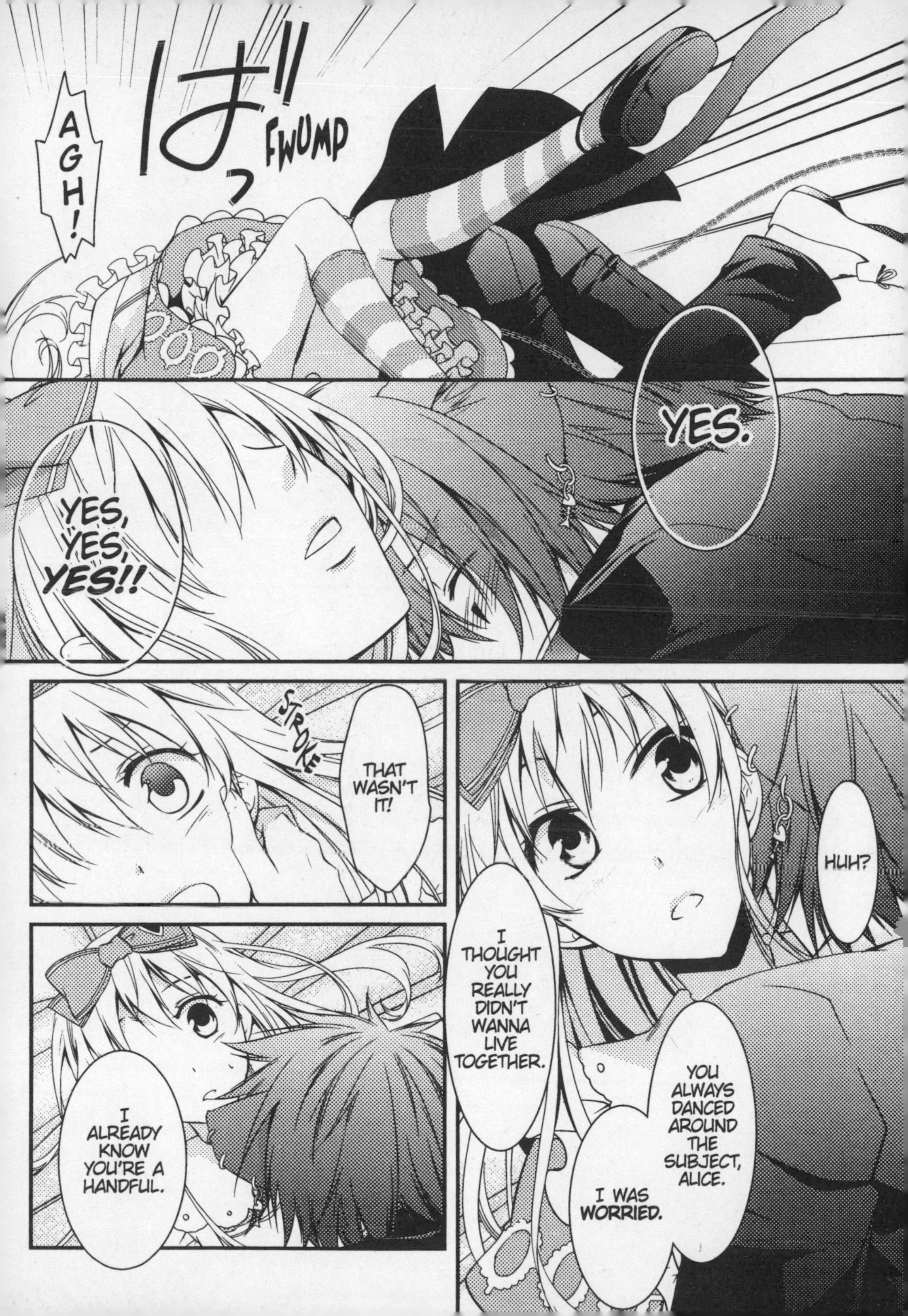
ぱっ
FWUMP
AGH!
YES.
YES, YES, YES!!
HUH?
I THOUGHT YOU REALLY DIDN'T WANNA LIVE TOGETHER.
YOU ALWAYS DANCED AROUND THE SUBJECT, ALICE.
I WAS WORRIED.
STROKE
THAT WASN'T IT!
I ALREADY KNOW YOU'RE A HANDFUL.

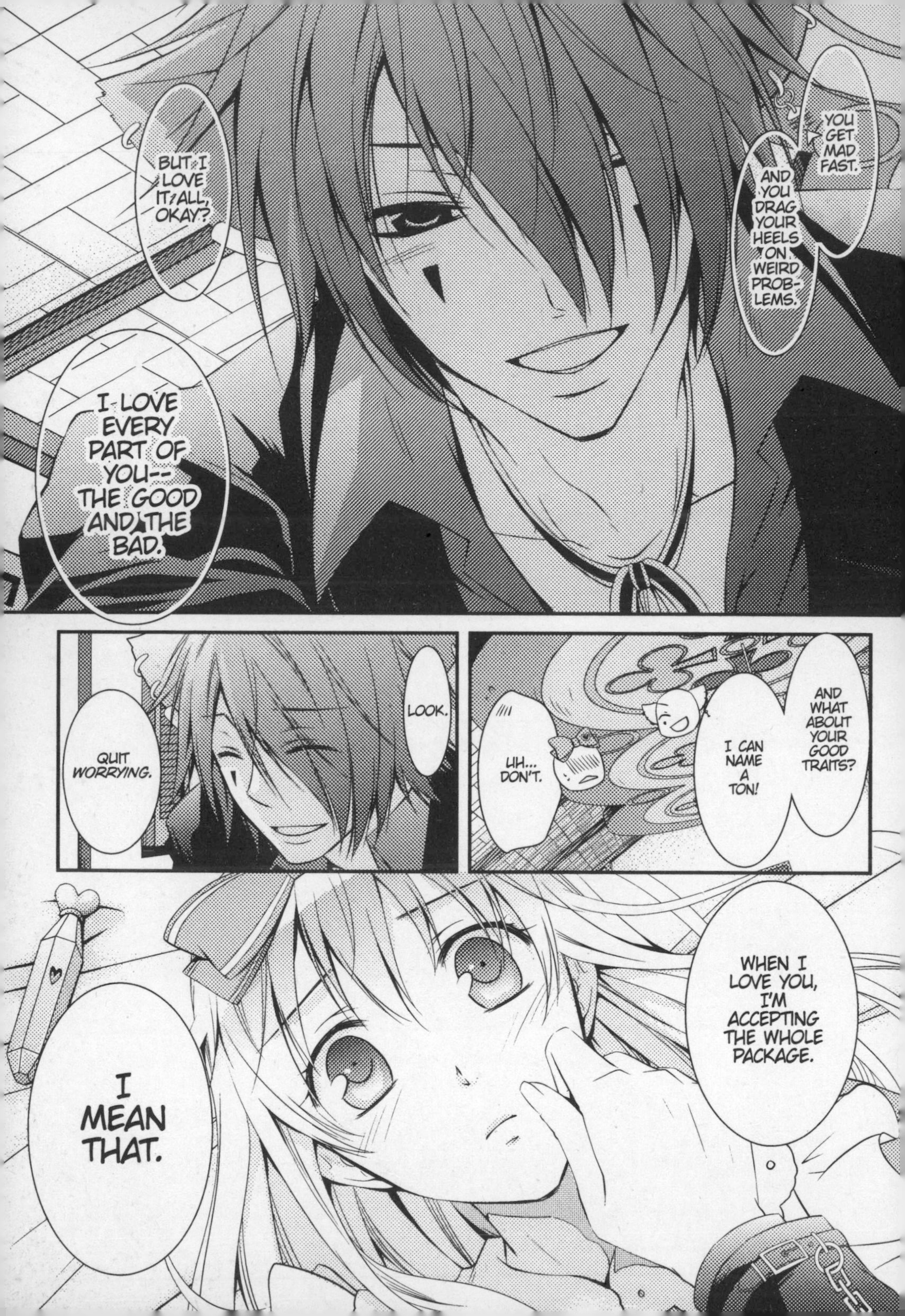
YOU GET MAD FAST.
AND YOU DRAG YOUR HEELS ON WEIRD PROB-LEMS.
BUT I LOVE IT ALL, OKAY?
I LOVE EVERY PART OF YOU-- THE GOOD AND THE BAD.
AND WHAT ABOUT YOUR GOOD TRAITS?
I CAN NAME A TON!
UH... DON'T.
LOOK.
QUIT *WORRYING.*
WHEN I LOVE YOU, I'M ACCEPTING THE WHOLE PACKAGE.
I MEAN THAT.

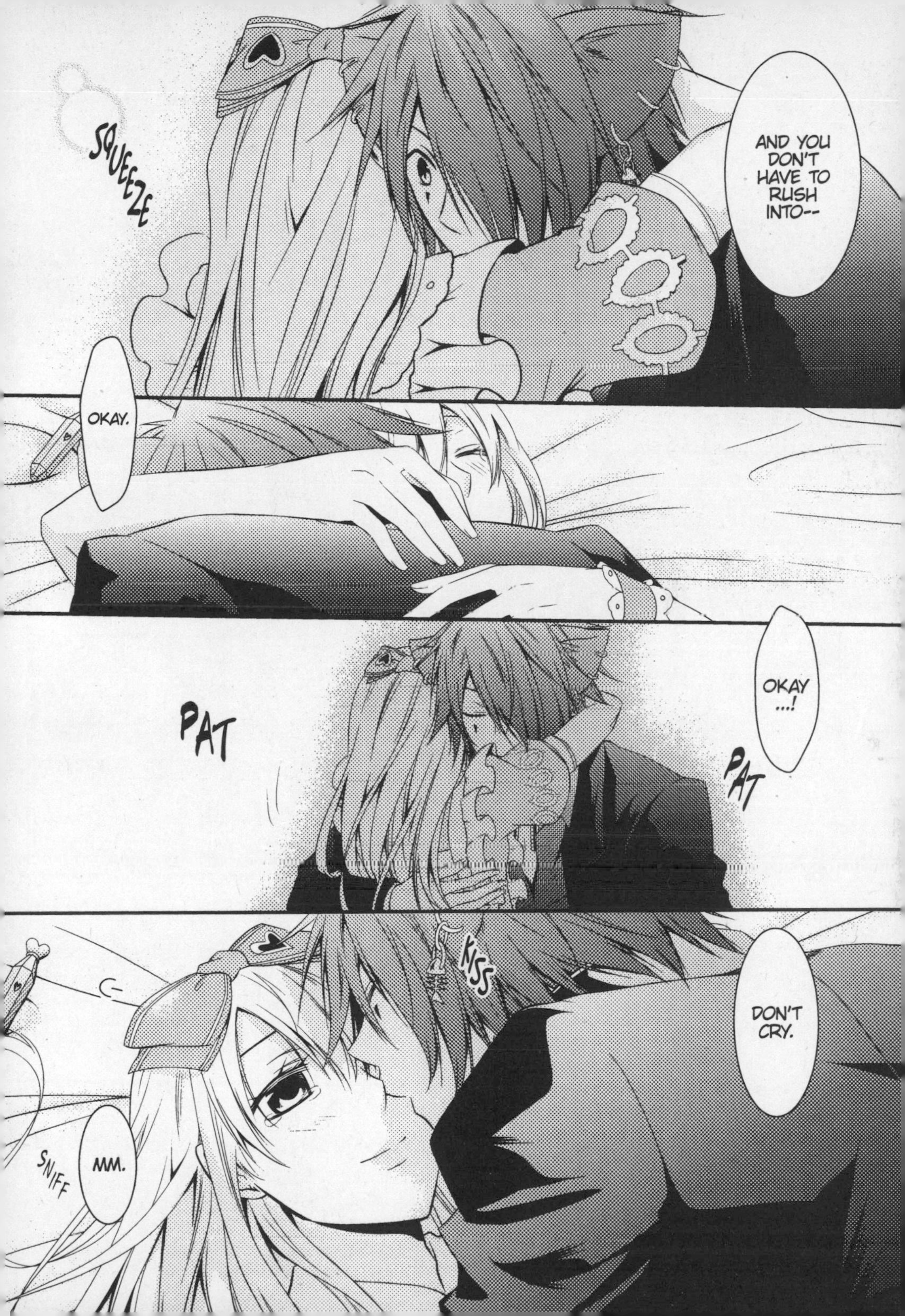
AND YOU DON'T HAVE TO RUSH INTO--
SQUEEZE
OKAY.
OKAY ...!
PAT
PAT
DON'T CRY.
KISS
MM.
SNIFF

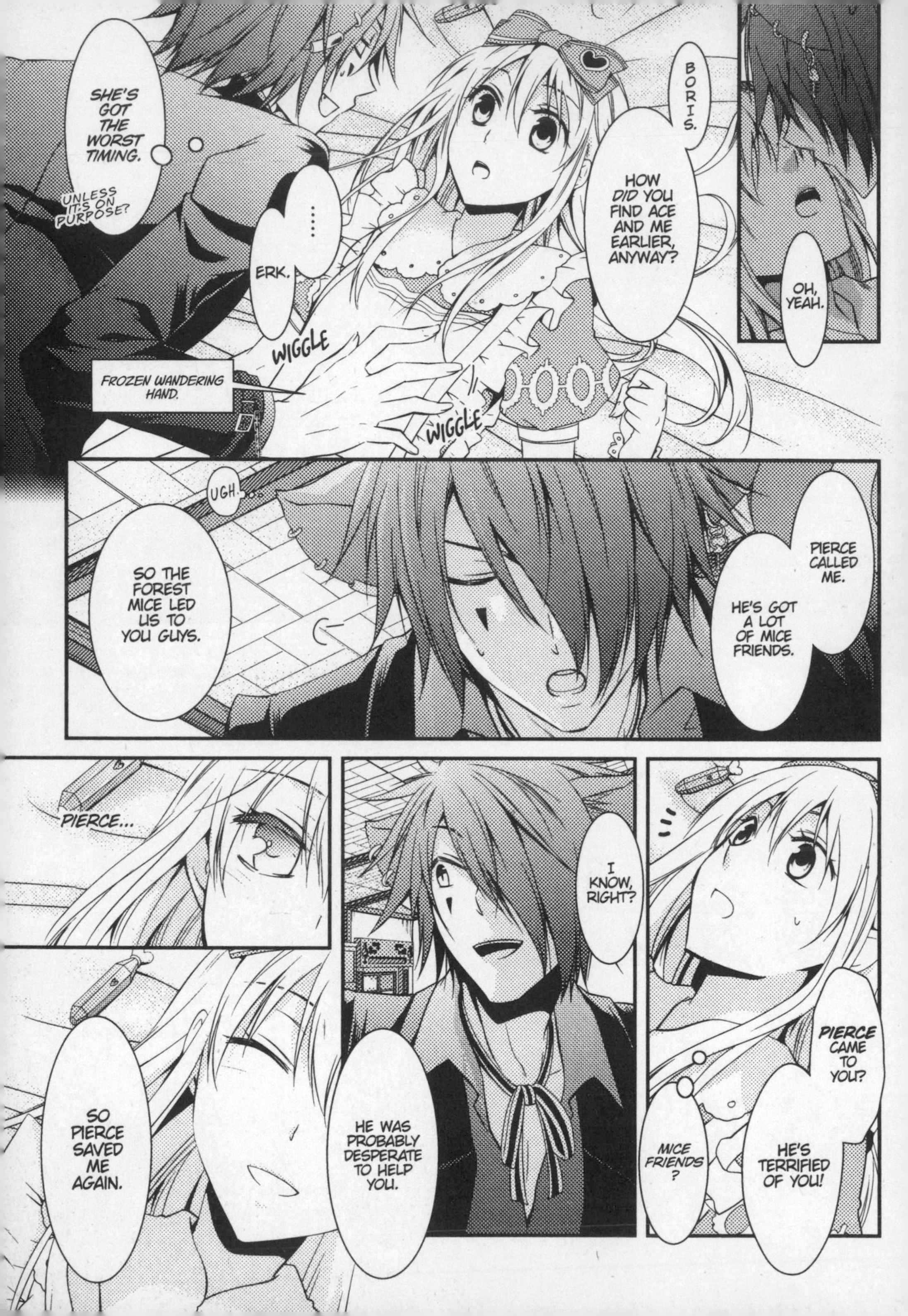
OH, YEAH.
BORIS.
HOW DID YOU FIND ACE AND ME EARLIER, ANYWAY?
.....
ERK.
SHE'S GOT THE WORST TIMING.
UNLESS IT'S ON PURPOSE?
WIGGLE
FROZEN WANDERING HAND.
WIGGLE
PIERCE CALLED ME.
HE'S GOT A LOT OF MICE FRIENDS.
SO THE FOREST MICE LED US TO YOU GUYS.
UGH.
PIERCE CAME TO YOU?
HE'S TERRIFIED OF YOU!
MICE FRIENDS?
I KNOW, RIGHT?
HE WAS PROBABLY DESPERATE TO HELP YOU.
PIERCE...
SO PIERCE SAVED ME AGAIN.

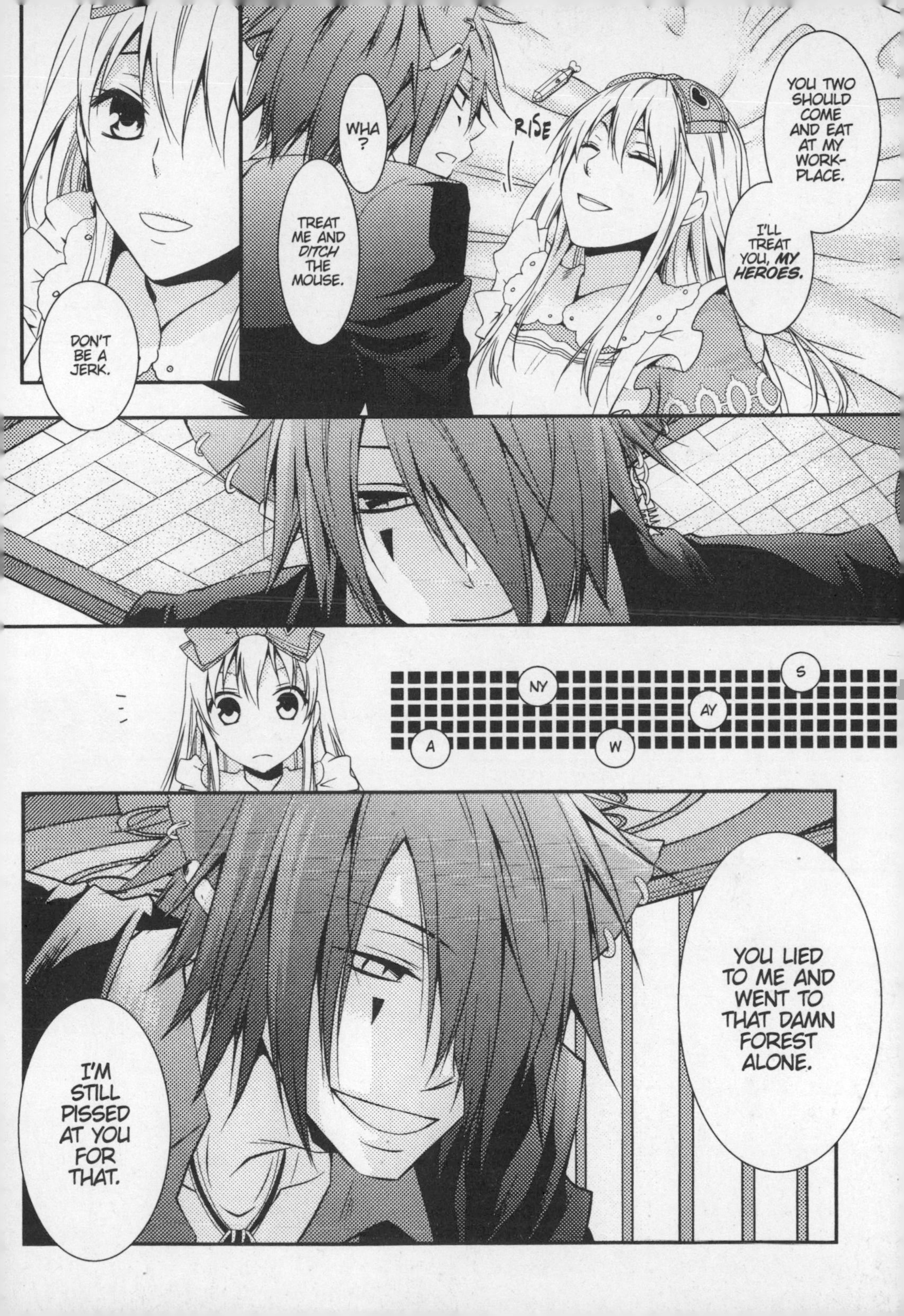
YOU TWO SHOULD COME AND EAT AT MY WORK-PLACE.
I'LL TREAT YOU, **MY HEROES.**
RISE
WHA?
TREAT ME AND *DITCH* THE MOUSE.
DON'T BE A JERK.
S
NY
AY
W
A
YOU LIED TO ME AND WENT TO THAT DAMN FOREST ALONE.
I'M STILL PISSED AT YOU FOR THAT.

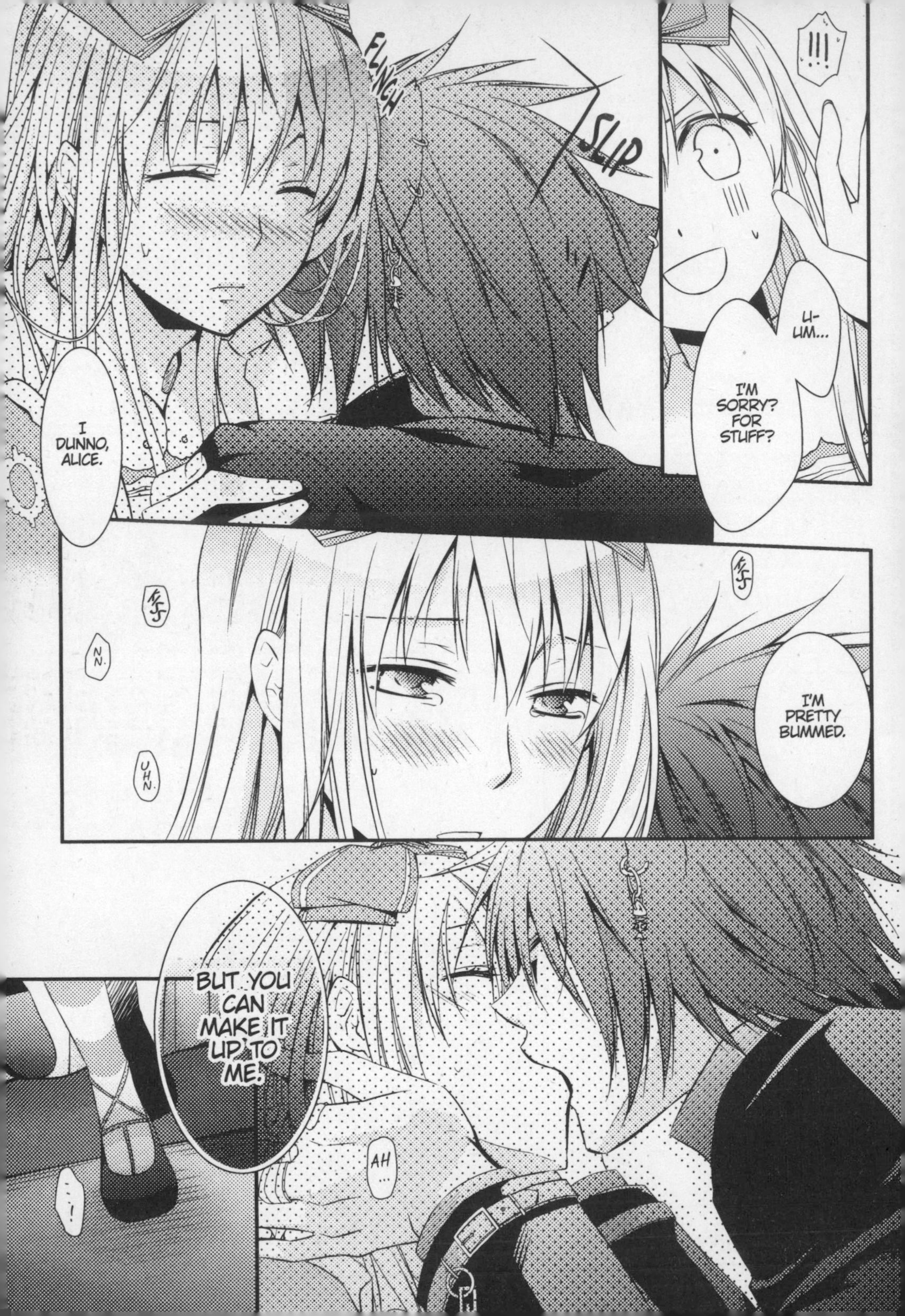
!!!
U-UM...
I'M SORRY? FOR STUFF?
SLIP
FLINCH
I DUNNO, ALICE.
I'M PRETTY BUMMED.
NN.
UHN.
BUT YOU CAN MAKE IT UP TO ME.
AH...
...!

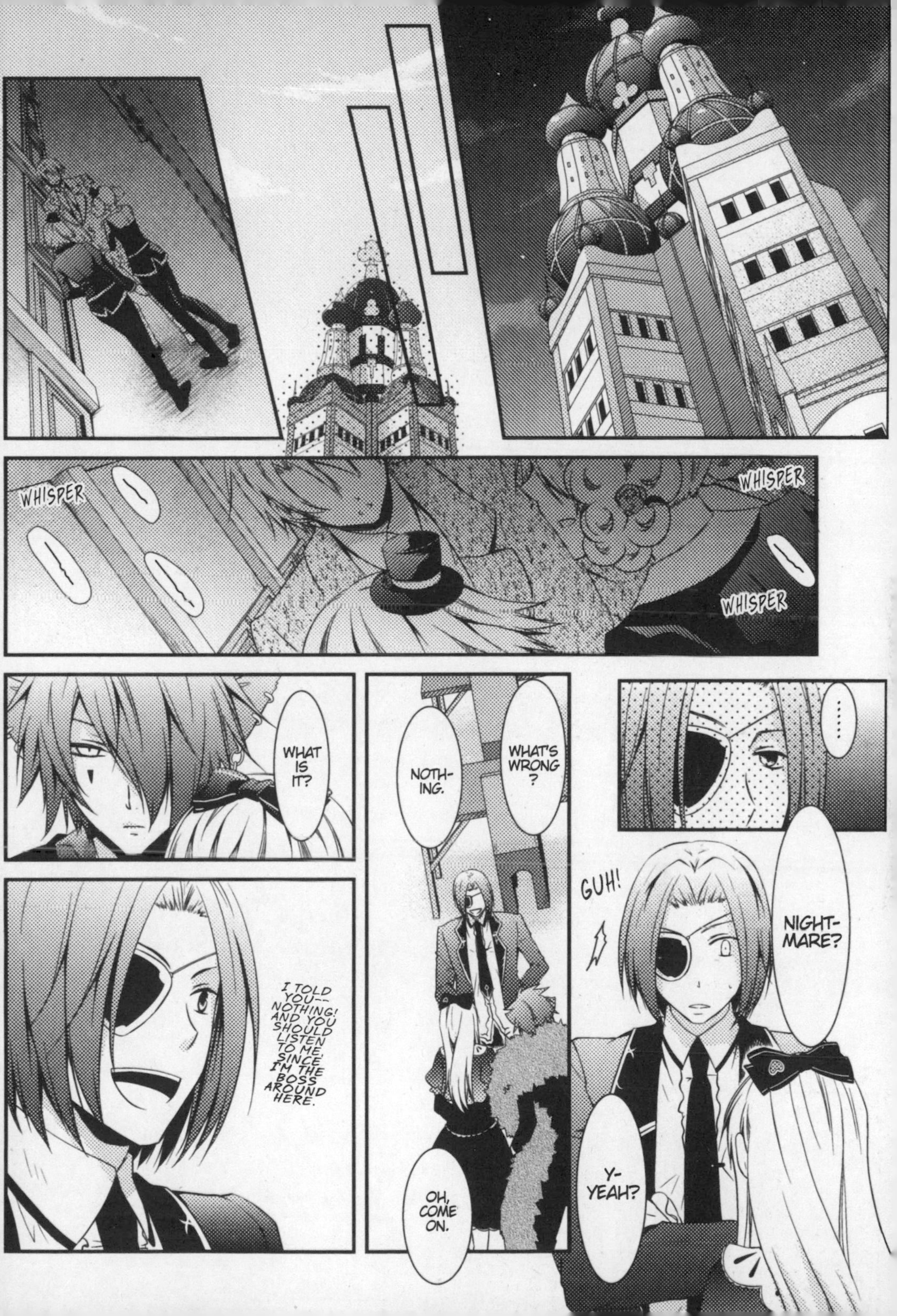
WHISPER
WHISPER
WHISPER
......
WHAT'S WRONG?
NOTHING.
NIGHT-MARE?
GUH!
Y-YEAH?
OH, COME ON.
WHAT IS IT?
I TOLD YOU-- NOTHING! AND YOU SHOULD LISTEN TO ME, SINCE I'M THE BOSS AROUND HERE.

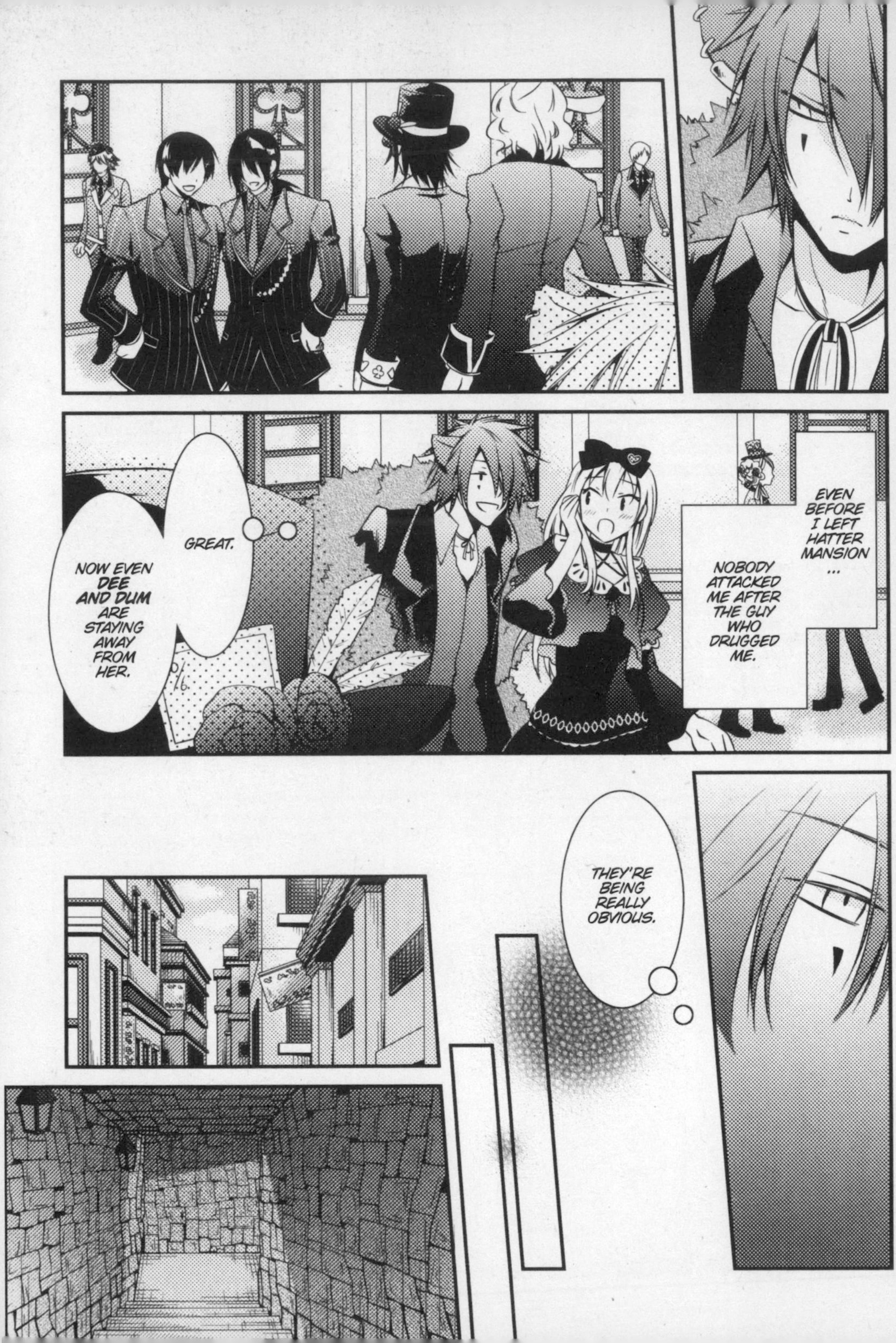

EVEN BEFORE I LEFT HATTER MANSION ...
NOBODY ATTACKED ME AFTER THE GUY WHO DRUGGED ME.
GREAT.
NOW EVEN DEE AND DUM ARE STAYING AWAY FROM HER.
THEY'RE BEING REALLY OBVIOUS.

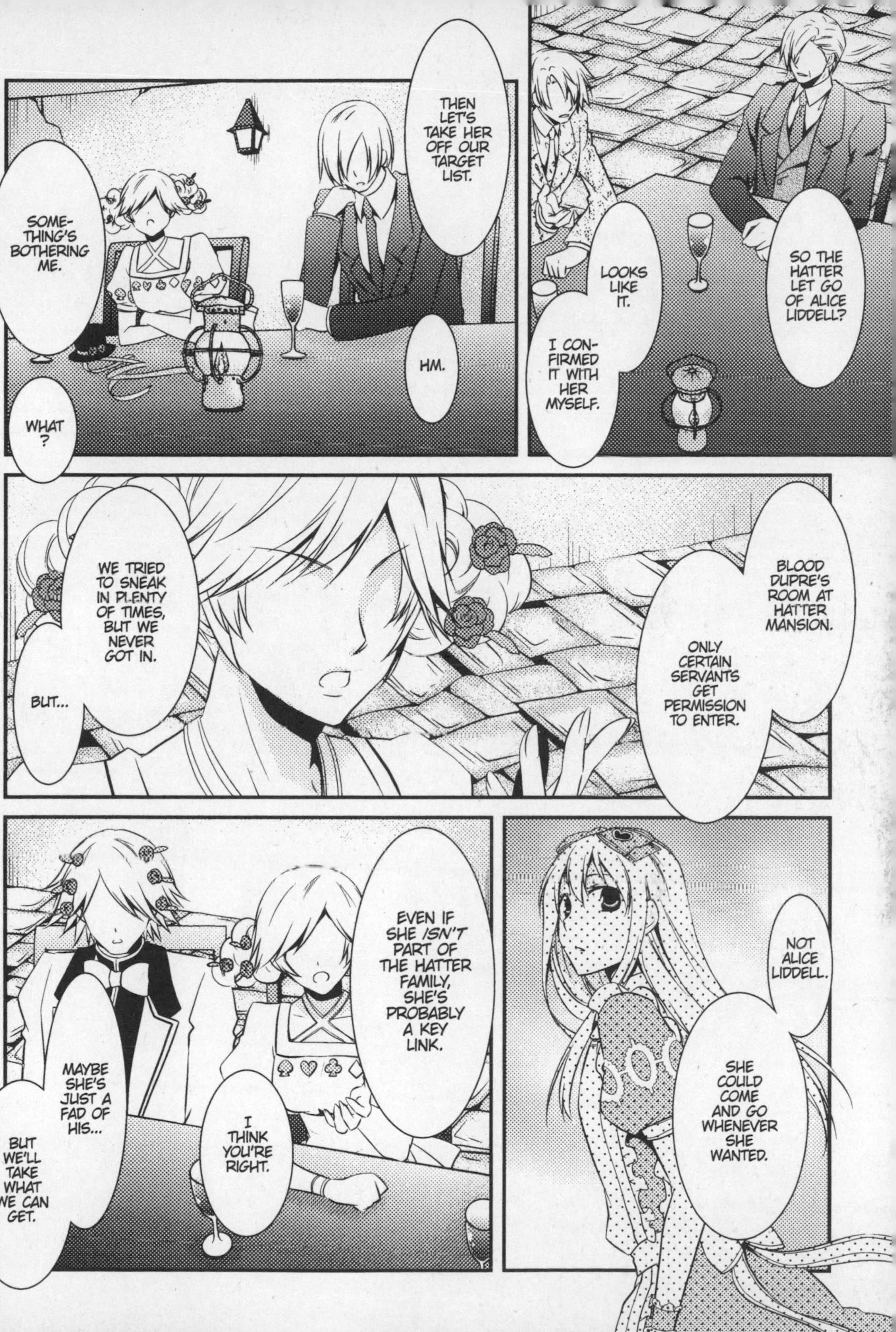
SO THE HATTER LET GO OF ALICE LIDDELL?
LOOKS LIKE IT.
I CONFIRMED IT WITH HER MYSELF.
THEN LET'S TAKE HER OFF OUR TARGET LIST.
HM.
SOMETHING'S BOTHERING ME.
WHAT?
BLOOD DUPRE'S ROOM AT HATTER MANSION.
ONLY CERTAIN SERVANTS GET PERMISSION TO ENTER.
WE TRIED TO SNEAK IN PLENTY OF TIMES, BUT WE NEVER GOT IN.
BUT...
NOT ALICE LIDDELL.
SHE COULD COME AND GO WHENEVER SHE WANTED.
EVEN IF SHE *ISN'T* PART OF THE HATTER FAMILY, SHE'S PROBABLY A KEY LINK.
I THINK YOU'RE RIGHT.
MAYBE SHE'S JUST A FAD OF HIS...
BUT WE'LL TAKE WHAT WE CAN GET.

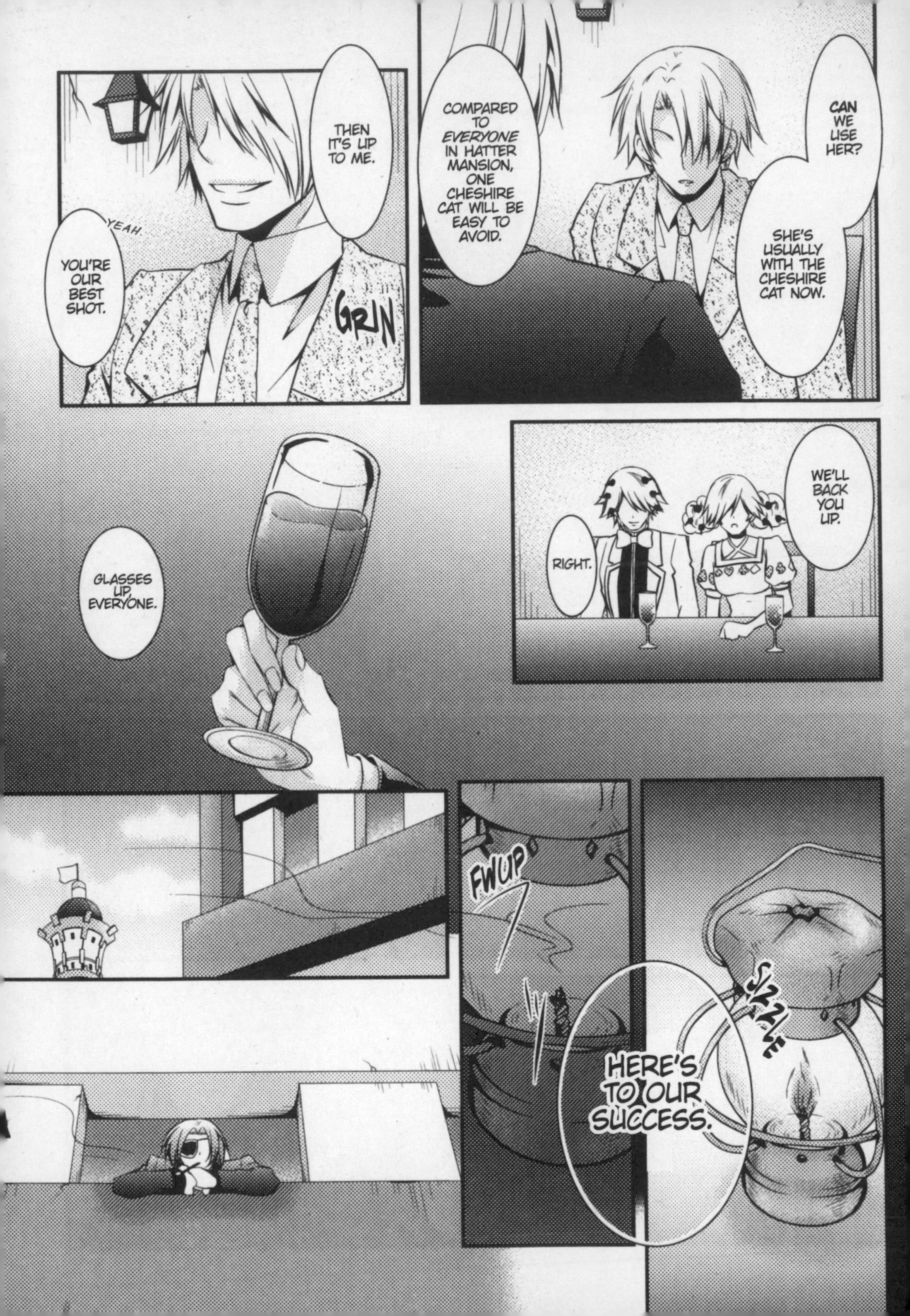
CAN WE USE HER?
SHE'S USUALLY WITH THE CHESHIRE CAT NOW.
COMPARED TO *EVERYONE* IN HATTER MANSION, ONE CHESHIRE CAT WILL BE EASY TO AVOID.
THEN IT'S UP TO ME.
GRIN
YEAH.
YOU'RE OUR BEST SHOT.
WE'LL BACK YOU UP.
RIGHT.
GLASSES UP, EVERYONE.
SIZZLE
FWUP
HERE'S TO OUR SUCCESS.

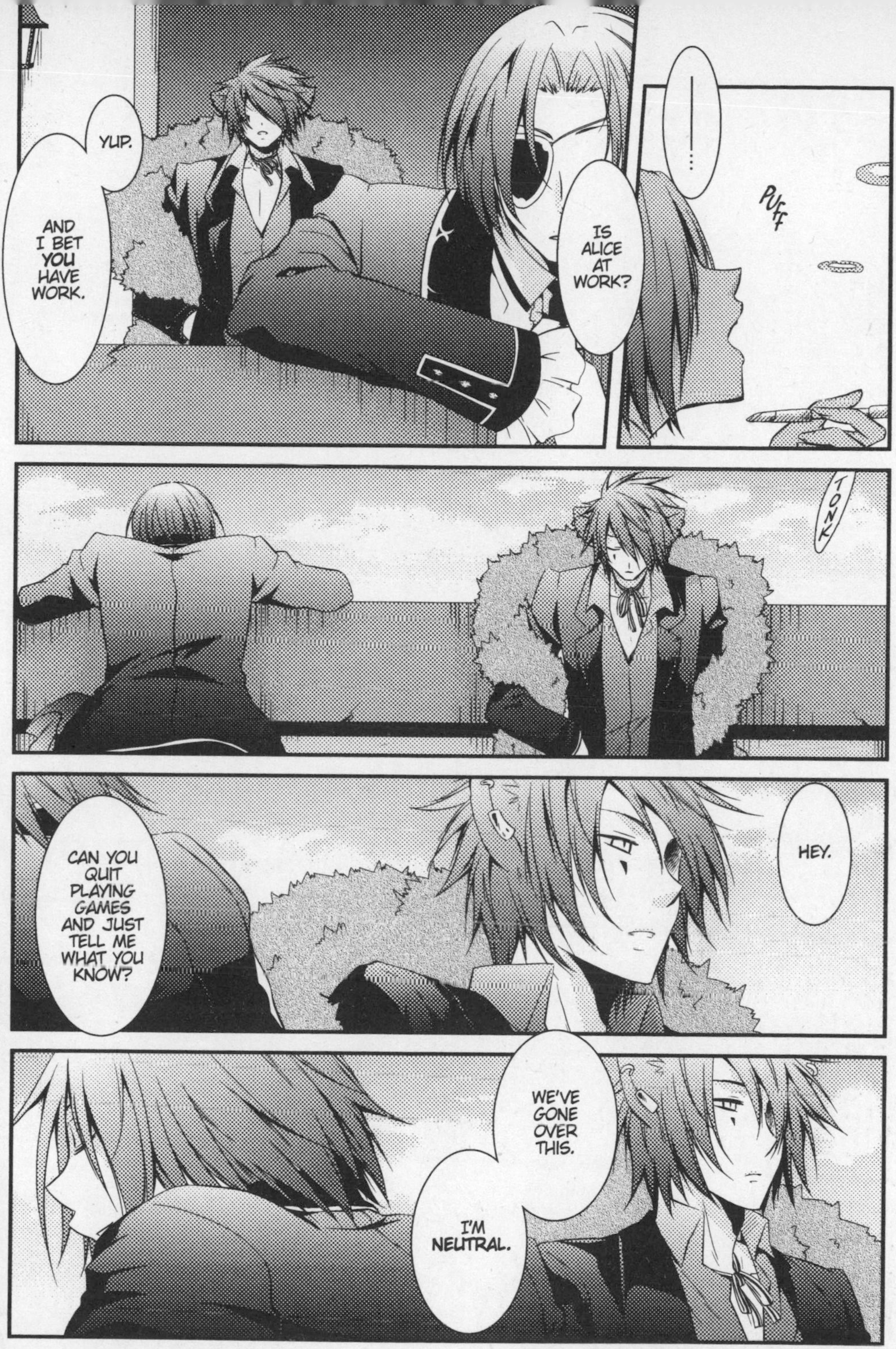
......
PUFF
IS ALICE AT WORK?
YUP.
AND I BET YOU HAVE WORK.
TONK
HEY.
CAN YOU QUIT PLAYING GAMES AND JUST TELL ME WHAT YOU KNOW?
WE'VE GONE OVER THIS.
I'M NEUTRAL.

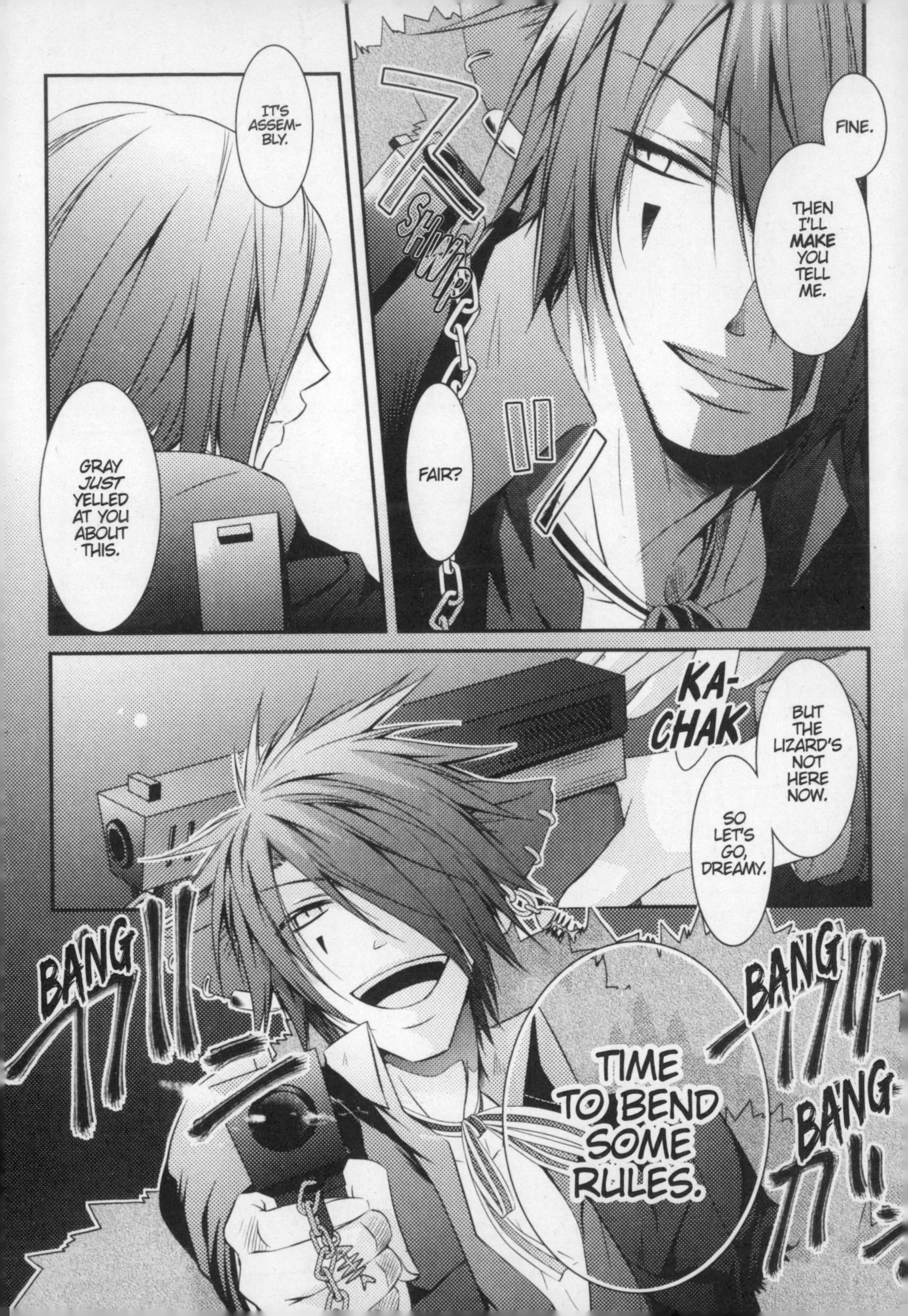
FINE.
THEN I'LL MAKE YOU TELL ME.
SHWIP
FAIR?
IT'S ASSEM-BLY.
GRAY JUST YELLED AT YOU ABOUT THIS.
KA-CHAK
BUT THE LIZARD'S NOT HERE NOW.
SO LET'S GO, DREAMY.
BANG
BANG
BANG
TIME TO BEND SOME RULES.

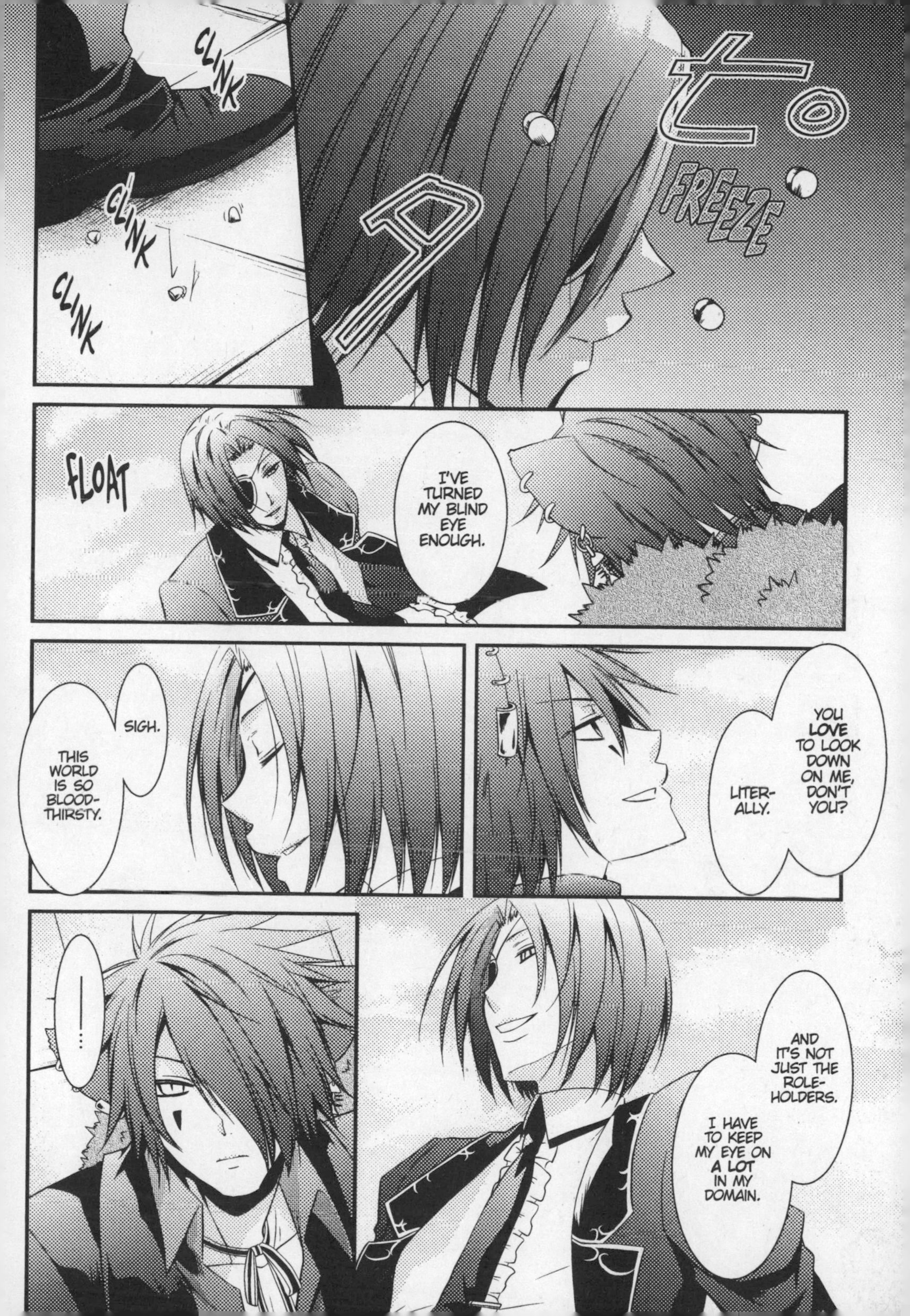
FREEZE
CLINK
CLINK
CLINK
CLINK
FLOAT
I'VE TURNED MY BLIND EYE ENOUGH.
YOU **LOVE** TO LOOK DOWN ON ME, DON'T YOU?
LITER-ALLY.
SIGH.
THIS WORLD IS SO BLOOD-THIRSTY.
AND IT'S NOT JUST THE ROLE-HOLDERS.
I HAVE TO KEEP MY EYE ON **A LOT** IN MY DOMAIN.
......

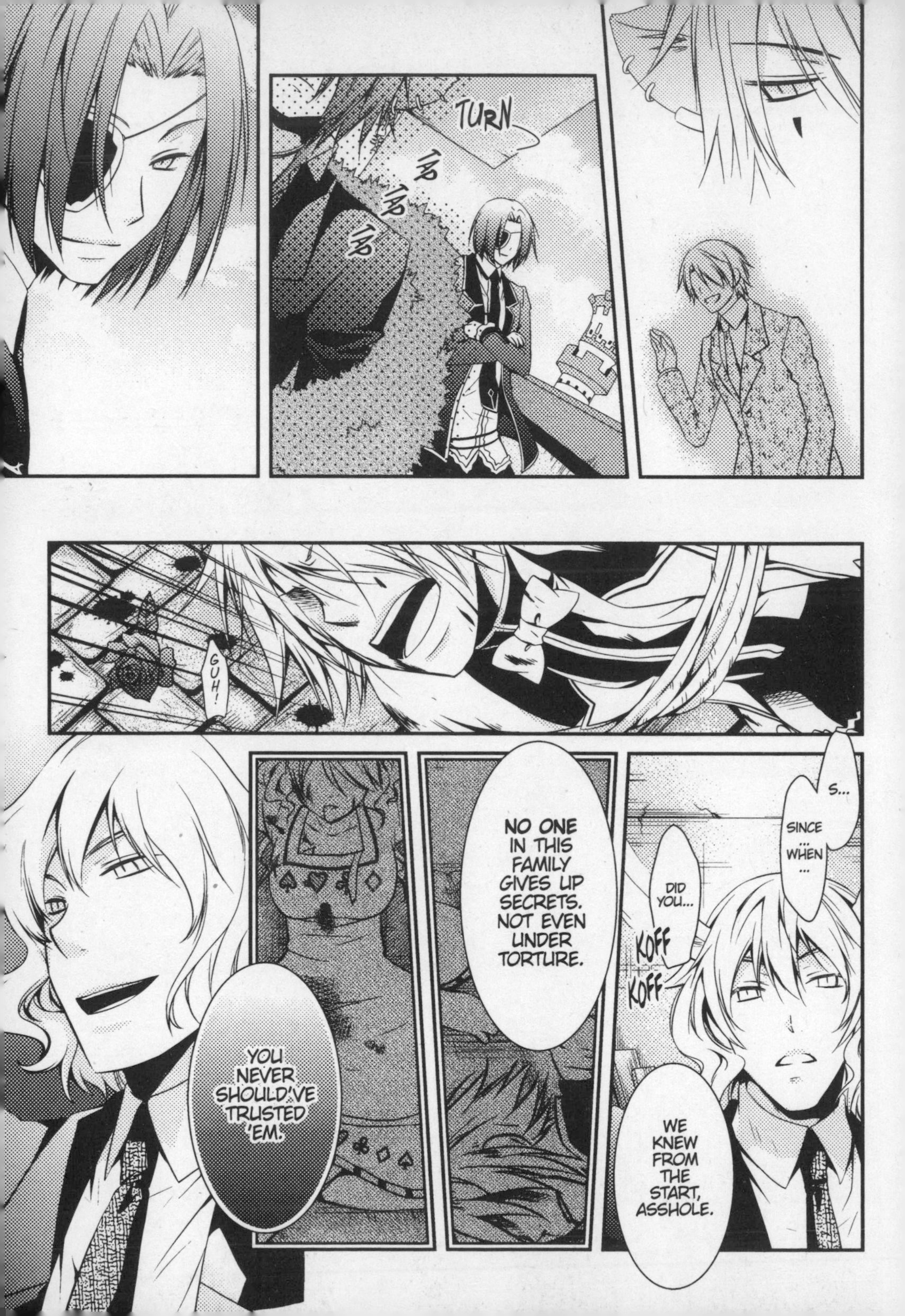
TURN
TAP
TAP
TAP
GUH!
S...
SINCE ... WHEN ...
DID YOU...
KOFF
KOFF
WE KNEW FROM THE START, ASSHOLE.
NO ONE IN THIS FAMILY GIVES UP SECRETS. NOT EVEN UNDER TORTURE.
YOU NEVER SHOULD'VE TRUSTED 'EM.

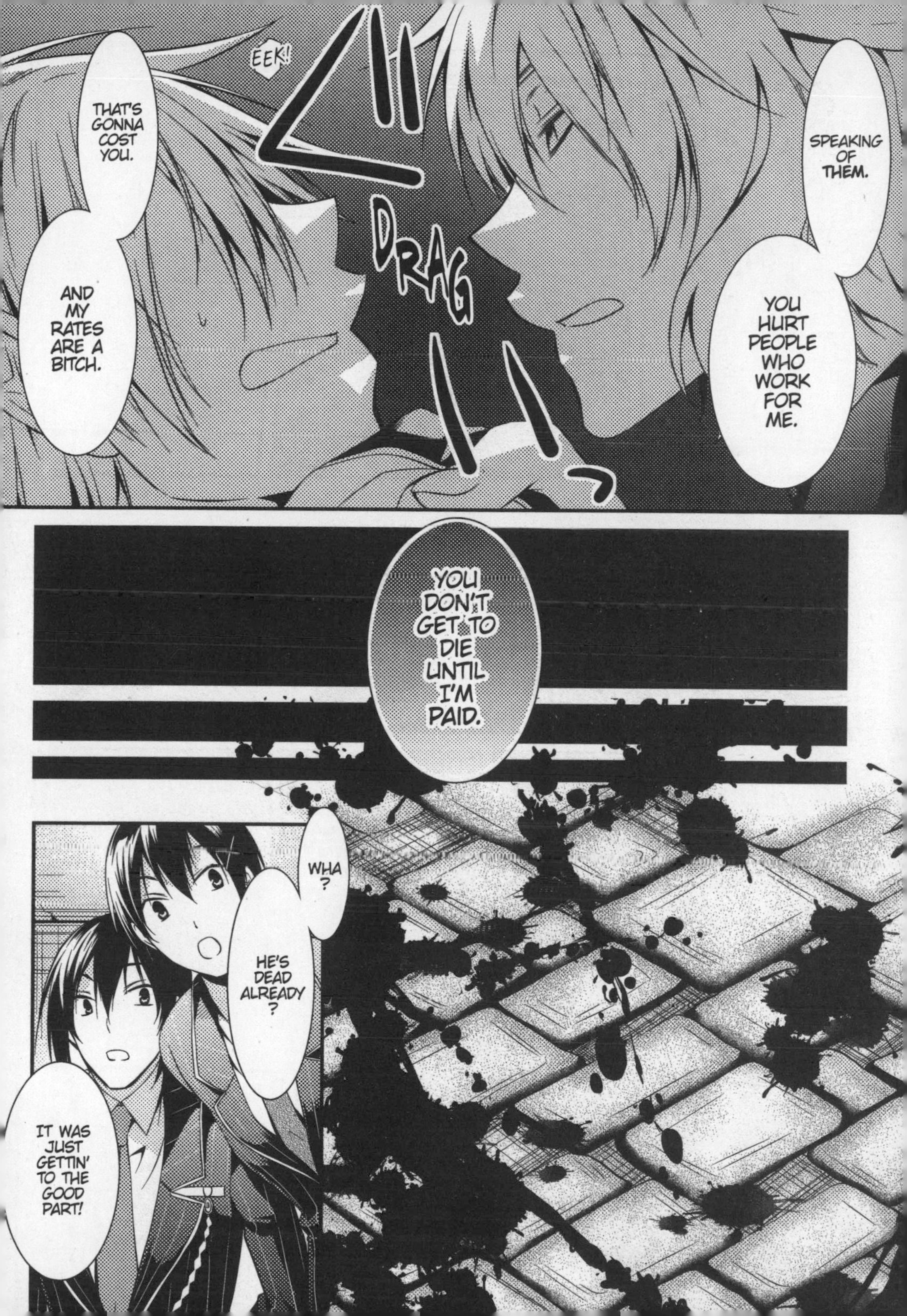
SPEAKING OF THEM.
YOU HURT PEOPLE WHO WORK FOR ME.
DRAG
EEK!
THAT'S GONNA COST YOU.
AND MY RATES ARE A BITCH.
YOU DON'T GET TO DIE UNTIL I'M PAID.
WHA?
HE'S DEAD ALREADY?
IT WAS JUST GETTIN' TO THE GOOD PART!

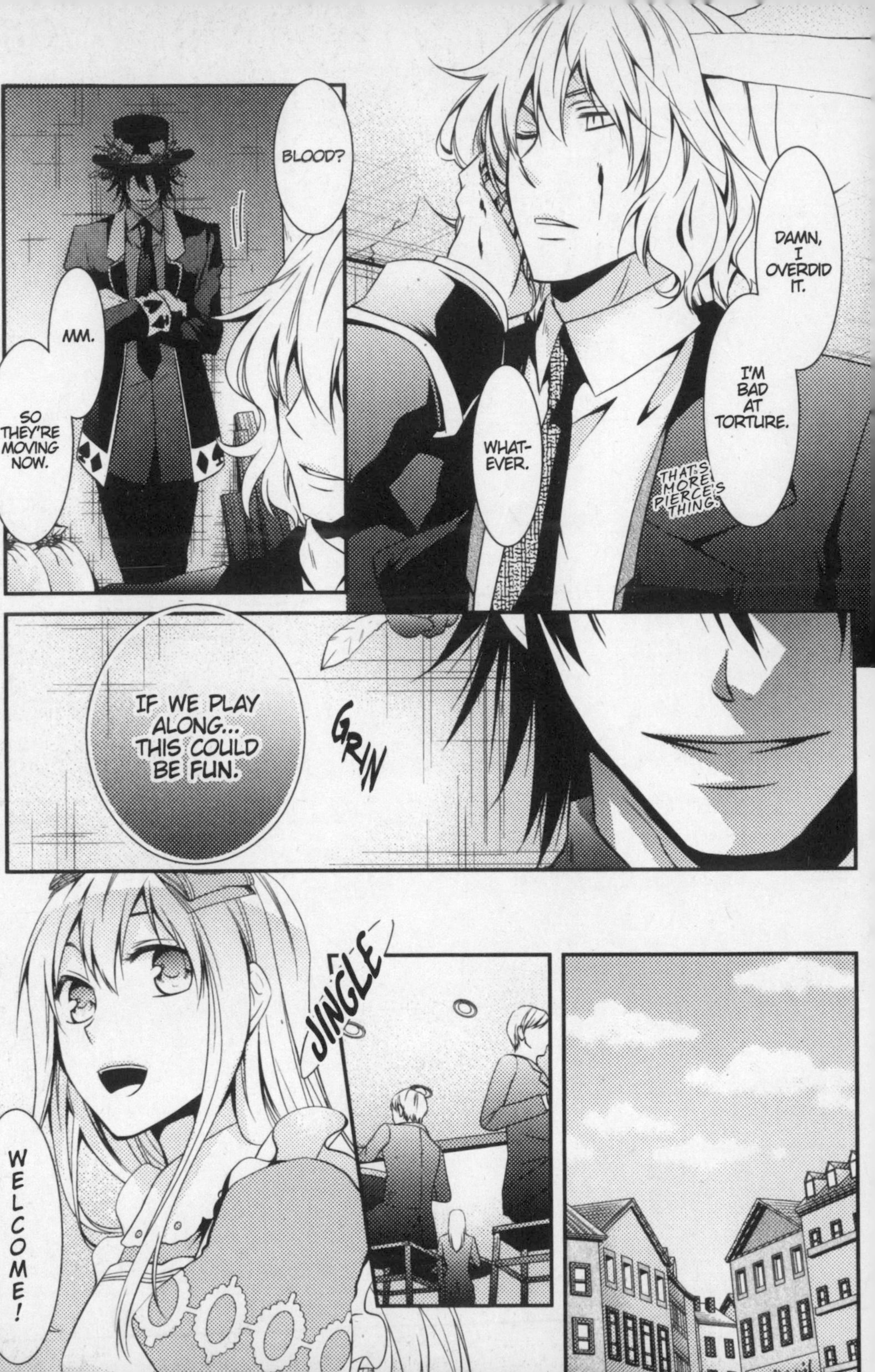
DAMN, I OVERDID IT.
I'M BAD AT TORTURE.
THAT'S MORE PIERCE'S THING.
WHAT-EVER.
BLOOD?
MM.
SO THEY'RE MOVING NOW.
IF WE PLAY ALONG... THIS COULD BE FUN.
GRIN
JINGLE
WELCOME!

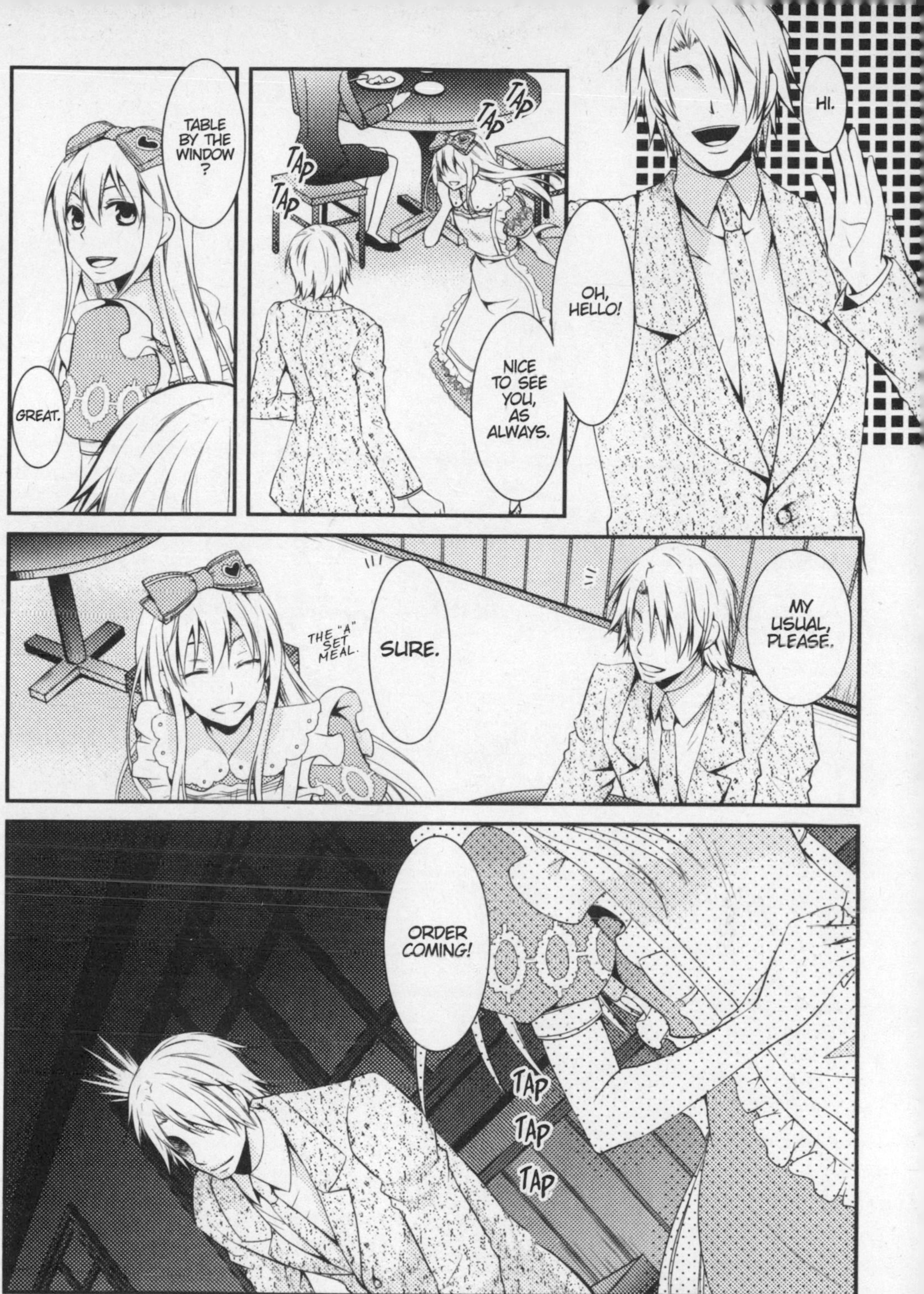
HI.
OH, HELLO!
NICE TO SEE YOU, AS ALWAYS.
TAP TAP
TAP TAP
TABLE BY THE WINDOW ?
GREAT.
MY USUAL, PLEASE.
SURE.
THE "A" SET MEAL.
ORDER COMING!
TAP TAP TAP

To Be Continued

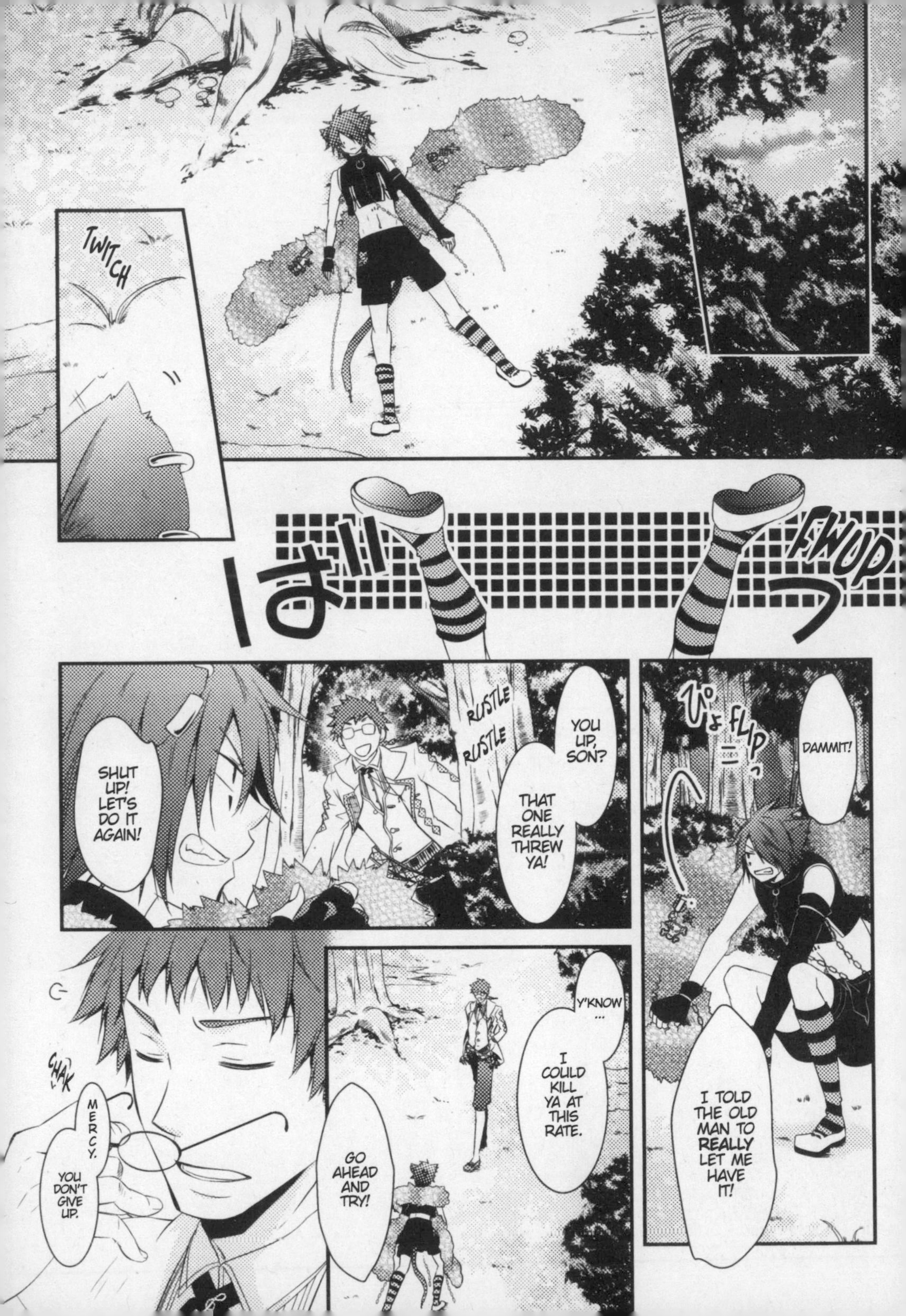
TWITCH
ばっ
FWUP
ぴょ FLIP
DAMMIT!
I TOLD THE OLD MAN TO REALLY LET ME HAVE IT!
RUSTLE
RUSTLE
YOU UP, SON?
THAT ONE REALLY THREW YA!
SHUT UP! LET'S DO IT AGAIN!
Y'KNOW...
I COULD KILL YA AT THIS RATE.
GO AHEAD AND TRY!
CHAK
MERCY.
YOU DON'T GIVE UP.

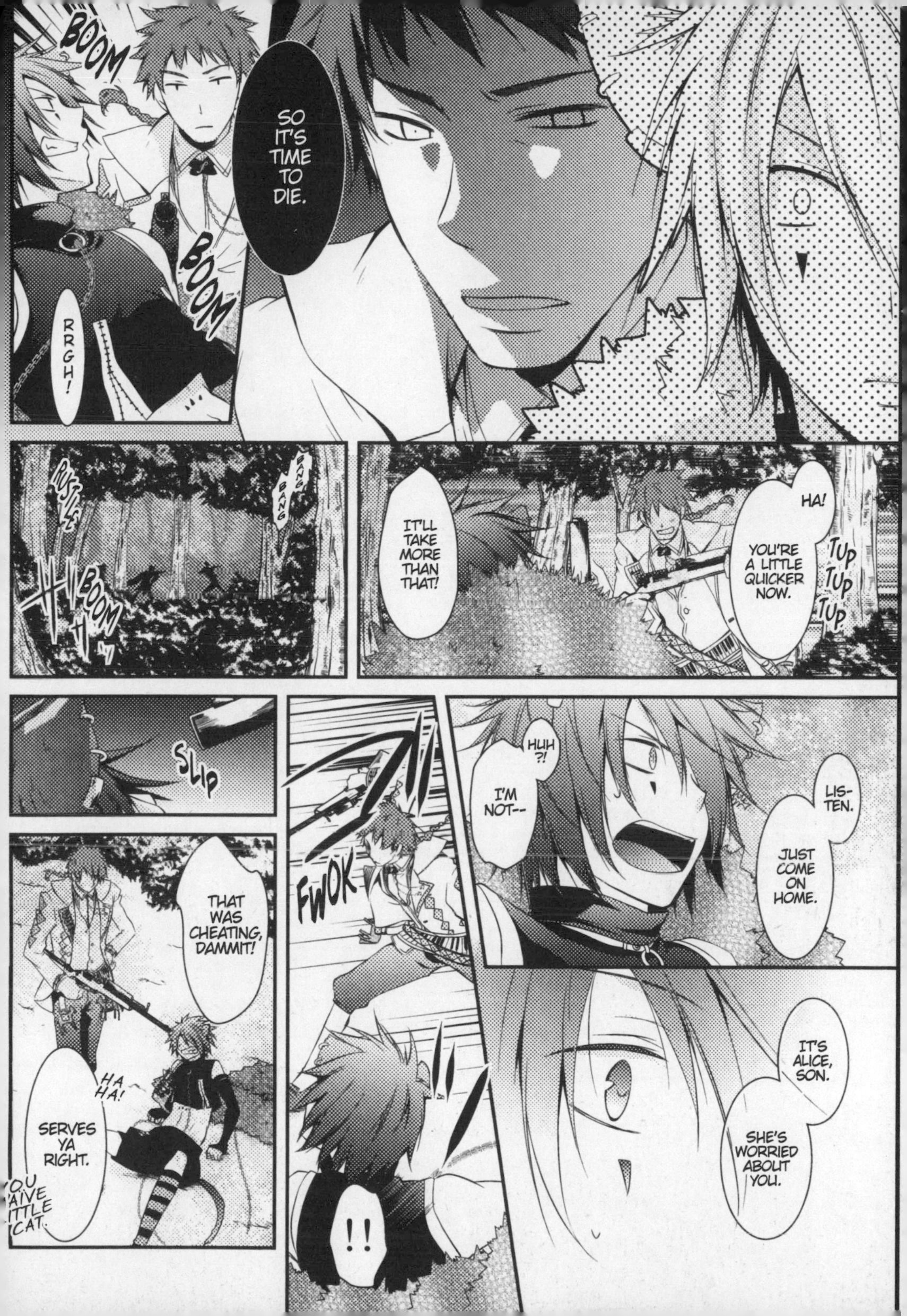
SO IT'S TIME TO DIE.
BOOM
BOOM
RRGH!
HA!
YOU'RE A LITTLE QUICKER NOW.
TUP TUP TUP
IT'LL TAKE MORE THAN THAT!
BANG BANG
RUSTLE
BOOM
LIS-TEN.
JUST COME ON HOME.
HUH?!
I'M NOT--
IT'S ALICE, SON.
SHE'S WORRIED ABOUT YOU.
!!
FWOK
SLIP
THAT WAS CHEATING, DAMMIT!
HA HA!
SERVES YA RIGHT.
OU AIVE ITTLE CAT.

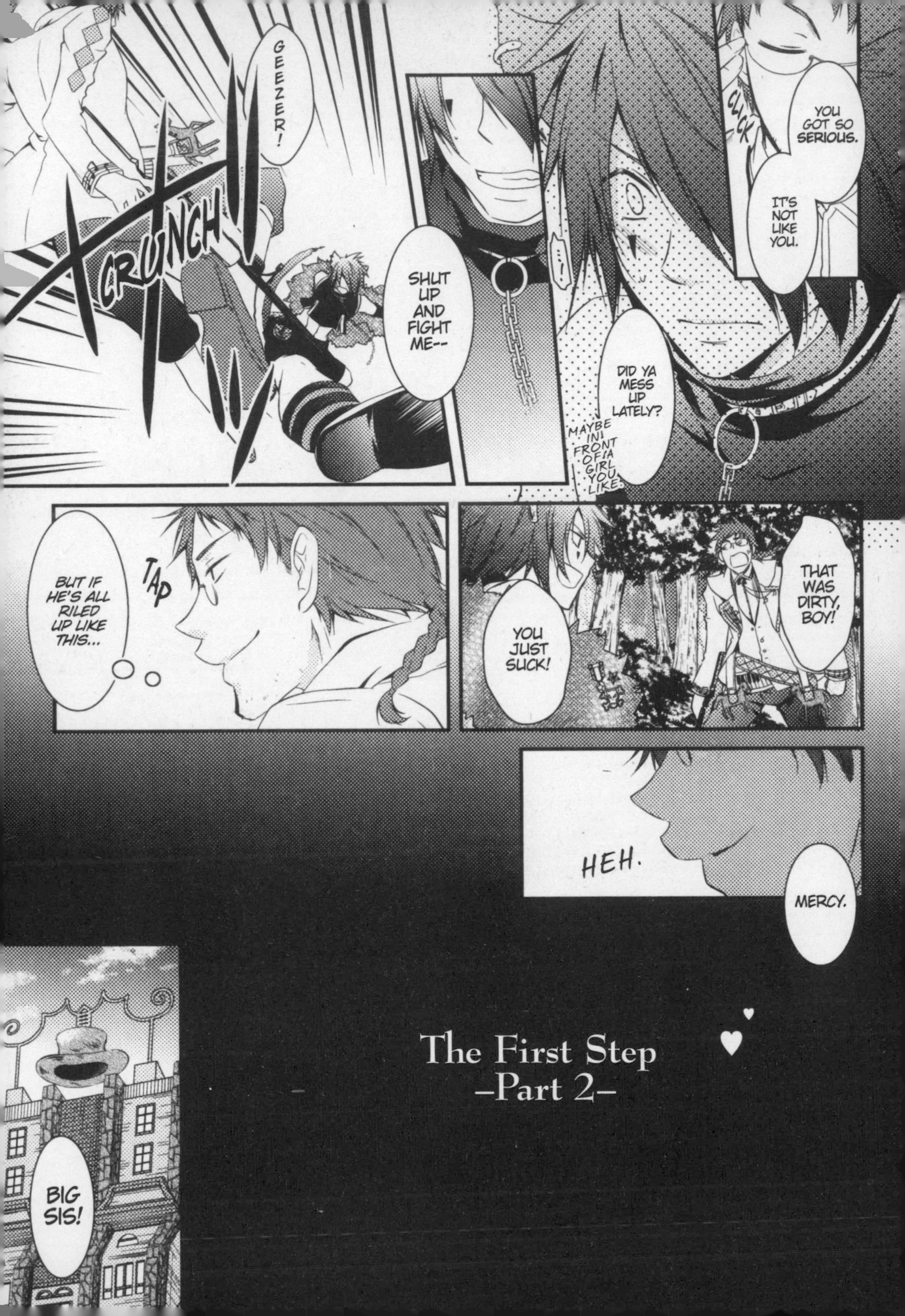
CLICK
YOU GOT SO SERIOUS.
IT'S NOT LIKE YOU.
DID YA MESS UP LATELY?
MAYBE IN FRONT OF A GIRL YOU LIKE.
SHUT UP AND FIGHT ME--
GEEZER!
CRUNCH
THAT WAS DIRTY, BOY!
YOU JUST SUCK!
BUT IF HE'S ALL RILED UP LIKE THIS...
TAP
HEH.
MERCY.
The First Step
-Part 2-
BIG SIS!

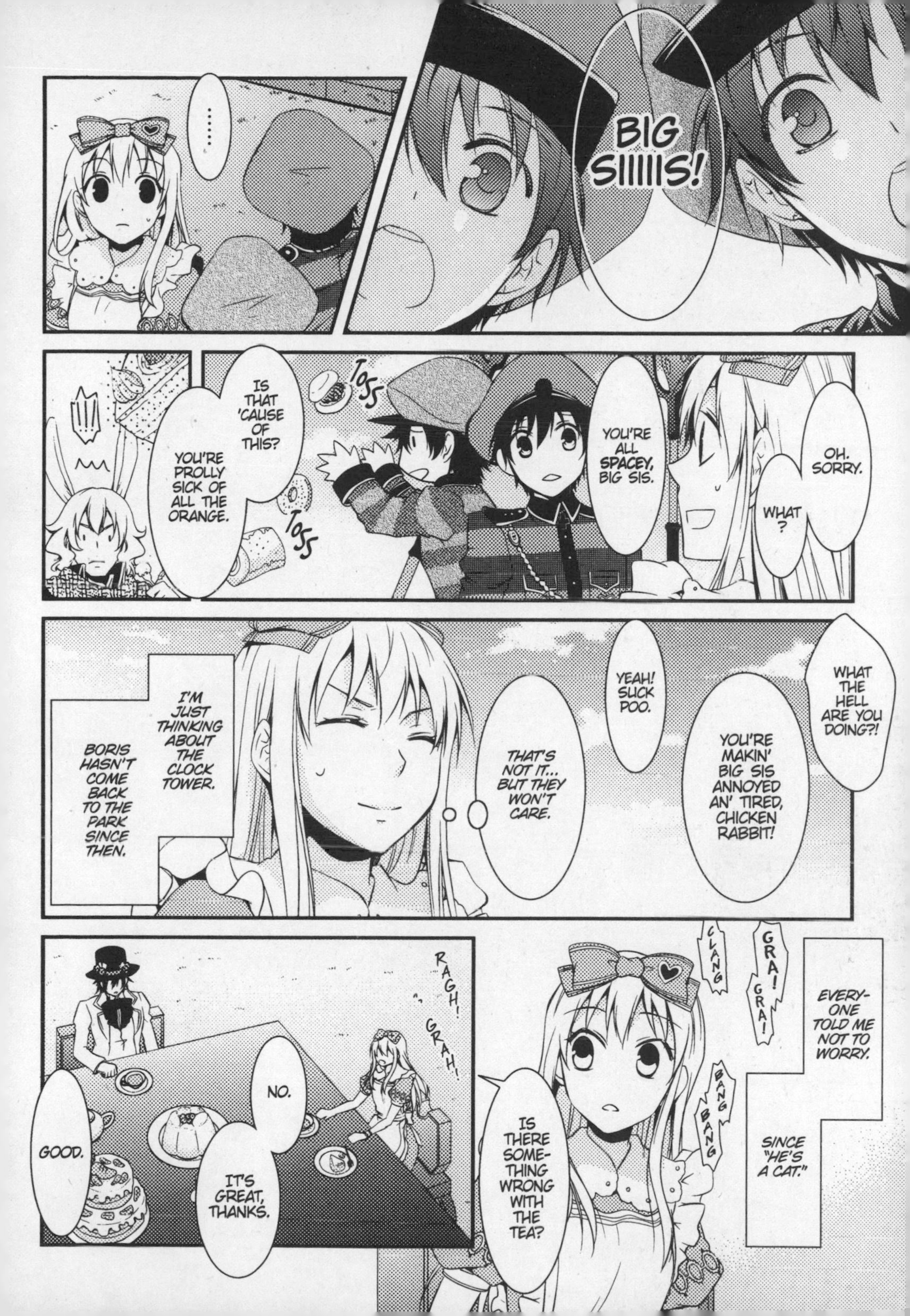
BIG SIIIIIS!
......
OH. SORRY.
WHAT?
YOU'RE ALL SPACEY, BIG SIS.
TOSS
TOSS
IS THAT 'CAUSE OF THIS?
YOU'RE PROLLY SICK OF ALL THE ORANGE.
!!!
WHAT THE HELL ARE YOU DOING?!
YOU'RE MAKIN' BIG SIS ANNOYED AN' TIRED, CHICKEN RABBIT!
YEAH! SUCK POO.
THAT'S NOT IT... BUT THEY WON'T CARE.
I'M JUST THINKING ABOUT THE CLOCK TOWER.
BORIS HASN'T COME BACK TO THE PARK SINCE THEN.
EVERY-ONE TOLD ME NOT TO WORRY.
SINCE "HE'S A CAT."
GRA! GRA!
CLANG
BANG BANG
IS THERE SOME-THING WRONG WITH THE TEA?
RAGH!
GRAH!
NO.
IT'S GREAT, THANKS.
GOOD.

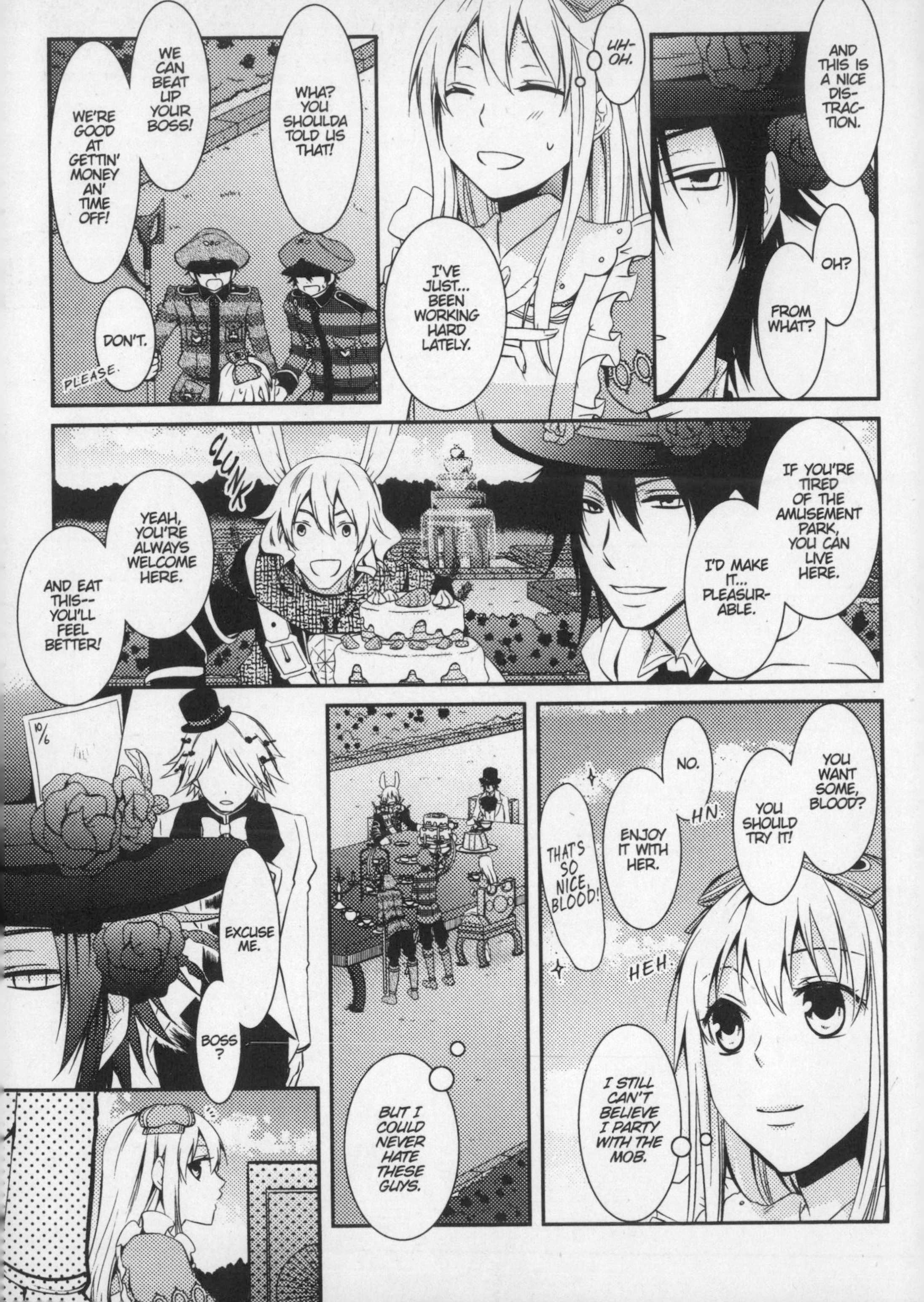
AND THIS IS A NICE DISTRACTION.
UH-OH.
OH?
FROM WHAT?
I'VE JUST... BEEN WORKING HARD LATELY.
WHA? YOU SHOULDA TOLD US THAT!
WE CAN BEAT UP YOUR BOSS!
WE'RE GOOD AT GETTIN' MONEY AN' TIME OFF!
DON'T.
PLEASE.
IF YOU'RE TIRED OF THE AMUSEMENT PARK, YOU CAN LIVE HERE.
I'D MAKE IT... PLEASURABLE.
CLUNK
YEAH, YOU'RE ALWAYS WELCOME HERE.
AND EAT THIS-- YOU'LL FEEL BETTER!
YOU WANT SOME, BLOOD?
YOU SHOULD TRY IT!
NO.
HN.
ENJOY IT WITH HER.
THAT'S SO NICE, BLOOD!
HEH
I STILL CAN'T BELIEVE I PARTY WITH THE MOB.
BUT I COULD NEVER HATE THESE GUYS.
10/6
EXCUSE ME.
BOSS?

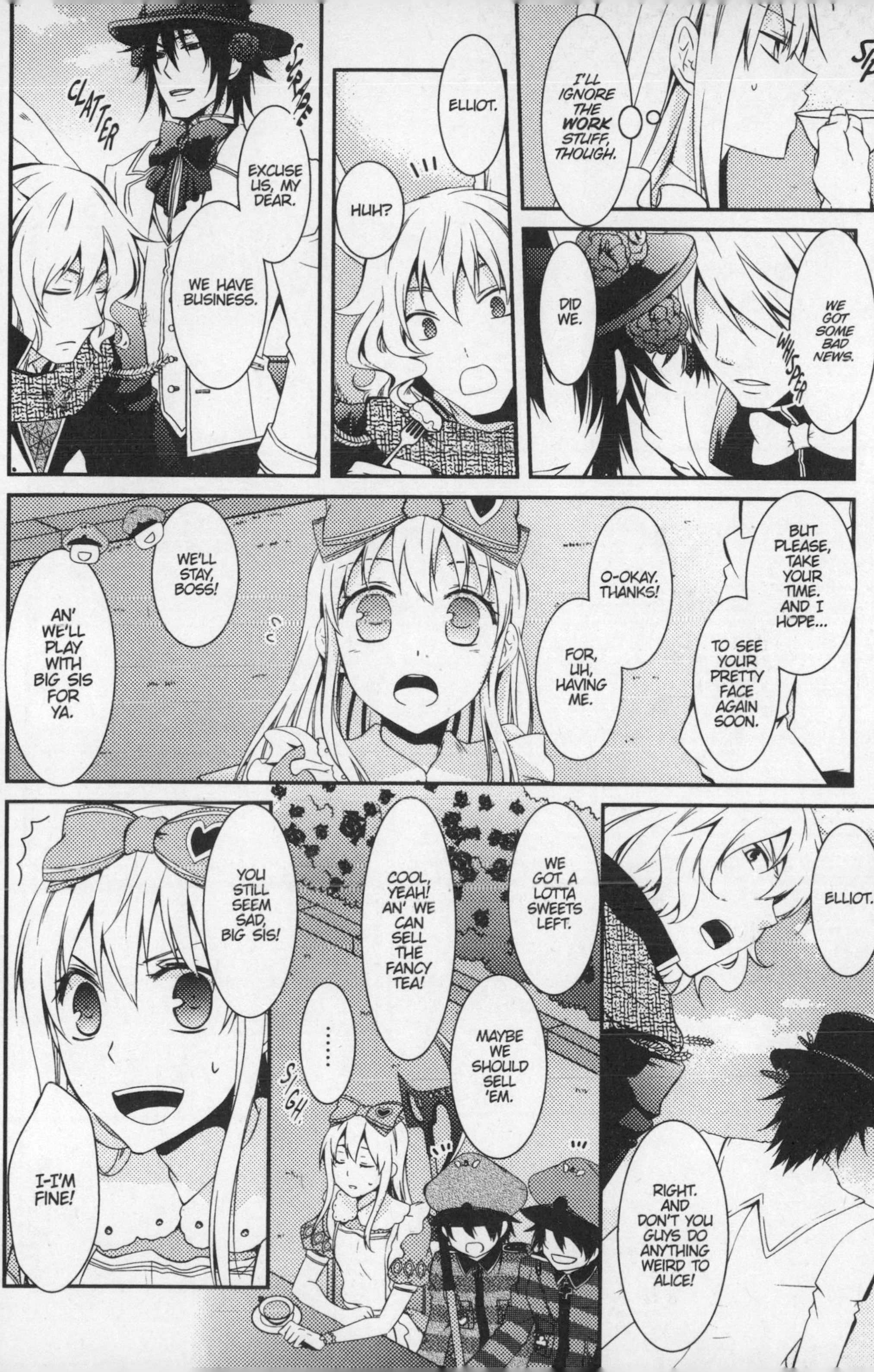
SIP
I'LL IGNORE THE WORK STUFF, THOUGH.
WE GOT SOME BAD NEWS.
WHISPER
DID WE.
ELLIOT.
HUH?
EXCUSE US, MY DEAR.
SCRAPE
CLATTER
WE HAVE BUSINESS.
BUT PLEASE, TAKE YOUR TIME. AND I HOPE...
TO SEE YOUR PRETTY FACE AGAIN SOON.
O-OKAY. THANKS!
FOR, UH, HAVING ME.
WE'LL STAY, BOSS!
AN' WE'LL PLAY WITH BIG SIS FOR YA.
ELLIOT.
RIGHT. AND DON'T YOU GUYS DO ANYTHING WEIRD TO ALICE!
WE GOT A LOTTA SWEETS LEFT.
COOL, YEAH! AN' WE CAN SELL THE FANCY TEA!
MAYBE WE SHOULD SELL 'EM.
......
SIGH.
YOU STILL SEEM SAD, BIG SIS!
I-I'M FINE!

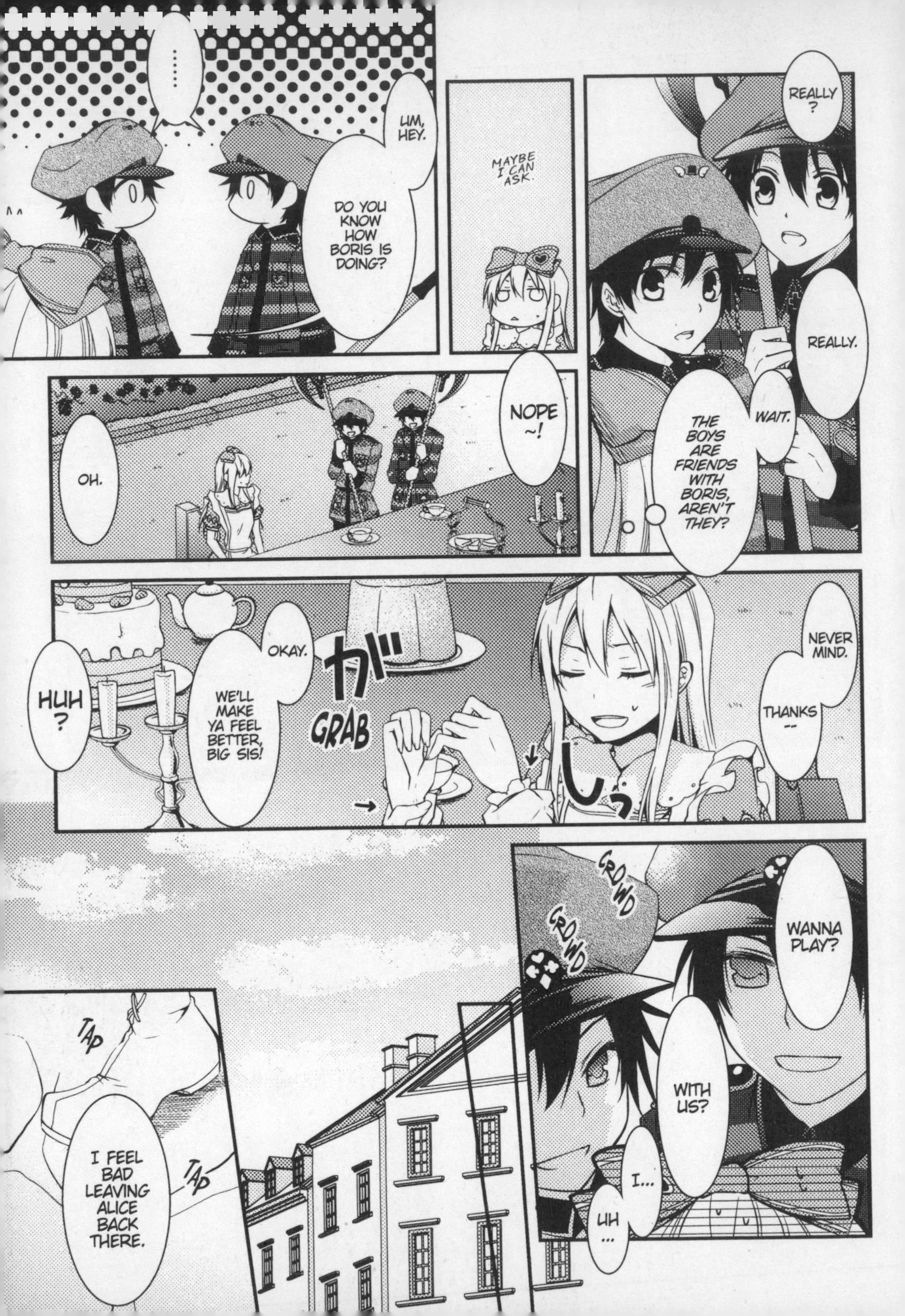

REALLY?
REALLY.
WAIT.
THE BOYS ARE FRIENDS WITH BORIS, AREN'T THEY?
MAYBE I CAN ASK.
UM, HEY.
DO YOU KNOW HOW BORIS IS DOING?
......
NOPE~!
OH.
NEVER MIND.
THANKS--
GRAB
OKAY.
WE'LL MAKE YA FEEL BETTER, BIG SIS!
HUH?
WANNA PLAY?
CROWD
CROWD
WITH US?
I...
UH...
TAP
TAP
I FEEL BAD LEAVING ALICE BACK THERE.

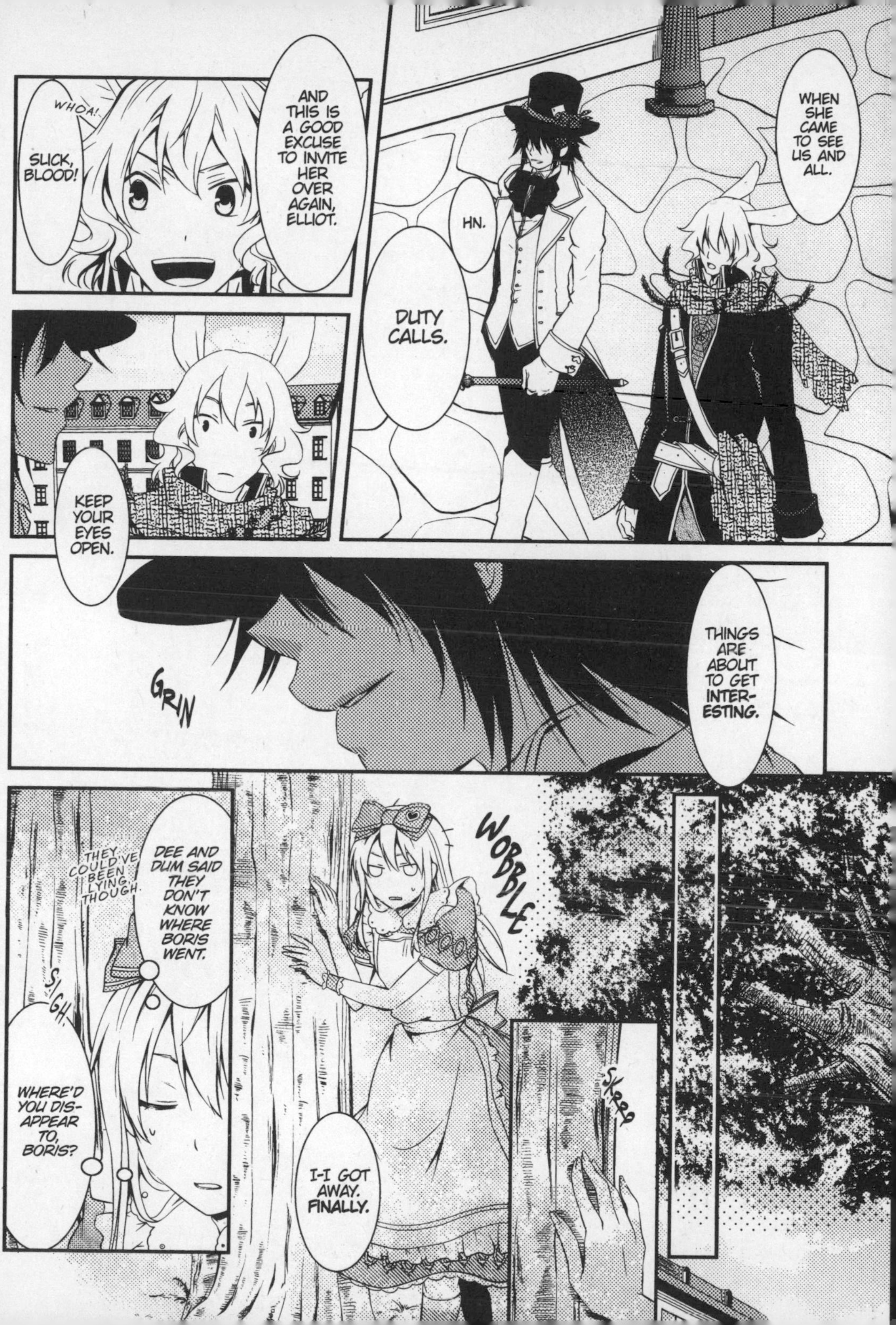
WHEN SHE CAME TO SEE US AND ALL.
HN.
DUTY CALLS.
AND THIS IS A GOOD EXCUSE TO INVITE HER OVER AGAIN, ELLIOT.
WHOA!
SLICK, BLOOD!
KEEP YOUR EYES OPEN.
THINGS ARE ABOUT TO GET INTERESTING.
GRIN
SKRRP
WOBBLE
I-I GOT AWAY. FINALLY.
DEE AND DUM SAID THEY DON'T KNOW WHERE BORIS WENT.
THEY COULD'VE BEEN LYING THOUGH.
SIGH.
WHERE'D YOU DIS-APPEAR TO, BORIS?

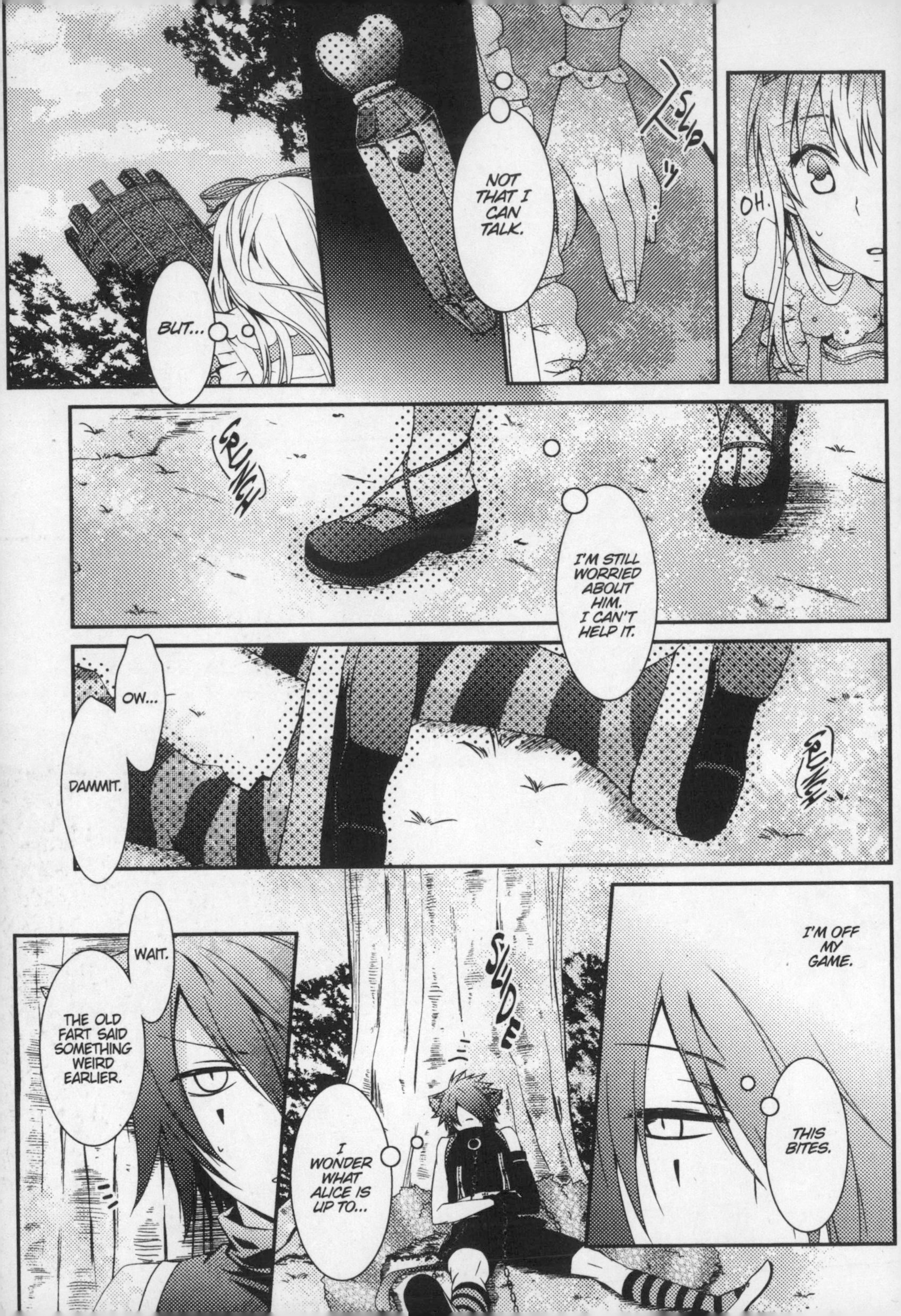
OH.
SLIP
NOT THAT I CAN TALK.
BUT...
I'M STILL WORRIED ABOUT HIM. I CAN'T HELP IT.
CRUNCH
CRUNCH
OW...
DAMMIT.
I'M OFF MY GAME.
THIS BITES.
SLIDE
I WONDER WHAT ALICE IS UP TO...
WAIT.
THE OLD FART SAID SOMETHING WEIRD EARLIER.

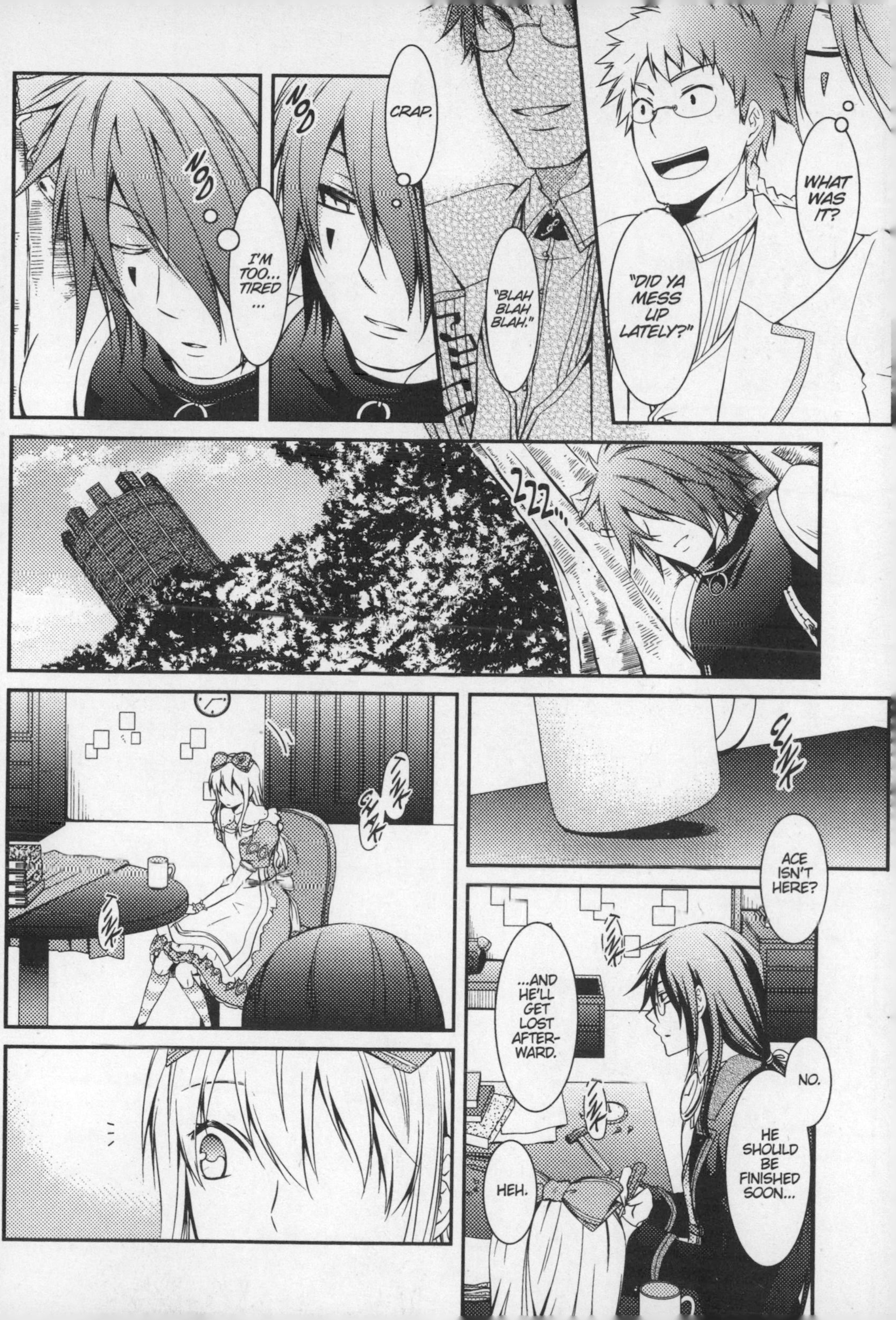
WHAT WAS IT?
"DID YA MESS UP LATELY?"
"BLAH BLAH BLAH."
NOD
CRAP.
NOD
I'M TOO... TIRED ...
ZZZ...
CLINK
ACE ISN'T HERE?
TINK
NO.
HE SHOULD BE FINISHED SOON...
...AND HE'LL GET LOST AFTERWARD.
TINK
HEH.
TINK
CHAK
TINK

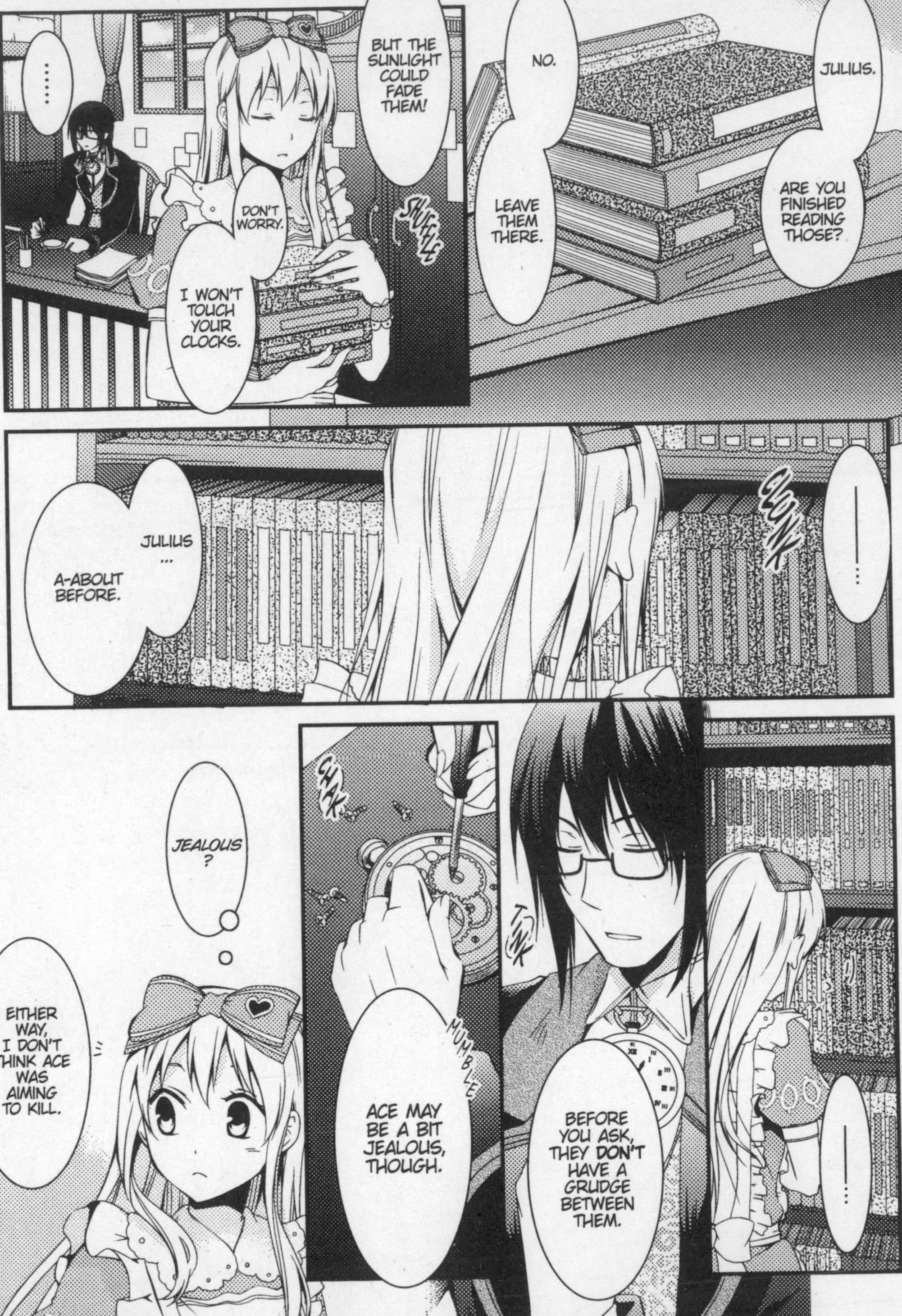

JULIUS.
ARE YOU FINISHED READING THOSE?
NO.
LEAVE THEM THERE.
BUT THE SUNLIGHT COULD FADE THEM!
......
DON'T WORRY.
SHUFFLE
I WON'T TOUCH YOUR CLOCKS.
......
CLONK
JULIUS...
A-ABOUT BEFORE.
......
BEFORE YOU ASK, THEY DON'T HAVE A GRUDGE BETWEEN THEM.
TINK
MUMBLE
ACE MAY BE A BIT JEALOUS, THOUGH.
CHAK
JEALOUS?
EITHER WAY, I DON'T THINK ACE WAS AIMING TO KILL.

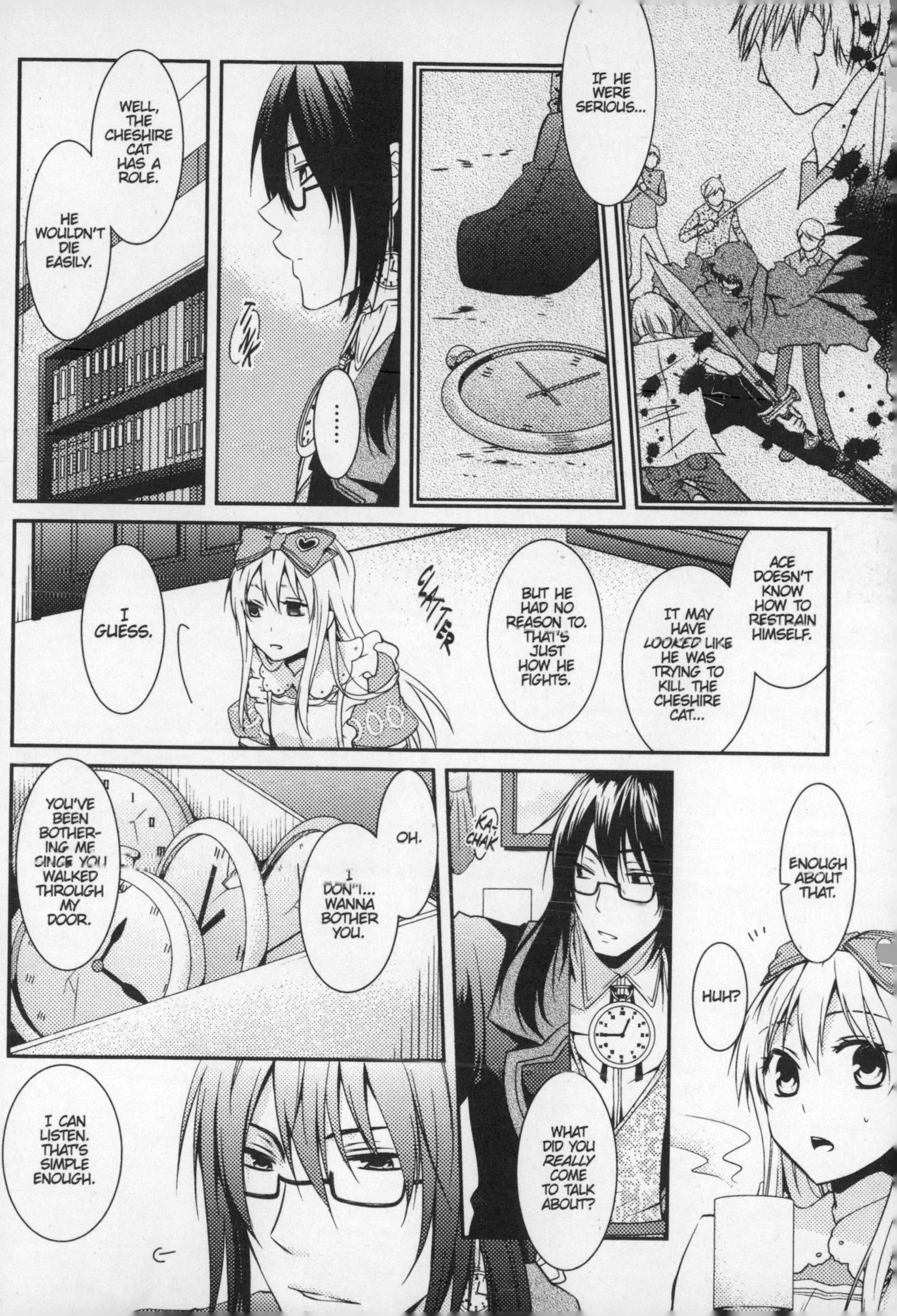
IF HE WERE SERIOUS...
TINK
......
WELL, THE CHESHIRE CAT HAS A ROLE.
HE WOULDN'T DIE EASILY.
ACE DOESN'T KNOW HOW TO RESTRAIN HIMSELF.
IT MAY HAVE LOOKED LIKE HE WAS TRYING TO KILL THE CHESHIRE CAT...
BUT HE HAD NO REASON TO. THAT'S JUST HOW HE FIGHTS.
CLATTER
I GUESS.
ENOUGH ABOUT THAT.
HUH?
KA-CHAK
WHAT DID YOU REALLY COME TO TALK ABOUT?
OH.
I DON'T... WANNA BOTHER YOU.
YOU'VE BEEN BOTHERING ME SINCE YOU WALKED THROUGH MY DOOR.
I CAN LISTEN. THAT'S SIMPLE ENOUGH.

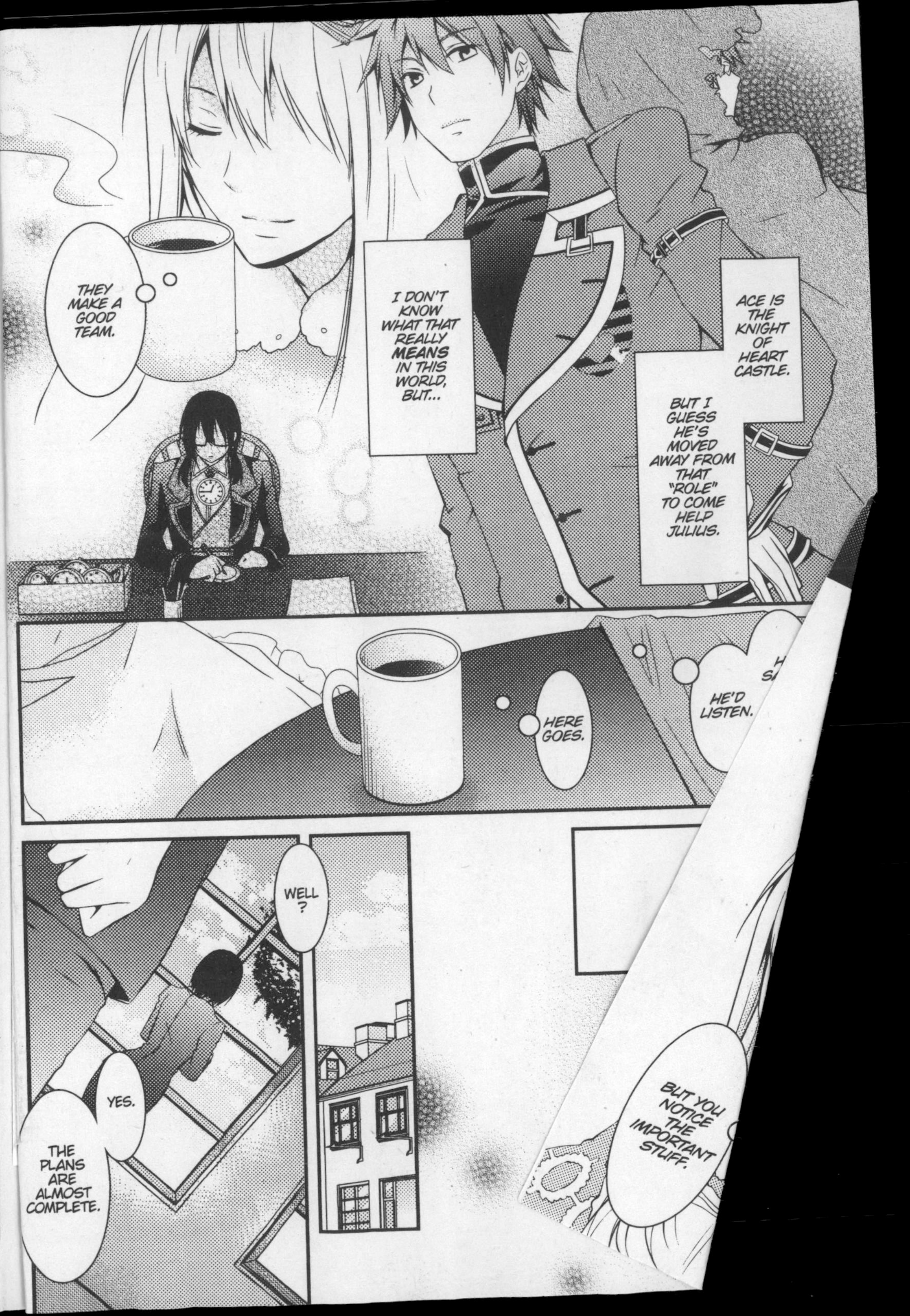
ACE IS THE KNIGHT OF HEART CASTLE.
BUT I GUESS HE'S MOVED AWAY FROM THAT "ROLE" TO COME HELP JULIUS.
I DON'T KNOW WHAT THAT REALLY MEANS IN THIS WORLD, BUT...
THEY MAKE A GOOD TEAM.
HE'D LISTEN.
HERE GOES.
BUT YOU NOTICE THE IMPORTANT STUFF.
WELL?
YES.
THE PLANS ARE ALMOST COMPLETE.

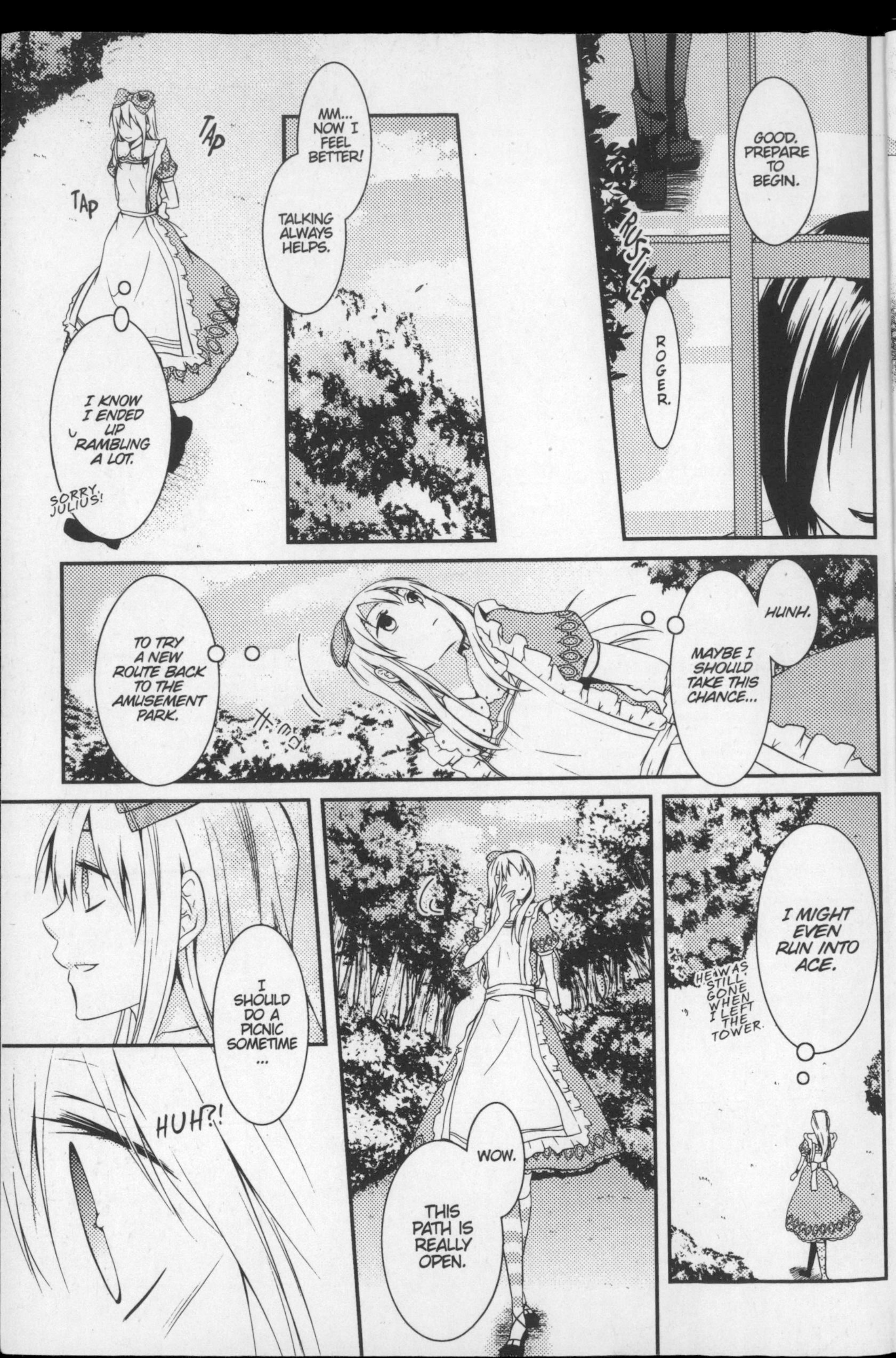
GOOD. PREPARE TO BEGIN.
RUSTLE
ROGER.
MM... NOW I FEEL BETTER!
TALKING ALWAYS HELPS.
TAP
TAP
I KNOW I ENDED UP RAMBLING A LOT.
SORRY, JULIUS!
HUNH.
MAYBE I SHOULD TAKE THIS CHANCE...
TO TRY A NEW ROUTE BACK TO THE AMUSEMENT PARK.
I MIGHT EVEN RUN INTO ACE.
HE WAS STILL GONE WHEN I LEFT THE TOWER.
WOW.
THIS PATH IS REALLY OPEN.
I SHOULD DO A PICNIC SOMETIME...
HUH?!

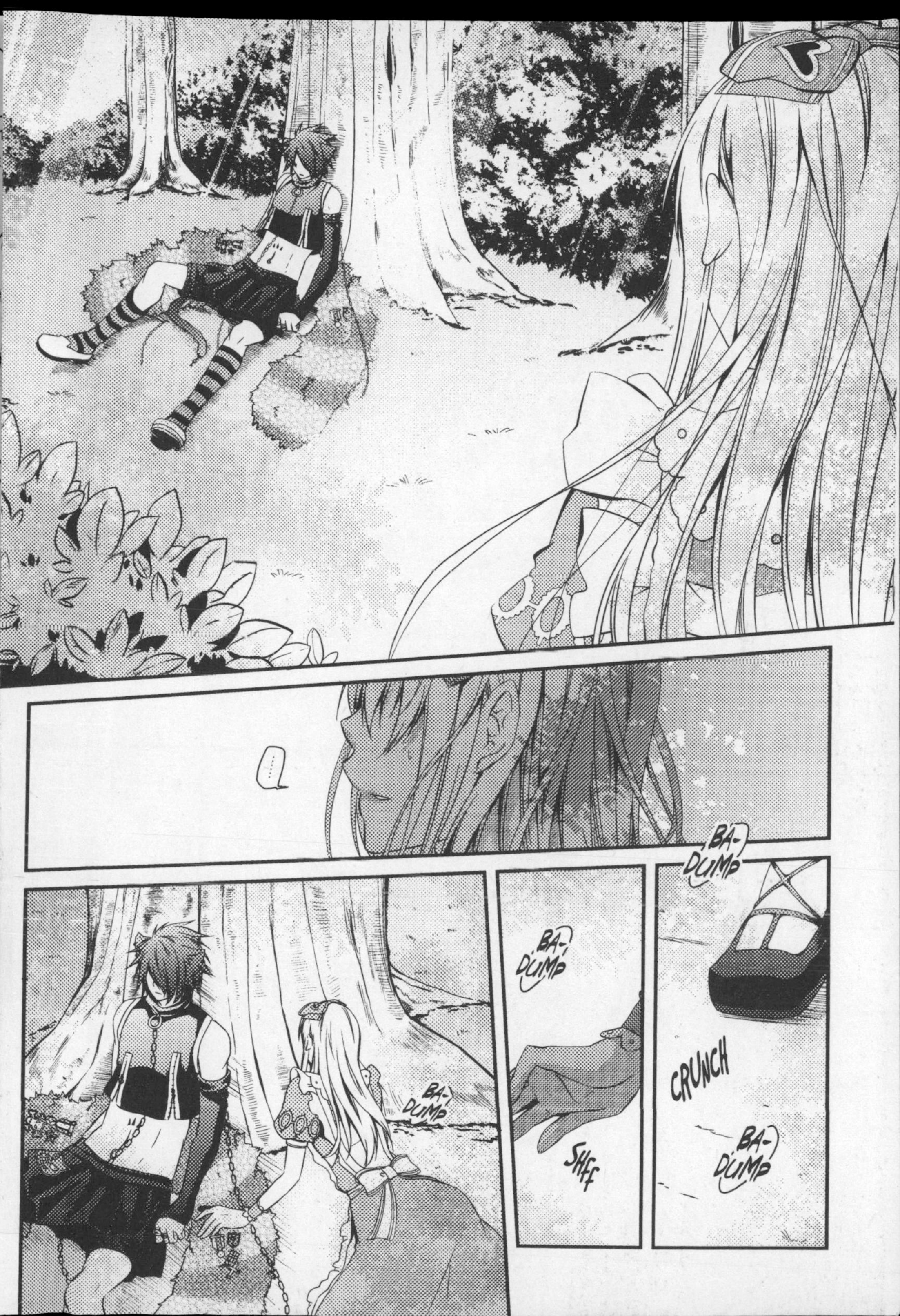
...
BA-DUMP
CRUNCH
BA-DUMP
BA-DUMP
SHFF
BA-DUMP

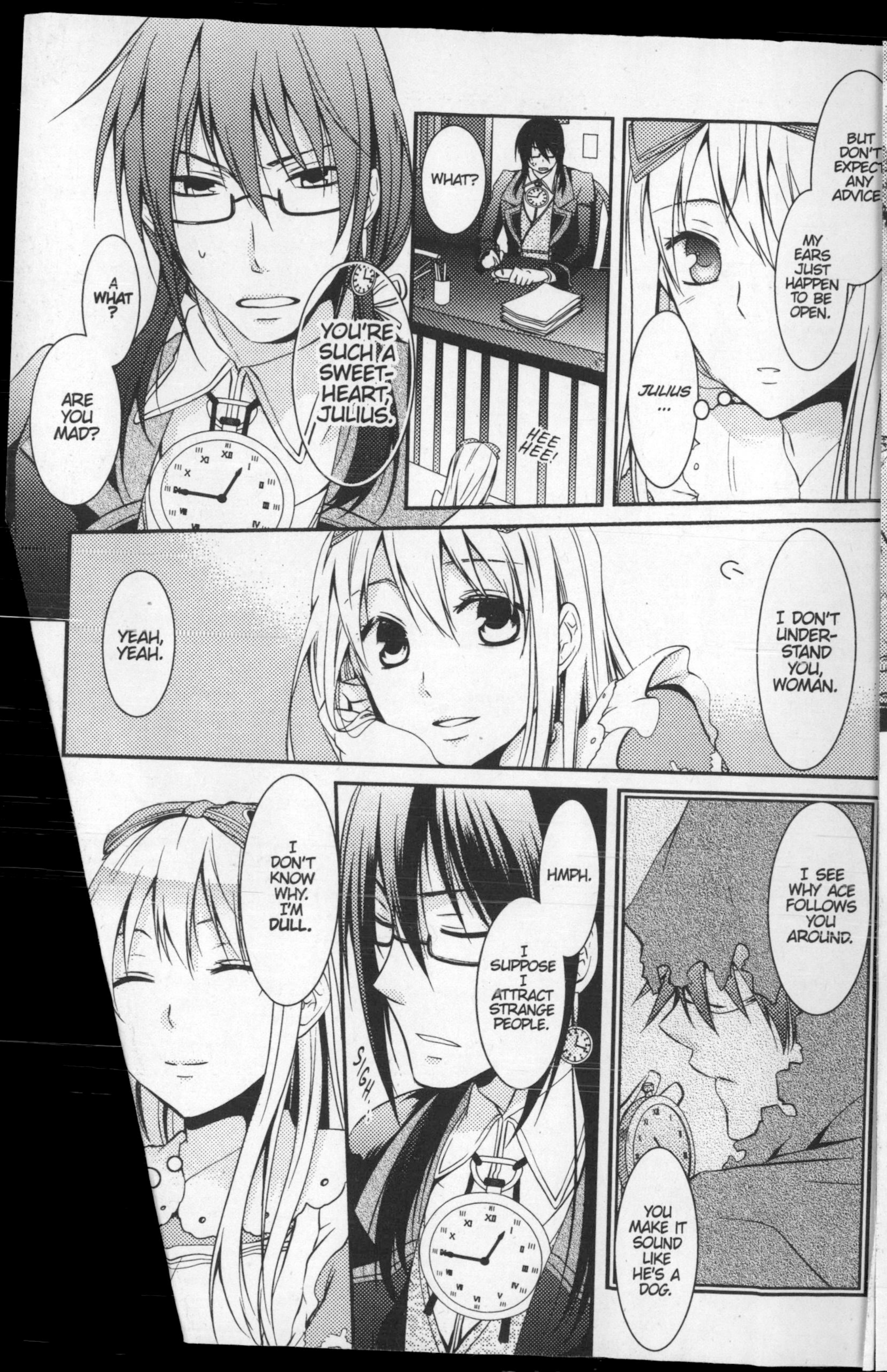
BUT DON'T EXPECT ANY ADVICE.
MY EARS JUST HAPPEN TO BE OPEN.
JULIUS...
WHAT?
YOU'RE SUCH A SWEET-HEART, JULIUS.
HEE HEE!
A WHAT?
ARE YOU MAD?
I DON'T UNDER-STAND YOU, WOMAN.
YEAH, YEAH.
I SEE WHY ACE FOLLOWS YOU AROUND.
YOU MAKE IT SOUND LIKE HE'S A DOG.
HMPH.
I SUPPOSE I ATTRACT STRANGE PEOPLE.
SIGH...
I DON'T KNOW WHY. I'M DULL.

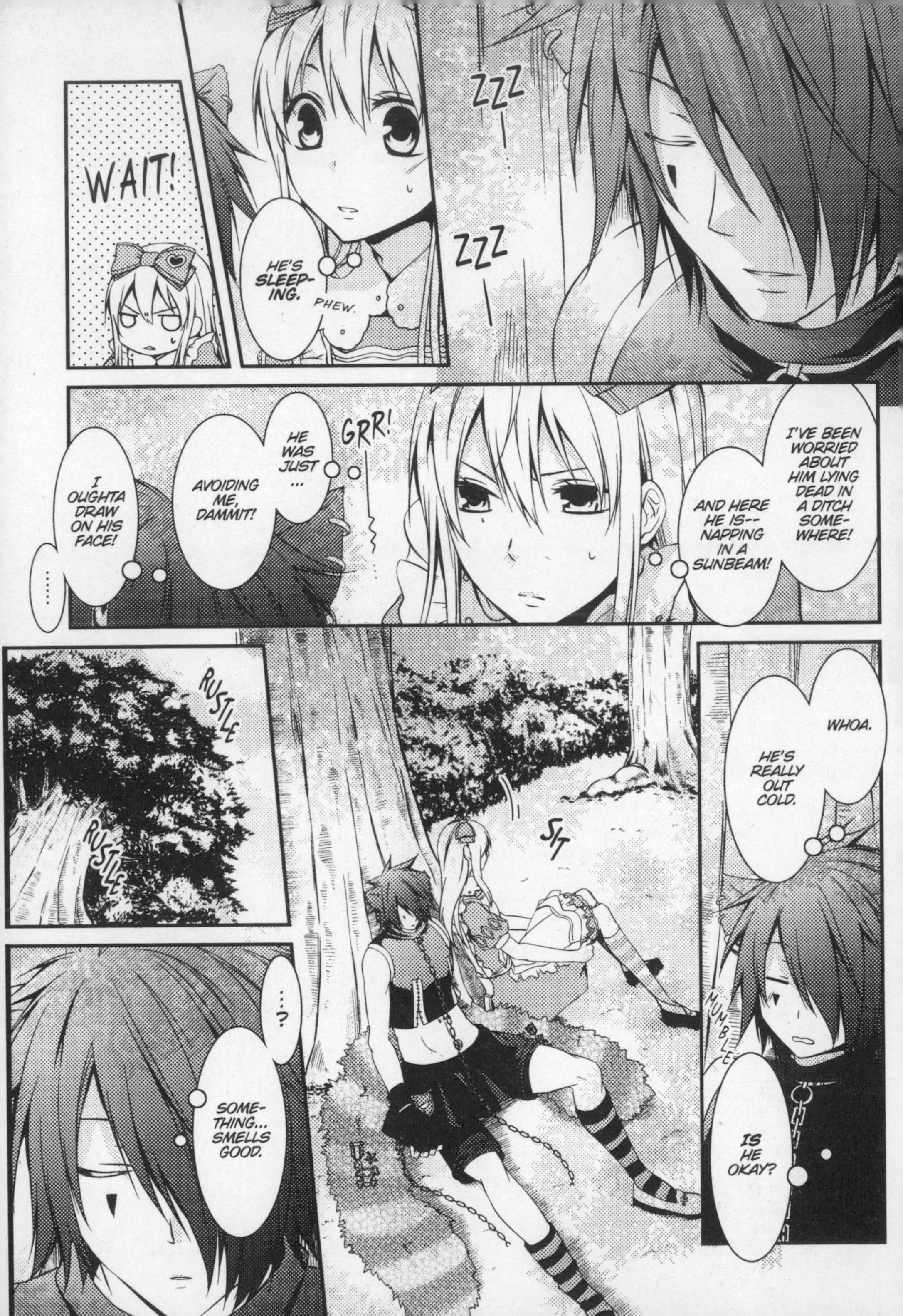
ZZZ
ZZZ
HE'S SLEEPING.
PHEW.
WAIT!
I'VE BEEN WORRIED ABOUT HIM LYING DEAD IN A DITCH SOMEWHERE!
AND HERE HE IS-- NAPPING IN A SUNBEAM!
GRR!
HE WAS JUST...
AVOIDING ME, DAMMIT!
I OUGHTA DRAW ON HIS FACE!
......
WHOA.
HE'S REALLY OUT COLD.
MUMBLE
IS HE OKAY?
SIT
RUSTLE
RUSTLE
...?
SOMETHING... SMELLS GOOD.

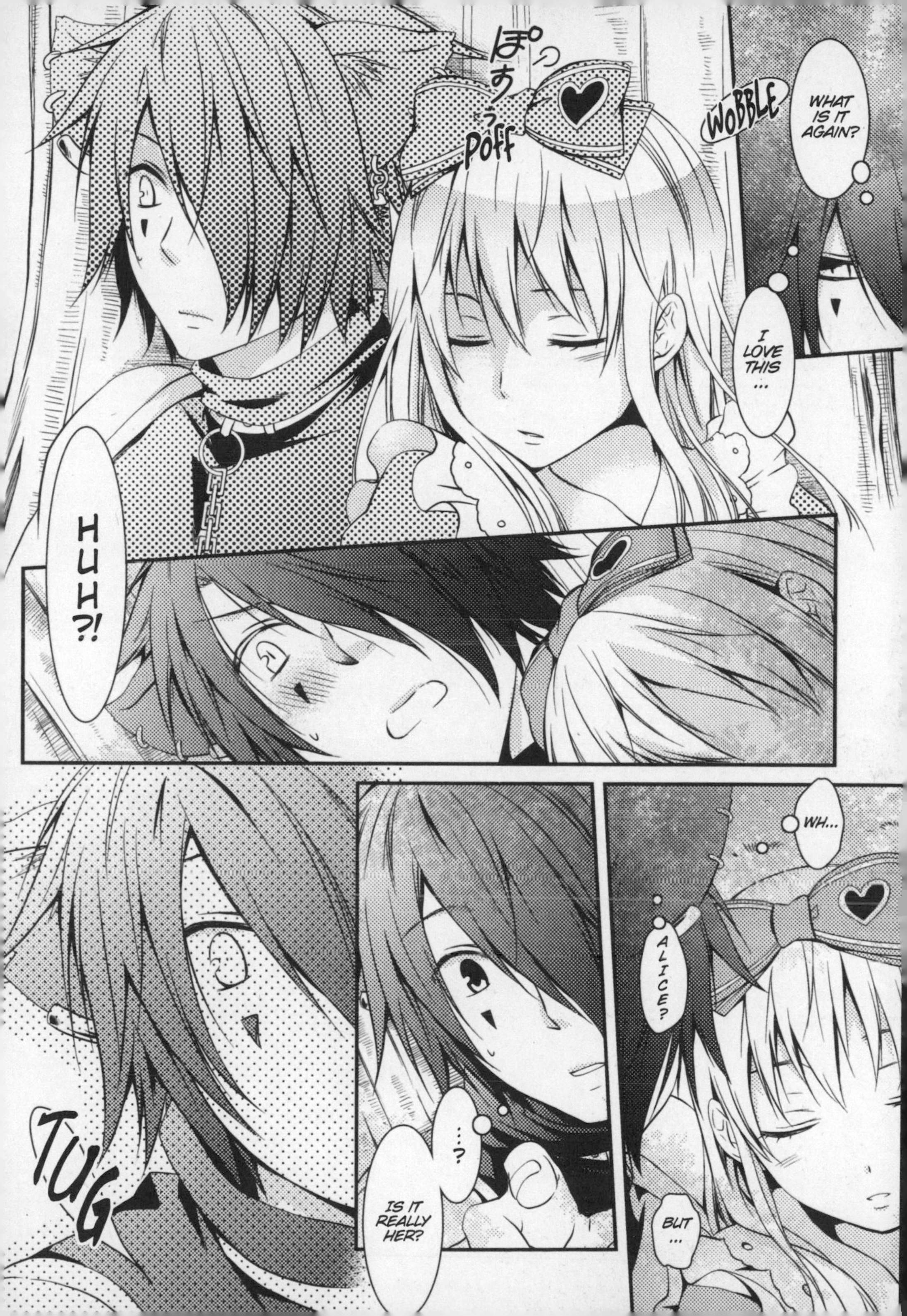
WOBBLE
WHAT IS IT AGAIN?
ぽすっ
POFF
I LOVE THIS ...
HUH?!
WH...
ALICE?
BUT ...
...?
IS IT REALLY HER?
TUG

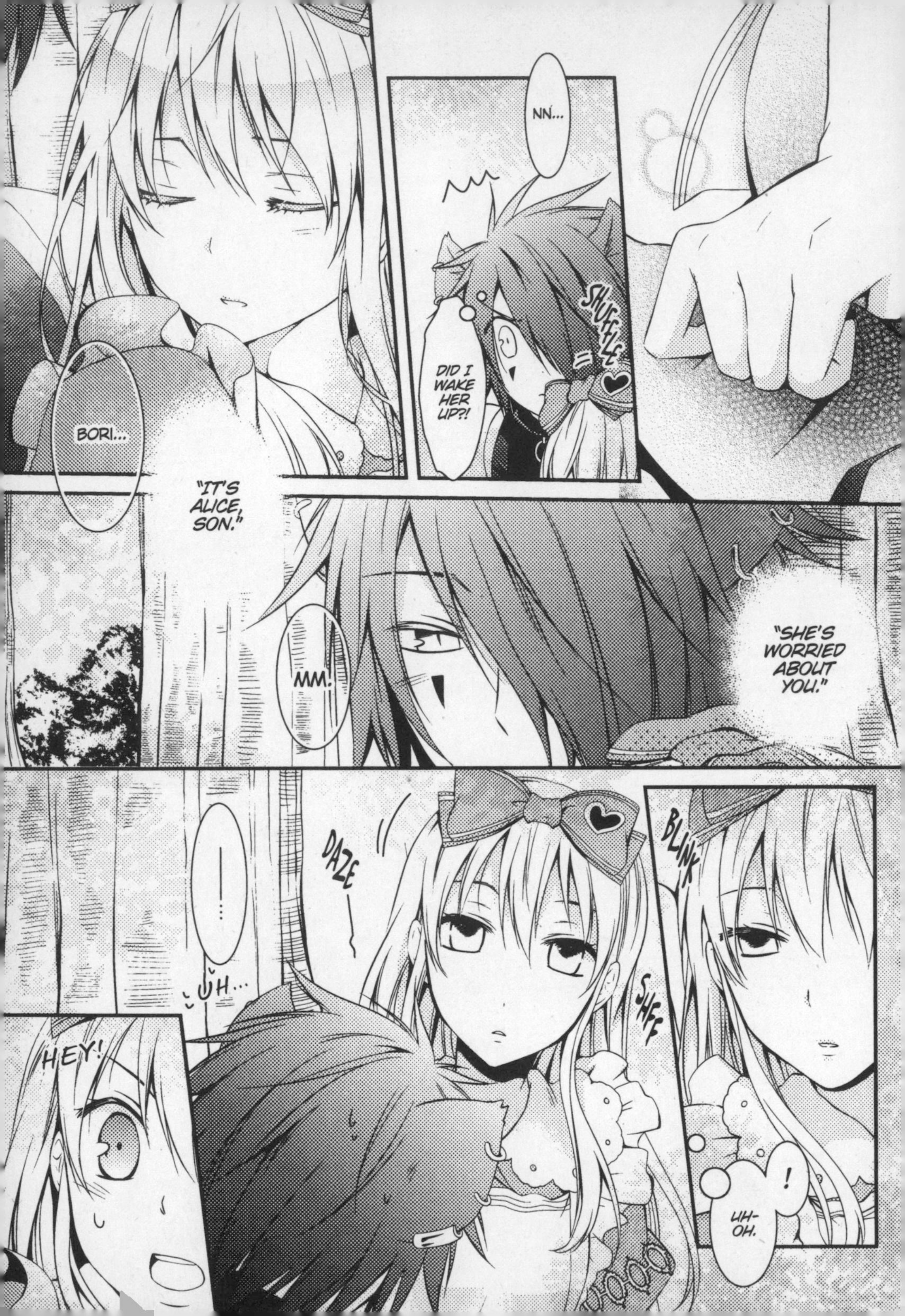
NN...
SHUFFLE
DID I WAKE HER UP?!
BORI...
"SHE'S WORRIED ABOUT YOU."
MM!
"IT'S ALICE, SON."
BLINK
SHFF
!
UH-OH.
DAZE
...!
UH...
HEY!

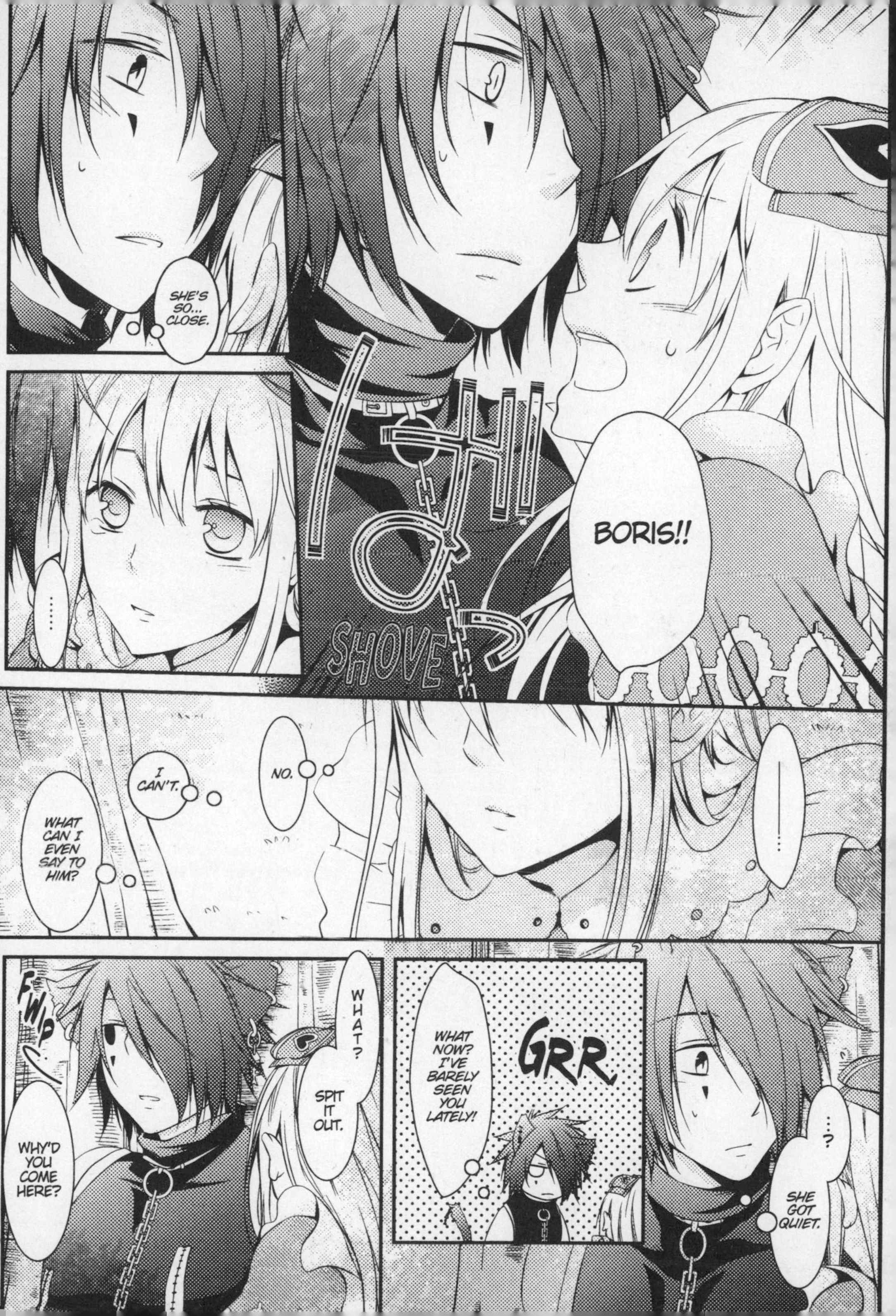

BORIS!!
SHOVE
SHE'S SO... CLOSE.
......
...
NO.
I CAN'T.
WHAT CAN I EVEN SAY TO HIM?
...?
SHE GOT QUIET.
GRR.
WHAT NOW? I'VE BARELY SEEN YOU LATELY!
WHAT?
SPIT IT OUT.
WHY'D YOU COME HERE?
FWIP

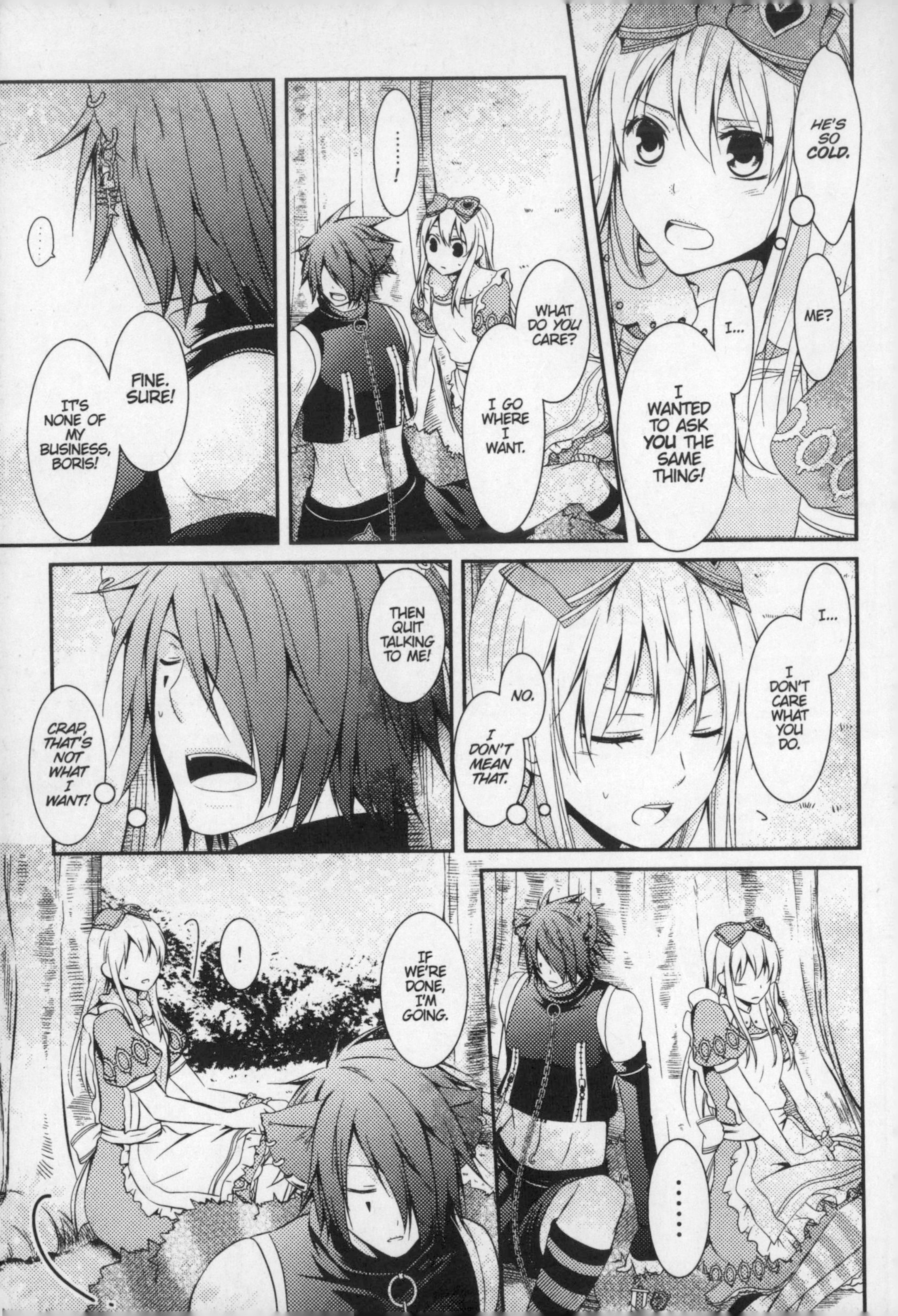
HE'S SO COLD.
ME?
I...
I WANTED TO ASK YOU THE SAME THING!
......!
WHAT DO YOU CARE?
I GO WHERE I WANT.
...
FINE. SURE!
IT'S NONE OF MY BUSINESS, BORIS!
I...
I DON'T CARE WHAT YOU DO.
NO.
I DON'T MEAN THAT.
THEN QUIT TALKING TO ME!
CRAP, THAT'S NOT WHAT I WANT!
......
IF WE'RE DONE, I'M GOING.
!

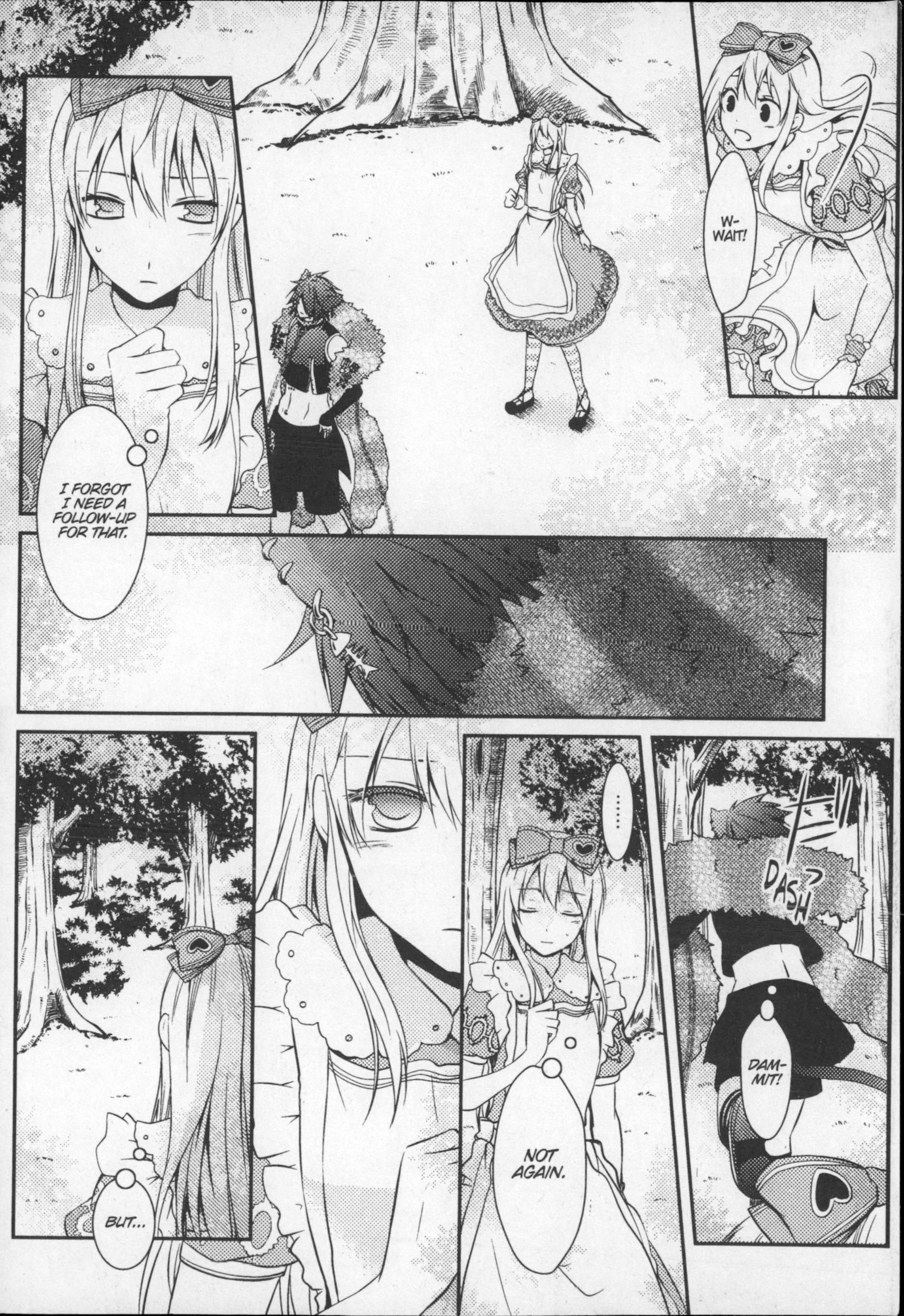
W-WAIT!
I FORGOT I NEED A FOLLOW-UP FOR THAT.
DASH?
DAM-MIT!
......
NOT AGAIN.
BUT...

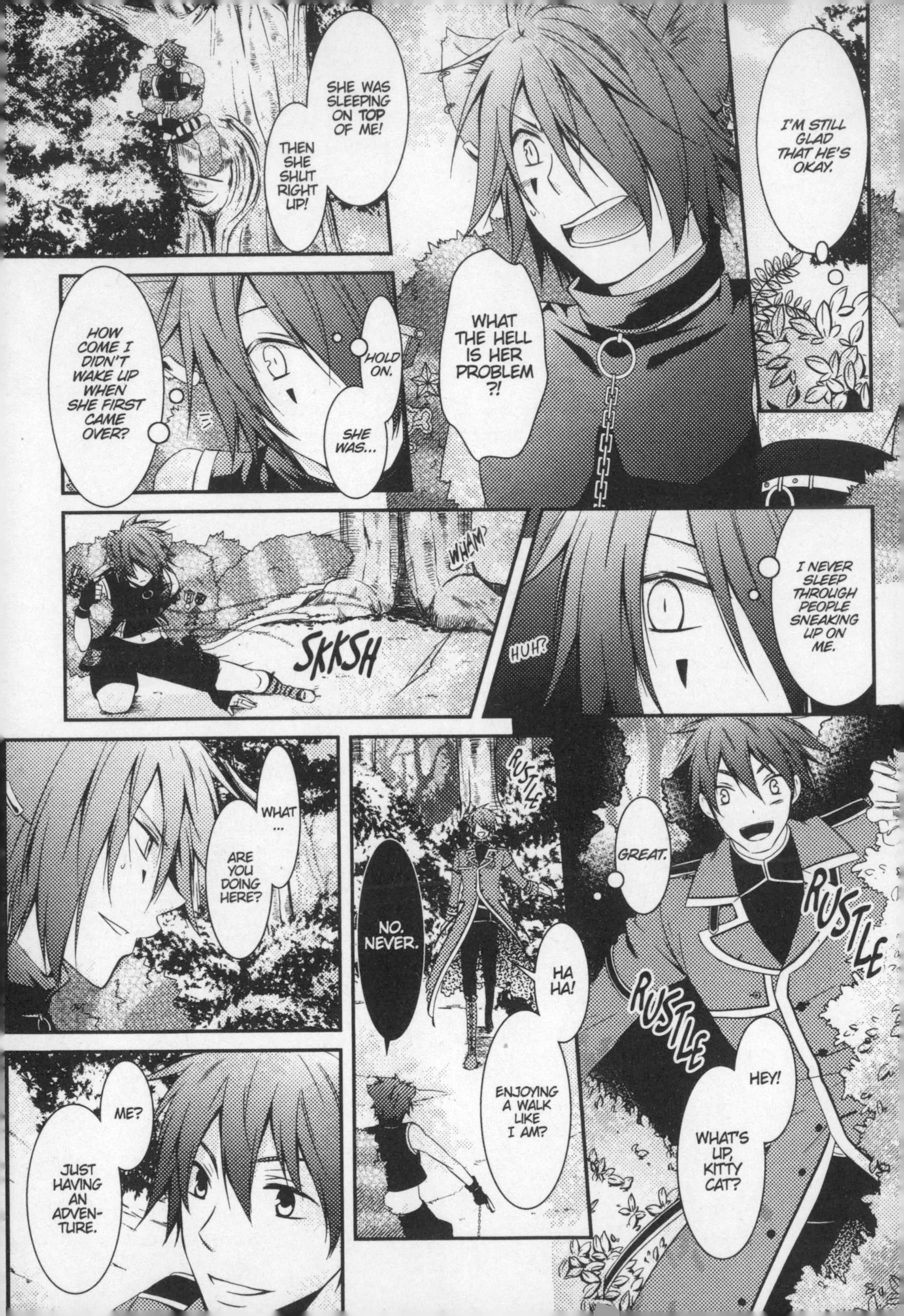
I'M STILL GLAD THAT HE'S OKAY.
SHE WAS SLEEPING ON TOP OF ME!
THEN SHE SHUT RIGHT UP!
WHAT THE HELL IS HER PROBLEM?!
HOLD ON.
SHE WAS...
HOW COME I DIDN'T WAKE UP WHEN SHE FIRST CAME OVER?
HUH?
I NEVER SLEEP THROUGH PEOPLE SNEAKING UP ON ME.
WHAM
SKKSH
RUSTLE
GREAT.
RUSTLE
RUSTLE
HEY!
WHAT'S UP, KITTY CAT?
HA HA!
ENJOYING A WALK LIKE I AM?
NO. NEVER.
WHAT ...
ARE YOU DOING HERE?
ME?
JUST HAVING AN ADVEN-TURE.

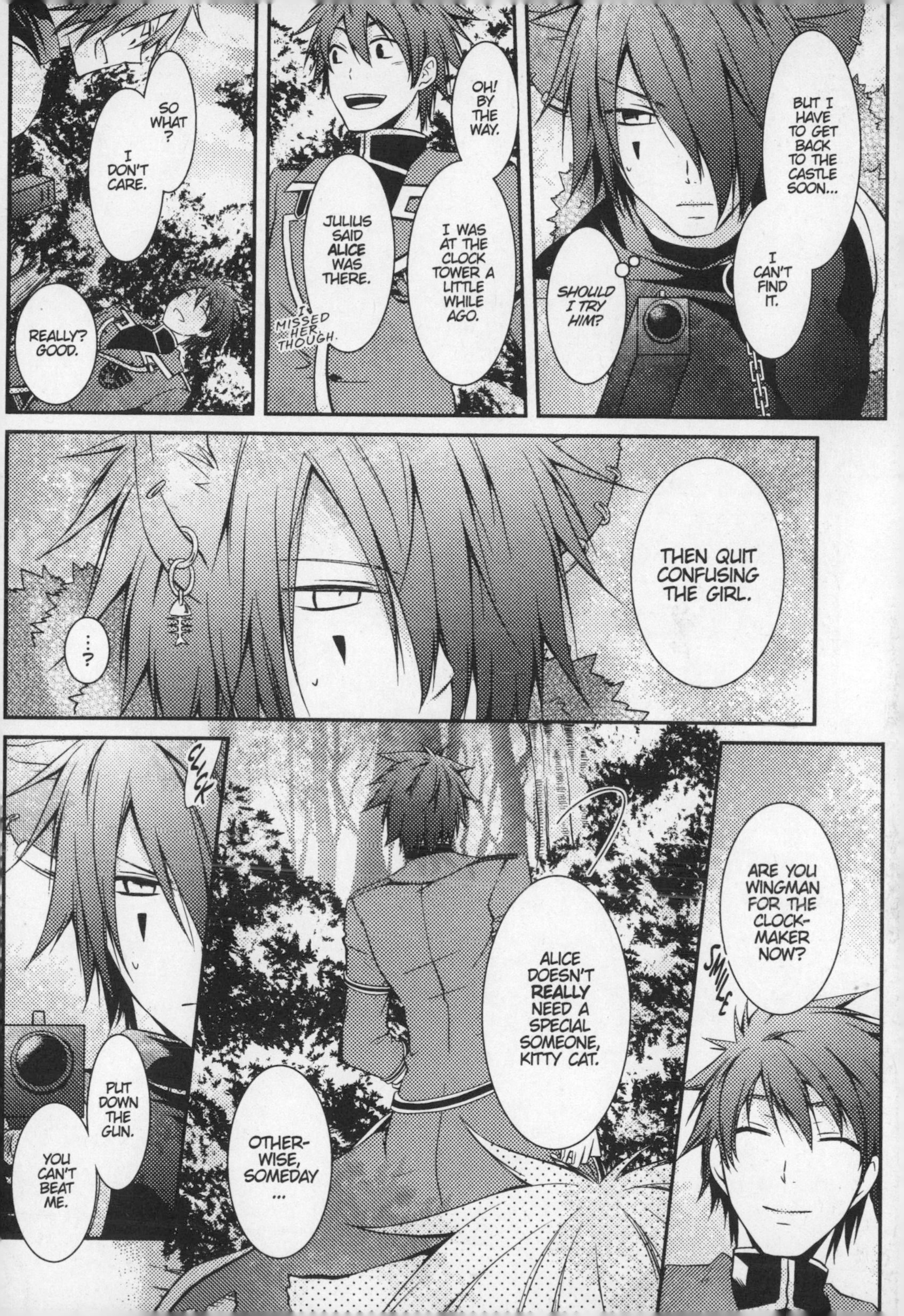
BUT I HAVE TO GET BACK TO THE CASTLE SOON...
I CAN'T FIND IT.
SHOULD I TRY HIM?
OH! BY THE WAY.
I WAS AT THE CLOCK TOWER A LITTLE WHILE AGO.
JULIUS SAID ALICE WAS THERE.
I MISSED HER THOUGH.
SO WHAT?
I DON'T CARE.
REALLY? GOOD.
THEN QUIT CONFUSING THE GIRL.
...?
ARE YOU WINGMAN FOR THE CLOCK-MAKER NOW?
SMILE
ALICE DOESN'T REALLY NEED A SPECIAL SOMEONE, KITTY CAT.
OTHER-WISE, SOMEDAY ...
CLICK
PUT DOWN THE GUN.
YOU CAN'T BEAT ME.

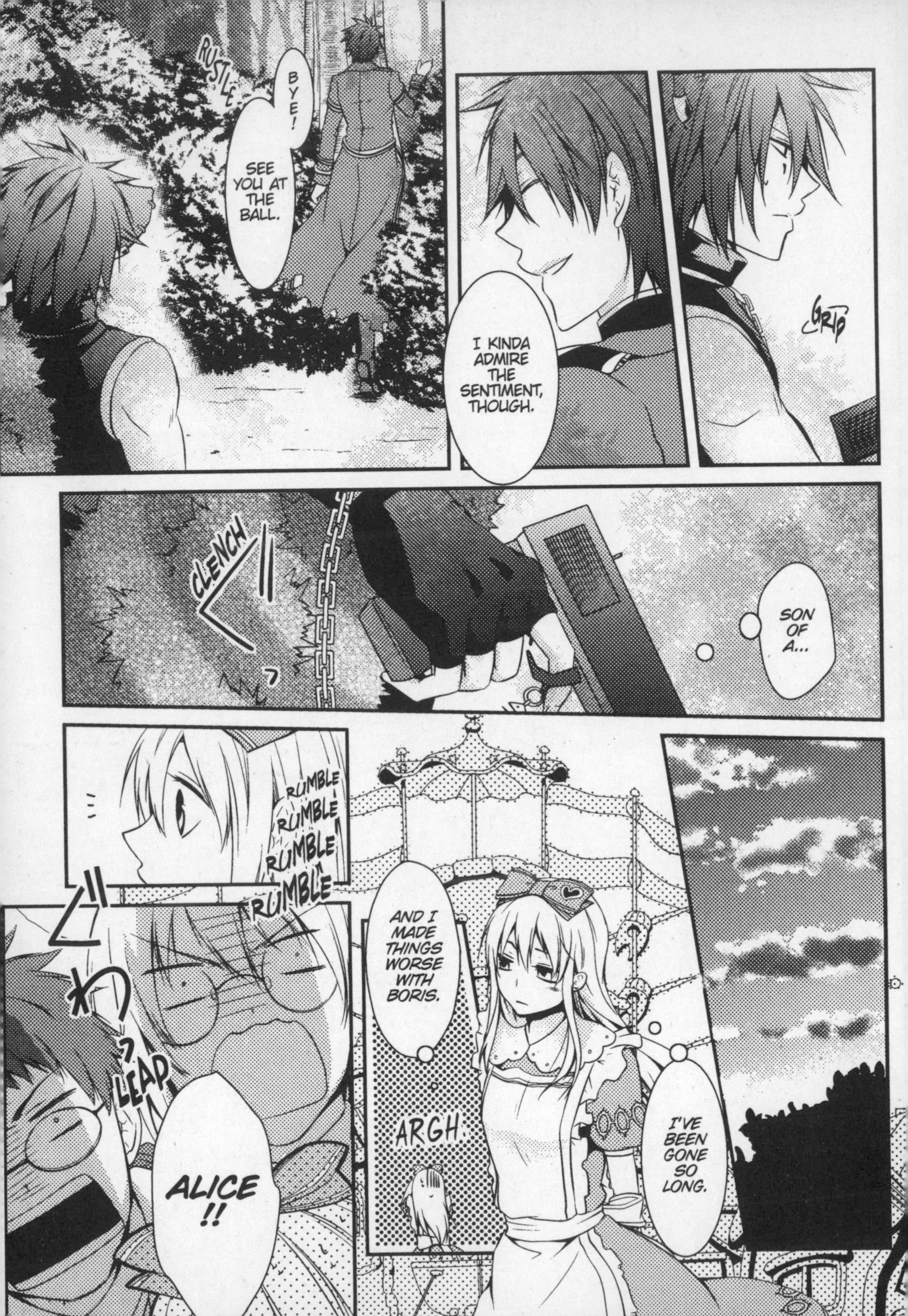

GRIP
I KINDA ADMIRE THE SENTIMENT, THOUGH.
RUSTLE
BYE!
SEE YOU AT THE BALL.
CLENCH
SON OF A...
I'VE BEEN GONE SO LONG.
AND I MADE THINGS WORSE WITH BORIS.
ARGH.
RUMBLE RUMBLE RUMBLE RUMBLE
LEAP
ALICE!!

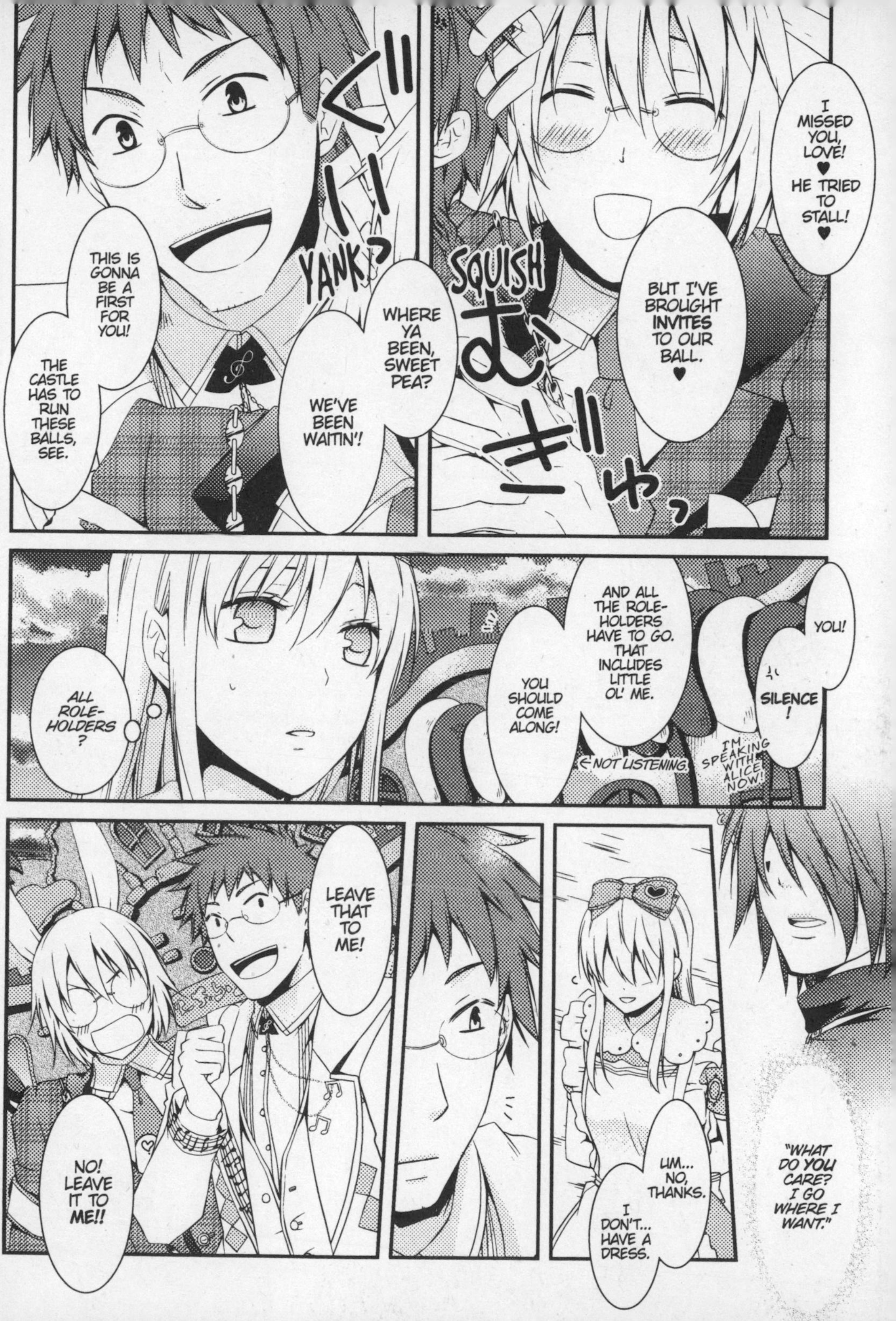
I MISSED YOU, LOVE! ♥
HE TRIED TO STALL! ♥
BUT I'VE BROUGHT INVITES TO OUR BALL. ♥
SQUISH
YANK
WHERE YA BEEN, SWEET PEA?
WE'VE BEEN WAITIN'!
THIS IS GONNA BE A FIRST FOR YOU!
THE CASTLE HAS TO RUN THESE BALLS, SEE.
YOU!
SILENCE!
I'M SPEAKING WITH ALICE NOW!
AND ALL THE ROLE-HOLDERS HAVE TO GO. THAT INCLUDES LITTLE OL' ME.
YOU SHOULD COME ALONG!
← NOT LISTENING.
ALL ROLE-HOLDERS?
"WHAT DO YOU CARE? I GO WHERE I WANT."
UM... NO, THANKS.
I DON'T... HAVE A DRESS.
LEAVE THAT TO ME!
NO! LEAVE IT TO ME!!

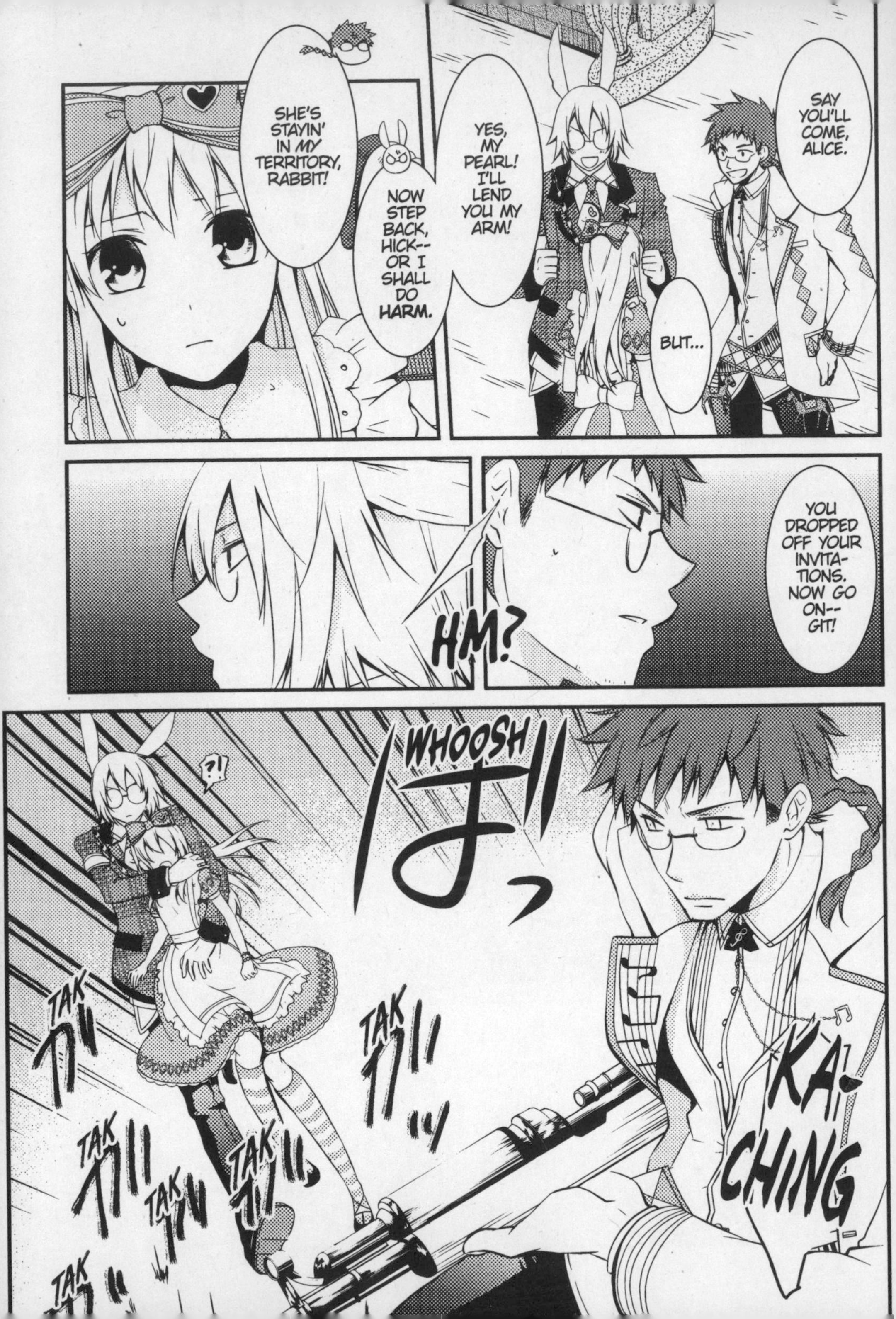
SAY YOU'LL COME, ALICE.
YES, MY PEARL! I'LL LEND YOU MY ARM!
BUT...
SHE'S STAYIN' IN *MY* TERRITORY, RABBIT!
NOW STEP BACK, HICK-- OR I SHALL DO **HARM.**
YOU DROPPED OFF YOUR INVITATIONS. NOW GO ON-- GIT!
HM?
WHOOSH
?!
KA-CHING
TAK
TAK
TAK
TAK
TAK
TAK

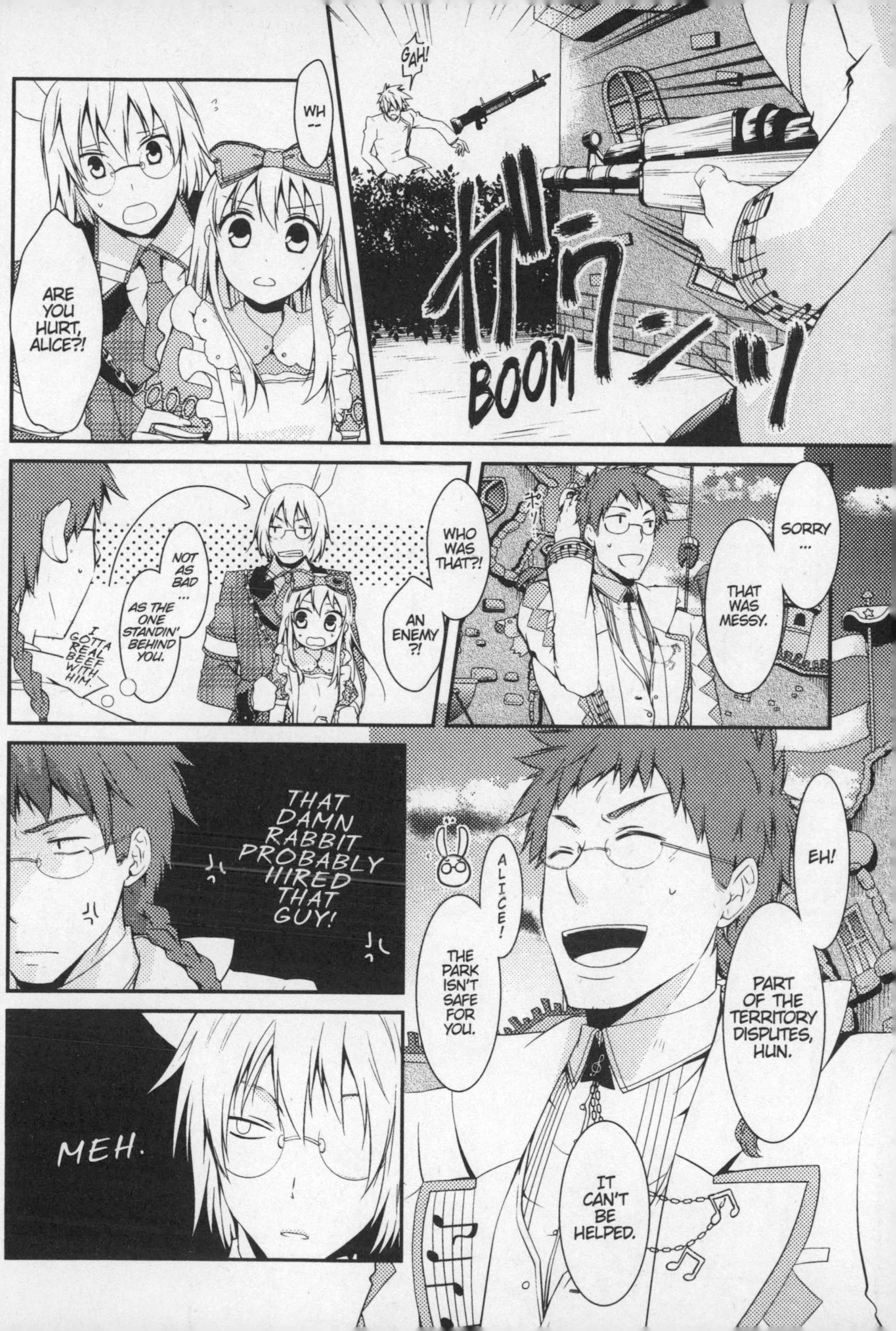
GAH!
BOOM
WH--
ARE YOU HURT, ALICE?!
SORRY... THAT WAS MESSY.
WHO WAS THAT?!
AN ENEMY?!
NOT AS BAD...
AS THE ONE STANDIN' BEHIND YOU.
I GOTTA REAL BEEF WITH HIM.
EH!
PART OF THE TERRITORY DISPUTES, HUN.
ALICE!
THE PARK ISN'T SAFE FOR YOU.
IT CAN'T BE HELPED.
THAT DAMN RABBIT PROBABLY HIRED THAT GUY!
MEH.

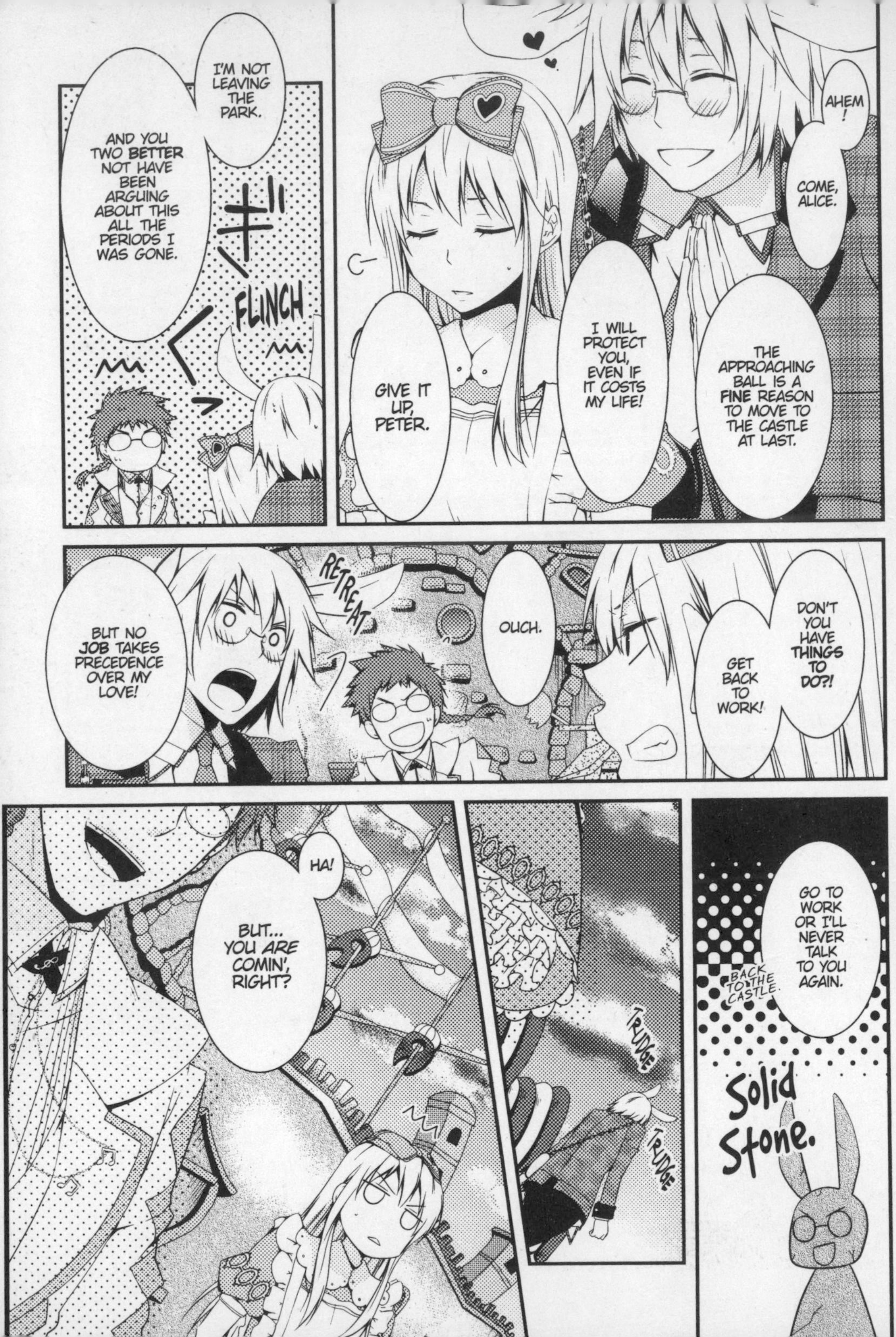
AHEM!
COME, ALICE.
THE APPROACHING BALL IS A FINE REASON TO MOVE TO THE CASTLE AT LAST.
I WILL PROTECT YOU, EVEN IF IT COSTS MY LIFE!
GIVE IT UP, PETER.
I'M NOT LEAVING THE PARK.
AND YOU TWO BETTER NOT HAVE BEEN ARGUING ABOUT THIS ALL THE PERIODS I WAS GONE.
FLINCH
DON'T YOU HAVE THINGS TO DO?!
GET BACK TO WORK!
OUCH.
RETREAT
BUT NO JOB TAKES PRECEDENCE OVER MY LOVE!
GO TO WORK OR I'LL NEVER TALK TO YOU AGAIN.
BACK TO THE CASTLE.
Solid Stone.
TRUDGE
TRUDGE
HA!
BUT... YOU ARE COMIN', RIGHT?

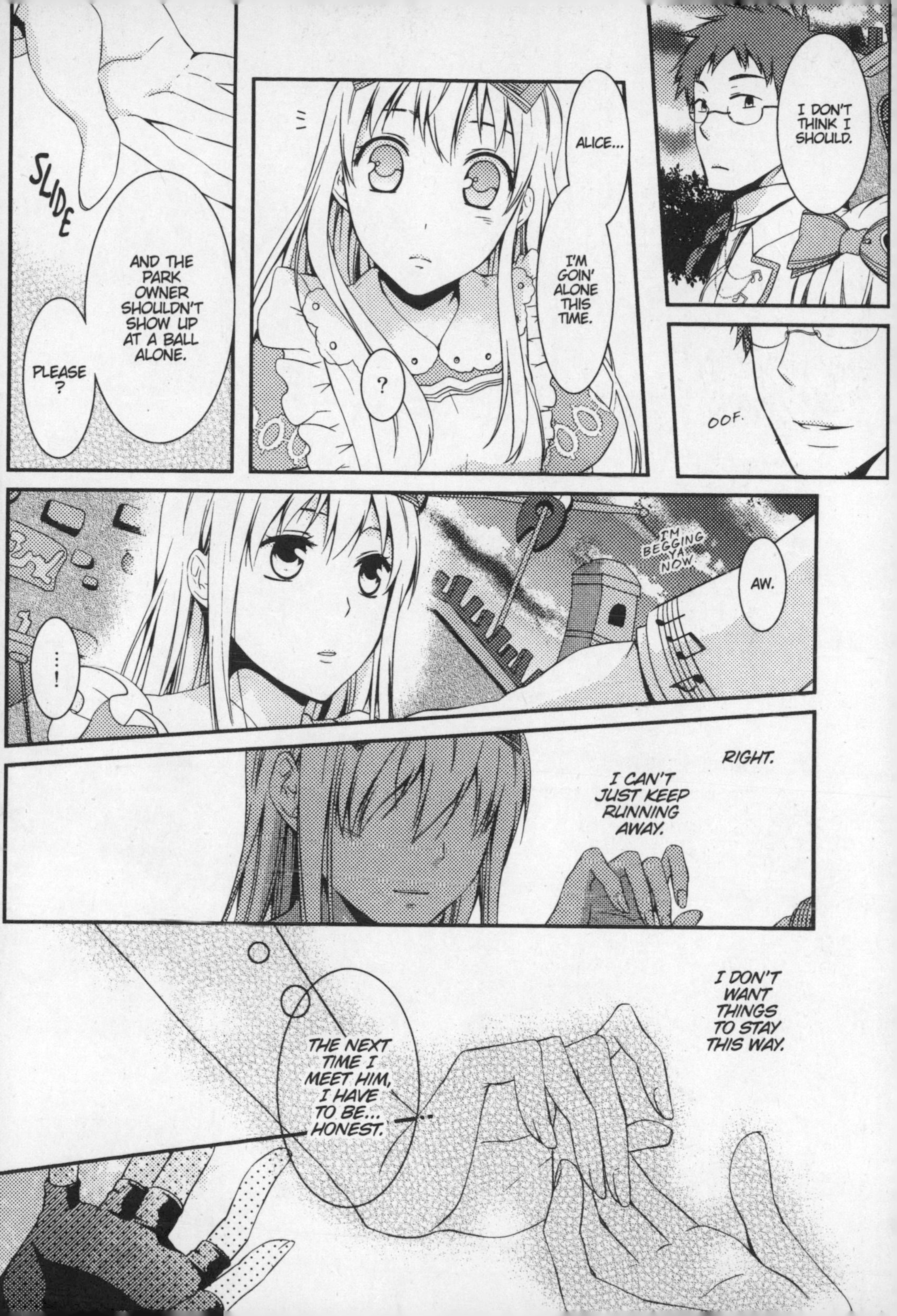
I DON'T THINK I SHOULD.
OOF.
ALICE...
I'M GOIN' ALONE THIS TIME.
?
SLIDE
AND THE PARK OWNER SHOULDN'T SHOW UP AT A BALL ALONE.
PLEASE?
I'M BEGGING YA NOW.
AW.
...!
RIGHT.
I CAN'T JUST KEEP RUNNING AWAY.
I DON'T WANT THINGS TO STAY THIS WAY.
THE NEXT TIME I MEET HIM, I HAVE TO BE... HONEST.

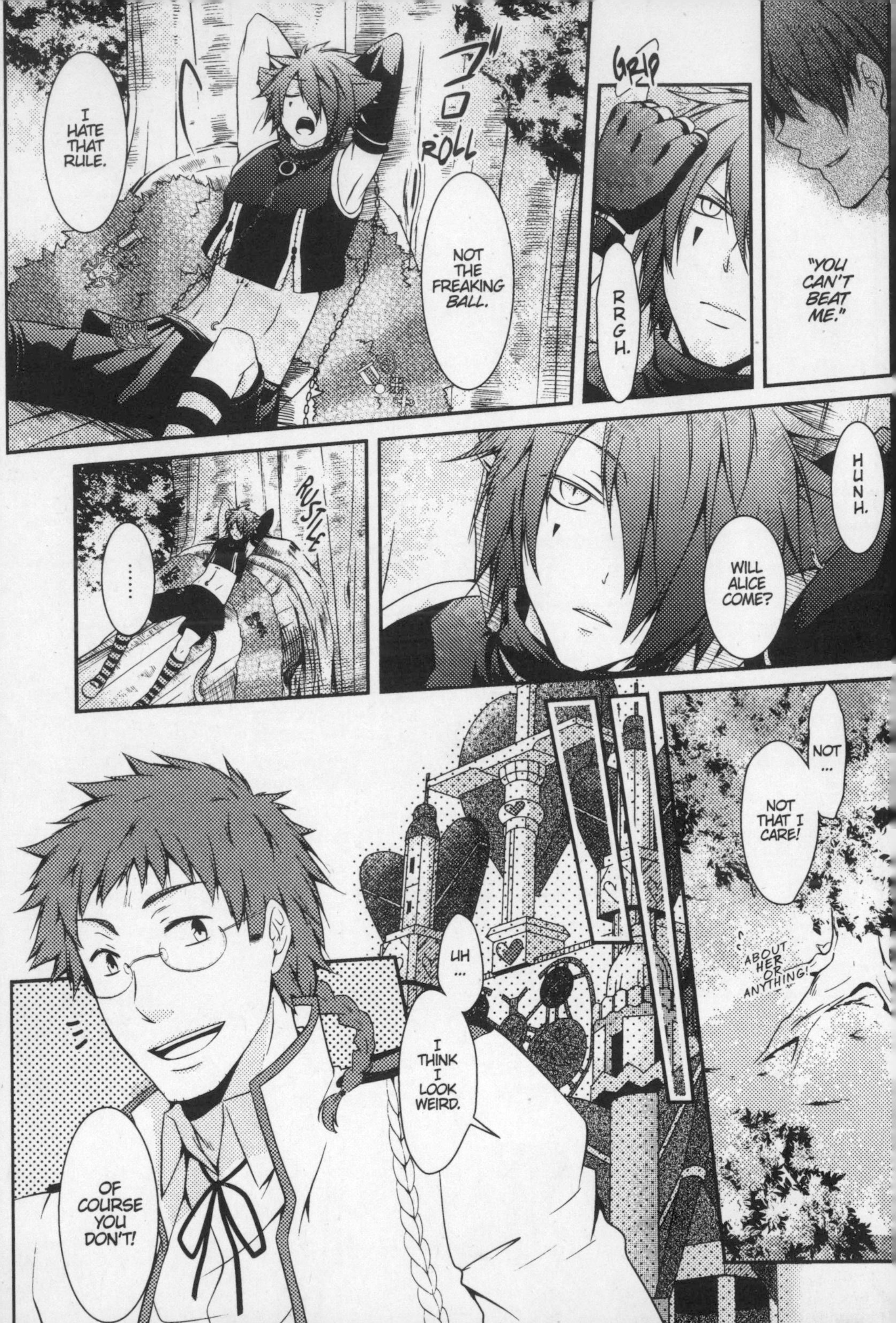
"YOU CAN'T BEAT ME."
GRIP
RRGH.
NOT THE FREAKING BALL.
ROLL
I HATE THAT RULE.
HUNH.
WILL ALICE COME?
RUSTLE
......
NOT...
NOT THAT I CARE!
ABOUT HER OR ANYTHING!
UH...
I THINK I LOOK WEIRD.
OF COURSE YOU DON'T!

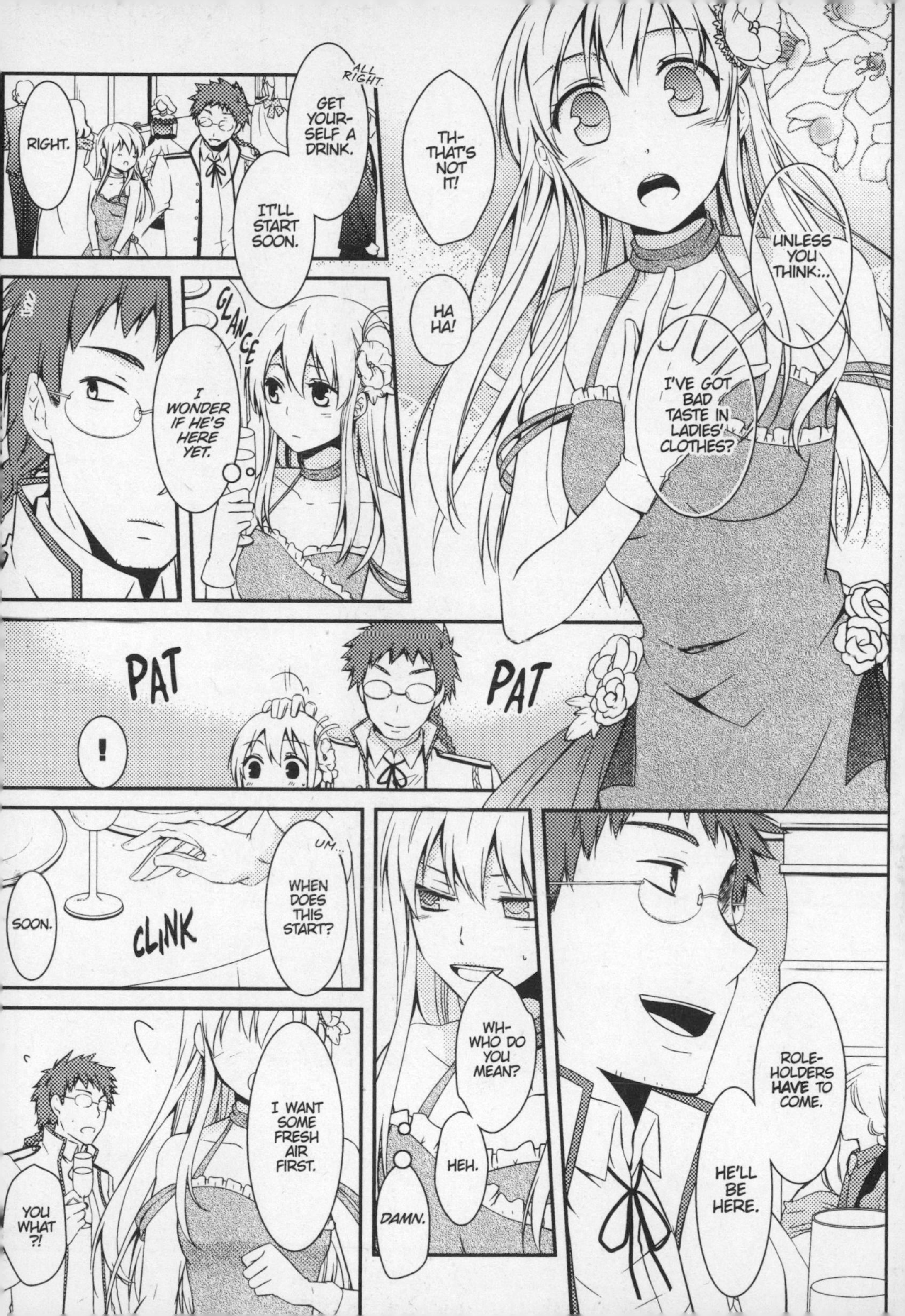
UNLESS YOU THINK...
I'VE GOT BAD TASTE IN LADIES' CLOTHES?
TH-THAT'S NOT IT!
HA HA!
ALL RIGHT.
GET YOURSELF A DRINK.
IT'LL START SOON.
RIGHT.
GLANCE
I WONDER IF HE'S HERE YET.
PAT
PAT
!
ROLE-HOLDERS HAVE TO COME.
HE'LL BE HERE.
WH-WHO DO YOU MEAN?
HEH.
DAMN.
UM...
WHEN DOES THIS START?
CLINK
SOON.
I WANT SOME FRESH AIR FIRST.
YOU WHAT?!

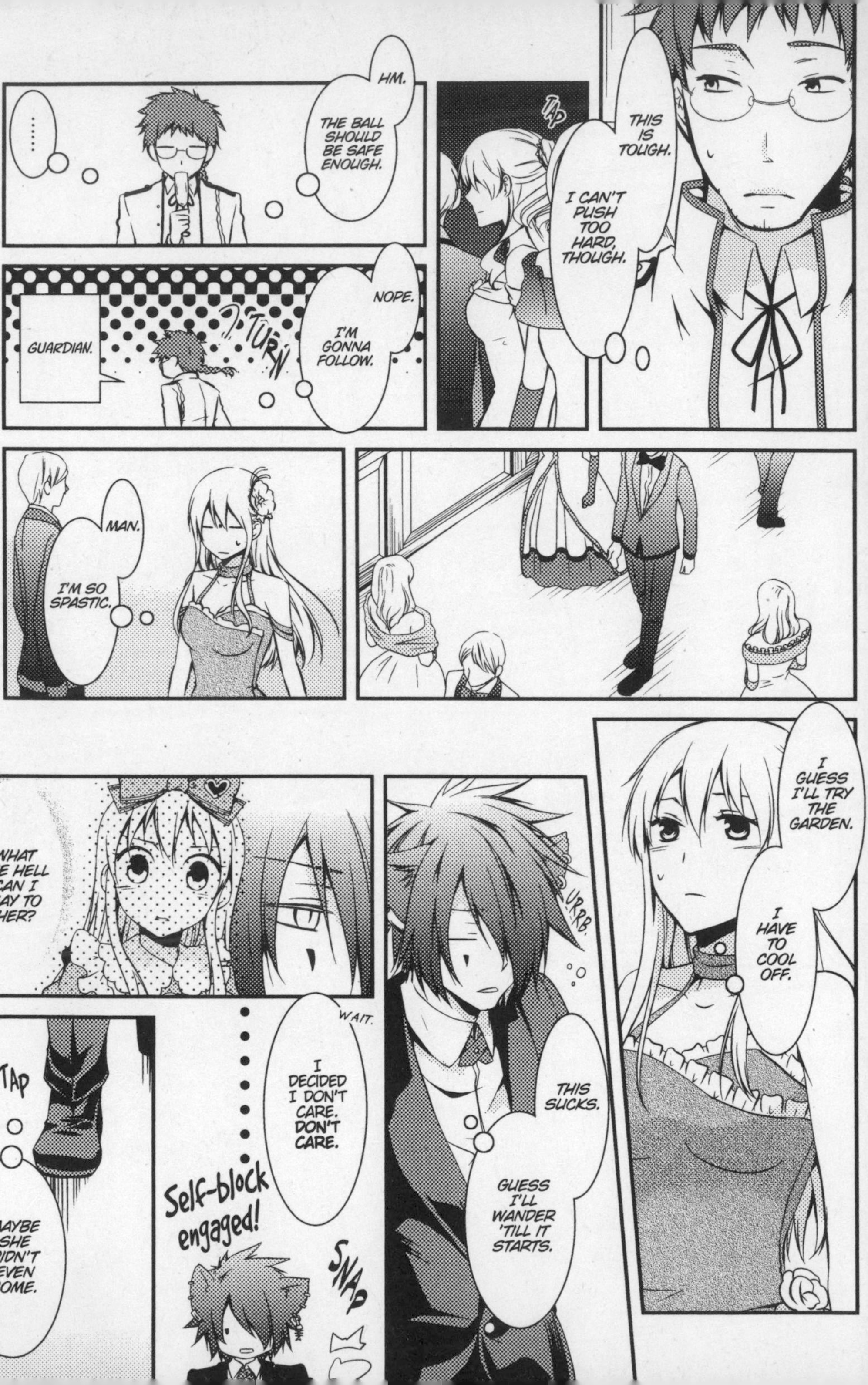
THIS IS TOUGH.
I CAN'T PUSH TOO HARD, THOUGH.
TAP
HM.
THE BALL SHOULD BE SAFE ENOUGH.
......
NOPE.
I'M GONNA FOLLOW.
TURN
GUARDIAN.
MAN.
I'M SO SPASTIC.
I GUESS I'LL TRY THE GARDEN.
I HAVE TO COOL OFF.
URRB.
THIS SUCKS.
GUESS I'LL WANDER 'TILL IT STARTS.
WHAT THE HELL CAN I SAY TO HER?
WAIT.
I DECIDED I DON'T CARE. DON'T CARE.
Self-block engaged!
SNAP
TAP
MAYBE SHE DIDN'T EVEN COME.

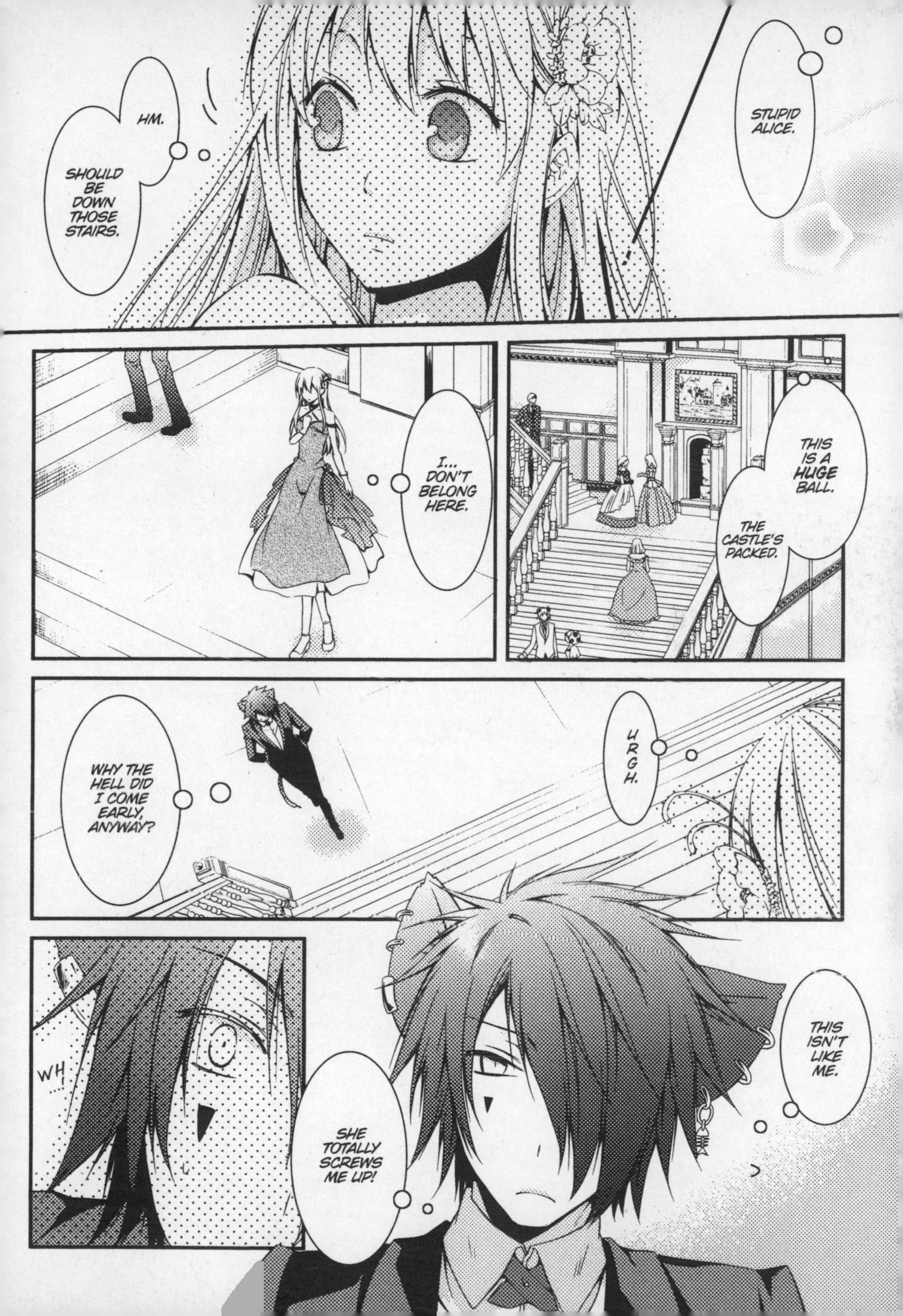
STUPID ALICE.
HM.
SHOULD BE DOWN THOSE STAIRS.
THIS IS A HUGE BALL.
THE CASTLE'S PACKED.
I... DON'T BELONG HERE.
URGH.
WHY THE HELL DID I COME EARLY, ANYWAY?
THIS ISN'T LIKE ME.
SHE TOTALLY SCREWS ME UP!
WH...!

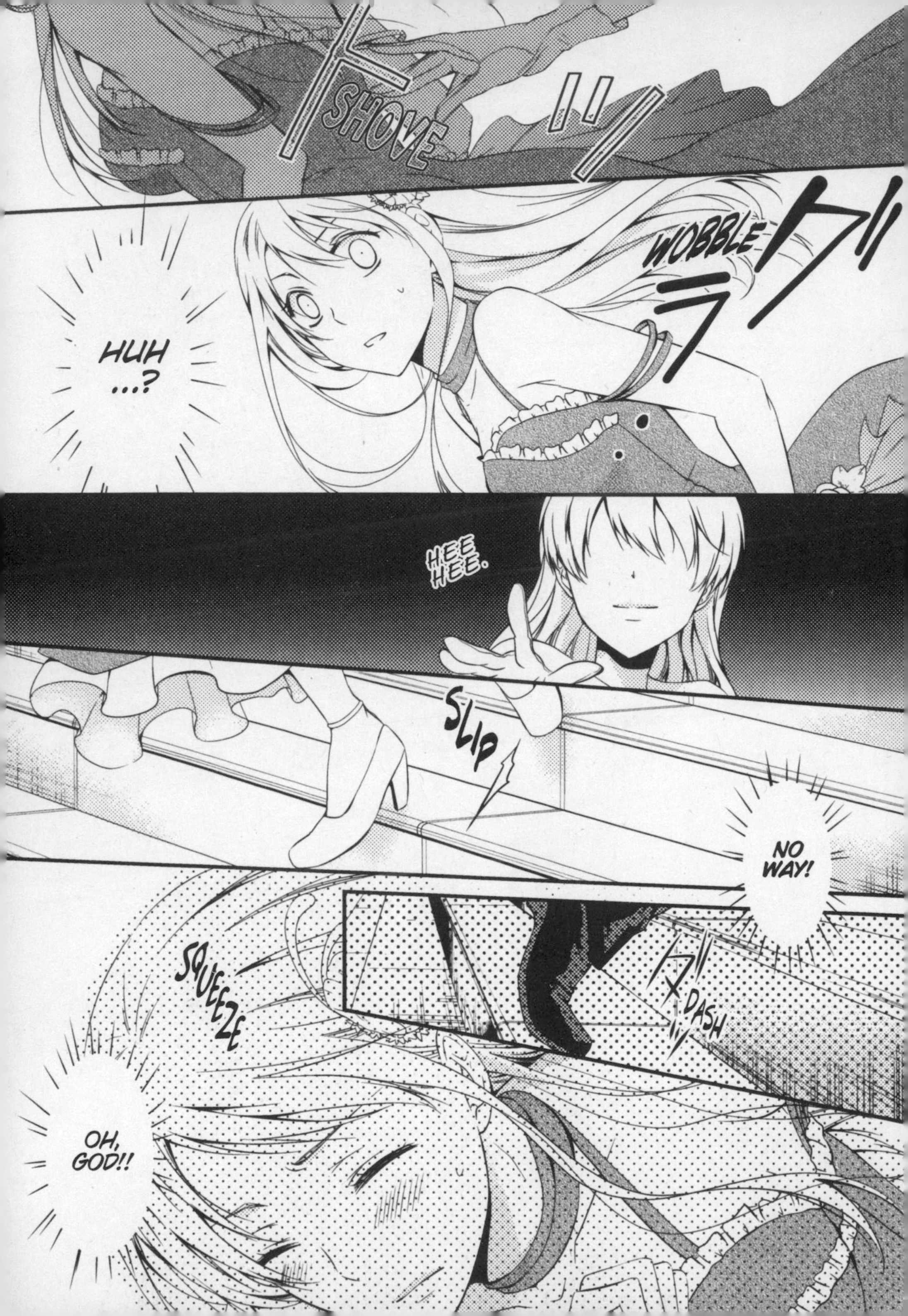
SHOVE
WOBBLE
HUH ...?
HEE HEE.
SLIP
NO WAY!
DASH
SQUEEZE
OH, GOD!!

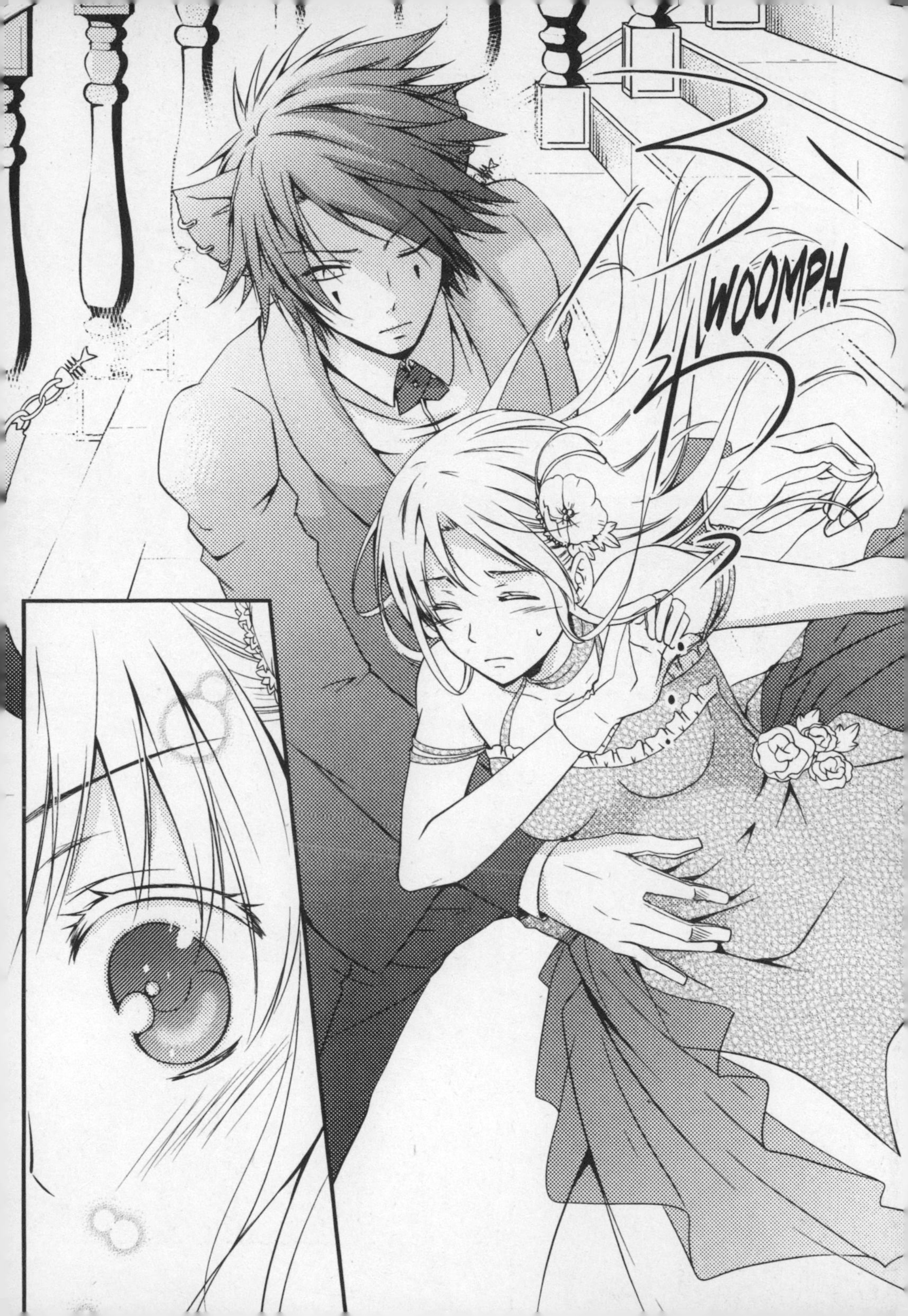
WOOMPH

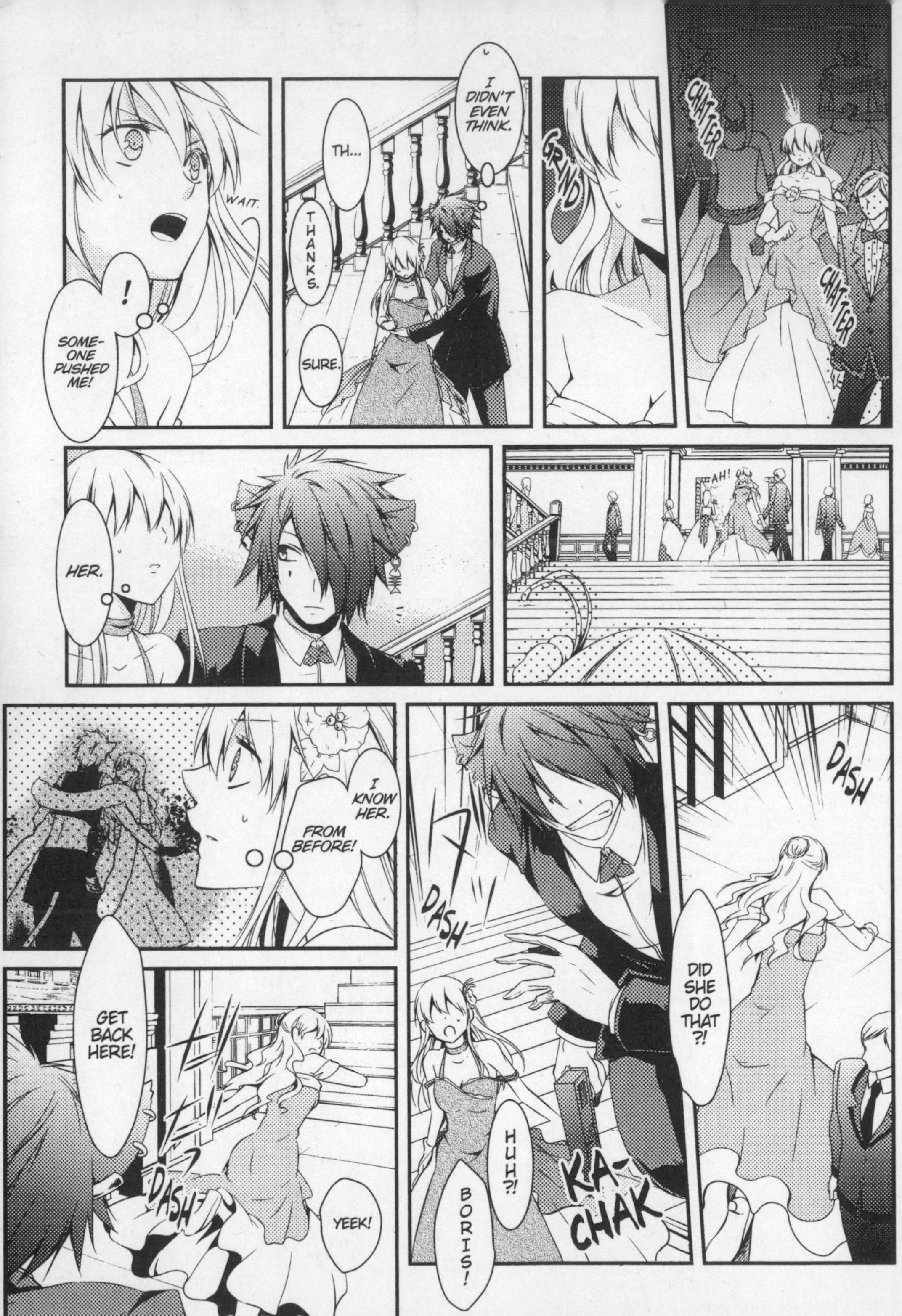
CHATTER
CHATTER
GRIND
I DIDN'T EVEN THINK.
TH...
THANKS.
SURE.
WAIT.
!
SOME-ONE PUSHED ME!
AH!
HER.
DASH
DID SHE DO THAT?!
DASH
HUH?!
KA-CHAK
BORIS!
I KNOW HER.
FROM BEFORE!
GET BACK HERE!
DASH
YEEK!

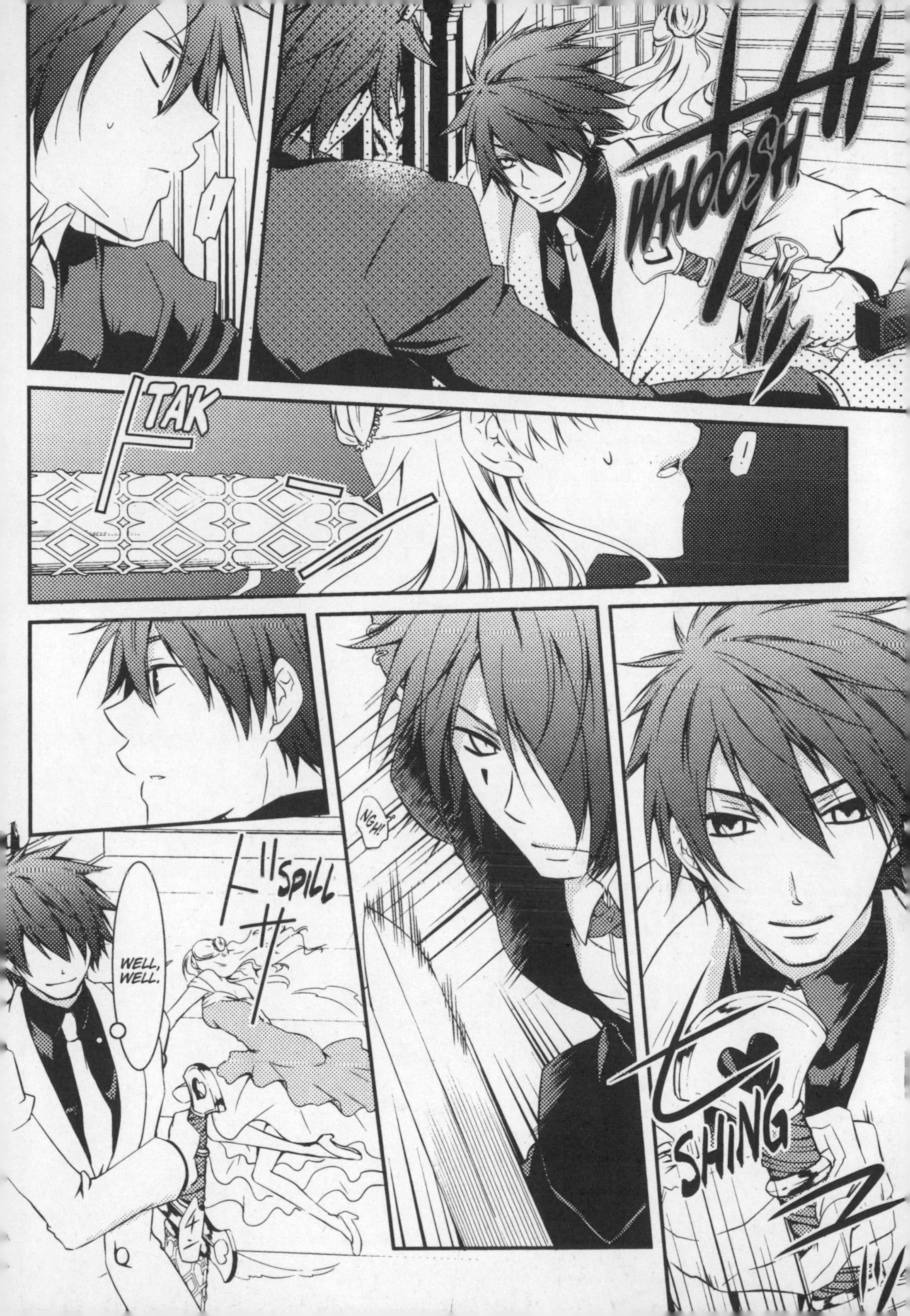
WHOOSH
!
!
TAK
SHING
NGH!
SPILL
WELL, WELL.

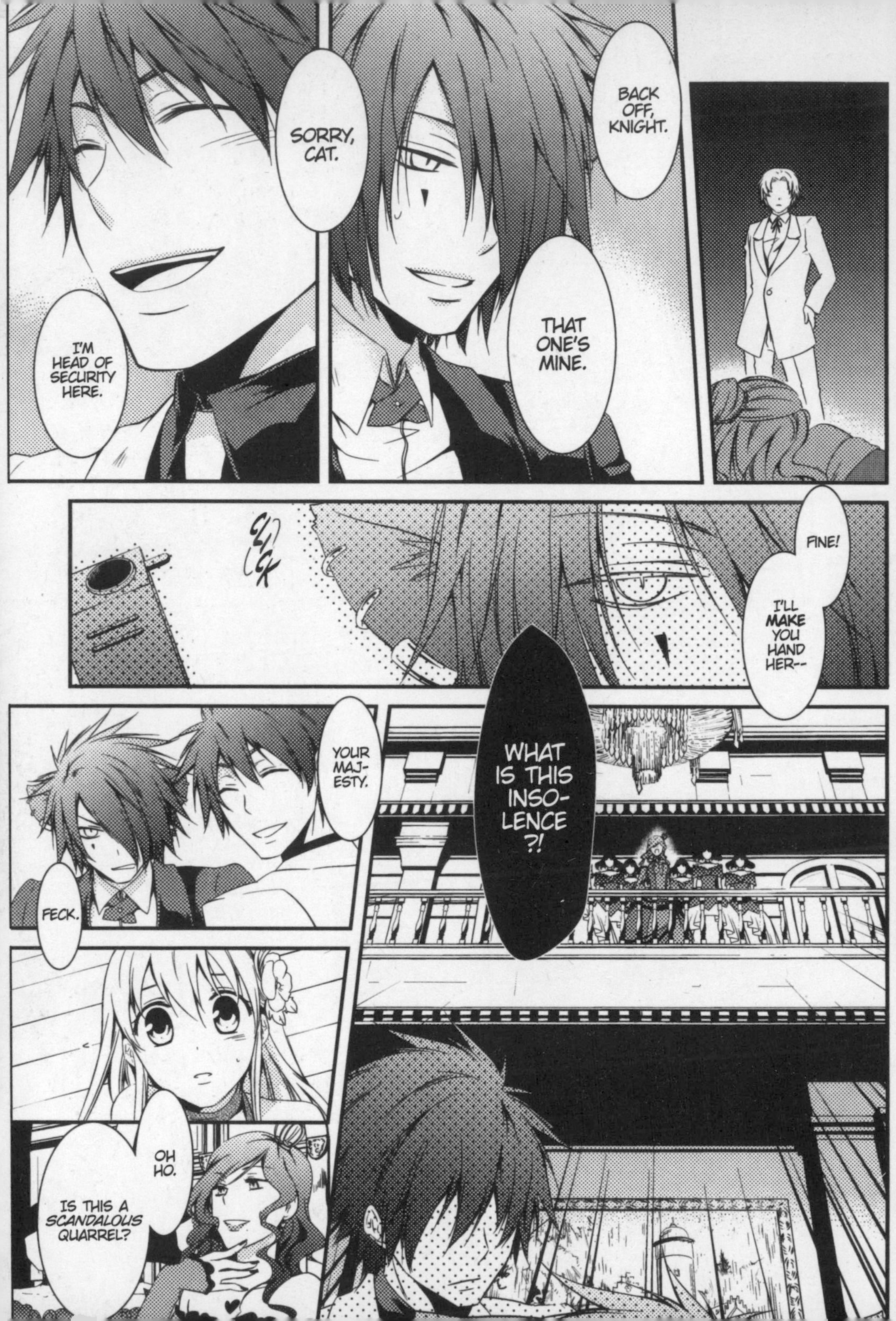
BACK OFF, KNIGHT.
THAT ONE'S MINE.
SORRY, CAT.
I'M HEAD OF SECURITY HERE.
FINE!
I'LL MAKE YOU HAND HER--
CLICK
WHAT IS THIS INSOLENCE?!
YOUR MAJESTY.
FECK.
OH HO.
IS THIS A SCANDALOUS QUARREL?

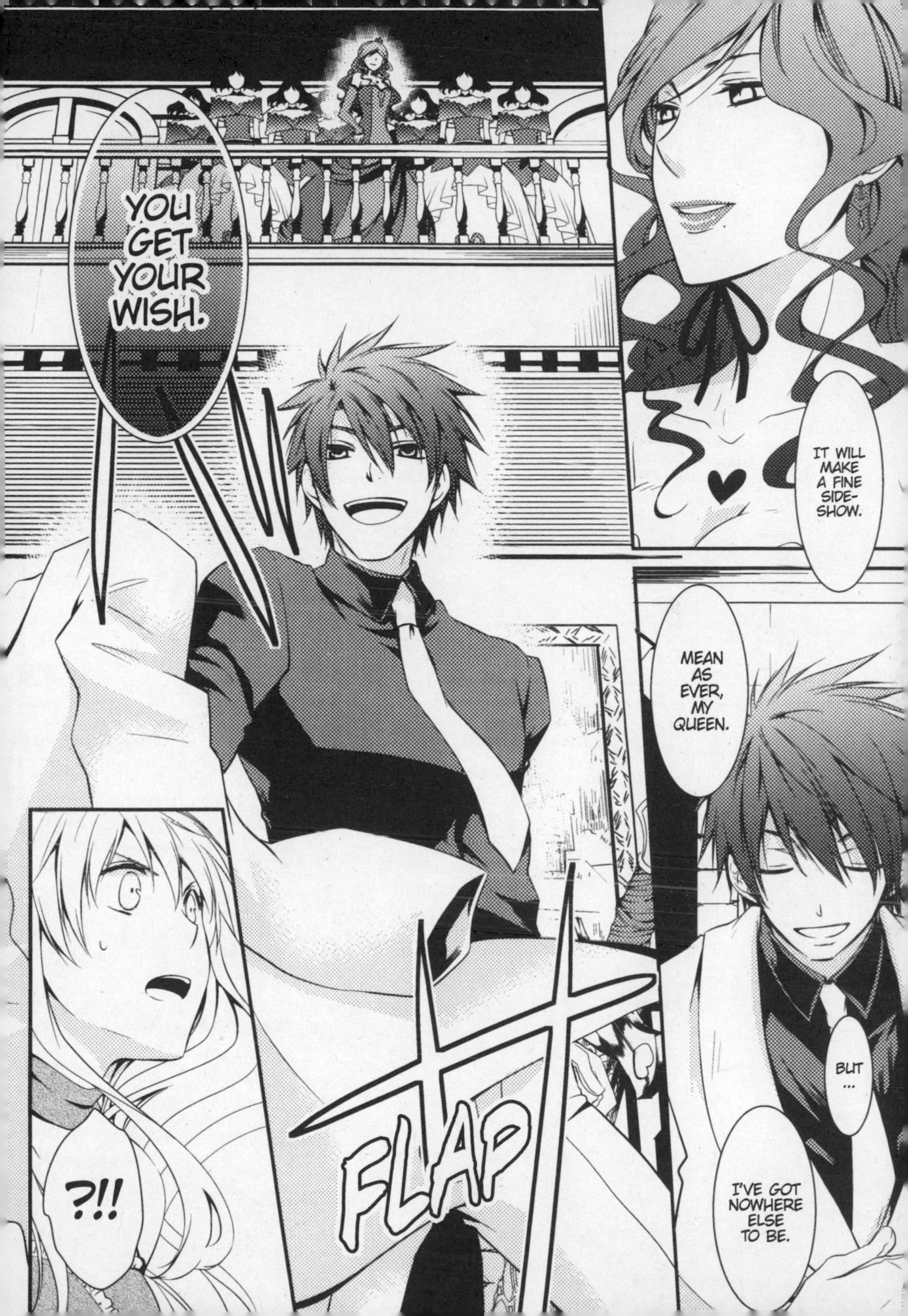
IT WILL MAKE A FINE SIDE-SHOW.
YOU GET YOUR WISH.
MEAN AS EVER, MY QUEEN.
BUT ...
I'VE GOT NOWHERE ELSE TO BE.
FLAP
?!!

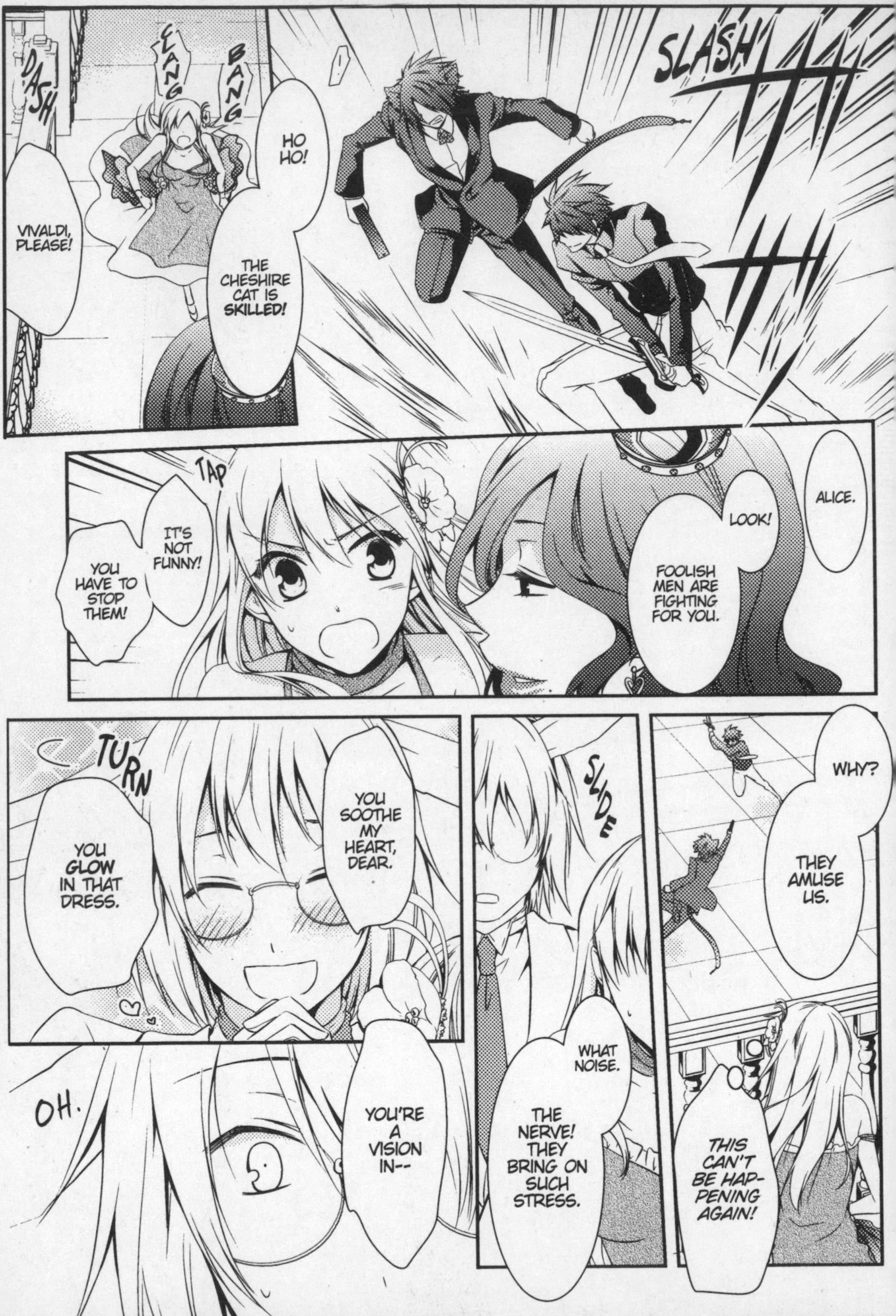
SLASH
!
BANG
HO HO!
THE CHESHIRE CAT IS SKILLED!
CLANG
DASH
VIVALDI, PLEASE!
ALICE.
LOOK!
FOOLISH MEN ARE FIGHTING FOR YOU.
TAP
IT'S NOT FUNNY!
YOU HAVE TO STOP THEM!
WHY?
THEY AMUSE US.
THIS CAN'T BE HAP-PENING AGAIN!
SLIDE
WHAT NOISE.
THE NERVE! THEY BRING ON SUCH STRESS.
TURN
YOU SOOTHE MY HEART, DEAR.
YOU GLOW IN THAT DRESS.
YOU'RE A VISION IN--
OH.

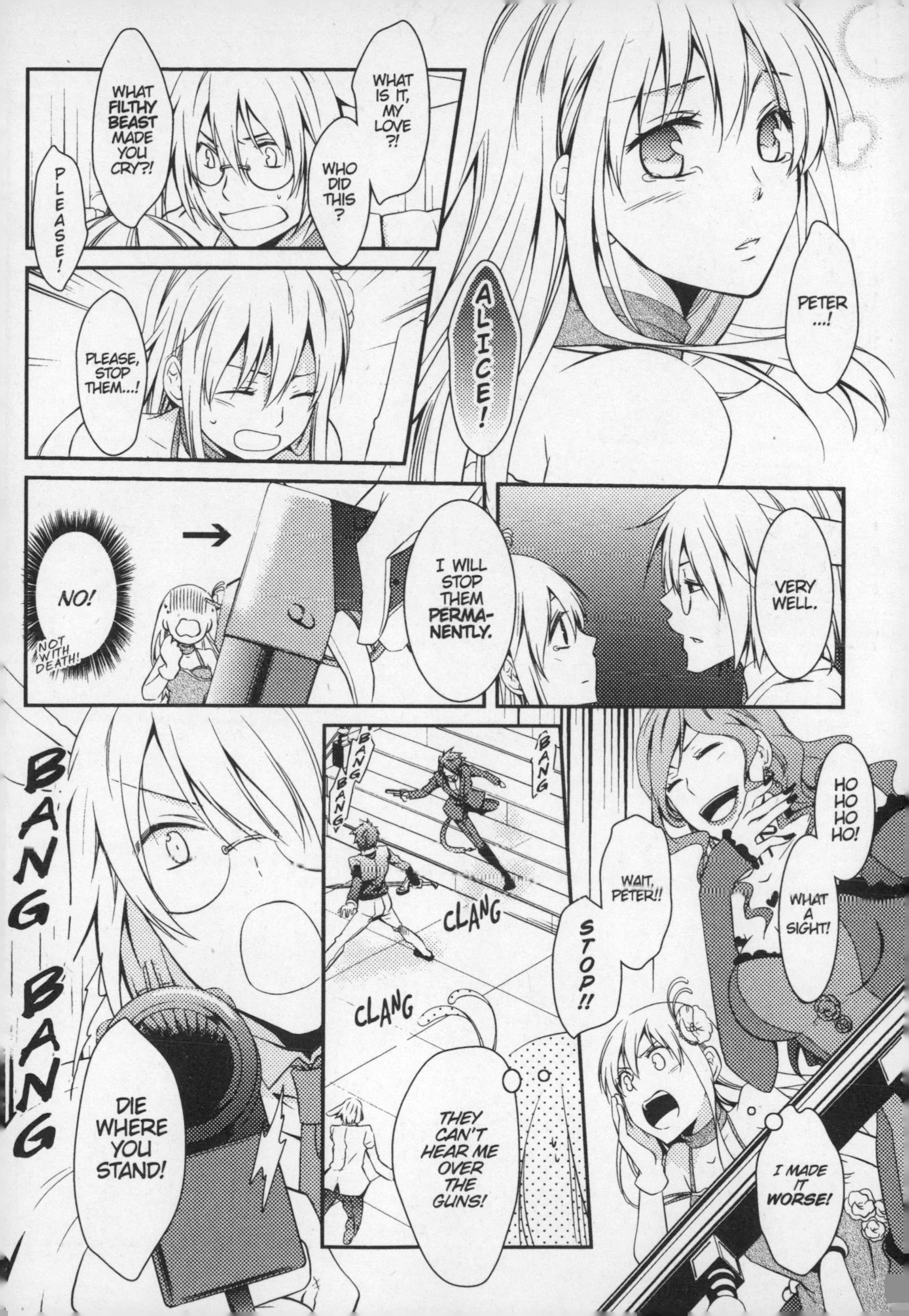

PETER ...!
ALICE!
WHAT IS IT, MY LOVE?!
WHO DID THIS?
WHAT FILTHY BEAST MADE YOU CRY?!
PLEASE!
PLEASE, STOP THEM...!
VERY WELL.
I WILL STOP THEM PERMANENTLY.
NO!
NOT WITH DEATH!
HO HO HO HO!
WHAT A SIGHT!
WAIT, PETER!!
STOP!!
I MADE IT WORSE!
BANG
BANG
BANG
CLANG
CLANG
THEY CAN'T HEAR ME OVER THE GUNS!
BANG BANG BANG
DIE WHERE YOU STAND!

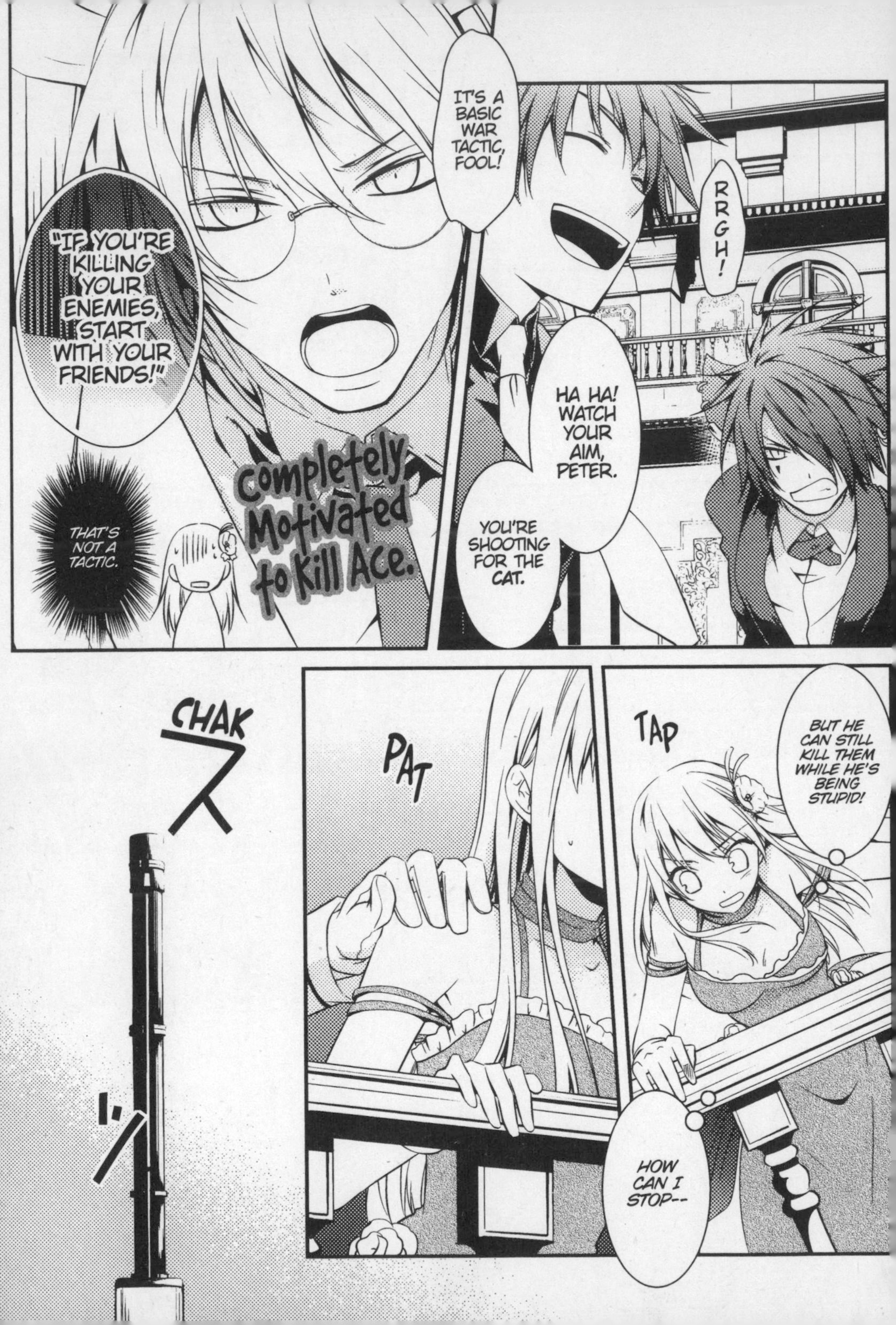
IT'S A BASIC WAR TACTIC, FOOL!
RRGH!
HA HA! WATCH YOUR AIM, PETER.
YOU'RE SHOOTING FOR THE CAT.
"IF YOU'RE KILLING YOUR ENEMIES, START WITH YOUR FRIENDS!"
completely Motivated to Kill Ace.
THAT'S NOT A TACTIC.
TAP
BUT HE CAN STILL KILL THEM WHILE HE'S BEING STUPID!
HOW CAN I STOP--
PAT
CHAK

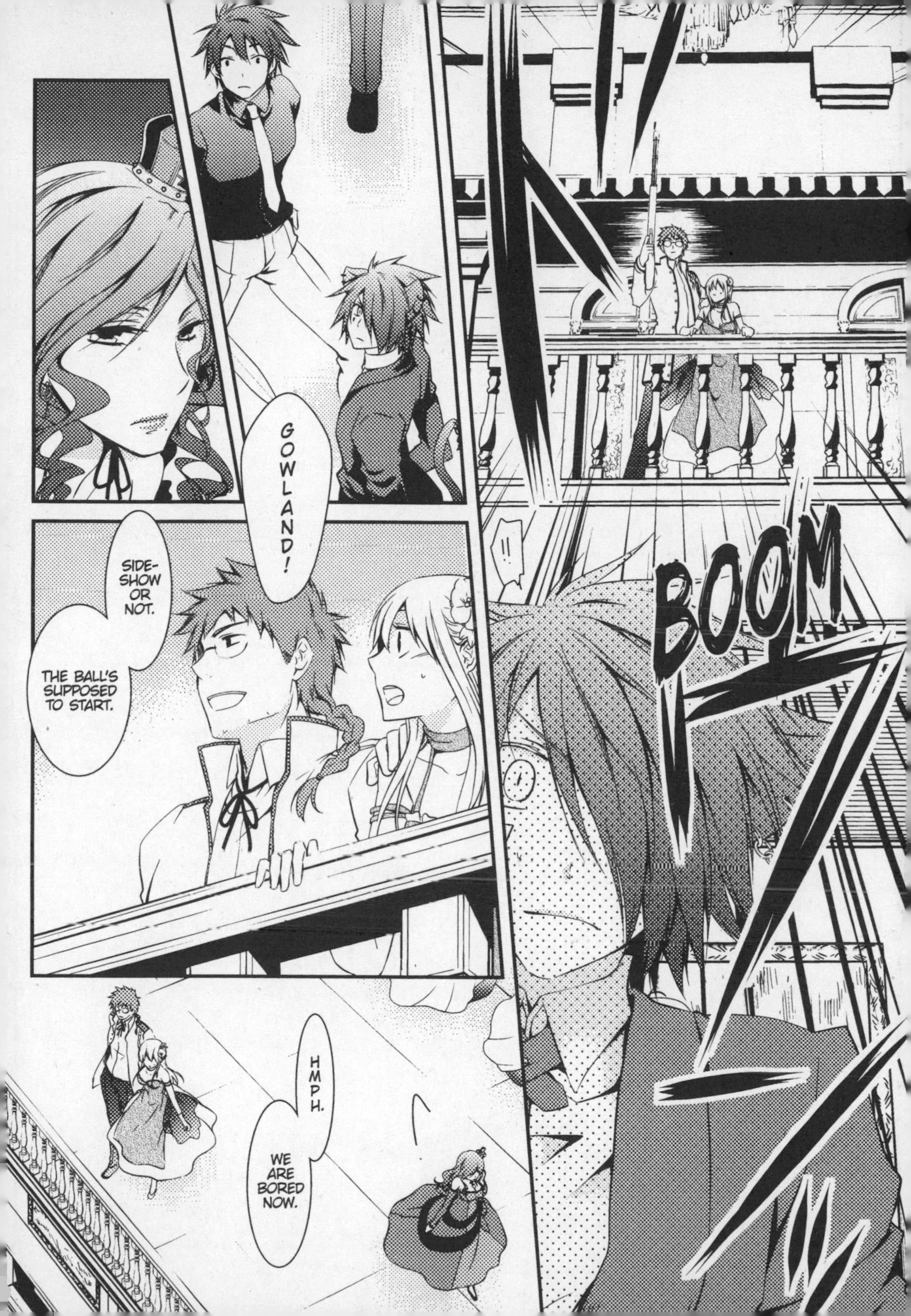
!!
BOOM
!
GOWLAND!
SIDE-SHOW OR NOT.
THE BALL'S SUPPOSED TO START.
HMPH.
WE ARE BORED NOW.

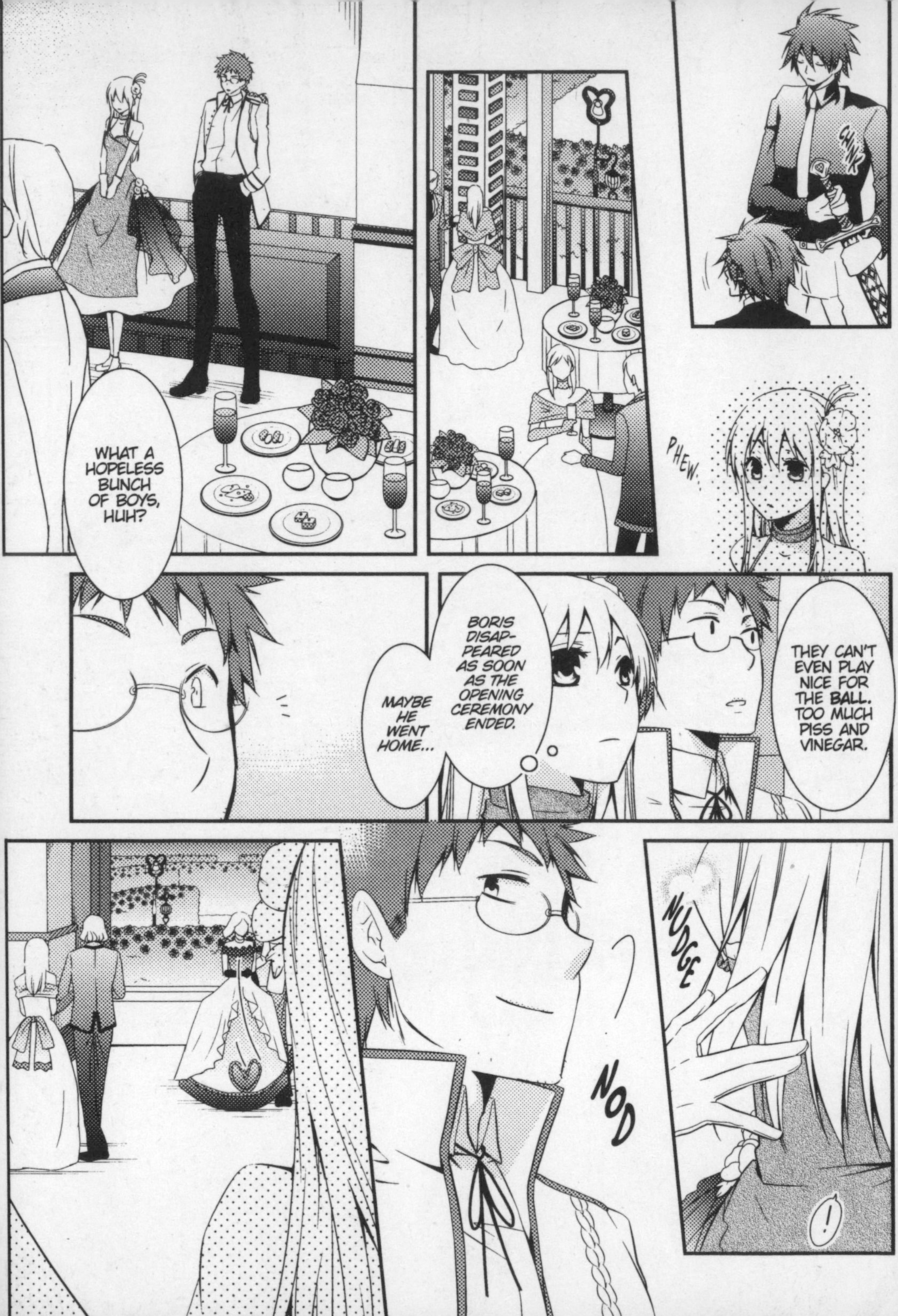
CHINK
PHEW...
WHAT A HOPELESS BUNCH OF BOYS, HUH?
THEY CAN'T EVEN PLAY NICE FOR THE BALL. TOO MUCH PISS AND VINEGAR.
BORIS DISAPPEARED AS SOON AS THE OPENING CEREMONY ENDED.
MAYBE HE WENT HOME...
NUDGE
!
NOD

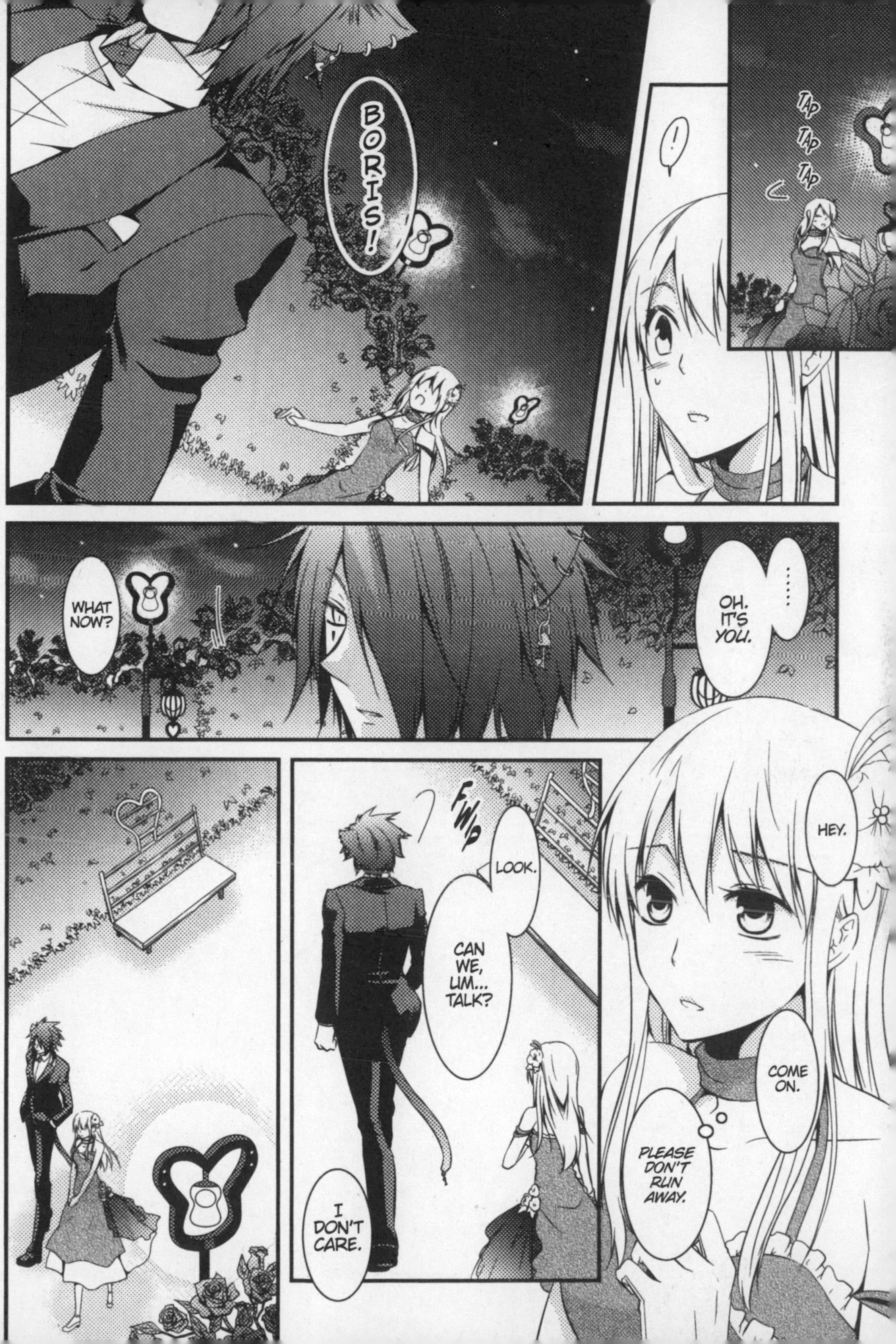
TAP
TAP
TAP
!
BORIS!
......
OH. IT'S YOU.
WHAT NOW?
HEY.
COME ON.
PLEASE DON'T RUN AWAY.
FWIP
LOOK.
CAN WE, UM... TALK?
I DON'T CARE.

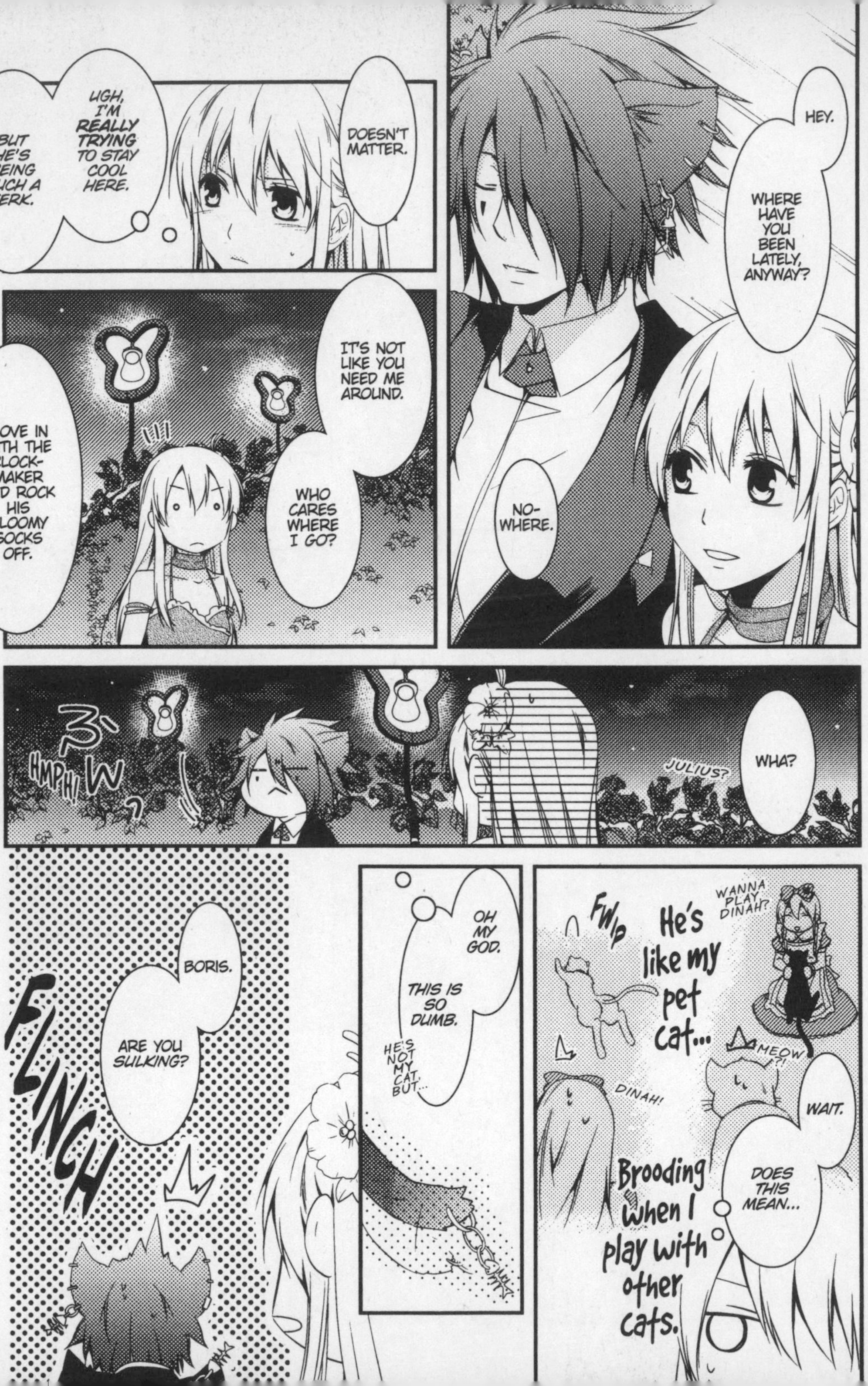
HEY.
WHERE HAVE YOU BEEN LATELY, ANYWAY?
NO-WHERE.
DOESN'T MATTER.
UGH, I'M REALLY TRYING TO STAY COOL HERE.
BUT HE'S BEING SUCH A JERK.
IT'S NOT LIKE YOU NEED ME AROUND.
WHO CARES WHERE I GO?
MOVE IN WITH THE CLOCK-MAKER AND ROCK HIS GLOOMY SOCKS OFF.
!!!
WHA?
JULIUS?
HMPH!
WANNA PLAY DINAH?
FWIP
He's like my pet cat...
MEOW?!
DINAH!
WAIT.
DOES THIS MEAN...
Brooding when I play with other cats.
OH MY GOD.
THIS IS SO DUMB.
HE'S NOT MY CAT, BUT...
BORIS.
ARE YOU SULKING?
FLINCH

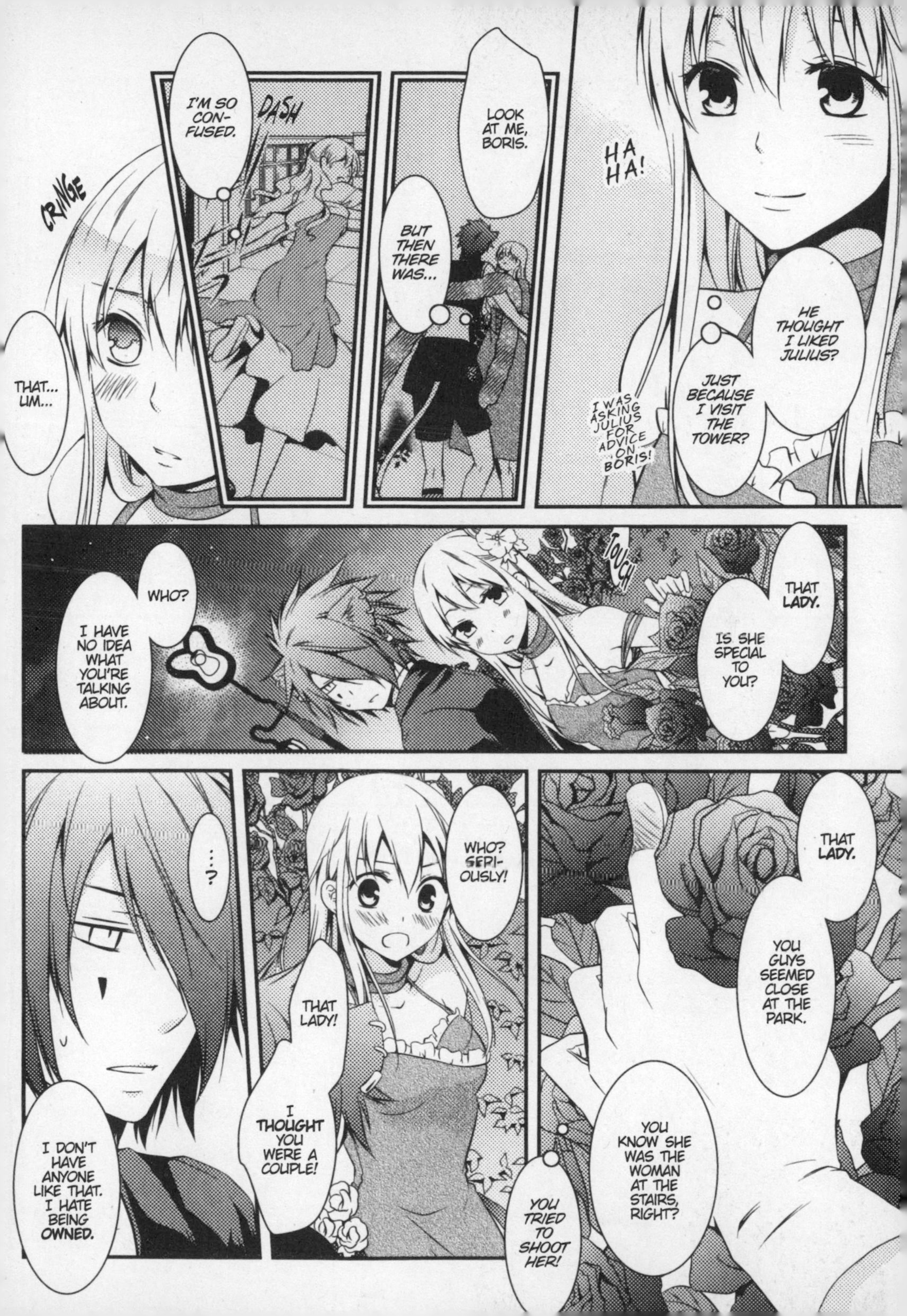
HA HA!
HE THOUGHT I LIKED JULIUS?
JUST BECAUSE I VISIT THE TOWER?
I WAS ASKING JULIUS FOR ADVICE ON BORIS!
LOOK AT ME, BORIS.
BUT THEN THERE WAS...
DASH
I'M SO CONFUSED.
CRINGE
THAT... UM...
TOUCH
THAT LADY.
IS SHE SPECIAL TO YOU?
WHO?
I HAVE NO IDEA WHAT YOU'RE TALKING ABOUT.
THAT LADY.
YOU GUYS SEEMED CLOSE AT THE PARK.
YOU KNOW SHE WAS THE WOMAN AT THE STAIRS, RIGHT?
YOU TRIED TO SHOOT HER!
WHO? SERIOUSLY!
THAT LADY!
I THOUGHT YOU WERE A COUPLE!
...?
I DON'T HAVE ANYONE LIKE THAT. I HATE BEING OWNED.

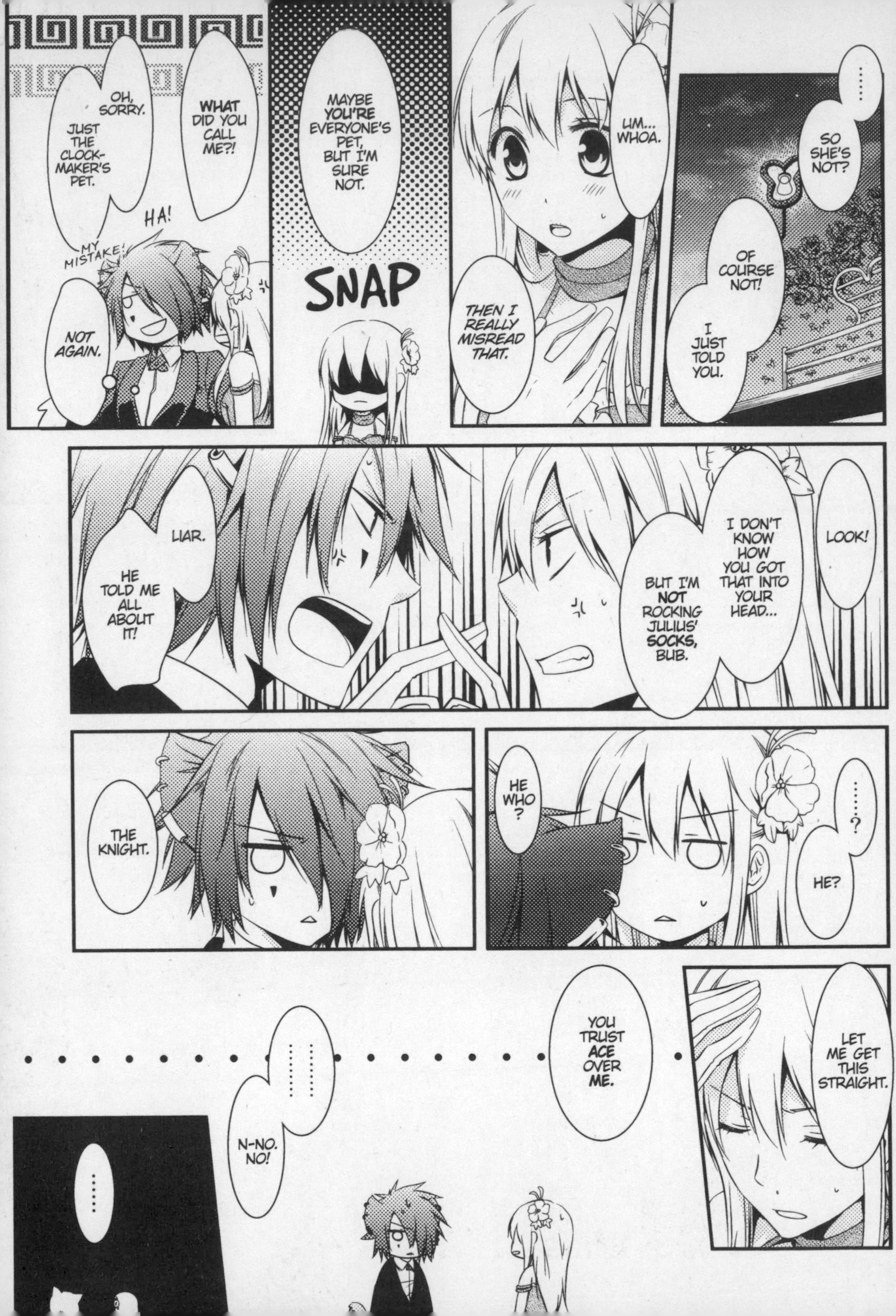
......
SO SHE'S NOT?
OF COURSE NOT!
I JUST TOLD YOU.
UM... WHOA.
THEN I REALLY MISREAD THAT.
MAYBE YOU'RE EVERYONE'S PET, BUT I'M SURE NOT.
SNAP
WHAT DID YOU CALL ME?!
OH, SORRY. JUST THE CLOCK-MAKER'S PET.
HA! MY MISTAKE!
NOT AGAIN.
LOOK!
I DON'T KNOW HOW YOU GOT THAT INTO YOUR HEAD...
BUT I'M NOT ROCKING JULIUS' SOCKS, BUB.
LIAR.
HE TOLD ME ALL ABOUT IT!
......?
HE?
HE WHO?
THE KNIGHT.
LET ME GET THIS STRAIGHT.
YOU TRUST ACE OVER ME.
......
N-NO. NO!
......

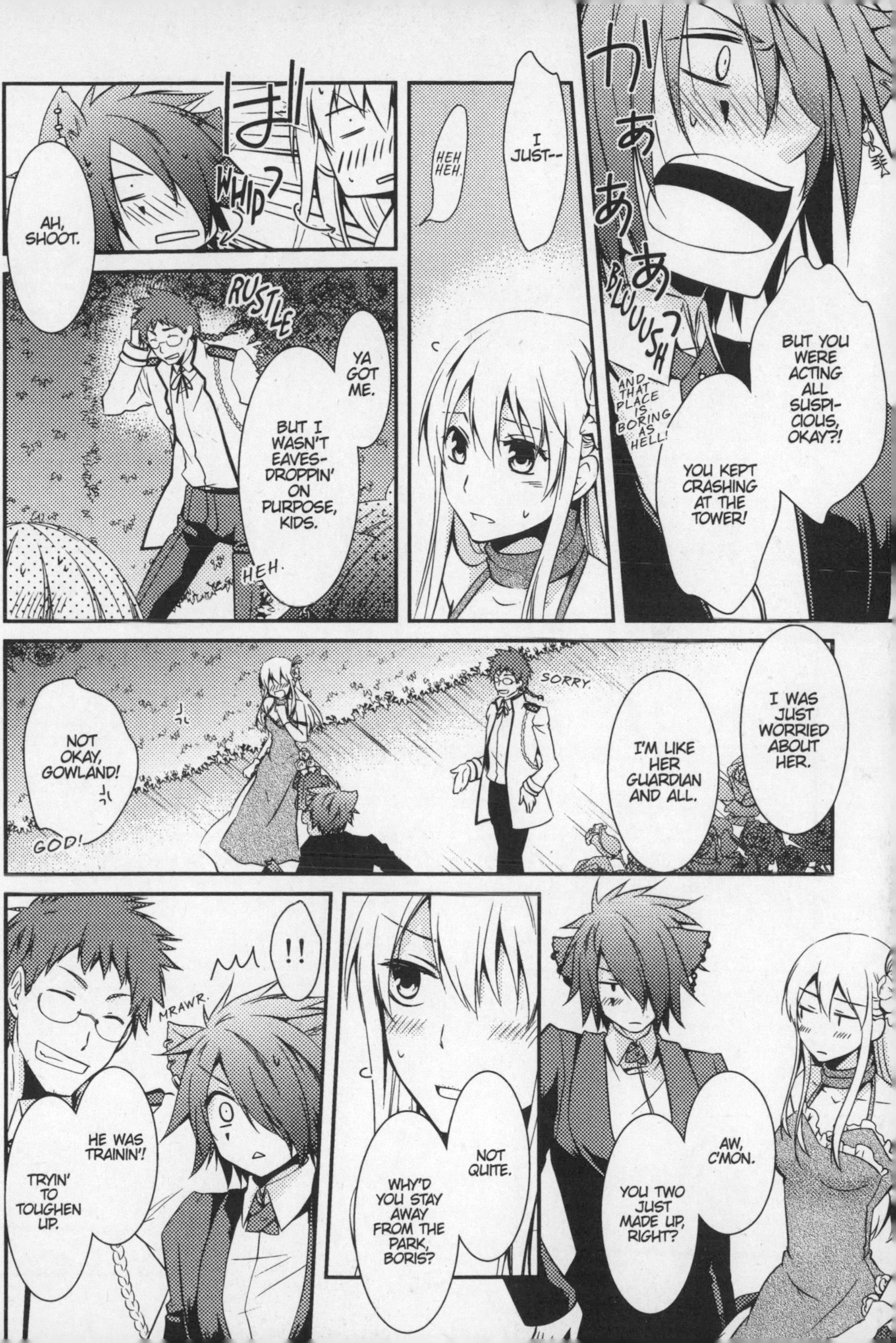
かぁぁぁ
BLUUUSH
BUT YOU WERE ACTING ALL SUSPICIOUS, OKAY?!
AND THAT PLACE IS BORING AS HELL!
YOU KEPT CRASHING AT THE TOWER!
I JUST--
HEH HEH.
は!!
WHIP
AH, SHOOT.
RUSTLE
YA GOT ME.
BUT I WASN'T EAVES-DROPPIN' ON PURPOSE, KIDS.
HEH.
I WAS JUST WORRIED ABOUT HER.
I'M LIKE HER GUARDIAN AND ALL.
SORRY.
NOT OKAY, GOWLAND!
GOD!
AW, C'MON.
YOU TWO JUST MADE UP, RIGHT?
NOT QUITE.
WHY'D YOU STAY AWAY FROM THE PARK, BORIS?
!!
MRAWR.
HE WAS TRAININ'!
TRYIN' TO TOUGHEN UP.

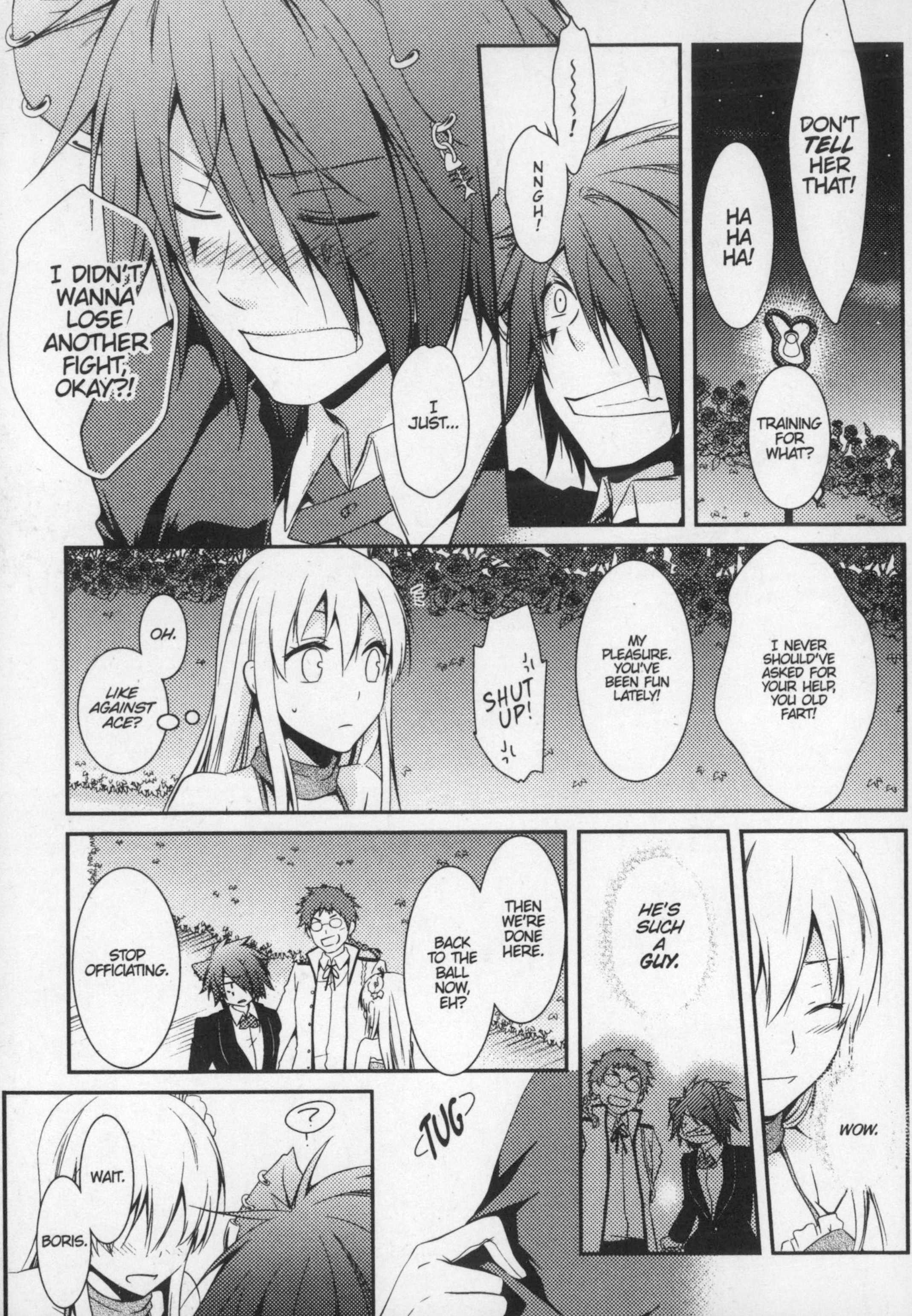
DON'T TELL HER THAT!
HA HA HA HA!
TRAINING FOR WHAT?
NNGH!
I JUST...
I DIDN'T WANNA LOSE ANOTHER FIGHT, OKAY?!
I NEVER SHOULD'VE ASKED FOR YOUR HELP, YOU OLD FART!
MY PLEASURE. YOU'VE BEEN FUN LATELY!
SHUT UP!
OH.
LIKE AGAINST ACE?
HE'S SUCH A GUY.
WOW.
THEN WE'RE DONE HERE.
BACK TO THE BALL NOW, EH?
STOP OFFICIATING.
TUG
?
WAIT.
BORIS.

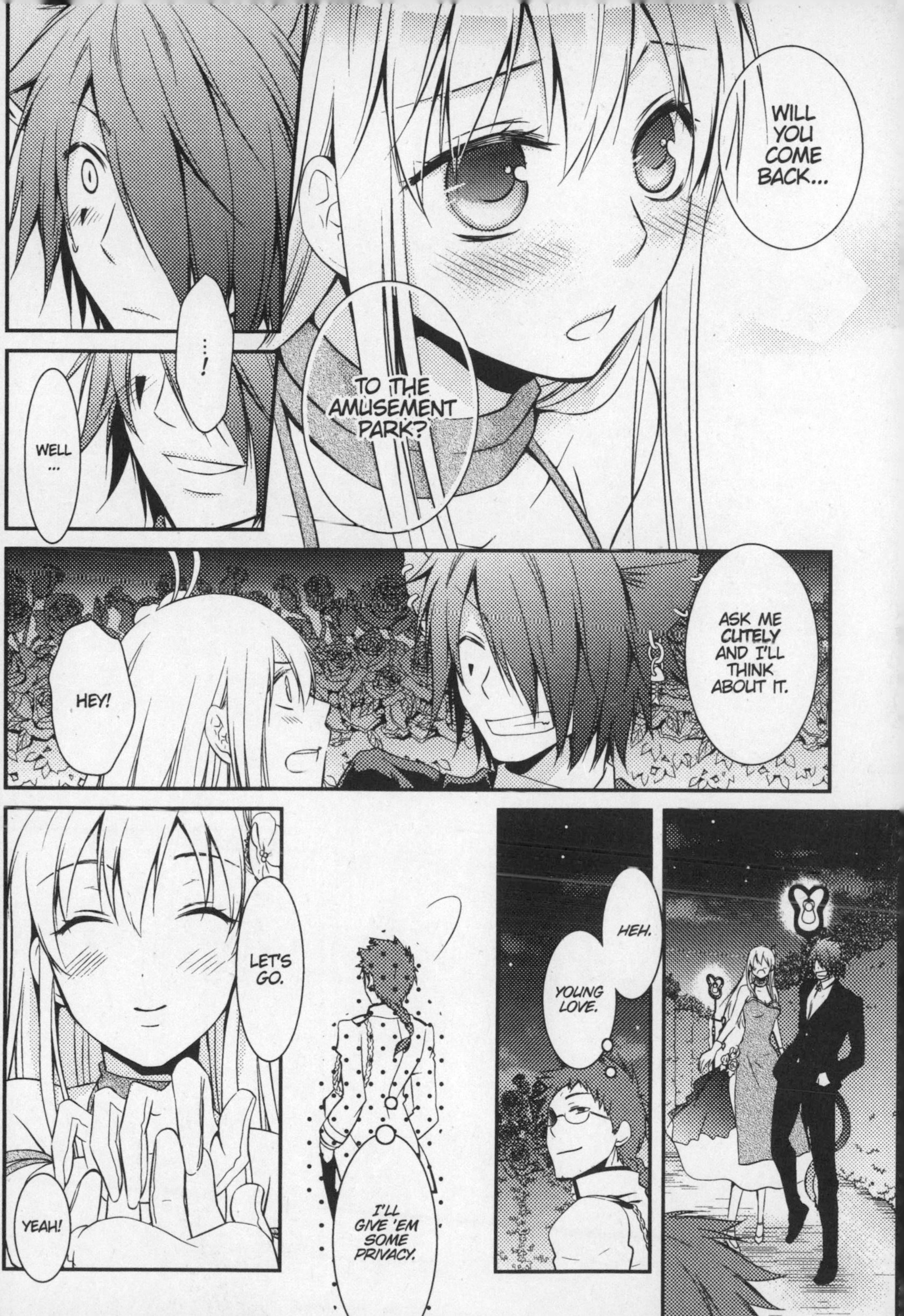
WILL YOU COME BACK...
TO THE AMUSEMENT PARK?
...!
WELL ...
ASK ME CUTELY AND I'LL THINK ABOUT IT.
HEY!
HEH.
YOUNG LOVE.
I'LL GIVE 'EM SOME PRIVACY.
LET'S GO.
YEAH!

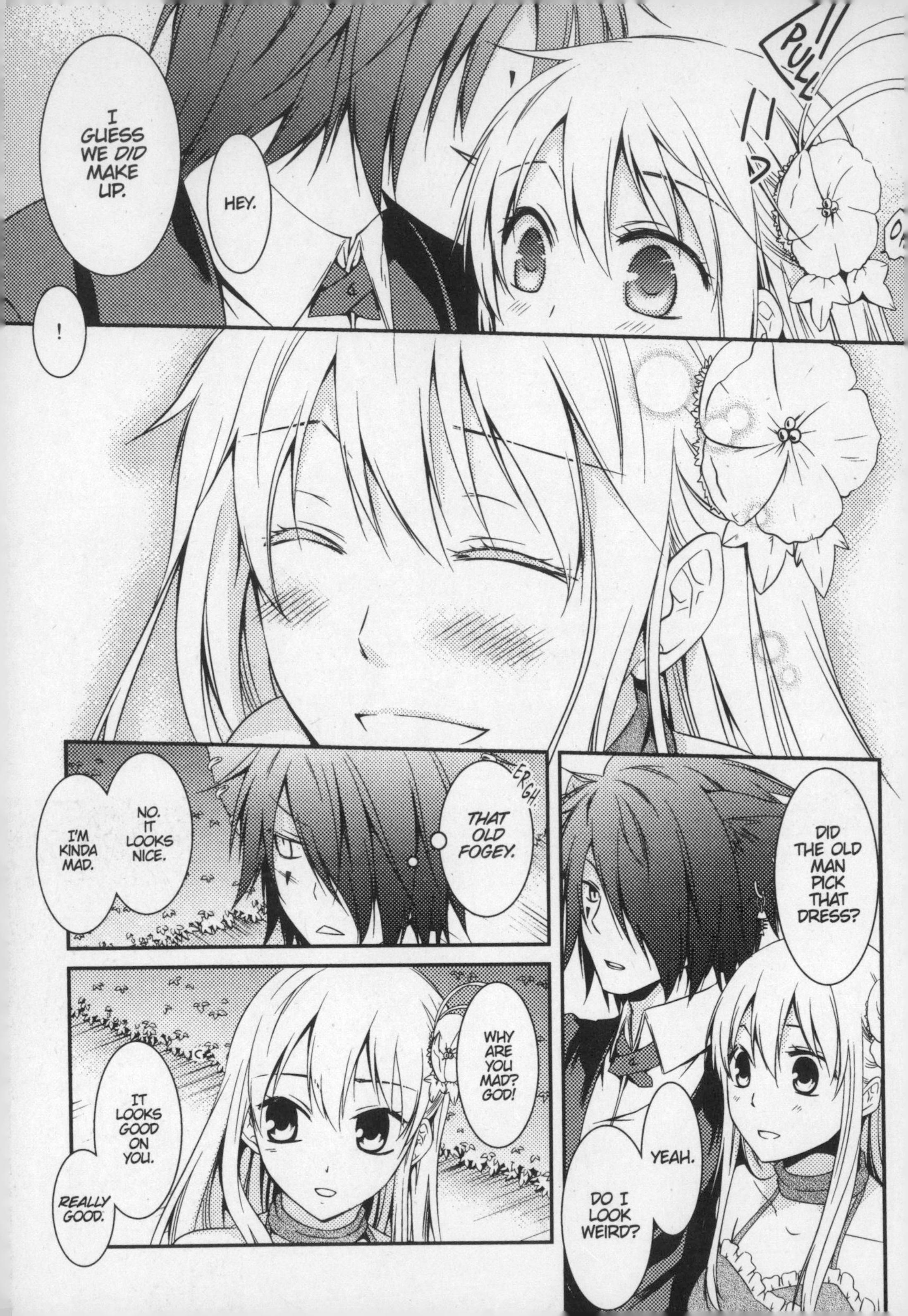
PULL
HEY.
I GUESS WE DID MAKE UP.
!
DID THE OLD MAN PICK THAT DRESS?
YEAH.
DO I LOOK WEIRD?
ERGH.
THAT OLD FOGEY.
NO. IT LOOKS NICE.
I'M KINDA MAD.
WHY ARE YOU MAD? GOD!
IT LOOKS GOOD ON YOU.
REALLY GOOD.

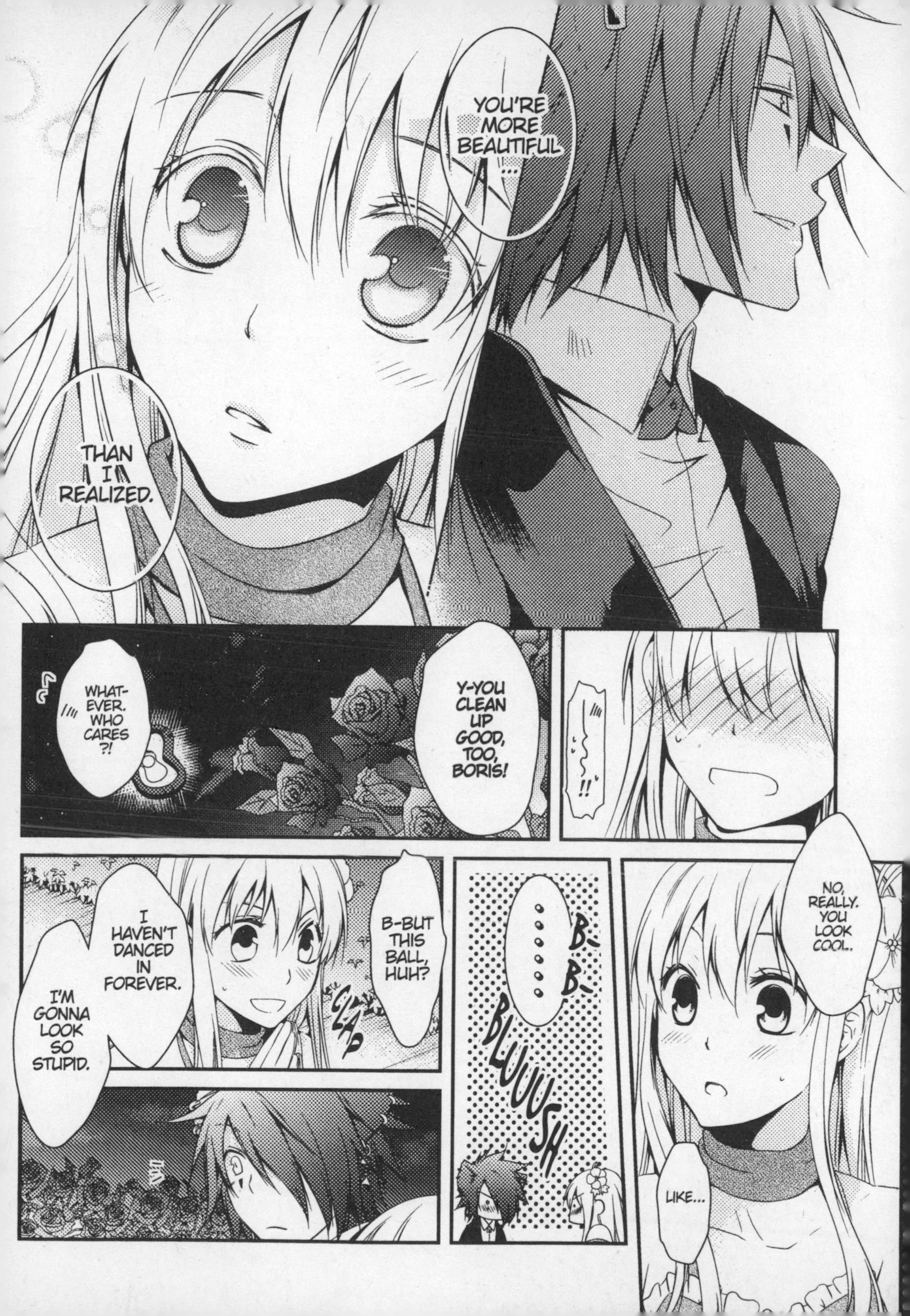
YOU'RE MORE BEAUTIFUL...
THAN I REALIZED.
Y-YOU CLEAN UP GOOD, TOO, BORIS!
WHAT-EVER. WHO CARES?!
NO, REALLY. YOU LOOK COOL.
LIKE...
......
B-B-BLUUUSH
B-BUT THIS BALL, HUH?
I HAVEN'T DANCED IN FOREVER.
I'M GONNA LOOK SO STUPID.
CLAP

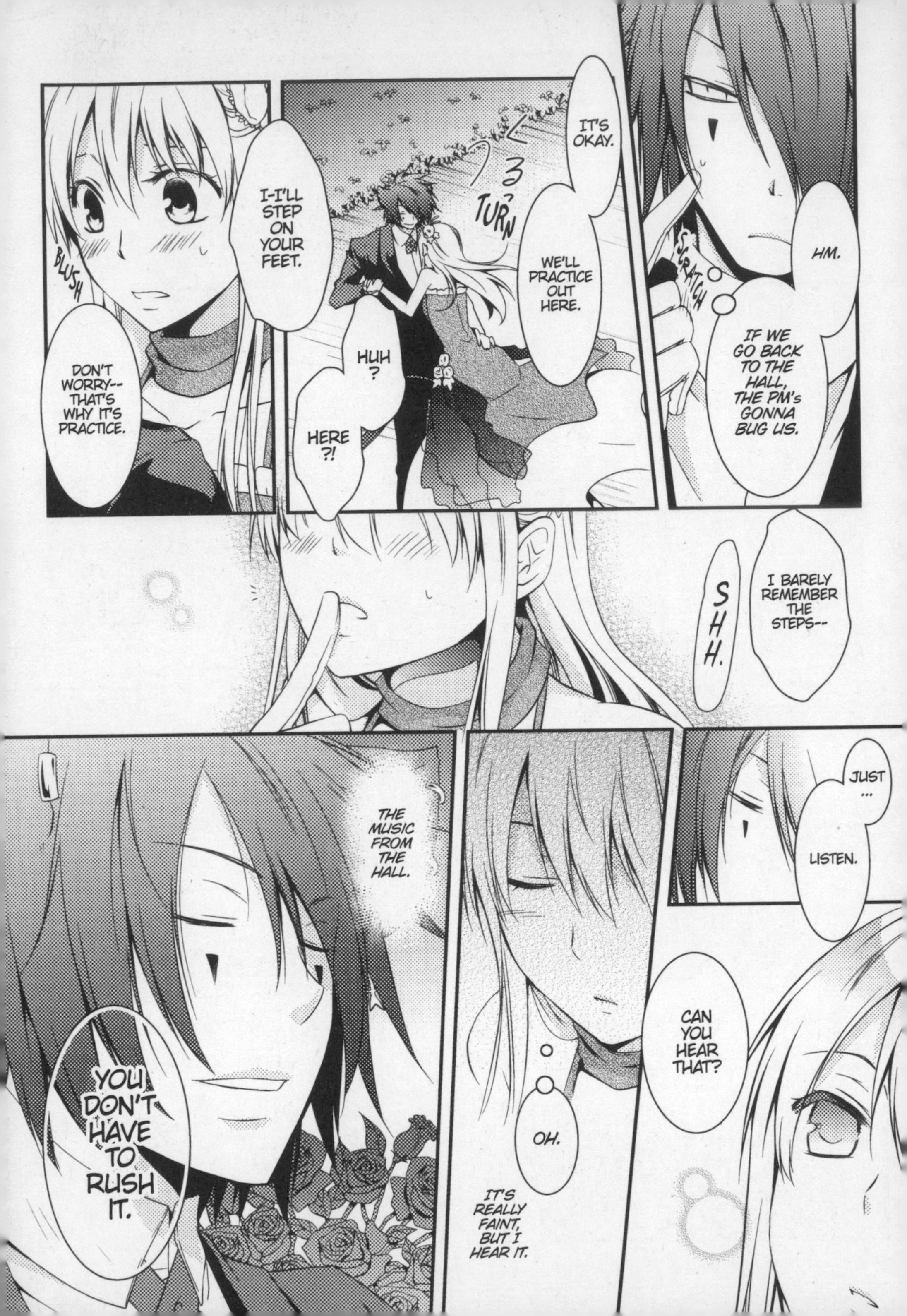
HM.
SCRATCH
IF WE GO BACK TO THE HALL, THE PM's GONNA BUG US.
IT'S OKAY.
WE'LL PRACTICE OUT HERE.
TURN
HUH?
HERE?!
I-I'LL STEP ON YOUR FEET.
BLUSH
DON'T WORRY--THAT'S WHY IT'S PRACTICE.
I BARELY REMEMBER THE STEPS--
SHH.
JUST...
LISTEN.
CAN YOU HEAR THAT?
OH.
IT'S REALLY FAINT, BUT I HEAR IT.
THE MUSIC FROM THE HALL.
YOU DON'T HAVE TO RUSH IT.

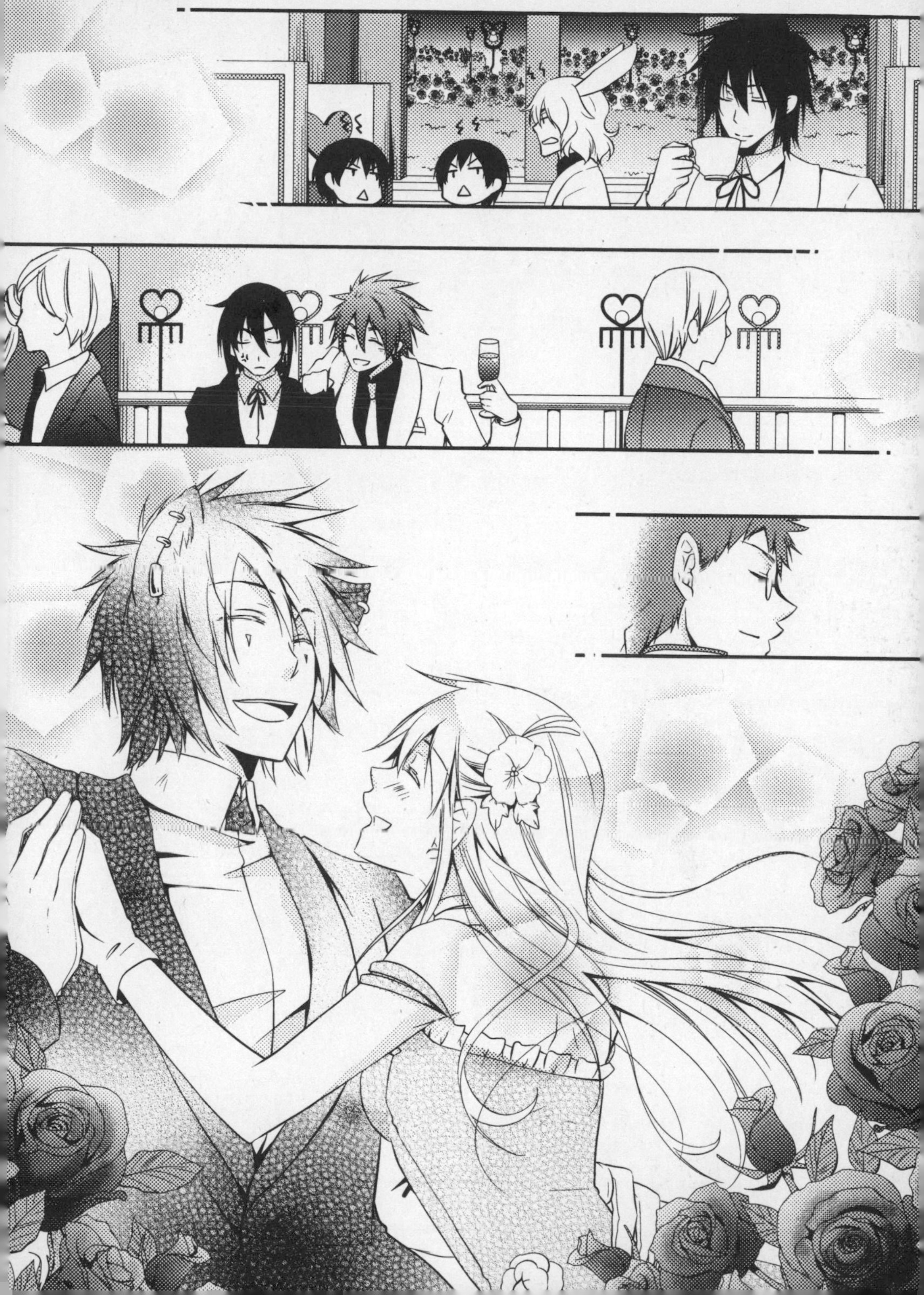

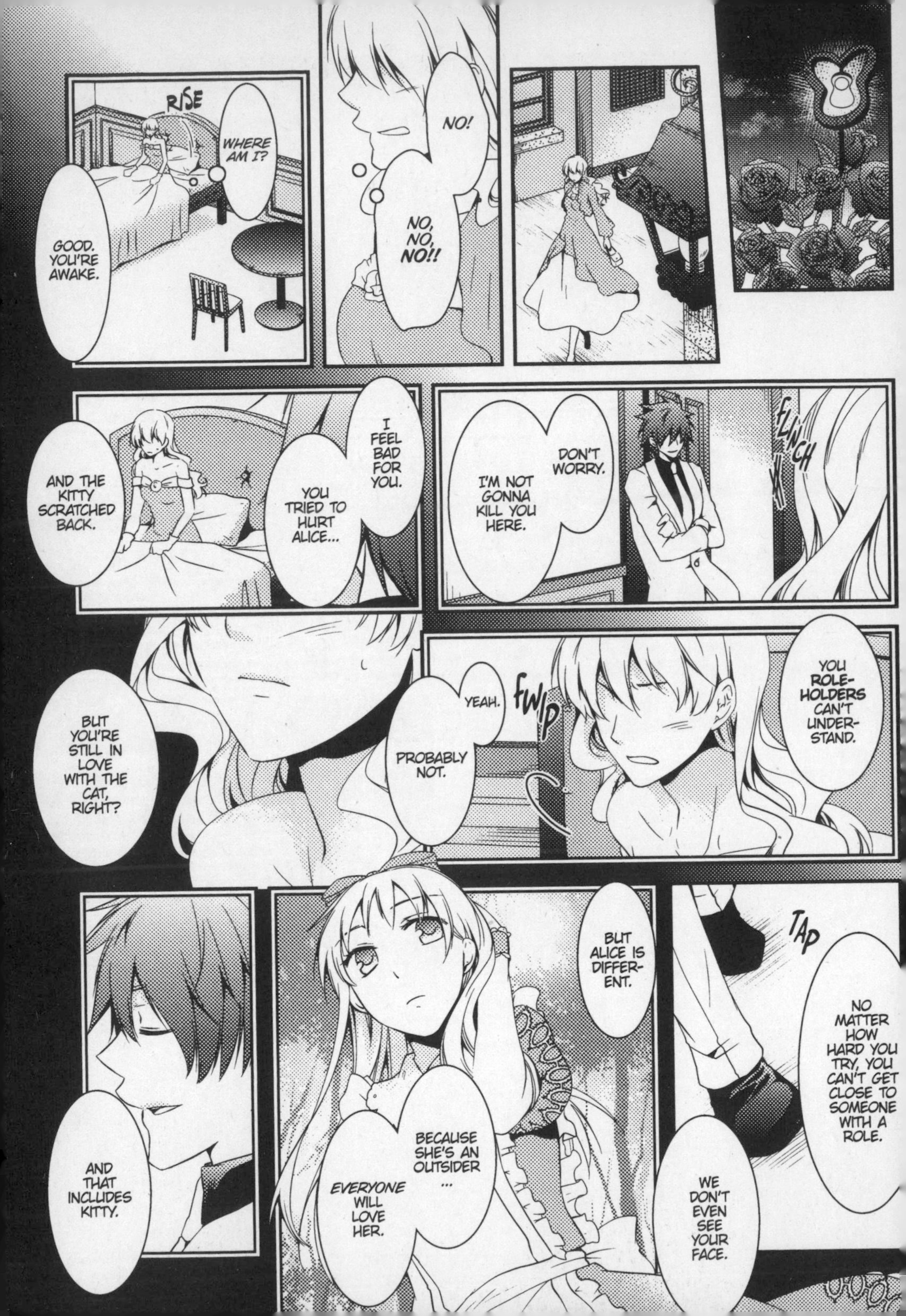
NO!
NO, NO, NO!!
RISE
WHERE AM I?
GOOD. YOU'RE AWAKE.
FLINCH
DON'T WORRY.
I'M NOT GONNA KILL YOU HERE.
I FEEL BAD FOR YOU.
YOU TRIED TO HURT ALICE...
AND THE KITTY SCRATCHED BACK.
YOU ROLE-HOLDERS CAN'T UNDER-STAND.
FWIP
YEAH.
PROBABLY NOT.
BUT YOU'RE STILL IN LOVE WITH THE CAT, RIGHT?
TAP
NO MATTER HOW HARD YOU TRY, YOU CAN'T GET CLOSE TO SOMEONE WITH A ROLE.
WE DON'T EVEN SEE YOUR FACE.
BUT ALICE IS DIFFER-ENT.
BECAUSE SHE'S AN OUTSIDER ...
EVERYONE WILL LOVE HER.
AND THAT INCLUDES KITTY.

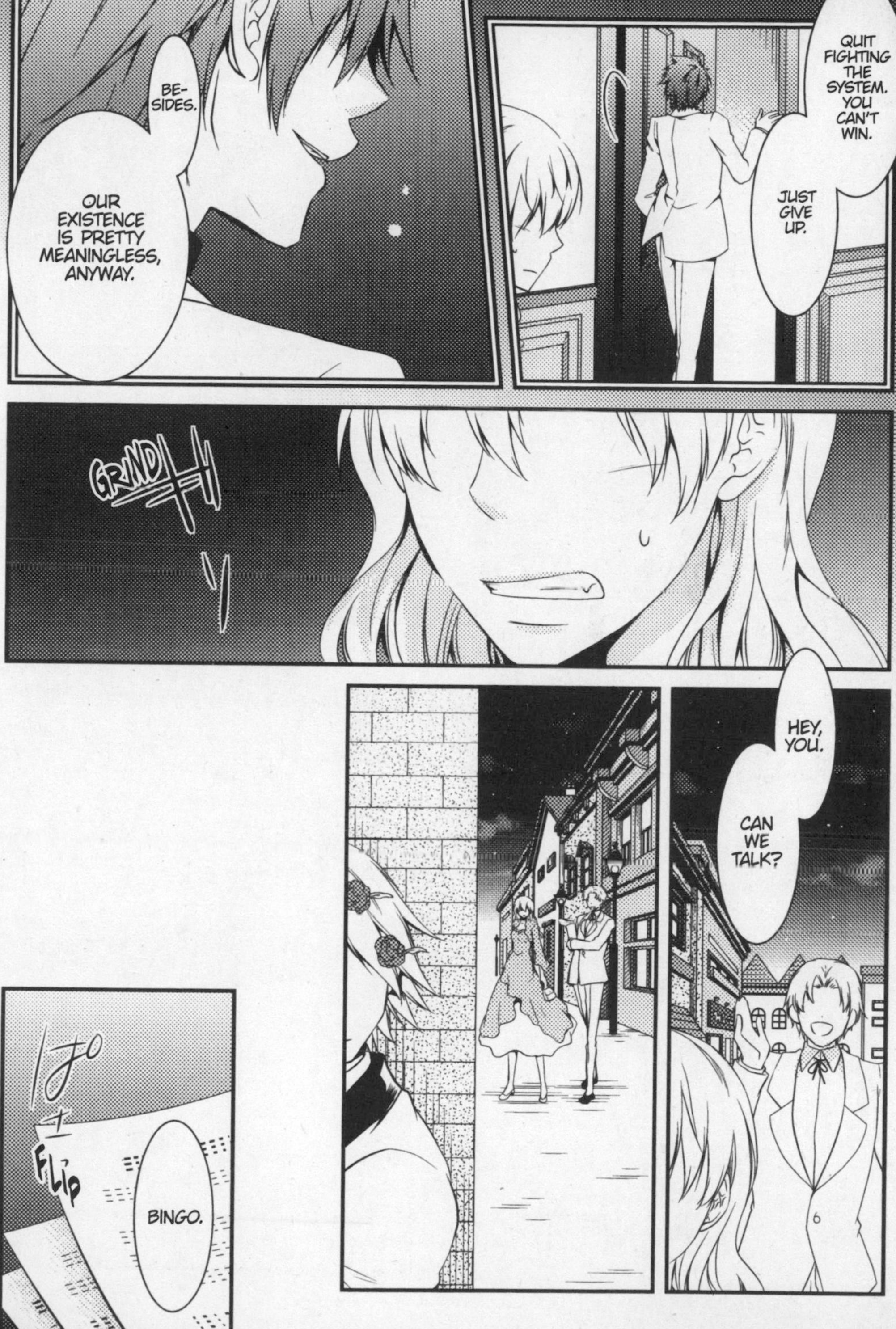
QUIT FIGHTING THE SYSTEM. YOU CAN'T WIN.
JUST GIVE UP.
BE-SIDES.
OUR EXISTENCE IS PRETTY MEANINGLESS, ANYWAY.
GRIND
HEY, YOU.
CAN WE TALK?
FLIP
BINGO.

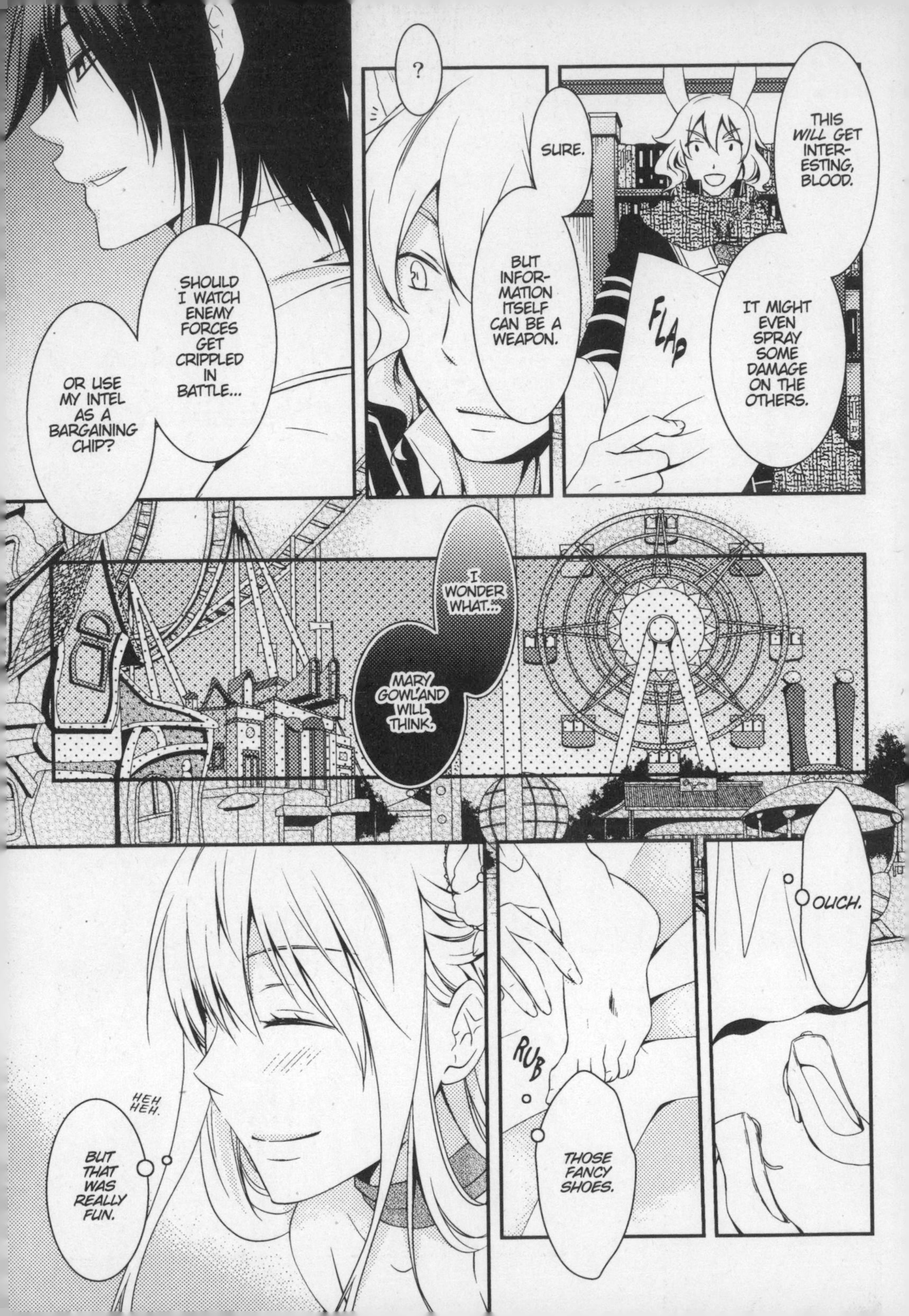
THIS WILL GET INTER-ESTING, BLOOD.
IT MIGHT EVEN SPRAY SOME DAMAGE ON THE OTHERS.
FLAP
?
SURE.
BUT INFOR-MATION ITSELF CAN BE A WEAPON.
SHOULD I WATCH ENEMY FORCES GET CRIPPLED IN BATTLE...
OR USE MY INTEL AS A BARGAINING CHIP?
I WONDER WHAT...
MARY GOWL'AND WILL THINK.
OUCH.
RUB
THOSE FANCY SHOES.
HEH HEH.
BUT THAT WAS REALLY FUN.

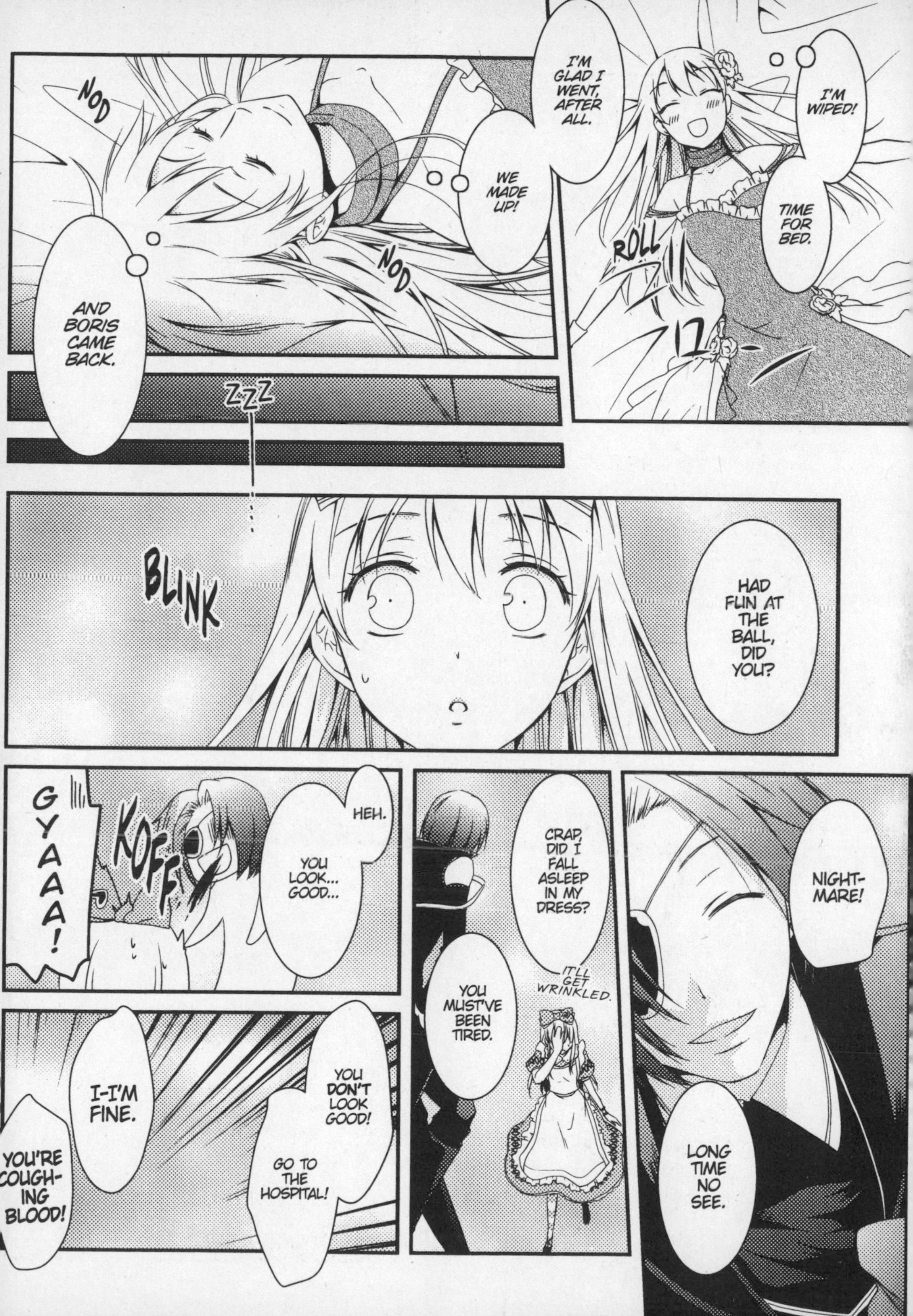
I'M WIPED!
I'M GLAD I WENT, AFTER ALL.
TIME FOR BED.
ROLL
WE MADE UP!
NOD
NOD
AND BORIS CAME BACK.
ZZZ
HAD FUN AT THE BALL, DID YOU?
BLINK
NIGHT-MARE!
LONG TIME NO SEE.
CRAP, DID I FALL ASLEEP IN MY DRESS?
IT'LL GET WRINKLED.
YOU MUST'VE BEEN TIRED.
HEH.
YOU LOOK... GOOD...
KOFF
GYAAAA!
YOU DON'T LOOK GOOD!
GO TO THE HOSPITAL!
I-I'M FINE.
YOU'RE COUGH-ING BLOOD!

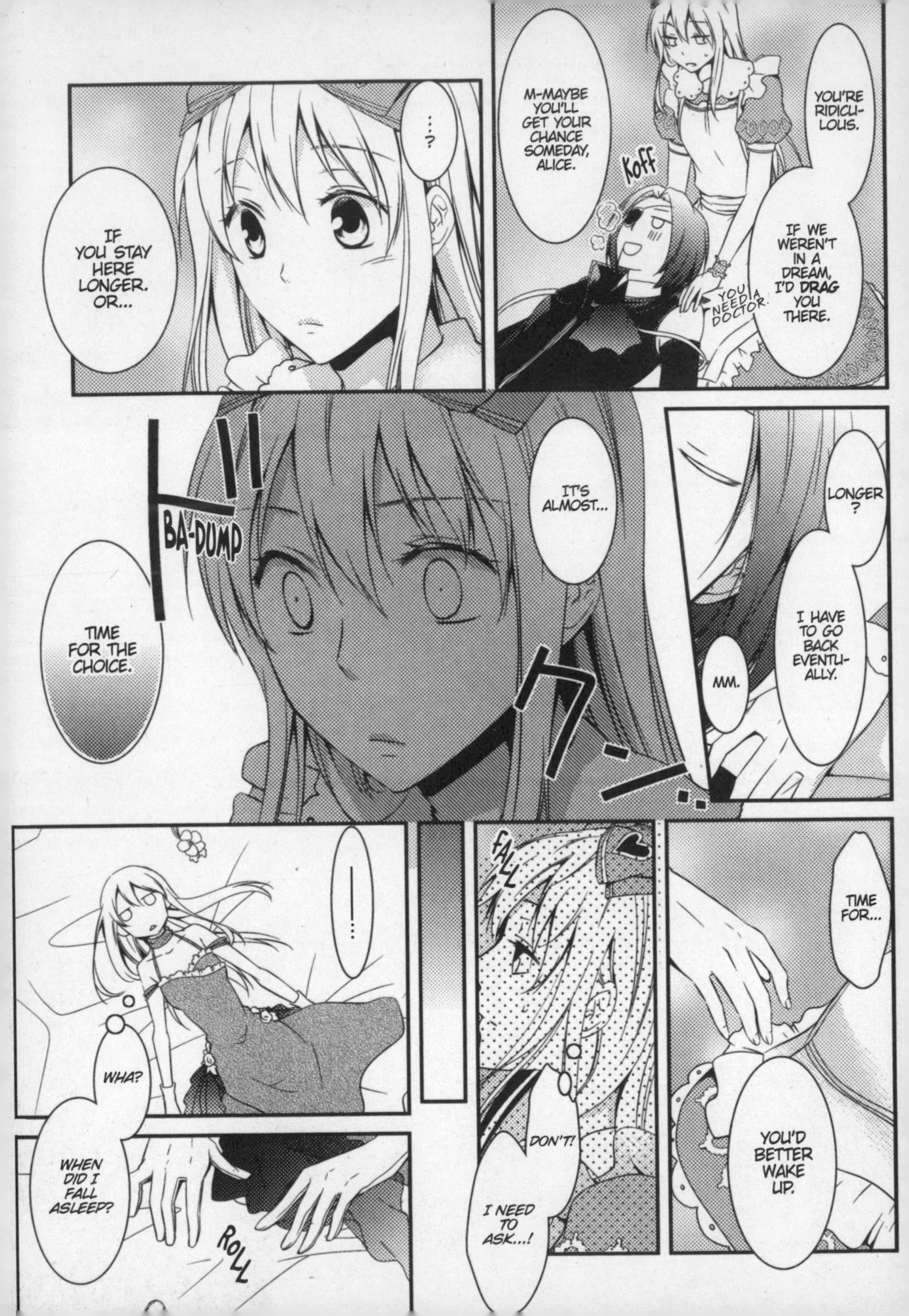
YOU'RE RIDICULOUS.
IF WE WEREN'T IN A DREAM, I'D DRAG YOU THERE.
YOU NEED A DOCTOR.
Koff
M-MAYBE YOU'LL GET YOUR CHANCE SOMEDAY, ALICE.
...?
IF YOU STAY HERE LONGER. OR...
LONGER?
I HAVE TO GO BACK EVENTUALLY.
MM.
IT'S ALMOST...
BA-DUMP
TIME FOR THE CHOICE.
TIME FOR...
YOU'D BETTER WAKE UP.
FALL
DON'T!
I NEED TO ASK...!
—!...
WHA?
WHEN DID I FALL ASLEEP?
ROLL

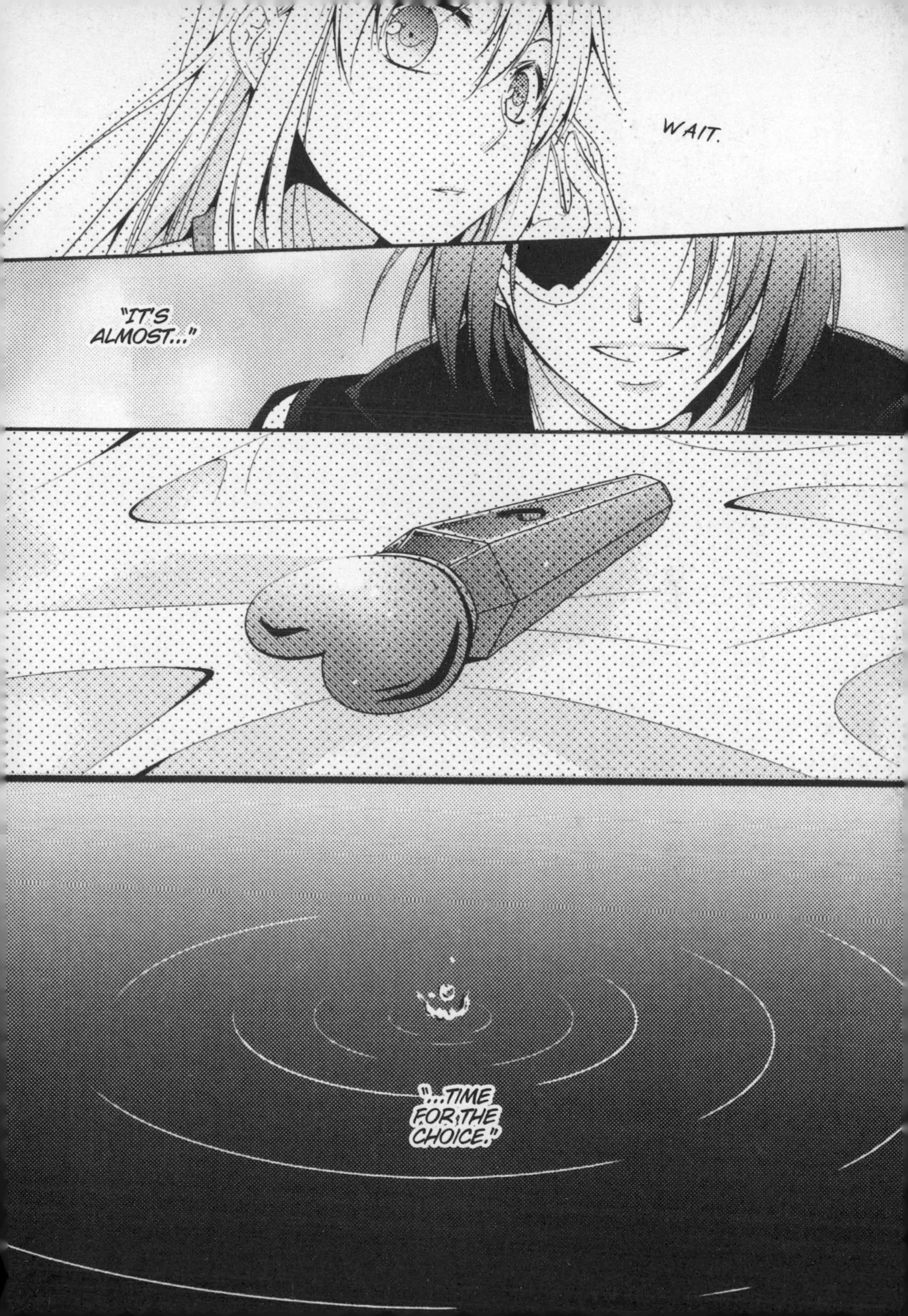
WAIT.
"IT'S ALMOST..."
"...TIME FOR THE CHOICE."

■ Next Volume Preview ■

ORDER COMING!
TAP
TAP
TAP
GASP!
ズルッ
SLIP
GLEAM

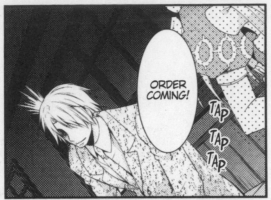

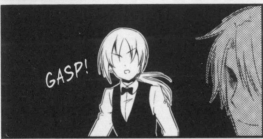

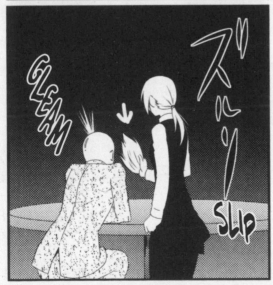

*Actual contents may change without notice.

THE NEXT VOLUME IS THE LAST ONE.
I HOPE YOU STICK WITH ME UNTIL THE END!

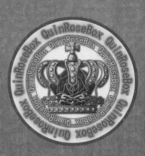

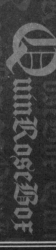

CHESHIRE CAT WALTZ VOL. 6 - POST-MORTEM

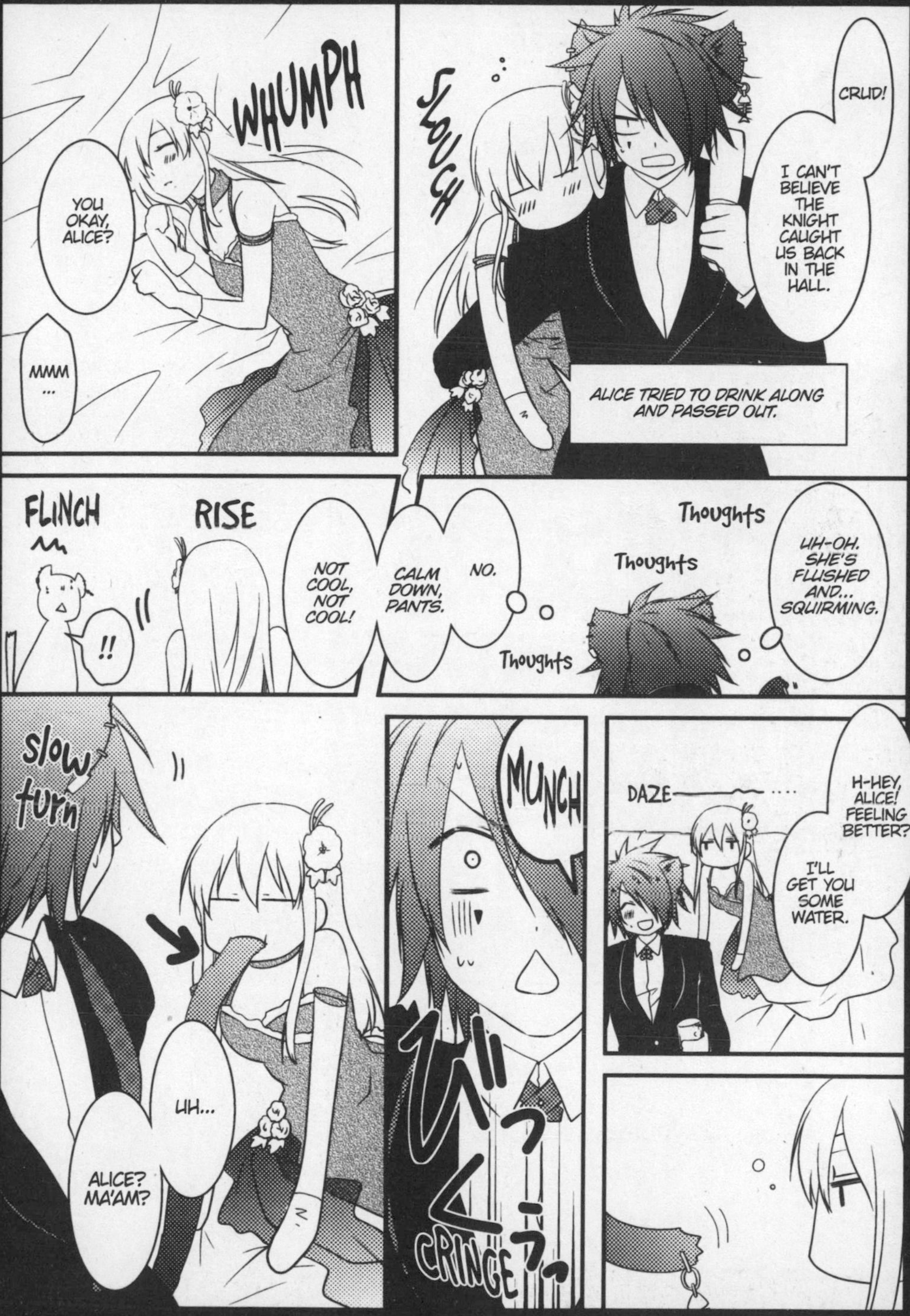
SLOUCH
CRUD!
I CAN'T BELIEVE THE KNIGHT CAUGHT US BACK IN THE HALL.
ALICE TRIED TO DRINK ALONG AND PASSED OUT.
WHUMPH
YOU OKAY, ALICE?
MMM ...
Thoughts
UH-OH. SHE'S FLUSHED AND... SQUIRMING.
Thoughts
Thoughts
NO.
CALM DOWN, PANTS.
NOT COOL, NOT COOL!
RISE
FLINCH
!!
H-HEY, ALICE! FEELING BETTER?
I'LL GET YOU SOME WATER.
DAZE
MUNCH
CRINGE
slow turn
UH...
ALICE? MA'AM?

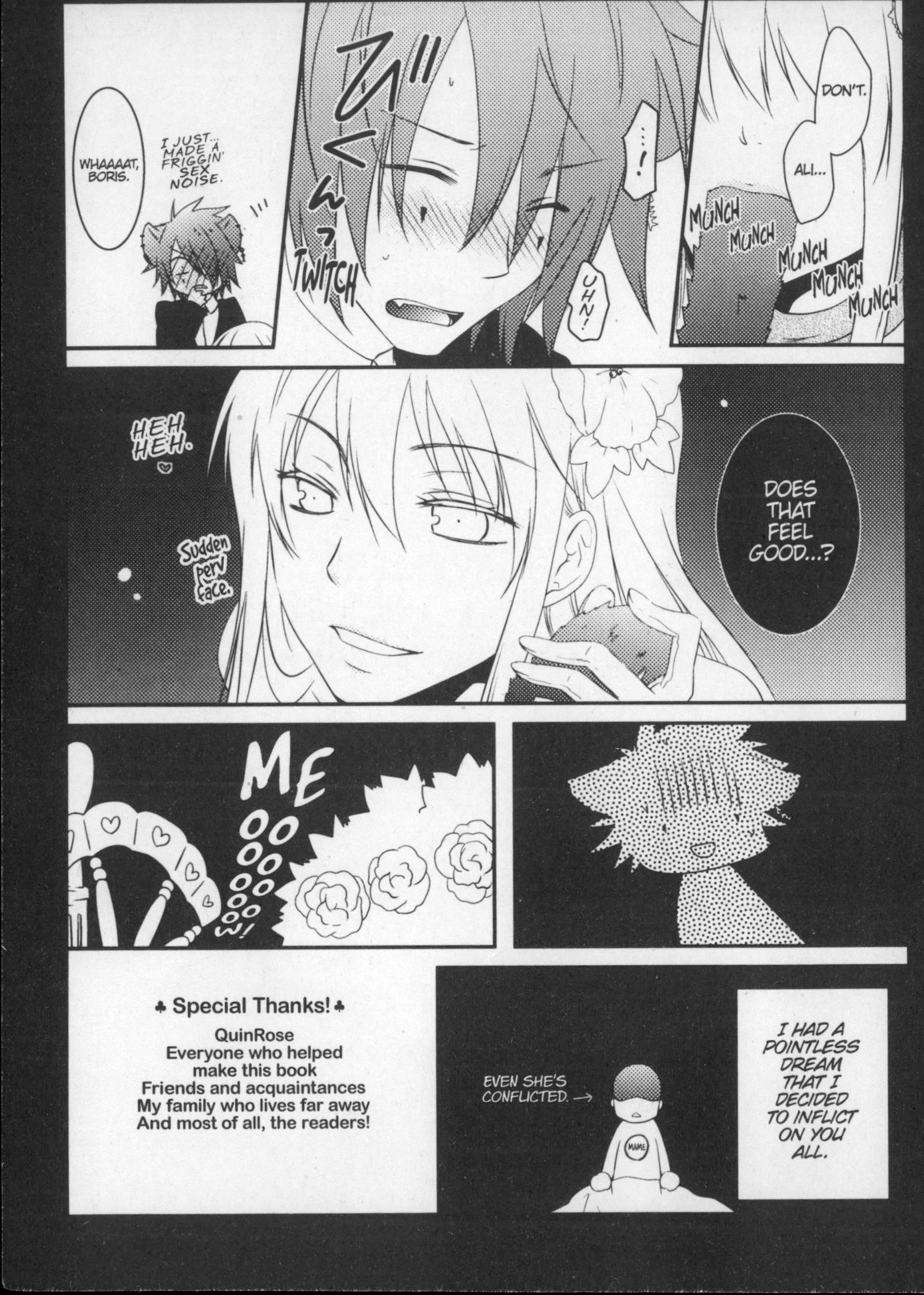
DON'T.
ALI...
MUNCH MUNCH MUNCH MUNCH MUNCH
...!
UHN!
TWITCH
WHAAAAT, BORIS.
I JUST... MADE A FRIGGIN' SEX NOISE.
DOES THAT FEEL GOOD...?
HEH HEH.
Sudden perv face.
MEOOOOOOOOOOOOOOW!
I HAD A POINTLESS DREAM THAT I DECIDED TO INFLICT ON YOU ALL.
EVEN SHE'S CONFLICTED. →
MAME

♣ Special Thanks! ♣

QuinRose
Everyone who helped make this book
Friends and acquaintances
My family who lives far away
And most of all, the readers!

COMING SOON

OCTOBER 2013
Alice in the Country of Joker:
Circus and Liars Game Vol. 3

NOVEMBER 2013
Alice in the Country of Clover:
Cheshire Cat Waltz Vol. 7

Alice in the Country of Hearts:
The Mad Hatter's Late Night
Tea Party Vol. 1

DECEMBER 2013
Alice Love Fables: Toy Box

Crimson Empire Vol. 3

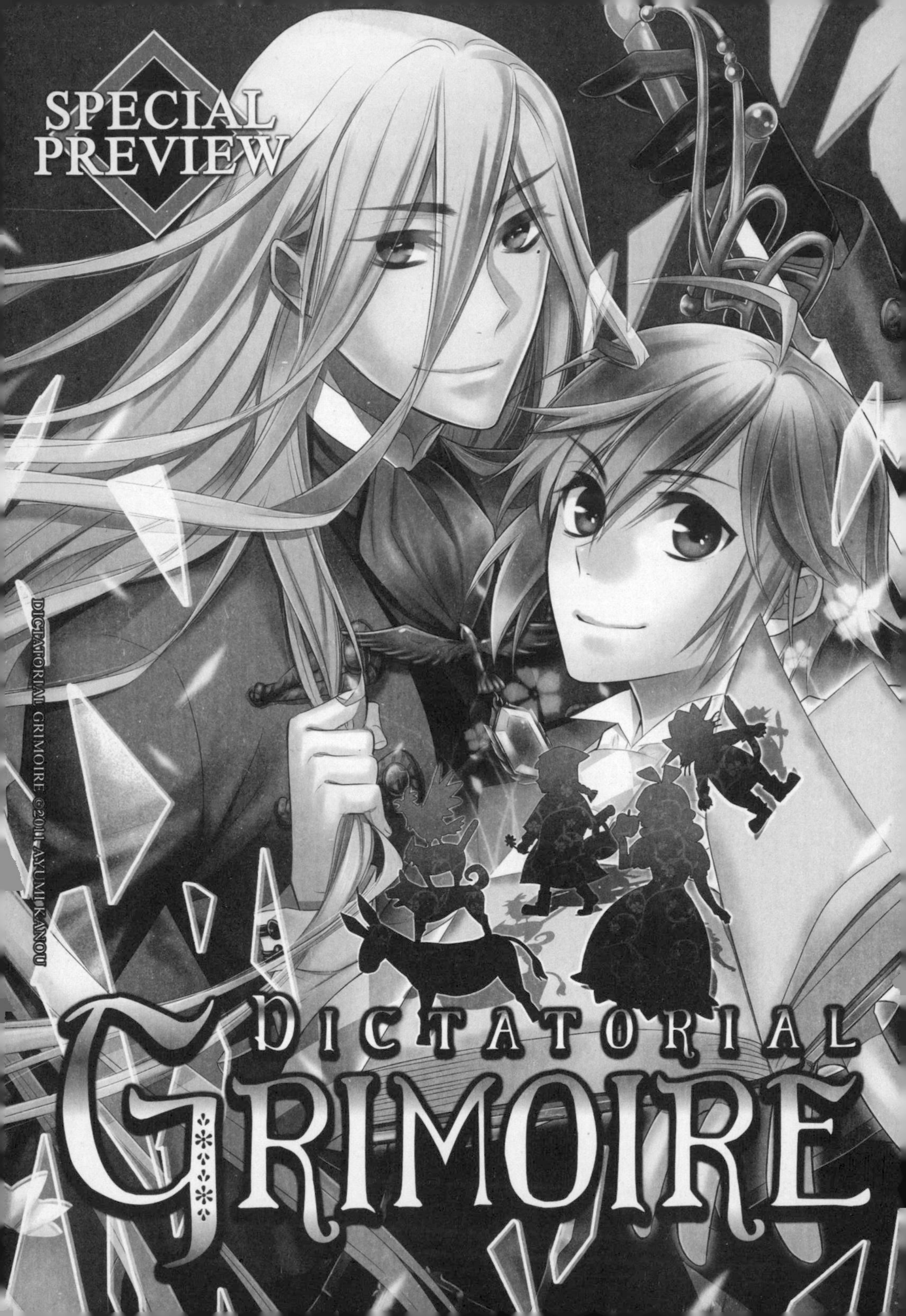
SPECIAL PREVIEW
DICTATORIAL GRIMOIRE
DICTATORIAL GRIMOIRE ©2011 AYUMI KANOU

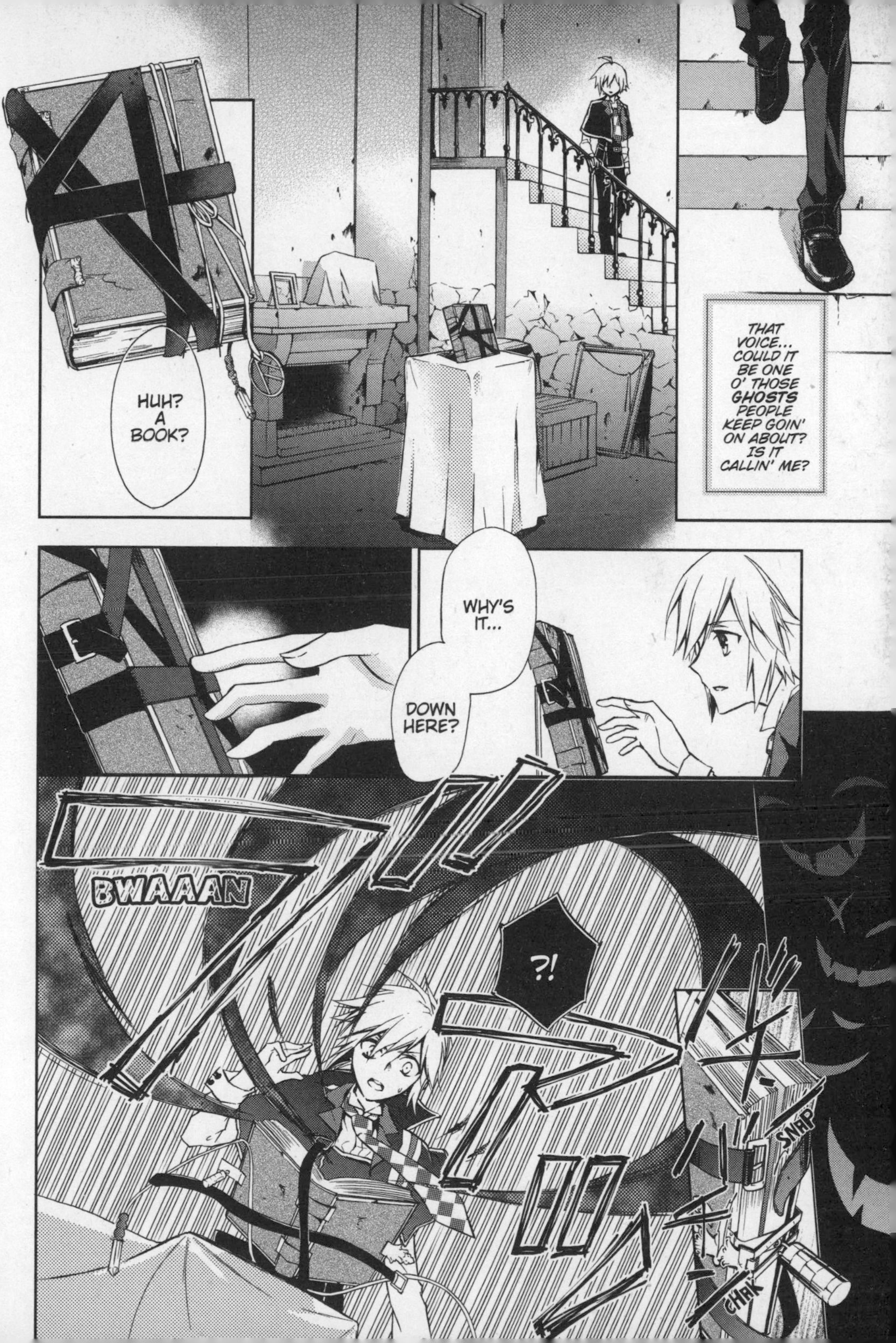
THAT VOICE... COULD IT BE ONE O' THOSE GHOSTS PEOPLE KEEP GOIN' ON ABOUT? IS IT CALLIN' ME?
HUH? A BOOK?
WHY'S IT...
DOWN HERE?
BWAAAN
?!
SNAP
CHAK

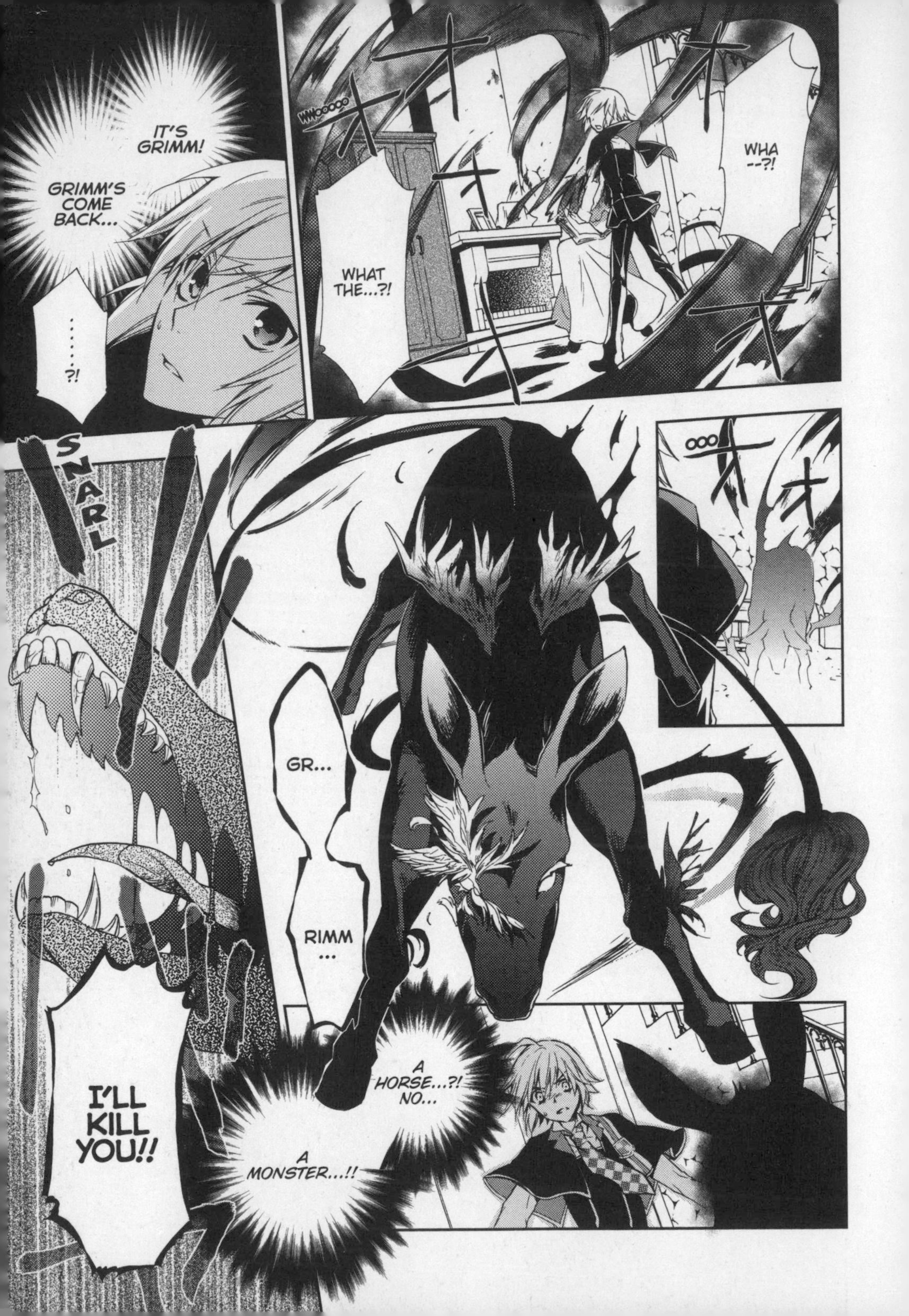
WHOOOOO
WHA --?!
WHAT THE...?!
IT'S GRIMM!
GRIMM'S COME BACK...
......?!
OOO
GR...
RIMM ...
A HORSE...?! NO...
A MONSTER...!!
SNARL
I'LL KILL YOU!!

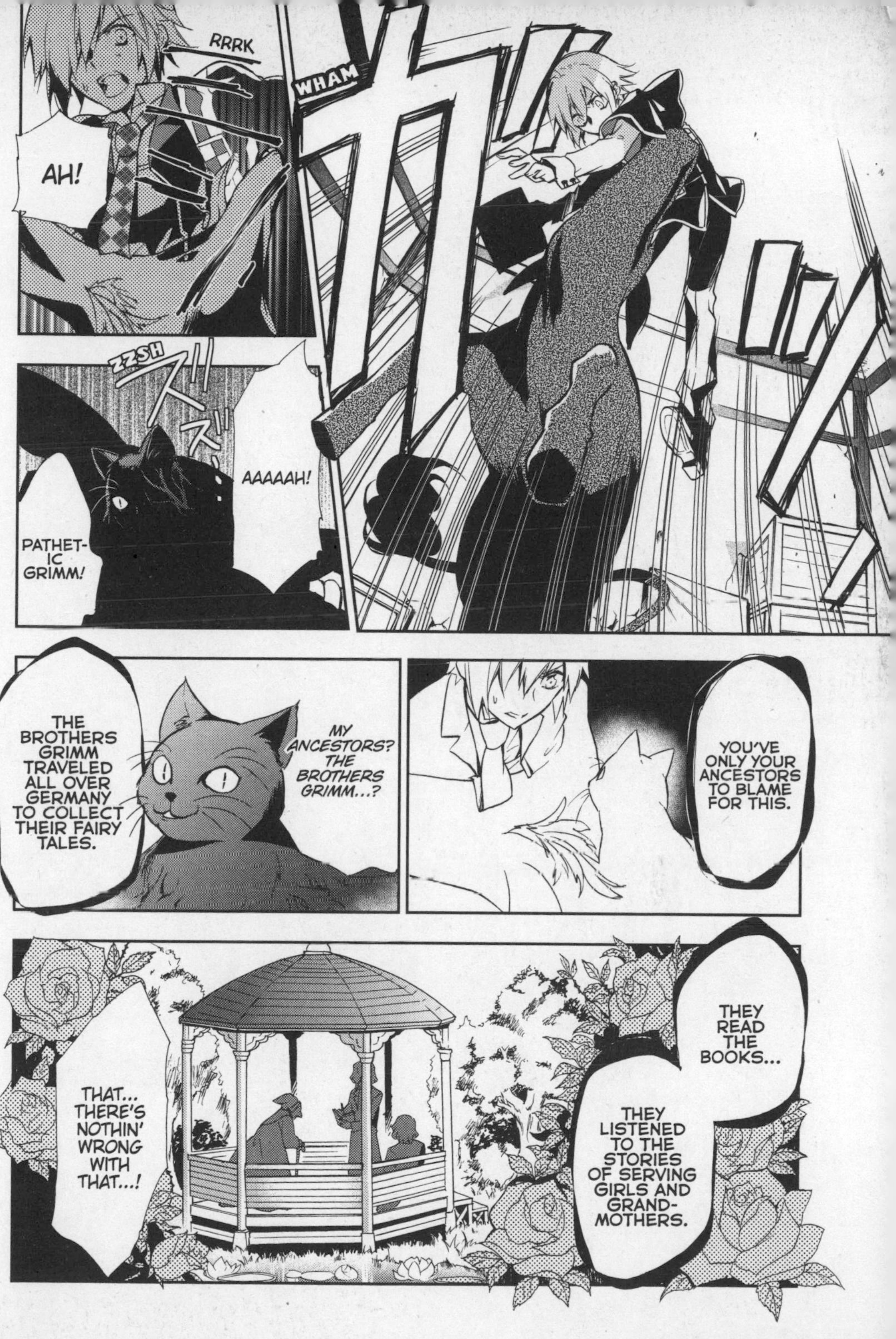
WHAM
RRRK
AH!
ZZSH
AAAAAH!
PATHETIC GRIMM!
YOU'VE ONLY YOUR ANCESTORS TO BLAME FOR THIS.
MY ANCESTORS? THE BROTHERS GRIMM...?
THE BROTHERS GRIMM TRAVELED ALL OVER GERMANY TO COLLECT THEIR FAIRY TALES.
THEY READ THE BOOKS...
THEY LISTENED TO THE STORIES OF SERVING GIRLS AND GRANDMOTHERS.
THAT... THERE'S NOTHIN' WRONG WITH THAT...!

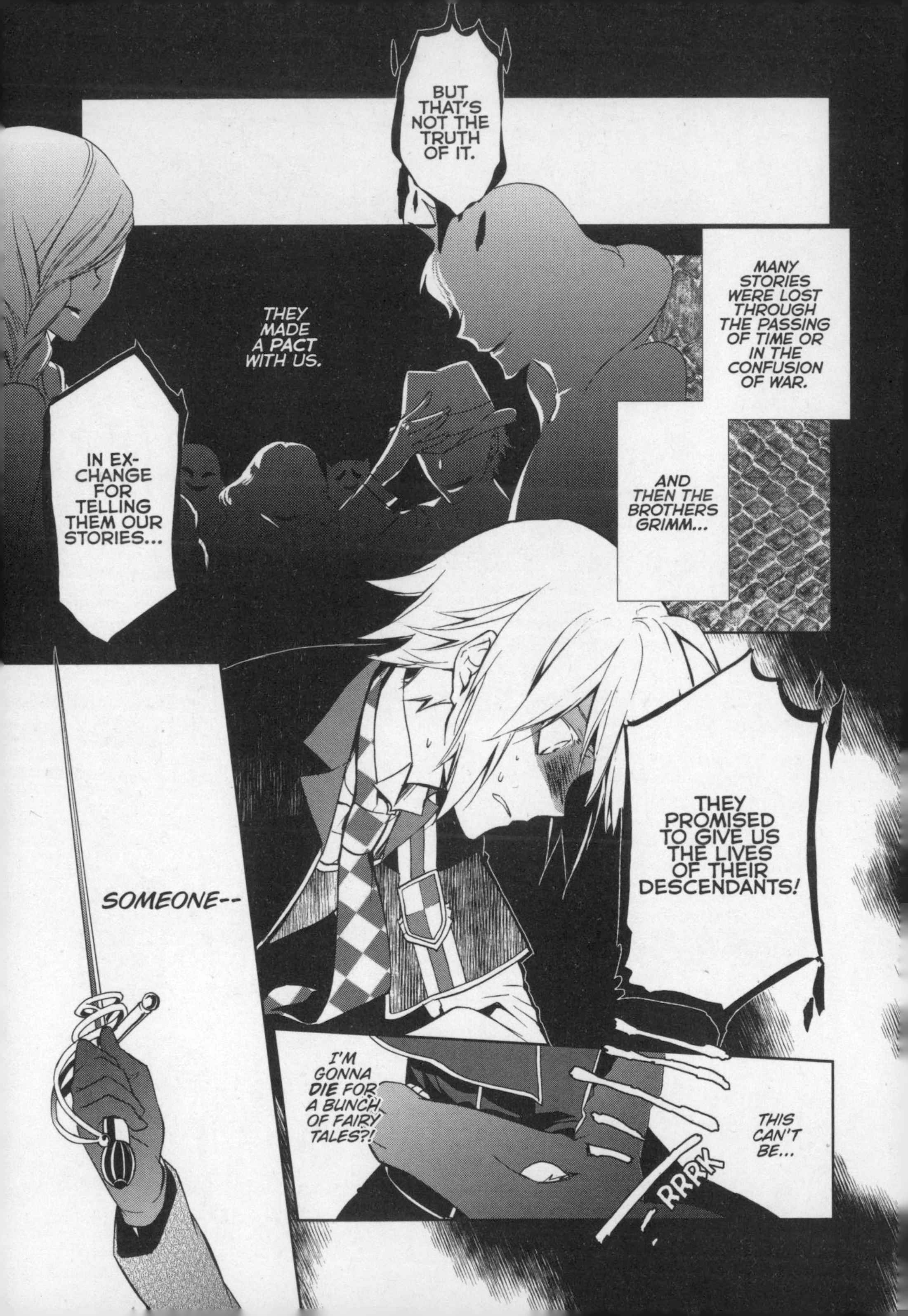

BUT THAT'S NOT THE TRUTH OF IT.
MANY STORIES WERE LOST THROUGH THE PASSING OF TIME OR IN THE CONFUSION OF WAR.
AND THEN THE BROTHERS GRIMM...
THEY MADE A PACT WITH US.
IN EX-CHANGE FOR TELLING THEM OUR STORIES...
THEY PROMISED TO GIVE US THE LIVES OF THEIR DESCENDANTS!
THIS CAN'T BE...
I'M GONNA DIE FOR A BUNCH OF FAIRY TALES?!
RRRK
SOMEONE--

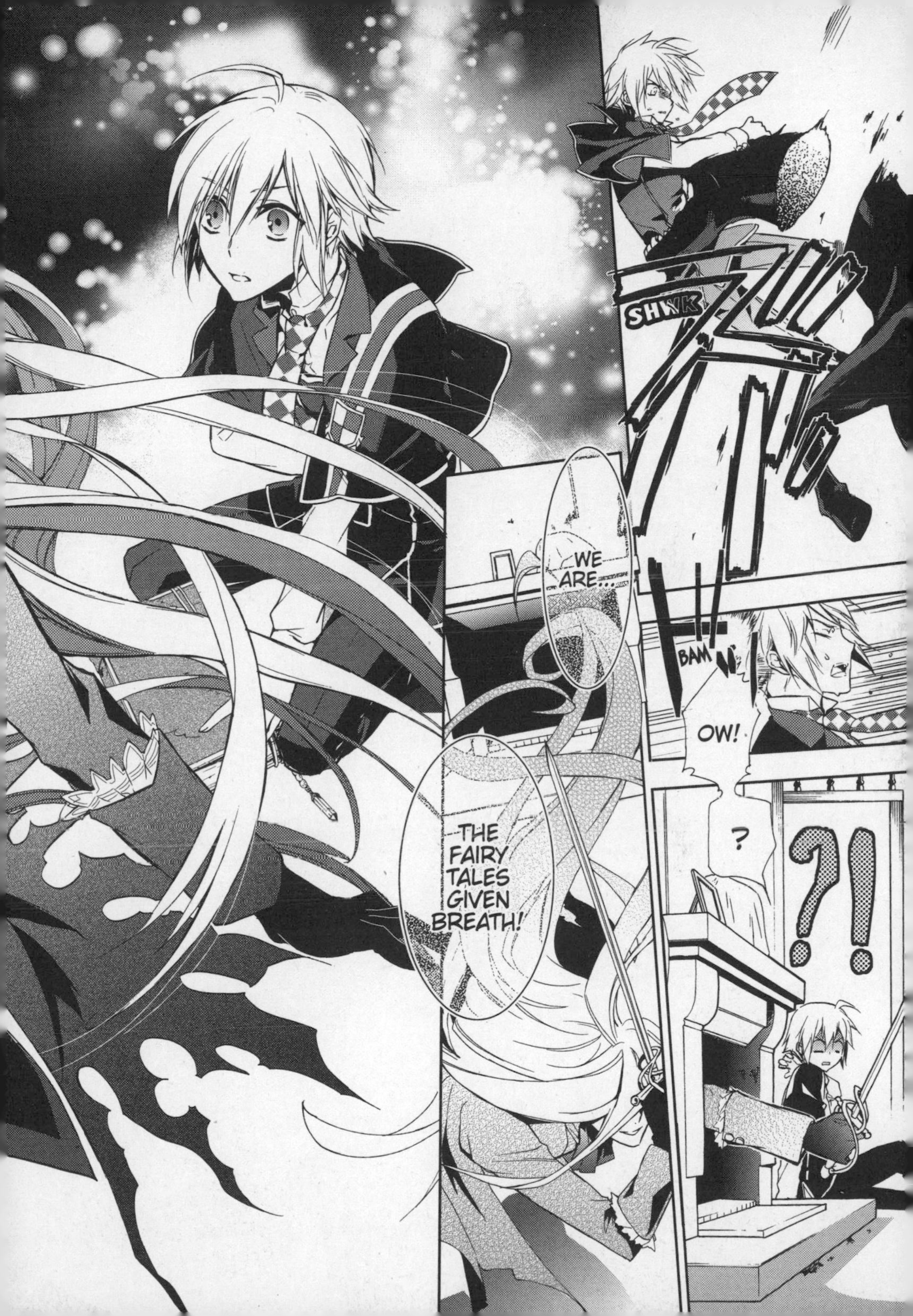
SHWK
BAM
OW!
?!
?
WE ARE...
THE FAIRY TALES GIVEN BREATH!

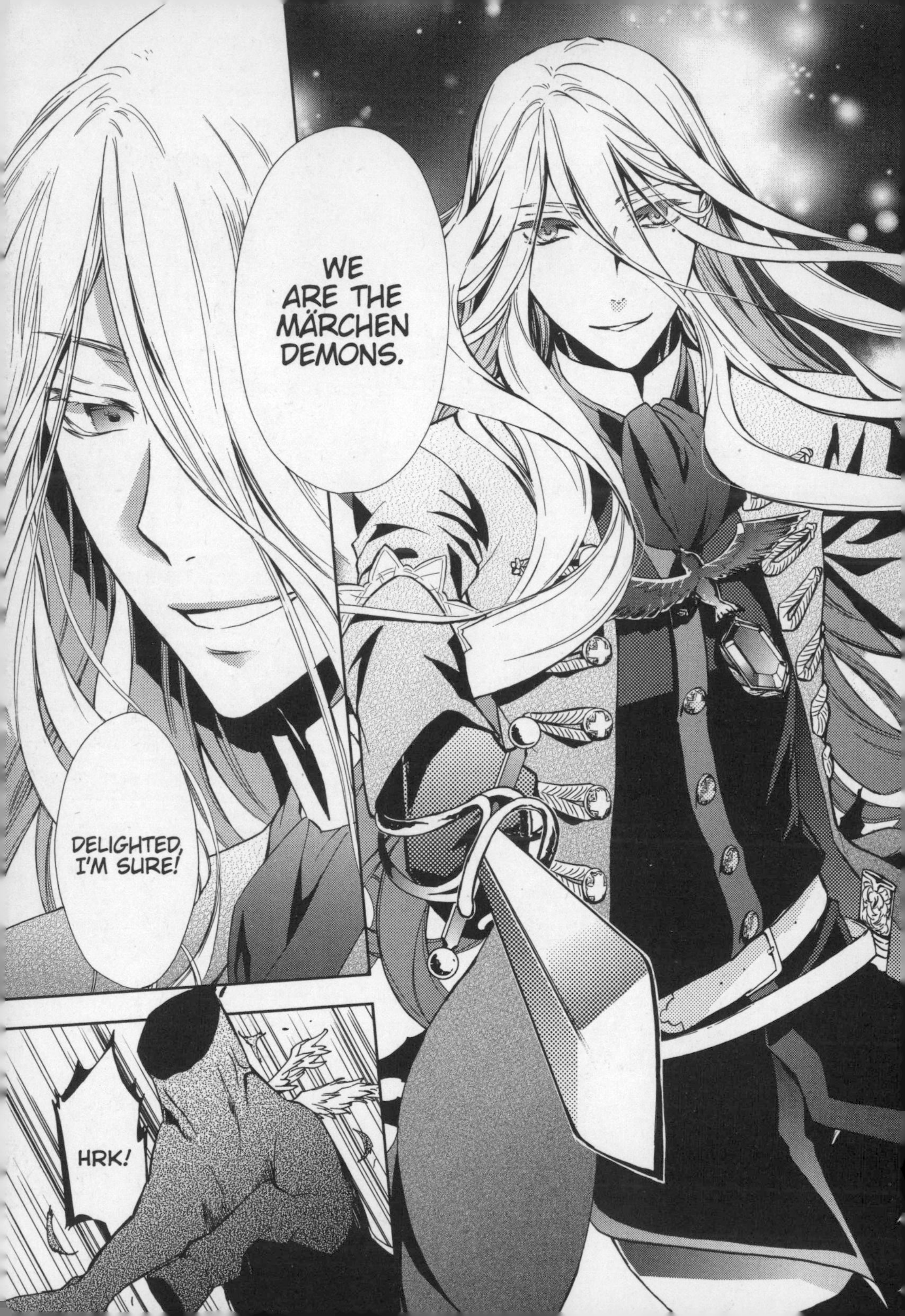
WE ARE THE MÄRCHEN DEMONS.
DELIGHTED, I'M SURE!
HRK!

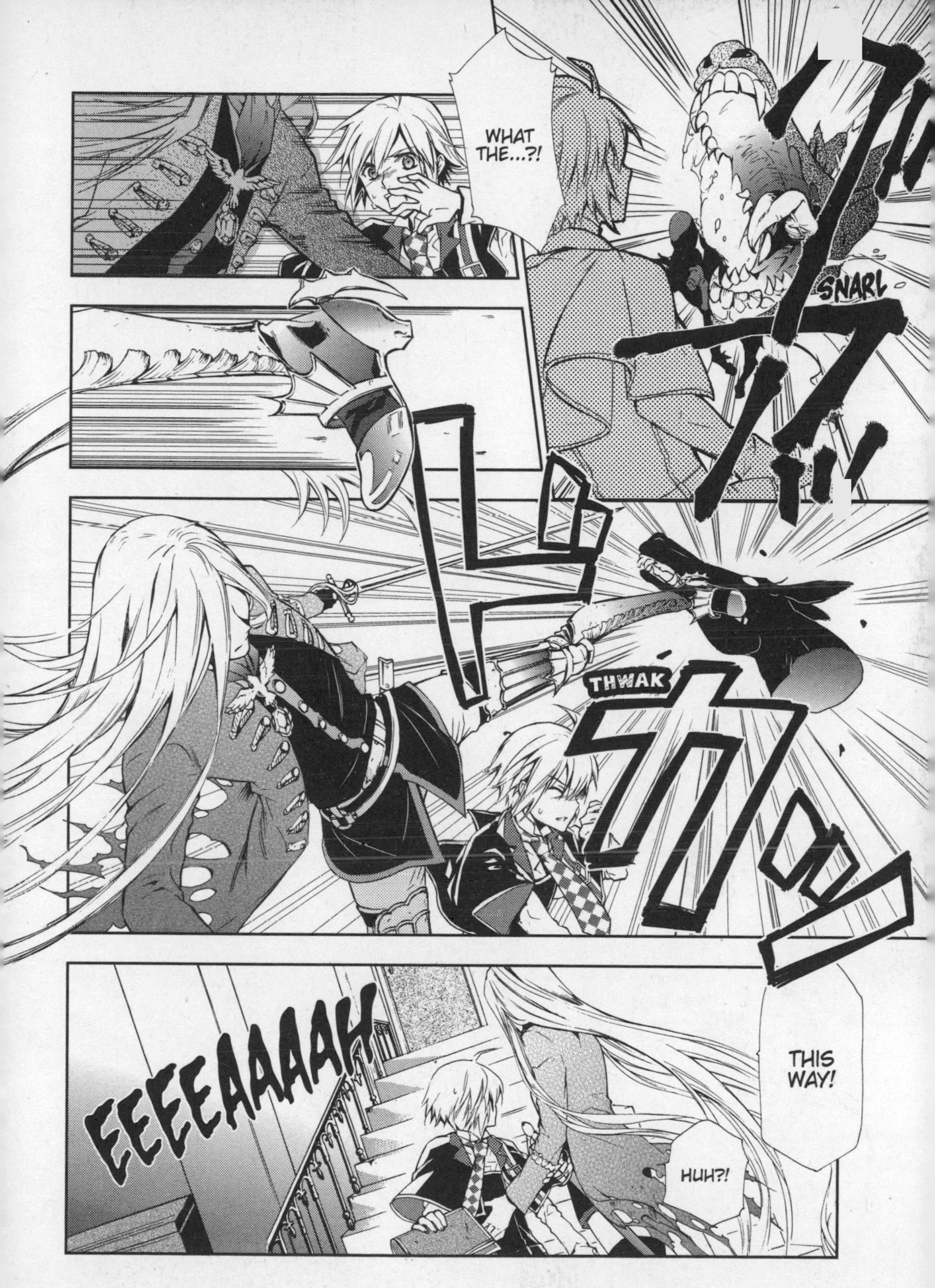
WHAT THE...?!
SNARL
THWAK
THIS WAY!
HUH?!
EEEEAAAAH

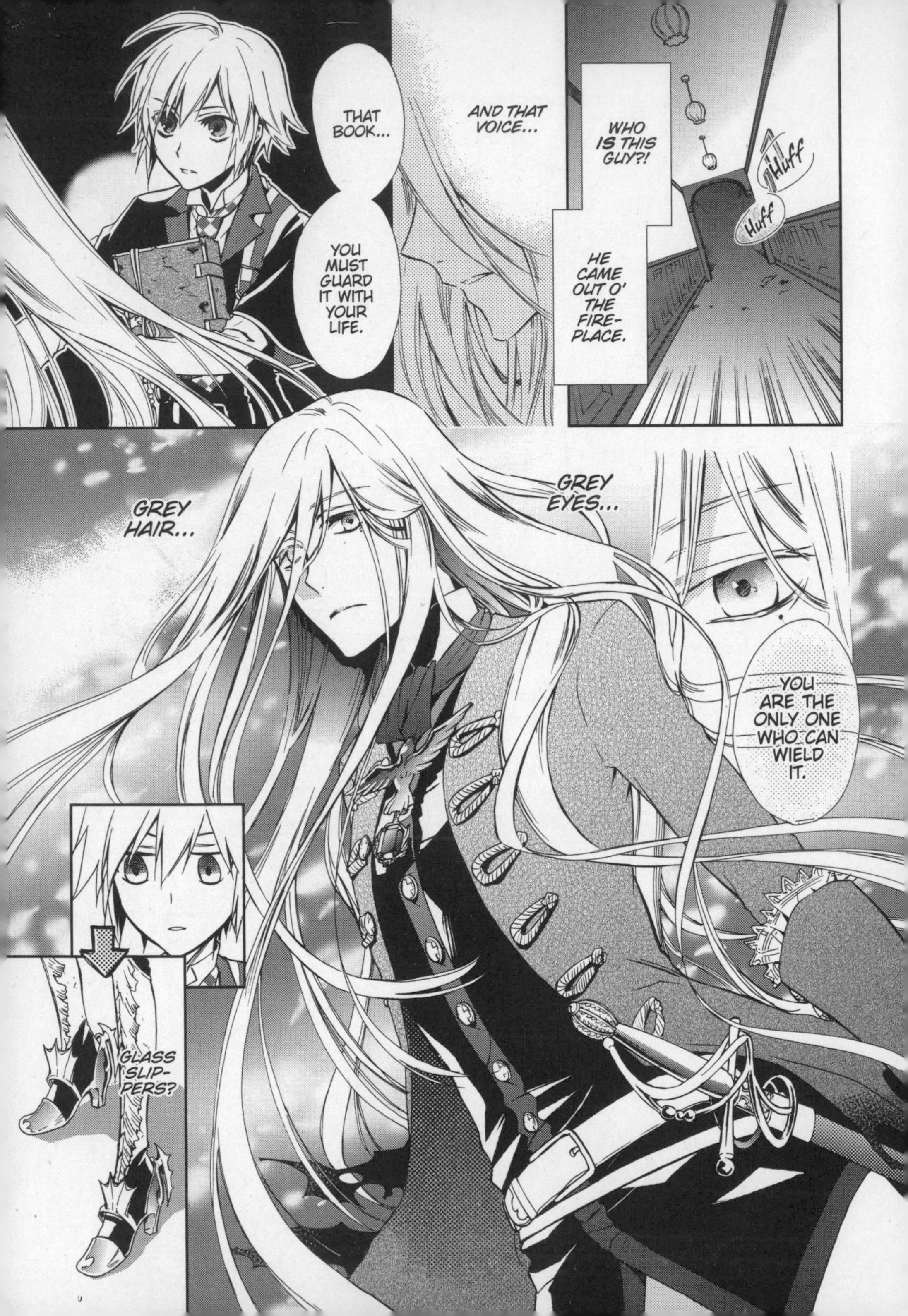
WHO IS THIS GUY?!
Huff
Huff
HE CAME OUT O' THE FIRE-PLACE.
AND THAT VOICE...
THAT BOOK...
YOU MUST GUARD IT WITH YOUR LIFE.
YOU ARE THE ONLY ONE WHO CAN WIELD IT.
GREY EYES...
GREY HAIR...
GLASS SLIP-PERS?

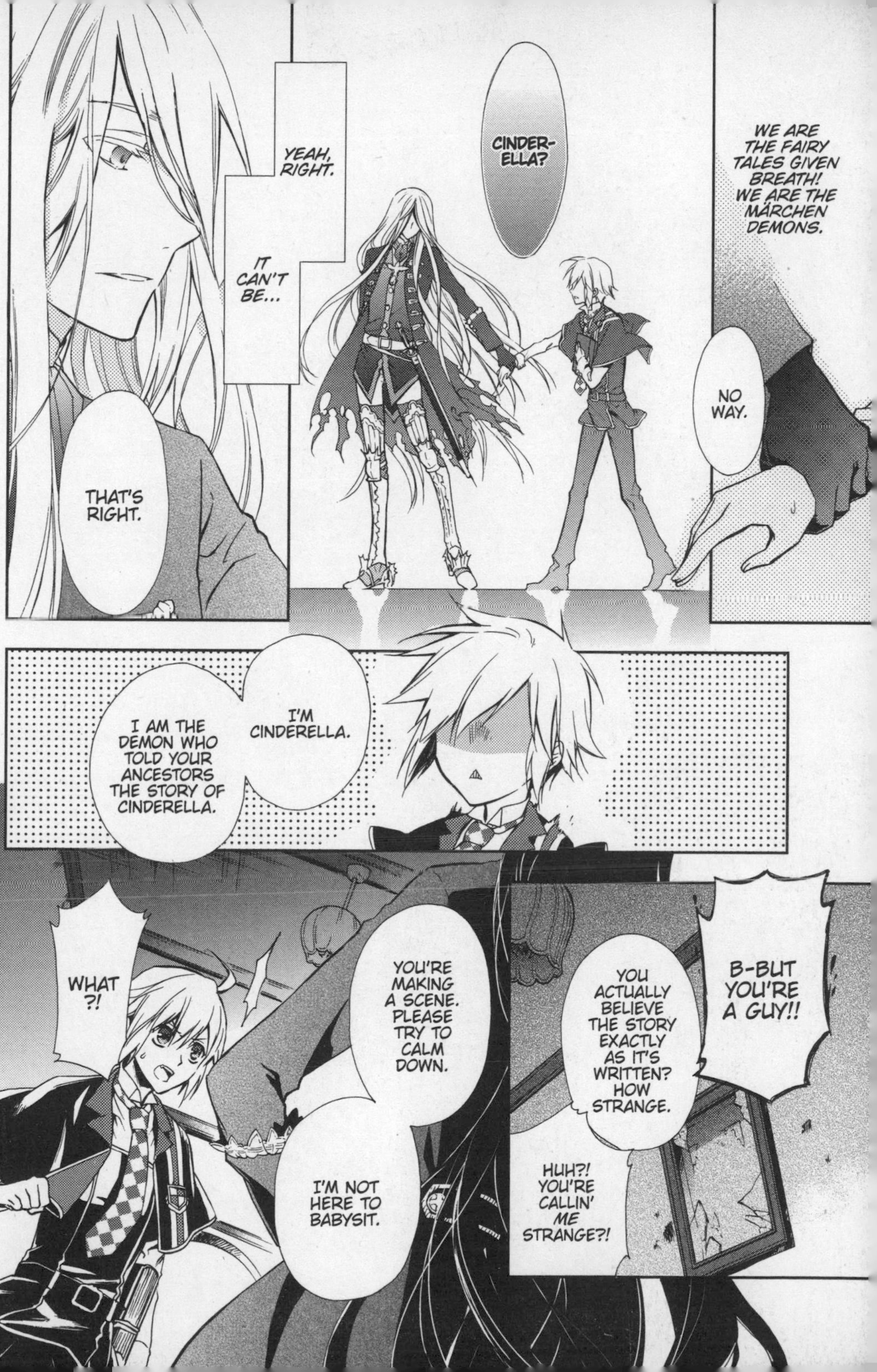
WE ARE THE FAIRY TALES GIVEN BREATH! WE ARE THE MÄRCHEN DEMONS.
NO WAY.
CINDER-ELLA?
YEAH, RIGHT.
IT CAN'T BE...
THAT'S RIGHT.
I'M CINDERELLA.
I AM THE DEMON WHO TOLD YOUR ANCESTORS THE STORY OF CINDERELLA.
B-BUT YOU'RE A GUY!!
YOU ACTUALLY BELIEVE THE STORY EXACTLY AS IT'S WRITTEN? HOW STRANGE.
HUH?! YOU'RE CALLIN' ME STRANGE?!
YOU'RE MAKING A SCENE. PLEASE TRY TO CALM DOWN.
WHAT?!
I'M NOT HERE TO BABYSIT.

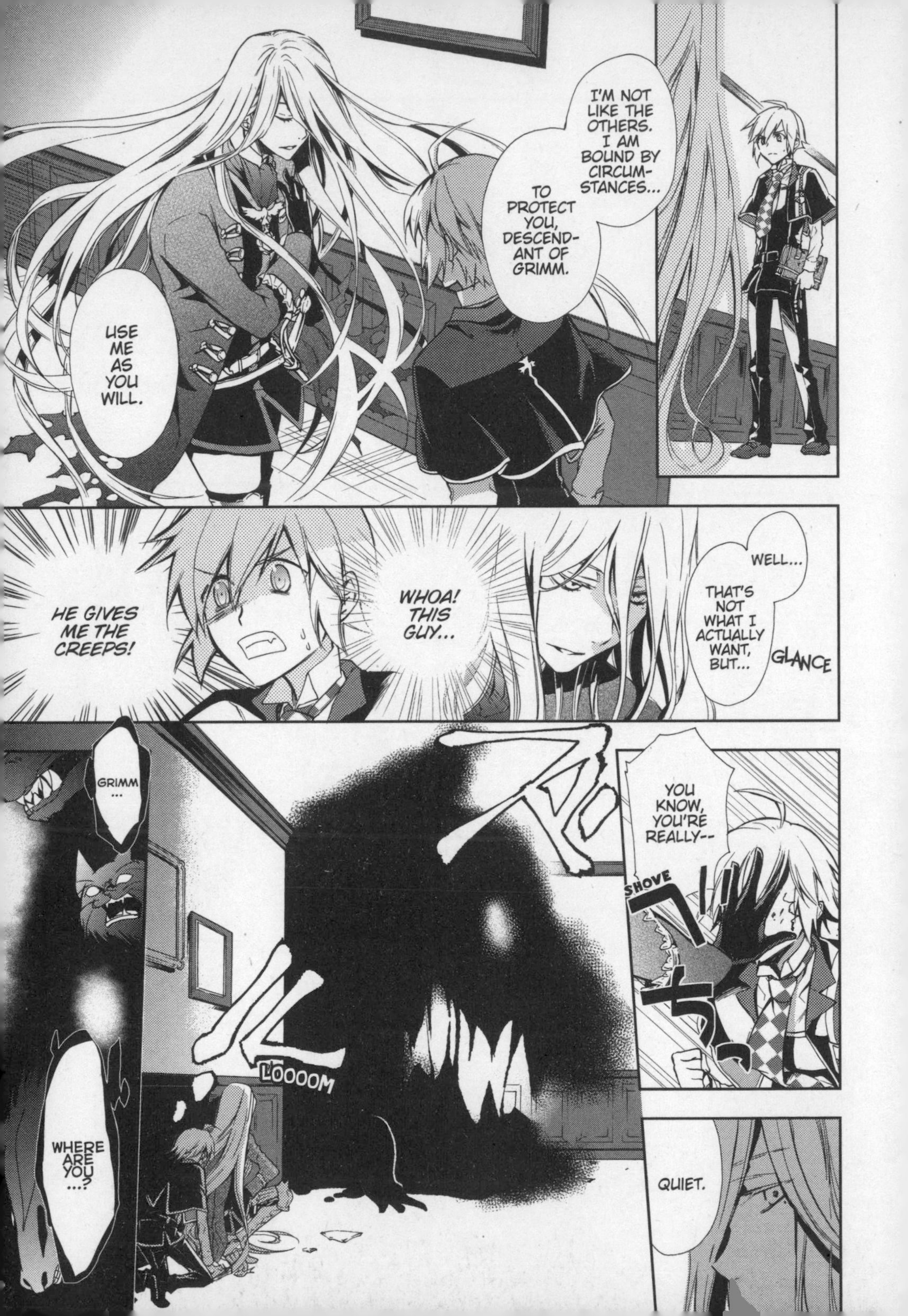
I'M NOT LIKE THE OTHERS. I AM BOUND BY CIRCUM-STANCES...
TO PROTECT YOU, DESCEND-ANT OF GRIMM.
USE ME AS YOU WILL.
WELL...
THAT'S NOT WHAT I ACTUALLY WANT, BUT...
GLANCE
WHOA! THIS GUY...
HE GIVES ME THE CREEPS!
YOU KNOW, YOU'RE REALLY--
SHOVE
QUIET.
GRIMM...
LOOOOM
WHERE ARE YOU...?

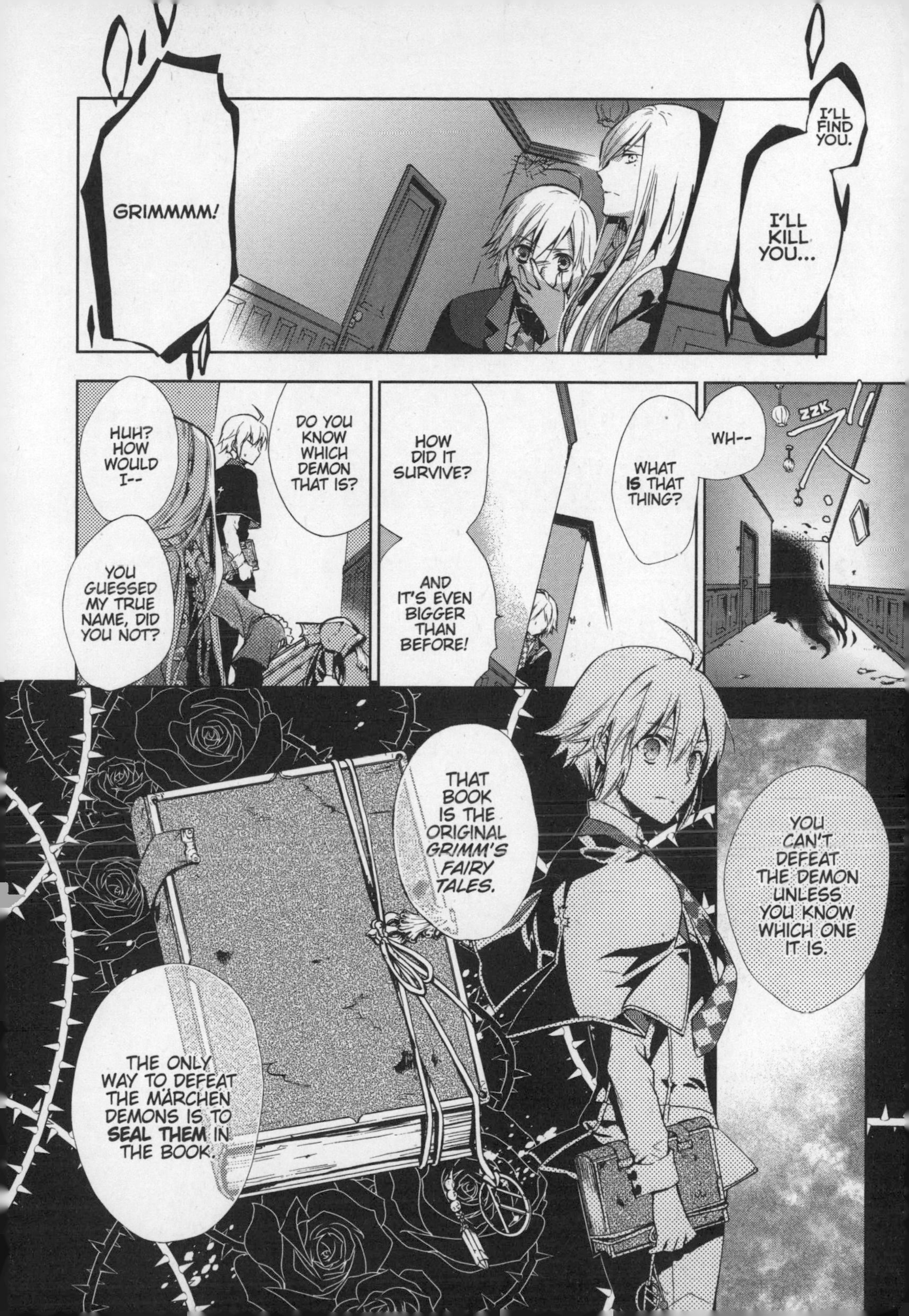
I'LL FIND YOU.
I'LL KILL YOU...
GRIMMMM!
ZZK
WH--
WHAT IS THAT THING?
HOW DID IT SURVIVE?
AND IT'S EVEN BIGGER THAN BEFORE!
DO YOU KNOW WHICH DEMON THAT IS?
HUH? HOW WOULD I--
YOU GUESSED MY TRUE NAME, DID YOU NOT?
YOU CAN'T DEFEAT THE DEMON UNLESS YOU KNOW WHICH ONE IT IS.
THAT BOOK IS THE ORIGINAL GRIMM'S FAIRY TALES.
THE ONLY WAY TO DEFEAT THE MÄRCHEN DEMONS IS TO SEAL THEM IN THE BOOK.

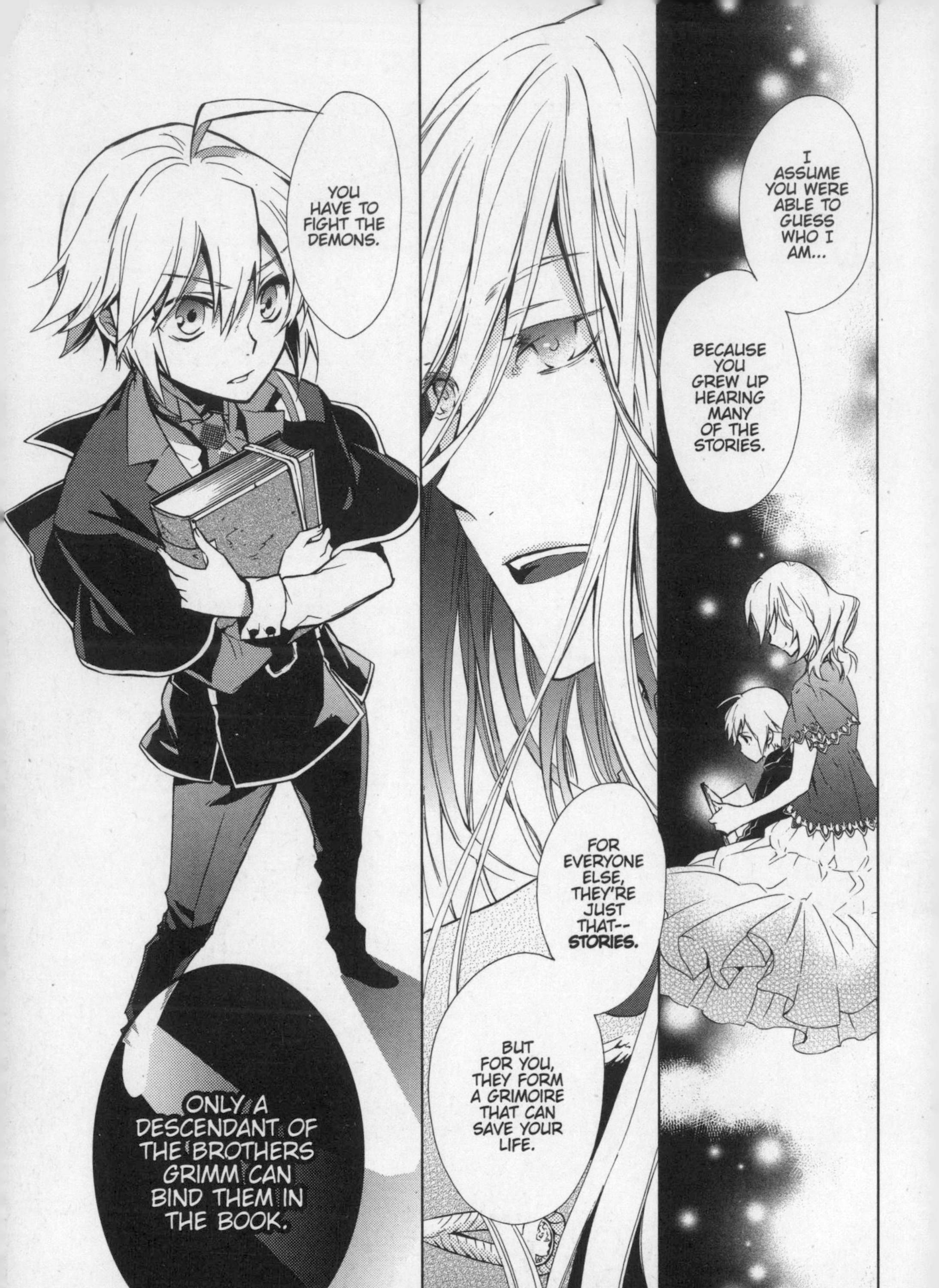
I ASSUME YOU WERE ABLE TO GUESS WHO I AM...
BECAUSE YOU GREW UP HEARING MANY OF THE STORIES.
FOR EVERYONE ELSE, THEY'RE JUST THAT--**STORIES.**
BUT FOR YOU, THEY FORM A GRIMOIRE THAT CAN SAVE YOUR LIFE.
YOU HAVE TO FIGHT THE DEMONS.
ONLY A DESCENDANT OF THE BROTHERS GRIMM CAN BIND THEM IN THE BOOK.

Continued in *Dictatorial Grimoire* Vol. 1

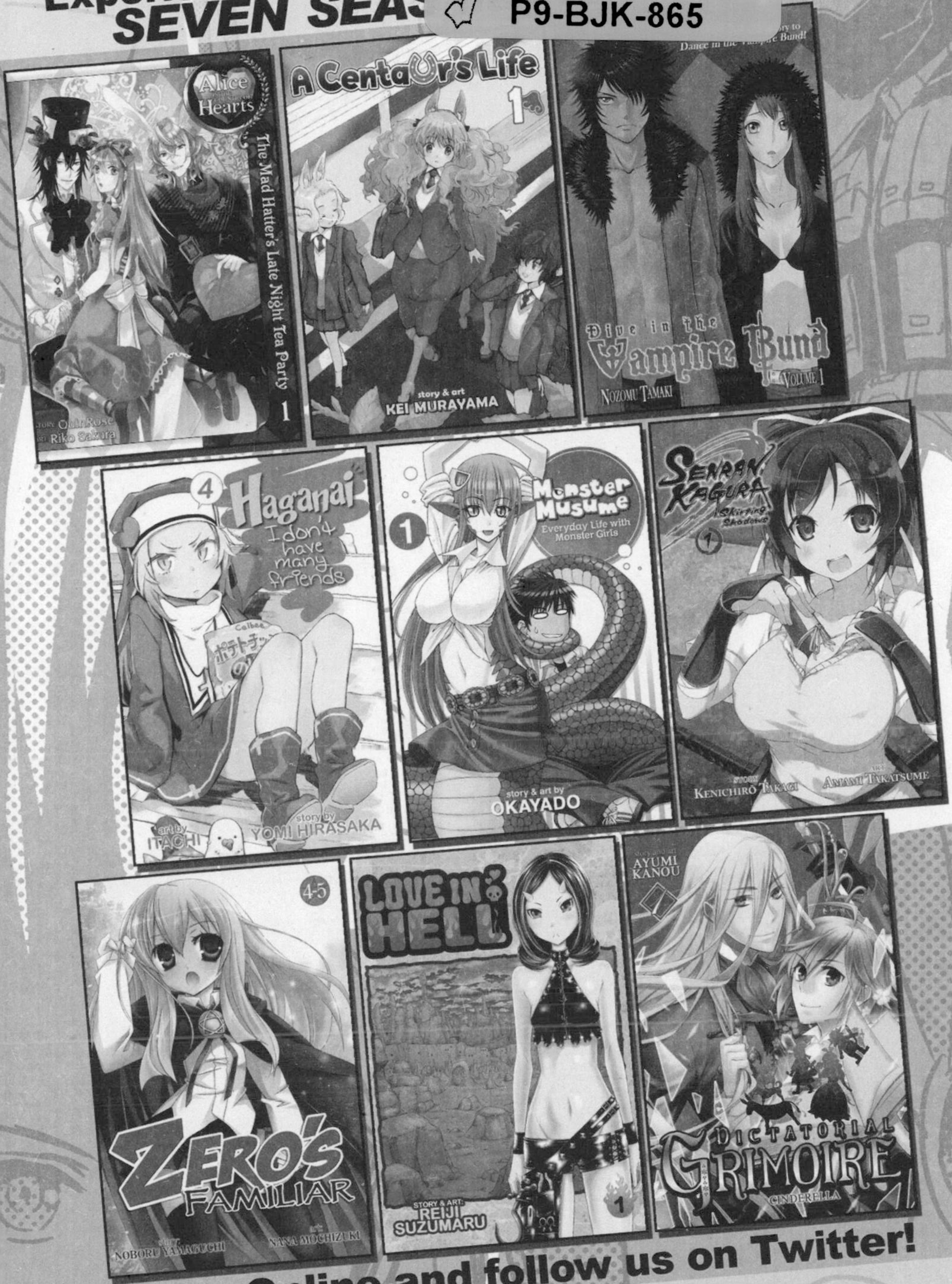
Alice in the Country of Hearts
The Mad Hatter's Late Night Tea Party
1
Riko Sakura
A Centaur's Life
1
story & art
KEI MURAYAMA
Dance in the Vampire Bund!
Dive in the Vampire Bund
NOZOMU TAMAKI
VOLUME 1
4
Haganai
I don't have many friends
art by
ITACHI
story by
YOMI HIRASAKA
1
Monster Musume
Everyday Life with Monster Girls
story & art by
OKAYADO
SENRAN KAGURA
Skirting Shadows
1
KENICHIRO TAKAGI
AMAMI TAKATSUME
4-5
ZERO'S FAMILIAR
NOBORU YAMAGUCHI
NANA MOCHIZUKI
LOVE IN HELL
STORY & ART:
REIJI SUZUMARU
1
AYUMI KANOU
DICTATORIAL GRIMOIRE
CINDERELLA